Kenneth and Helen Durant

THE ADIRONDACK GUIDE-BOAT

With Plans and Commentary by John Gardner

THE ADIRONDACK MUSEUM   BLUE MOUNTAIN LAKE, NEW YORK

End sheet map by Norma Whitman

To CARLOS G. OTIS, M.D.
of Townshend, Vermont

To the earliest men stretches of water were formidable barriers; as man mastered the skill of boatbuilding, they began to venture forth. . . .

G. Frank Mitchell, President, Royal Irish Academy
Treasures of Early Irish Art

Contents

Foreword by John Gardner

My first contact with Kenneth Durant came about as the result of several articles I had written on the Whitehall boat, which were published in the *Maine Coast Fisherman* in 1953. Durant ran across them on microfilm in the New York Public Library in the spring of 1958 in the course of his inquiry into guide-boat origins, on which he had been engaged for the previous two years. Here, in these articles, he received, for the first time, a suggestion that the Whitehall might have been very important in the background of the Adirondack boat, and he wrote to me asking if I could help him to secure some good photographs of authentic Whitehalls. As he later explained to me, as part of his guide-boat project he was compiling for the Adirondack Museum "a portfolio of pictures, ancient and modern, of small boats in many types, native to the waters of northeastern U.S. and Canada."[1]

This was to be in triplicate—one copy for the Museum, one copy for his own use, and one to circulate privately among small craft specialists "to evoke memories and provoke suggestions, leading to a solution of the riddle of the Adirondack guide-boat."

Thus was begun an acquaintance that soon ripened into friendship and collaboration, and a correspondence that continued until Durant's death in 1972, during which time upwards of a thousand letters were exchanged, aggregating considerably more than half a million words.

Both of us had been deeply involved in small craft history prior to our meeting, and very soon we fell into an arrangement whereby we shared our research freely, exchanging materials and ideas without stint or reservation, an arrangement by which I believe I was clearly the gainer. Durant's scholarship was prodigious, his learning encyclopedic. But what stood out above all was his integrity, the high standards he set for himself, his unflagging persistence in searching out the facts, and his refusal to accept anything less.

At the outset, Durant was not writing a book. He quite definitely said so himself in July 1958, in replying to an inquiry I had made as to what restrictions, if any, there were on materials I had received from him. "You need not return anything I sent you," he informed me, "Photostats, etc., were made for you. Nothing is reserved, so far as I am concerned, *I am not writing a book* [emphasis mine—JG]. I am making a preliminary survey for the Adirondack Museum, which I hope will result in a comprehensive work on the Adirondack skiff (guide-boat). Meanwhile, the more published on this subject, the better. We need to provoke interest and discussion, to bring out the hidden materials from obscure corners."[2]

This was written in the summer of 1958, and it con-firmed and made explicit what Durant had stated two months earlier in the first letter he wrote me: "I am engaged in an inquiry into the origin of the Adiron-dack guide-boat. . . . My present research is prelim-inary to a larger study to be made by the [Adiron-dack] Museum."[3]

In 1957 Durant had placed his own guide-boat, which he had used and cherished for 50 years, in the Adirondack Museum. At that time it appeared to him, as to others, that the guide-boat in use was soon to vanish, "to the point of becoming a rare museum piece."[4]

"I spent a large part of my youth in a guide-boat," Durant explained, "without ever looking at the boat — unless it sprang a leak . . . and not until it was in the Museum, and I no longer in the boat, did I begin to look at it with attention and curiosity (as a Proust or Joyce begins to reflect on a familiar youth)."[5]

"It was then," Durant relates, that "I began to look for an answer to a question that I had never asked before: Where did it come from? The currently ac-cepted legend is that the Adirondack boat was 'in-vented' by an Indian guide [Mitchell Sabattis] — a prodigious fellow who killed many moose, panthers and bear, played the fiddle, and led singing in the church. I believe much that has been written about this Indian, but not that he invented the Adirondack skiff."[6]

Although Durant had never thought about it before, and although he claimed to have started out "completely illiterate in marine architecture,"[7] it was clear to him from the first that the guide-boat was not a canoe, and leaving out some superficial resemblances to the canoe in form, its materials were not Indian materials, and its construction not Indian either. It was the construction that particularly engaged Durant's attention even in the early stages of his inquiry, when his search for origins was still almost exclusively historical and confined to published sources. And as time went on he became more and more absorbed in exploring and recording the technical aspects of the guide-boat construction, un-til finally his efforts were centered on explaining how the guide-boat was built.

As a lifelong journalist and editor, Durant natu-rally began his search in the libraries and historical archives. Then, quite unexpectedly, in the summer

of 1958, his project took an abrupt turn. In a letter written on July 10 of that year, he casually mentions, "I am off next week to visit an old Adirondack boat-builder — 82 years — learned the craft from his father, who was a leader in his community, a guide, and a member of the legislature."

The "old boatbuilder" was Lewis Grant. Chance had presented Durant, as he was soon to realize, with a unique opportunity. In the Grant boat shop at Boonville, the guide-boat had attained the peak of its perfection. The shop, dating back to the 1870s, had survived unchanged, with patterns and tools intact. In addition, there were systematic records detailing the construction of every one of several hundred guide-boats built in that shop over a period of some 40 years. And there was Lewis Grant himself, a guide-boat builder, and one of the best.

Lewis Grant's mind was sharp, his recollection clear. He revered his father's memory and desired, above all else, to perpetuate a record of his father's achievement as a guide-boat builder. Moreover, Lewis was literate, as many of the old guide-boat builders were not, and capable of coherent and well-organized exposition of building procedures. He was eager to explain and to assist. From the first, he seems to have grasped the importance of Durant's inquiry, perceiving what it could do for the Boonville story, just as Durant's reporter's instinct recognized that in Boonville he had uncovered a mother lode of primary source material of unparalleled richness.

Henceforth, the direction and scope of Durant's study changed radically. His base of operation moved from the library to the boat shop. For the next two years, until Lewis's death in the fall of 1960, Durant devoted himself assiduously to learning all that Lewis could teach him. He immersed himself in the mys-teries of guide-boat construction. He recorded with-out stint the details of the building process as Lewis unveiled it.

Sometime during this interval, it appears that Durant changed his mind about writing a book. Just when this change of plans occurred and how it came about is unclear, yet the decision seems to have been made sometime before he wrote me in April 1959: "I am struggling with the attempt to reduce the building of a guide-boat to language comprehensible to the general reader, sufficiently precise and technically correct to satisfy the boat expert, and not offend the Adirondack builders who had a terminology all their own. . . . When I have finished my chapter on the building of the guide-boat and sent it to Lewis Grant in Boonville, and have it back with his revisions, I shall greatly need your advice and assistance."[8] There seems to be no doubt that now there were plans for a book. In the normal course of things one does not write a chapter, and refer to it specifically as such, unless one has plans to include it in a book, even though publication may lie vaguely distant in the future.

In the year that followed, work continued deliberately without deadlines or timetables. There were numerous distractions and side-excursions, and in September Lewis Grant passed away suddenly from a heart attack. In August 1960, Durant reported, "I plod along very slowly with the boat. It gradually gets on paper." And two months later the process of getting the boat on paper continued, in spite of involvement with a new and more immediate project, an anthology of selections from published guide-boat sources. "With encouragement from Bruce [Inverarity, Museum Director]," Durant wrote, "I am working on the [guide-boat] anthology. He sees it as I do, as a valuable introduction to, and source material for, *the definitive opus* [emphasis mine—JG], and now that I no longer have Lewis Grant as an excuse for indefinite prolongation, I work on that."[9] Of course the effort expended on the guide-boat anthology, published as *Guide-Boat Days and Ways*, did retard progress on "the definitive opus," but the anthology was nevertheless a worthy project in its own right, and a notable achievement both for Durant and for the Adirondack Museum.

Although the anthology did not come out between covers until late fall 1963, after numerous delays and considerable foot-dragging—on the part of others than Durant—it was in one sense completed before it was started. The research it embodied had already been done and was waiting. After 1960, such historical, and to some extent literary, research as went into the anthology ceased to occupy Durant to any significant extent. He now concentrated on the technology of guide-boat construction. How the guide-boat was built had become more important to him than where it had come from, and henceforth his principal aim did not shift or waver, although the completion of the definitive opus retreated ever before him.

Writing toward the end of November 1962, Durant laid it all out, making it quite clear what he now saw to be the task ahead, and what the priorities were. "Even at best I am not optimistic about spring publication [for the anthology]. But now it is out of my hands and on his [Inverarity's] desk—so I can proceed with the next volume. My attitude toward that has changed somewhat. Though I began full of zest for ancient history and origins and so forth, now I think that the actual boat, in construction and in use, is more important than the shadowy background. Lewis Grant is dead. It may be that I am the sole repository of detailed knowledge of how a guide-boat was built—which I learned chiefly from Lewis Grant and Hanmer, and from the son of my own builder, Warren Cole. You share this responsibility, because almost everything I know I have told you; and you have explained things which I might otherwise have not understood."[10]

Four months later Durant had more to say about the work in progress: "I have Brewington's book but have not had the time to read, or discover if it merely reprints the *Log Canoe*—which, with Morris's *Fore and Aft* [are] the two best jobs of research and summary known to me. My research is much less extensive because it was interrupted by my meeting with Lewis Grant and my immediate preoccupation with the builder, and the boat as built, which gave me release from the doubtful pursuit of origins. The documents for that research still remain for discovery. My document was the living Lewis Grant, and what good luck and good judgment that I gave him all my attention! I doubt if any reader will understand this. Why does Durant spend all his time in the boat shop while he ignores history and answers no questions—and writes a long, tedious book? I like to do it this way. Partly a reaction from a belly full of popularizers; partly thumbing my nose at commercial publishers. I made the anthology, I think, interesting and sometimes entertaining. This book I want to be important."[11]

Another four months passed and Durant was still involved with the anthology, as yet unpublished. "I am gradually working through proof as it comes to me from Blue Mt. At this rate I see little prospect of a book on the counter this summer. I am very disappointed with the typography, but cannot complain since I left it up to the Museum. . . . I am most envious of the beautiful Brewington job. On the second book I shall demand quality and to hell with the costs—using the *Log Canoe* as a club."[12]

It was not until October that finally and at

long last *Guide-Boat Days and Ways* was finished and out, and Durant could give full attention to his major work. At that stage he was deeply immersed in the structural make-up of the Grant boat, analyzing and reconstructing its fabric, step-by-step and in detail, from his notes and from the sketches and diagrams previously obtained from Lewis Grant. Then shortly after the onset of the new year, something new is introduced. "In three separate paragraphs of your letter," Durant wrote me, "you suggest that the book might be made useful for prospective builders, more than mere history, more than technical lines comprehensible to Chapelle. This is characteristic of you, and most proper, a long step beyond my original purpose to write of the development and use of the guide-boat and its construction. I had left out the 'how-to' chapter. This is your forte and I am glad you reminded me.

"It might be a chapter, or it might take another form. The book will be costly—much more than GBDW. Prospective builders are very destructive of such chapters. Try to find Stephens's plates in any library! What about a separate pamphlet for the 'how-to'? You must necessarily point out easier ways and new materials. No use telling the amateur to dig spruce roots. . . . So your treatment must include plywood, epoxy, fiberglass, etcetera. And there you are getting beyond the range of my book. A separate book or pamphlet seems indicated."[13]

This was not his final word, however. Two days later Durant had something additional to say. The idea, once planted, was growing. "My immediate reply was that you had introduced an idea which was not in my original plan for the book—a 'how-to' chapter. It was natural for you to assume that this study should have practical results, to produce not only dry bones of history, but a manual; literally, something for the hands. You are entirely right. I thank you for reminding me of this and I am thinking how to bring it into useful form."[14]

As Durant worked his way deeper into the technical complexities of guide-boat construction, there were dangers of leaving the general reader behind, and perhaps losing him entirely.

"I almost forgot an important question. This has to do with the problem of my reader, whom, as you may have observed, I make out to be a rather stupid fellow. I try to be fairly humble—in contrast to my spruce arrogance—because I would not know how to

fill a bucket with H_2O unless I had some water. For me, E equals MC^2 only as a vague threat; and I can't remember what C is. But this reader: he will be subjected to much inevitable jargon, including such a variety of curves, cambers, rockers, the hollow deadrise and the reverse curve. I insist that he must be told, or shown, what we mean. But just let him look in the dictionary for *hollow deadrise*. He will find it, but it won't tell him a thing. Does the guide-boat have hollow deadrise? Where is it, and how can we portray [it] most graphically? The reverse curve which gave Francis Herreshoff such erotic excitement, the curves on a beautiful woman in her prime! He may, of course, have been like the Frenchman who was asked why he said that the Eiffel Tower reminded him of Sex. 'Everything does.' Be that as it may, I shall want to mention the reverse curve, and want my stupid reader to know what I am talking about. It is not easy to see in a photograph, though recognizable if he knows what to look for. But I want him to see it quite clearly—even to be excited by it, as Herreshoff. That will give him a new interest in our boat, herself."[15]

The high point came in 1964. Prospects for the book loomed large. In April Durant informed me: "I hope to have a manuscript ready to submit by September 1st. Can you have the drawings complete a week before that?"[16] The drawings referred to here are those reproduced in Appendix C of this book. The boat is the *Virginia*, built by Lewis Grant in 1905 for Robert M. Jeffress of Big Moose, New York. Durant selected the *Virginia* as the best representative example of the guide-boat at the peak of its development available for study in the summer of 1959, when I accompanied him to Blue Mountain Lake. We took partial measurements at that time, from which I made drawings that were published in *Outdoor Maine* the following summer, the first guide-boat construction drawings to be printed. Four years later I returned to the Museum with the Durants, this time to do a complete job. A week was spent measuring the *Virginia* throughout and recording every construction detail. Later that year a full-size laydown was made of the boat, which was checked against notes and patterns previously obtained from Lewis Grant. From this a series of drawings exhibiting every detail of guide-boat construction was made for the book. Following the preliminary layout, each sheet was forwarded to Durant to be checked and revised, if necessary, after which it was returned to be redrawn and retraced, altogether an exacting and time-consuming process.

Each sheet of the drawings was studied and analyzed and checked line by line, and dimension by dimension, with the text. "I catch on very slowly. Now I know what the second curved line is, the one that passes through the 'S' at the top of the stem. I suppose this is a case where, as you suggest, the written text must supplement the drawing. It is, indeed, an important functional element in the construction of the stem. The guide-boat builders never permitted themselves any decorative extensions of the stem, in the manner of the Vikings and the gondoliers. Of necessity they could not. Every time you turn a guide-boat over, to empty water, or take shelter under it, or merely to leave it for a few days untended, it pivots on the tops of the stems. On the carry, setting it down for a brief rest, the weight is on the stern stem, with the bow in the fork of a tree. Or, in progress over the carry, it is the stem at the stern which takes a knock now and then, going over a log. . . . Therefore, to take these knocks and wear, the stem is made thicker at the top, and your curve represents the beginning of this thickening. What do you call that which is the opposite from a bearding line? And is there a convention in drawing by which the initiated will recognize that curved line for what it is, though you give no cross section? Or do you have to carry along an old guide-boat man to explain? Did you know all this when you drew it? I am encouraged to believe that, with some pains, the bridge between the two levels can be made smooth going. It was not until I rode the Trans-Siberian Railway that I learned there was no division between East and West.

"This is the stuff of which my book is composed. The technician, carpenter, serious student need to know why the stem is made so, and will be interested to learn. The other fellows will have to take it, or go jump in the lake."[17]

The finished manuscript was not ready for submission in September, nor in October, when a letter arrived on the 21st: "The visit to Blue Mountain was shorter than expected because working conditions were most unfavorable . . . was unable to check any measurements on the *Virginia*. . . ."

Finally, as the year was drawing to a close, word came: "Helen and I have settled down to a long, quiet winter. No Christmas festivities; no guests until Memorial Day. This is my chance to finish the book—if ever."[18] But it was not to be.

Spring found work still progressing, but at a slower pace. "What must appear to you as excessive fussiness with respect to obvious details, arises from difference in audience. You write almost exclusively for persons who know something about boat carpentry and who are generally competent in reading drawings. My audience includes such persons and a lot more, who, like myself, have no experience in carpentry and a very low ability to read drawings. Anything I do not understand at first glance, I must ask about and be prepared to explain to others equally under-privileged. I expect my book to be read, and your drawings to be inspected, by many who never built a boat and do not aspire to build one, but who merely wish to understand what they read and see. This company, which includes myself, has my careful regard."[19]

This is the last letter I can find in our correspondence in which Durant refers to his book as such, and to considerations that govern the selection and management of its content, or his aims and intentions. The exchange of ideas and information, or query and comment, flowed on as before, but the pattern for the book had been set, and what remained was the slow, exacting, painstaking labor of completing it, a process over which, unfortunately, Durant himself did not have complete control.

Notes

The following notes all refer to letters written by Kenneth Durant to John Gardner.

1. September 8, 1958.
2. July 28, 1958.
3. May 1958.
4. May 1958.
5. May 7, 1961.
6. July 10, 1958.
7. July 10, 1958.
8. April 26, 1959.
9. October 19, 1960.
10. November 26, 1962.
11. March 11, 1963.
12. July 4, 1963.
13. January 29, 1964.
14. January 31, 1964.
15. March 28, 1964.
16. April 1, 1964.
17. April 3, 1964.
18. December 19, 1964.
19. February 25, 1965.

Preface

Bundled in a pack basket strapped to the back of a guide, Kenneth Durant made his first trip to the Adirondacks in the summer of 1890 when he was less than a year old. His father was Frederick C. Durant, designer and proprietor of the Prospect House at Blue Mountain Lake Village. The family home was in Philadelphia, but summers were spent at Camp Cedars on Forked Lake. It was there that Kenneth Durant began his lifelong love affair with the north woods.

After he had learned to swim and had proved himself a responsible rower, he was given, at the age of approximately 12, his own guide-boat. In later years he remembered the subtle pleasures of long, solitary journeys through the narrow streams or across the wind-swept lakes, and spoke of going out in his guide-boat for fishing trips in the company of young friends, or of rowing into the sunset to call on the young ladies at a neighboring summer camp.

"I spent a large part of my youth in a guide-boat and made the daily 14 miles to get the mail," Kenneth Durant wrote in 1960, "but I paid little attention to it; kept it clean and varnished. When I went on the lake in sheer idleness, it was not the boat which concerned me, but the water, the woods and the sky."[1]

A guide-boat was part of life in the north woods — something one could not do without. The guides at Camp Cedars built their own boats or bought them from other guides at Long Lake or Saranac Lake. Guides simply knew how to build such a boat, much as the native Vermonter knows how to build a house without benefit of an architect's blueprint; one learns while growing up, helping father and neighbors.

Kenneth Durant's curiosity about the origin of the guide-boat was aroused during many conversations when the Adirondack Museum was being planned and then constructed in Blue Mountain Lake Village. When the Museum became a reality in 1957, Kenneth Durant began, for his own pleasure and satisfaction, an exhaustive inquiry into the history of the boat that had been so instrumental to life in the Adirondacks. "When I am done," he wrote in 1966 to the then-Director of the Adirondack Museum, Robert Bruce Inverarity, "it will be voluminous, yet [will be] only an outline sketch for the guidance of future seekers." His research was broad and all-inclusive. As it progressed his subject broadened. He would not limit himself to a restricted area or goal; his interest was all-encompassing. "The World is my Digs," he said.

From 1957 onward my husband and I spent most of our time, except winters, in the many private preserves and on the waterways of the Adirondacks, searching for the oldest surviving guide-boats, tracing their successive owners, the years the boats were built, where and by whom. Sometimes we were successful in convincing the owners to donate their treasures, often no longer used, to the Adirondack Museum to form, eventually, the nucleus of a small-boat exhibit. In 1965, through the generosity of Harold K. Hochschild, the Adirondack Museum opened its special Boat Building. Kenneth Durant did not complete his project—he died on November 29, 1972.

John Gardner, Associate Curator of Small Craft at Mystic Seaport in Connecticut, is a boat designer and builder as well as Technical Editor of the *National Fisherman* and a regular contributor of articles on small craft history and design since 1951. He has been my husband's friend and collaborator in general small-boat research since 1958, when they began a voluminous correspondence, freely exchanging ideas and knowledge.

John Gardner spent May 20–26, 1973, at our home in Jamaica, Vermont, reading the masses of documents and the partially finished draft chapters my husband had left. Reporting his findings to the Adirondack Museum in July 1973, Gardner wrote:

> In setting out to write the history of the guide-boat, Durant found himself in the situation of a pioneer. Not only had nothing previously been written about the guide-boat, but in general, comparatively little was available on small craft history. . . . Published material on small craft origins, both in this country and abroad, was, and still is, scattered, fragmentary, and often unreliable. Durant, as a first rate journalist of long experience and meticulous integrity, knew what facts were as distinguished from surmise, speculation, legend and fancy, and nothing short of the facts satisfied him. Yet in undertaking to explore and map the historical background of the guide-boat, he found himself in an overgrown wilderness without roads and few land marks, and just clearing away the underbrush became in some instances the labor of years.

It was Gardner's opinion that an informed and authoritative book could be edited without being definitive in the sense of having exhausted the subject or having covered it from every angle. "I consider it of primary importance," wrote Gardner, "that this book be so planned and organized as to provide both reading entertainment and instruction. There is no

incompatibility between the two, and in this case they can be made to merge quite naturally. . . . The book should be Durant's own book as much as it is possible to make it his." In Gardner's opinion this ruled out rewriting or extensively revising the draft chapters.

However much I agreed at the time with John's point of view, when I started to edit Kenneth Durant's documents, this proved impossible. In order to establish continuity it was necessary to rearrange the draft chapters, insert details, eliminate digressions, and add new chapters. It was inevitable, therefore, that, with the exception of the chapters written by John Gardner, the language of the book is mine. Since the entire content of the book is based on my husband's research and documents, the book remains Kenneth Durant's own book as much as it was possible to make it his.

The book presents the guide-boat in relation to its environment and its users and describes chiefly what was accomplished between 1880 and 1934 in the Boonville shop of H. Dwight Grant and his sons, Floyd and Lewis. There are occasional references to Theodore and Willard Hanmer of Saranac Lake Village, with intimate descriptions by Talbot Bissell of the boat shop of Warren Cole in Long Lake.

This is not a "how-to" book. With the exception of John Gardner, who builds boats, the authors are no carpenters and would not presume to tell those experienced with tools how to use them. Instead of giving precise details for the construction of a guide-boat we describe how the old builders fashioned their boats, emphasizing *what* they achieved rather than *how* they achieved it. Our concern is not concentrated on the earliest builders who improvised, adapted, and experimented, but on those who worked from established patterns and brought the guide-boat to perfection. We must assume a certain amount of experience and skill on the part of the reader interested in constructing a guide-boat. Therefore, some of the smaller problems are left to the reader's ingenuity, although we try to make clear what he must achieve.

Except in John Gardner's chapter, "Modern Materials and Tools," we do not deal with machinery. During Dwight Grant's days boat shops had no electricity. Besides hand tools, Warren Cole had only a foot-treadle jigsaw. Emerson had a similar one. The basic guide-boat was handmade. "There were no light highspeed woodworking machines in those days," said Willard Hanmer in his reminiscences. "Hand tools, like ratchet screw drivers, and better grade planes and chisels were not to be had. Even the sandpaper was of poor quality. I had to learn all the art of building by hand. . . ."[2] Machines contributed nothing essential to guide-boat design and little to their construction. They merely made easier and faster work that had been done the hard and slow way: by hand.

A considerable interest in guide-boat building is currently manifested by small craft enthusiasts. What was holding back the incipient guide-boat revival more than anything else was the lack of good working plans. The Gardner drawings, published in this book, are possibly the most complete yet drawn for any traditional American small boat and are exact to the most minute detail. We have added explanatory sketches made by Lewis Grant.

At the Adirondack Museum the interested builder can find a structural model from the Hanmer shop and study its components. He can read the transcript of a tape-recorded interview with Willard Hanmer and see a motion picture of Hanmer at work in his boat shop at Saranac Lake Village. There is also a wide selection of photographs in the Museum archives on details of guide-boat construction.

Unless otherwise specified, *the Museum* always refers to the Adirondack Museum at Blue Mountain Lake. The term *guide-boat* is generally used to apply to the *type,* even to those that appeared before the term came into use.

Acknowledgment must be made to Harold K. Hochschild for the many years during which he encouraged my husband in this project; to the past director of the Museum, H. J. Swinney, and his staff for their cooperation; to Lewis L. Grant, who so patiently explained to us all the details of guide-boat building; to Mrs. Talbot Bissell and her son, Thomas, of Long Lake, for permission to use excerpts from Talbot Bissell's manuscript, "Their Little Boats," and for permission to study their old guide-boats repeatedly.

We have a debt to the private camp owners of Bisby, Brandreth, and Hewitt, and other private preserves, who gave us free access to their boat houses; and to Floyde Gallagher, superintendent at Bisby, for being ever ready to assist us.

Of the Museum staff we want to single out Ralph Raymond, custodian for many years. Always willing to pull boats out of storage, he facilitated our investigations; Marcia Smith, librarian, who, in spite of constant demands on her time, nevertheless provided us promptly with requested documents. The present Director of the Museum, Craig A. Gilborn, met my husband only once; therefore, my debt to him is a deep personal one for encouragement and generosity in putting all of the Museum's resources at my disposal.

My own profession was that of a cineast, and I know that film-making is a collaborative venture. All participants, in degree, receive credit on the titles. With a book, only the author's name appears on the cover, yet a book, too, is a collaborative enterprise. It is impossible to mention all those who have contributed their individual skills; some of them are not even known to me. Editors usually work behind closed doors and get no public credit. Let us reverse the process. My editor, Alice Gilborn, gave unstintingly of her time. Her constructive criticism forced me to tighten composition, smooth the story line, and clarify the language. She, too, shares in the authorship.

And finally there remains the recognition of John Gardner. His knowledge of American small craft inspired my husband to further research. In turn, my husband's scholarly inquiries induced John Gardner to a continuous exchange of ideas. Looking over their correspondence covering 15 years, I am aware of the way ideas flew back and forth, unselfishly, with no holds barred. It was primarily John Gardner who suggested that I should finish my husband's work. This would have been impossible without his constant advice. For this I shall never be able to thank him enough.

Helen van Dongen Durant
"House on the Hill"
Jamaica, Vermont

March 1980

Notes

1. Letter to John Gardner, August 8, 1960.
2. Kenneth Durant, *Guide-Boat Days and Ways* (Blue Mountain Lake, N.Y.: The Adirondack Museum, 1963), p. 235.

I

The Guide-Boat: Its Time and Place

I/Introduction

*The region seems like a porcupine,
and the quills bristle in every direction.*

Reverend John Todd[1]

The time: before 1850. The place: the north woods of New York State known as the Adirondacks, a region with few roads where most who traveled went by water. The South Branch of the Moose River, upstream from McKeever in Herkimer County, connects with a tributary leading to Nicks Lake. This is the threshold of the Brown's Tract, a trail leading to the eight lakes of the Fulton Chain. These lakes, in turn, lead to Raquette Lake, which flows into Forked Lake and farther on to Long Lake. So wander all the waterways of this wilderness, branching and joining, through narrow inlets, all the way to the borders of Canada and beyond to the St. Lawrence River. Dense forests, laced with waterways where falls and rapids constitute formidable obstacles, made the use of wagons or horses almost impossible.

An intelligence report of 1694 regarding an overland route from Albany to Montreal and Quebec for the invasion of French Canada advised Benjamin Fletcher, provincial governor of New York, that it was impossible to march with any party of men by land, as they would have to climb over rocky mountains or wade through swamps "cumbered with underwood, where men cannot go upright, but must creep through bushes for whole day's marches. . . ."[2]

An exaggeration, perhaps, but a deterrent. A man on foot was a prisoner of the shore line. He could not walk far in any direction without coming to water that must be crossed. He needed a boat.

Travel remained equally hard for those whose boats were too cumbersome to be carried over the numerous portages. The white settler who came to the Adirondacks at the end of the Revolutionary War in 1783 trapped or fished for a living. As he crossed the wilderness on foot, carrying his provisions, blanket, axe, and rifle, the daring searcher for pelts of sable and mink axe-marked the trees in order to find his way out of the deep forest again.[3]

Trout, the preferred fish for the commercial markets, swam in deep waters of the open lakes. To get them, the woodsman needed a boat. In the dense forest, the Indian birch canoe was by far the best portable boat, but when the Indian retreated to the interior and the canoe vanished with him, the white man was on his own. At first he made do with dugouts, crude skiffs, and other craft he found hidden at the lake shore. Most of these boats were too heavy in a region where boat and catch had to be carried from lake to lake over long and difficult portages.

The bateau, historically the most important American work boat, disappeared almost without a trace. (Helen Durant)

The trapper knew that he needed a light boat. Rowing and paddling or poling miscellaneous craft all day, during all kinds of weather, taught him how a boat responded. He learned what was good and what was bad. Like other country men of his day, he was exceedingly adept with the axe and possessed a variety of manual skills. Some worked with finer tools and were capable of expert joinery. Since no manuals were available for the construction of a portable boat, the trapper with the requisite skill might copy ribs, stem, and bottom board from an old wreck. Necessity compelled invention. Eventually, the trapper's boat developed refinements and acquired variants peculiar to builder and locale. When the trapper became a guide, his boat became his essential tool, his work boat, with which he earned his living.

The work boat eventually became a definable type: a narrow wooden craft roughly 16 feet long and 3 feet wide, which could be carried by one man. Square-sterned and clapboarded at first, the "guide-boat" reached its mature form when it became a true double-ender, pointed at both ends, and its clapboard planking gave way to a refined lapstrake in which skillful beveling produced a smooth skin inside and out. Thousands of these craft were built during the late 1800s and 1900s, in small shops scattered throughout the Adirondacks.

We know what the perfected guide-boat looks like and how it was built, but its origin eludes us. Its expert design and construction points to evolvement rather than to sudden invention by one man. Pioneer life leaves no written records. The guide-boat's origin, from whatever antecedents, cross-currents of migration, example or precedent, remains obscure. All we can say with certainty, for the time being, is that the Adirondack trapper did not learn boatbuilding from the Indians, who did not make plank boats.

When first reported by travelers at different times and from different places, the boat was in transition. Sometimes it was feared for its fragility and became the subject of tales of perilous escapes. At other times it attracted momentary attention when a guide carried it downside-up on his back. Early adventurers in the Adirondacks wrote about marvels seen only once in a lifetime but not about everyday things. Few had the interest or the trained eye to observe the craft that carried them through the wilderness and to report on its construction. Travel by boat in the Adirondacks was then so typical and commonplace that travelers neglected to record information that has become, for us, an elusive secret.

Artifacts made of wood, the most common of our primitive materials, are often the most transitory. The small boats in which the pioneers traveled lay outdoors, exposed to the sun, rain, and frost. Few survived the ravages of nature. We are lucky if we find an American work boat more than a hundred years old. Many a craft, like the bateau, historically the most important American work boat, has disappeared without a trace. The lack of reliable records makes the history of small boats in America highly speculative.

The guide-boat, outside a certain time and place, is inexplicable. It can only be defined in terms of function, form, and construction; therefore it becomes necessary to abandon, temporarily, the term *guide-boat,* which does not define and may, sometimes, even mislead. The earliest writers did not report guide-boats; they spoke of little skiffs, canoes, or carry-boats, and frequently used these terms indiscriminately for the same craft. The hunter called it a boat and so did the guide. (An exceptionally early use of the term *Adirondack guide-boat* occurs in *Forest and Stream* of March 9, 1876, in connection with a boat that was built by Caleb Chase of Newcomb.)

While many another craft has a variety of names according to locality, the term *guide-boat* did not reach the ears of the lexicographers. We have been unable to find it in any dictionary. This omission is indicative of the brief life span and narrow distribution of the guide-boat, a clearly defined type found in only one region: the Adirondacks.

Notes

1. John Todd, *Long Lake* (Pittsfield, Mass.: E.P. Little, 1845), p. 47.
2. William Pinhorne and N. Byard, "Report to Benjamin Fletcher, Governor of the Province of New York, July, 1694," N.Y. State Historical Society.
3. Verplanck Colvin, *Seventh Annual Report on the Progress of the Topographical Survey of the Adirondack Region of New York for the Year 1879,* Assembly Document no. 87, March 7, 1879 (Albany: Weed, Parsons & Co., 1880), p. 67.

II/Water Transport in Colonial America

We in the thirteen original states were lucky to have our skills in boat building handed down to us from several countries, for besides England and Scotland we have been influenced by the Dutch, French and Nordics, all of whom were among our early settlers.

L. Francis Herreshoff[1]

The early European explorers trying to sail up the inland waters of the North American continent in their oceangoing vessels, or in the small boats they carried aboard, were soon halted by rapids or river shoals, which the Indians, familiar with the climate and the local terrain, traversed easily in their canoes. These were of two kinds: the hollowed-out tree or dugout and those made of bark. In the Adirondacks, the birch canoe was the preferred means of travel.

The Indians who accompanied Samuel de Champlain during his voyage of exploration in 1603 conquered in their canoes all the impediments they encountered. Champlain, however, traveling in a light skiff built expressly for the swift waters of the St. Lawrence River, got only as far as the Lachine Rapids, where impassable rocks and dangerous reefs obstructed further progress. Champlain wrote that whoever wanted to pass through these rapids should fit himself with the canoes of the savages, which were easily carried. That way a man could travel freely and see all that was to be seen.[2]

When in 1609 Henry Hudson, the English mariner, finished exploring the river that now bears his name, Dutch settlers followed and established the Territory of New Netherland, granted to the Dutch West Indies Company. The Dutch did not come to farm; that was done around Manhattan by a group of blacks, emancipated for services to the Company. The white Dutch settlers could make more money trading with the Indians for beaver skins, which were sent to the Netherlands by the thousands.

Sailors of the Dutch ships had reported to Johannes de Laet, director of the West Indies Company, that the Hudson was navigable for oceangoing ships as far as Latitude 43, which is near Schuylerville. "Judging from appearance," reported De Laet, "this river extends to the great river of St. Lawrence, or Canada, since our skippers assure us that the natives come to the fort [Orange] from that river. . . ."[3]

De Laet stretched the headwaters of the Hudson beyond their northern limit, on the basis of circumstantial evidence: long before scientists fixed the points with their instruments, Indians knew the route from Canada and the St. Lawrence River to the Hudson and the Mohawk Rivers. Some brought their canoes by way of the Richelieu River, Lake Cham-

The hollowed-out tree or dugout. (Adirondack Museum)

plain, and Lake George; others traveled through the wilderness waters of the Oswegatchie, the Raquette River, and the Saranac Lakes and their tributaries.

The French explorers, in close connection with the military and the *coureurs de bois,* were probably the first white men to penetrate the north woods. Father Simon le Moine and his party were traveling from Quebec to the land of the Onondagas below Lake Ontario in the summer of 1654 when rain and storms forced them to land and search for a new route. While carrying canoes, baggage, and provisions, they found another waterway, but the river became so rapid at one point that they had to throw themselves into the stream dragging their canoes after them "as a cavalier, dismounting, leads his horse by the bridle."[4]

When the demands of trade and military supply began to exceed the capacity of the Indian's canoe, the conquerers set out to develop a boat better suited to their purposes. In 1657 Father Ragueneau and a band of 53 Frenchmen, trying to avoid capture by the Onondagas, had built, in secret, "two Batteaux of a novel and excellent structure" which drew very little water and could carry about 15 men each plus considerable freight.[5] With these, plus eight captured Indian canoes, they made good their escape over the portages to Lake Ontario and the St. Lawrence River. The report does not reveal how many men were needed to carry the bateaux around the rapids.

For their expedition against the Iroquois 10 years later, the French needed boats that they could also carry overland, since they had to walk six score leagues crossing lakes and rivers to meet the enemy. Of the 300 boats they had brought, 41 were "very light bateaux," the rest canoes. How "light" these bateaux really were may be deduced from the statement that they had to be carried "by main strength."[6] In 1685, realizing that canoes require too much attention and repair, the French, for their expedition against the Iroquois and Senecas, ordered planks "to be prepared for one hundred flat bateaux."[7]

By the middle of the eighteenth century the means of inland water transport had changed but little. Peter Kalm, the Swedish naturalist, left a catalog of

Indian birch canoe. (Adirondack Museum)

the boats he had seen on the Hudson at Albany in 1749. Among the boats listed were log dugouts, which were attached as tenders to the vessels plying the Hudson. The passengers sat on the bottom for greater stability. At Albany, which lacked wharves, two such log canoes lashed together served as lighters for the loading of freight boats. Battoes, furnished with seats and oars, had flat bottoms like Russian barges, for shallow drafts. They carried the trading goods up the river to the Indians wherever it was possible to pass through "without having to pull these battoes far across inland." Kalm found that the bark canoes, though easier to carry, lacked stability and capacity and were too fragile.[8]

Mrs. Anne Grant, an English lady who visited the American colonies at the dawning of the Revolution, supplemented Kalm's information. In her memoirs she reported that in the mid-eighteenth century around Albany every family had a canoe and that travel on the Mohawk River above Schenectady was generally by bateau. Mrs. Grant described a voyage of six bateaux, accompanied by Indians in their canoes, which were taking winter supplies to the British garrison at Oswego. Passage through Wood Creek was often obstructed by fallen trees. While the Indians were able to carry their canoes past the trees, the deep-loaded bateaux were halted. The soldiers had to chop away massive obstructions. It took the bateaux three days to proceed 14 miles.

According to Mrs. Grant, ambitious young lads from Albany eager to seek their fortune would set out singly or accompanied by a Negro slave, steering northward in a canoe toward the Canadian frontier. They usually carried about 50 dollars worth of rum and other trading goods for illegal barter for furs with the Indians. Ten miles above Albany, where three rivers unite in the famous Cohoes Falls, the canoes had to be unloaded and carried for about a mile. Then the travelers had to return to the rapids to pick up the cargo. Farther on, much longer carrying places were frequently encountered, where vessel and content had to be dragged through thickets "abounding with snakes and wild beasts."[9]

These romantic amateurs no doubt followed the routes traveled by professional smugglers who, always overburdened with pelts, trading goods, and armaments, were plagued by portages, soon to be known as

carries. These were exactly what the name implied: places where the boat had to be carried overland around falls and rapids, or from one lake to another.

Farther to the north, frontier men had earlier met similar problems. The first great fur trading enterprise in the far north was the Hudson's Bay Company, chartered as a monopoly by King Charles II in 1670 for the purpose of importing into Great Britain the furs and skins obtained from the Indians, chiefly by barter. The Algonquins were willing to exchange pelts for the guns they needed.[10]

Early inland trading from York Factory had been conducted in large birch canoes, 24 to 28 feet long, 4 feet wide, and drawing 8 inches of water. Since the outposts of the Hudson's Bay Company lay beyond the line of birch trees, canoes had to be purchased from the Indians to the south, but the supply was insufficient and the maintenance of canoes was costly. The lack of bark canoes placed the traders of the Hudson's Bay Company at a disadvantage in their rivalry with the *voyageurs* of the North West Fur Company of Montreal, who, usually with the help of Indian women, had developed large freighting canoes. They took along squaws for companionship as well as for the maintenance of the canoes. The more puritanical Hudson's Bay Company frowned upon such practices. By this time, however, sawn planks for light boats could be brought in from overseas. It is no great wonder, then, that the idea of a portable plank boat occurred to the men of the Hudson's Bay Company. One of their employees, Joseph

Hudson's Bay canoe. (Public Archives of Canada)

Isbister, a thrifty Orkneyman, complained in 1745: "There's no end to building canoes." He expressed the intention "to make triell to build a boat to Drawe as letle watter as a Canno and carie more goods."[11]

Mathew Cocking, another Hudson's Bay man, also had thoughts about replacing canoes. In 1776 he had written in his journal:

> I am fearful of being thought impertinent by presuming to point at any remedies, however with deference I think that Vessels in Canoe form made of Fir might be contrived of a small Draught of greater burden than the Indian's Canoes, and yet of such a Weight as to be carried occasionally by those who go in them. . . .[12]

Samuel Hearne, who explored the inland water routes for the Hudson's Bay Company and discovered the great ore deposits of the Coppermine River, also sought a solution for the perennial shortage of canoes. He made this entry in his journal in June 1776:

> the only method that remains is to try what can be done in light shells made of wood after the canoe-form; I am apt to believe that expert wherry builders could make vessels . . . so portable that two men may carry them one-fourth of a mile at least without resting . . . taking great care to avoid all superfluity of wood and iron. . . .[13]

The immediate need to replace the canoe was met for a time by the York boat, believed to have been developed in Canada in the early 1700s by Orkney carpenters. In the *National Fisherman* of March 1964, John Gardner described a York boat as closely resembling a bateau above the waterline, but with a scantling keel (instead of a bottom board), slack bilges, and a round bottom. The York boats were usually from 30 to 40 feet long overall, heavier than bateaux, and showed more Nordic influence than most native American boats. They had to be taken in brigades to the carries, where their combined crews dragged and pushed them across rollers. Yet, in spite of their increased weight, the York boats were more efficient than the overgrown freighting canoes. Four to eight oarsmen, occasionally assisted by sail, could pull more cargo than the same number using paddles. On a stormy lake York boats were more seaworthy and far sturdier than birch canoes that had

York boat. (Hudson's Bay Company)

been enlarged and overburdened beyond the intent of their original design.

Traders began to construct boat types of their own design, suitable for wilderness transport under stringent conditions. Perhaps the most important and widely used for commerce as well as for warfare was the bateau, the main vehicle for inland travel during two centuries. Bateaux were used for river freighting, particularly among rapids where their greater strength and resistance to damage from rocks made them superior to the large birch canoes. It is unlikely, however, that they penetrated far into the interior where conditions of travel required smaller and more portable craft.

With the close of the French and Indian Wars in 1763, the fur trade through the north woods was no longer illegal (and was therefore less profitable). After the American Revolution, demobilized scouts and Indian fighters, eager to challenge the red man on his own grounds, entered the woods with guns, traps, and fish lines. But the new settler lacked a boat that he could build and carry by himself. Plank boat construction depended upon sawmills and saw pits and these came slowly to the north woods. The so-much-desired carry-boat was still in the dim future.

The rivers of the Adirondacks (with the exception of the Hudson) flow into Lake Champlain, Lake Ontario, and the St. Lawrence River, all waters shared by Canada and New York. Traveling up these rivers, miscellaneous craft entered Adirondack waters from the north. Perhaps among them came the offspring of the fanciful thoughts of Isbister, Hearne, and Cocking on Hudson's Bay, to stimulate the imagination of the Adirondack woodsmen. The specifications these Hudson's Bay men wrote down in their journals are so amazingly close to those of the ultimate guide-boat that we can only wonder "what expert wherry makers" fashioned these "light shells after the canoe-form" for Adirondack waters.

Notes

1. *The Rudder,* October 1947, p. 31, "The Common Sense of Yacht Design" by L. Francis Herreshoff. Copyright 1947, Fawcett Publications, by permission of C.B.S. Publications.
2. *The Voyages and Explorations of Samuel de Champlain, 1604–1616, Narrated by Himself, Together with The Voyage of 1603,* ed. Edw. Gaylord Bourne (New York: Allerton Book Co., 1922), II, p. 198.
3. *Narratives of New Netherland, 1609–1664,* ed. J.F. Jameson (New York: Barnes & Noble, 1909), p. 47.
4. *The Documentary History of the State of New York,* ed. E.B. O'Callaghan, M.D. (Albany: Weed, Parsons & Co., Public Printers, 1849), I, pp. 33-34.
5. *Ibid.,* I, p. 52.
6. *Ibid.,* I, p. 69.
7. *Ibid.,* I, p. 201.
8. Peter Kalm, *Travels in North America,* ed. Adolph B. Benson, 1770 (New York: Dover Publications, 1937), I, pp. 333–371.
9. Anne Grant, *Memoirs of an American Lady with Sketches of Manners and Scenery in America, as They Existed Previous to the Revolution.* Foreword: London, 1808. (New York: George Dearborn, 1836), pp. 51, 55, 235, 248.
10. Daniel J. Boorstin, *The Americans* (New York: Random House, 1965), II, p. 59.
11. *The Beaver,* March 1949, p. 20.
12. *Journal of Mathew Cocking,* Master at Cumberland House, 1776, July 2, in *Journals of Samuel Hearne and Philip Turnor (1774–1792),* ed. J.B. Tyrell (Toronto: Champlain Society, 1934) [translated into modern English].
13. *Journals of Samuel Hearne and Philip Turnor (1774–1792),* ed. J.B. Tyrell (Toronto: The Champlain Society, 1934), pp. 188-189.

III/Early Portable Boats

All the different available forms [of portable boats] known to the world have been originated . . . either among savages with the first dawning of civilization or when civilization pushed out into the wilderness . . . where the narrow lanes of water and frequent landings and portages will not admit larger craft.

Verplanck Colvin[1]

Portable boats, ancient devices, generally fall into two classes according to circumstances: those needed by land travelers who meet occasional interruption by water; and those needed by water travelers to overcome occasional interruption by land. In the Adirondacks portable boats were needed for both contingencies.

Portable is a relative term. During the American Revolution, the bateau was considered portable; that is, the crew sprang into the water, raised the bateau by main force, and staggered up the bank. With the aid of a shore party, bateau and lading were carried beyond the rapids. We are concerned here, however, with boats that are meant to be carried, and especially those built to be carried by one man.

James Hornell suggested in his book, *Water Transport,* that since early man had nothing more serviceable than the rudest form of stone tools, he probably learned to snap reed stalks from the marshes and strip bark from a forest tree long before he was capable of felling a tree to make a dugout. The idea of bracing a bark (or skin) shell on the inside with reed or willow twigs laid across the bottom, then up the sides, to be held together at the top by a rounding strip serving as gunwale, was not beyond the mental processes of an intelligent hunter accustomed to using forest materials to fashion clothing and lodging.[2]

Skin boats are probably the earliest reported portable boats. Herodotus, writing in the second half of the fifth century B.C., mentioned the boats that floated down the Euphrates River from Armenia. They were round like a shield, constructed without stem or stern, and made of skin stretched over willow frames. Besides produce for the market at Babylon, each boat also carried a live ass aboard so that the crew could ride home, the upstream current being too strong to return by river. As soon as the cargo was unloaded the boats were taken apart. When produce and wicker frames were sold, the skins were folded and loaded on the backs of the asses. After their return to Armenia, the traders would build fresh frames to be used on their next voyage downstream.[3]

This form of boat was known to the Romans as a curuca, carracium, or caribus; to the Celts as a corwig or curach; to the Irish as a currach and to the British

Welsh coracle. (British Travel Association)

as a coracle. Julius Caesar had seen such boats in 55 B.C. during his campaign in Britain. He remembered them six years later while fighting a rival Roman army in Spain. When the bridges over the Sicoris (Segre) River could not be repaired, Caesar ordered his troops to build skin boats to carry them across.[4] The various shapes of the coracles, which are still in use near the Aran Islands, depended upon local conditions. Their size and proportions were dependent upon the height and weight of the bearer, and upon how much or how little he wanted to exert himself.

The only boats used by Eskimos prior to European contact were lightly framed craft covered with skin. The umiak was capable of carrying cargo and passengers; the light kayak, a sharp-ended canoe, usually accommodated but a single man. The American Plains Indians could fashion within a few hours a bull boat made of buffalo hide stretched over a frame of willow strips; it was crude but serviceable. Similar boats, using a different hide, were employed in 1778 by the southern traders of North America; white oak saplings were cut for frames whenever a stream was to be crossed.[5]

On his expedition to the headwaters of the Missouri River in 1804, Meriwether Lewis took along a collapsible metal frame that he planned to cover with buffalo or elk hide. The success of such a device, however carefully designed, depended upon the skill of the user. Lewis had to abandon his idea because he did not know how to waterproof the seams of the skins. John C. Fremont had an inflatable rubber boat that was wrecked in the rapids of the Platte River in 1842; a similar boat that he took on his expedition to Oregon the following year had to be abandoned because of defective seams.[6]

Verplanck Colvin, superintendent of the Topographical Survey of the Adirondack Region from 1870 to 1900, had to hold to overland travel. Seeking old markers, laying new lines, and looking for lost ponds, Colvin could not follow the vagrant waterways. "Often I have been annoyed in the course of

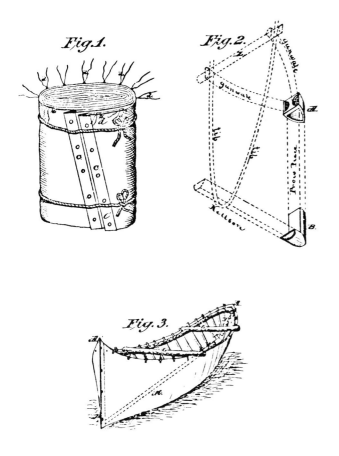

Fig. 1.

Fig. 2.

Fig. 3.

Verplanck Colvin's portable boat.

wilderness exploration by the sudden discovery of a lake where none was supposed to exist, and by finding myself without a boat in which to explore it," wrote Colvin.[7] After experiencing slow and difficult progress poling a primitive craft, he came to the conclusion that the first essential of a boat was a firm and strong shell. Testing several materials, he chose waterproof canvas and fashioned for himself an envelope that could be folded and carried as a small package. Whenever the "boat" was needed, Colvin would insert into the envelope a frame made of small saplings fastened with leather thongs. Since saplings were everywhere available, the frames could be discarded at every portage. But such inventions were no solution to the Adirondack woodsman who needed a stronger and more durable boat to carry with him.

W. S. Benchley, whose brothers George and Joseph were well-known trappers, with a line of shanties and marten traps from the Brown's Tract to Raquette

Lake, was a frequent visitor to another famous trapper, Nat Foster, who lived in the old Herreshoff Manor near Thendara. In a letter that Jeptha R. Simms published in *Trappers of New York,* this Benchley wrote that he had seen Foster at the age of 60 carry his skiff upon his shoulders over the three-quarter-mile carry between Fifth and Sixth Lakes of the Fulton Chain, "with but one stop."[8] If Benchley's chronology was correct, Foster, who was born in 1767, was backing his skiff across the carry in 1827; in any event, it was before 1833, when Foster left the Brown's Tract and retired to Boonville after having been accused and acquitted of murdering an Indian.

We know little about Foster's boat, except for one detail mentioned by a witness at the murder trial who testified that Foster was caulking his boat when threatened by the Indian.[9] A bark canoe may need caulking in July; but Benchley had called Foster's boat a "skiff." The witness gave no details about construction, shape, or weight.

On the day of the alleged murder, three boats were moving through First Lake. The Indian, Drid, was in a bark canoe, presumably birch. Two white trappers were in another bark canoe, and four fishermen were in a rowboat. A woodcut in Simms's book portrays these three boat types: the Indian's small canoe with curved stem characteristic of the birch canoe, the trapper's crude craft of spruce or elm bark, and the fisherman's rowboat with square transom. Since Foster was allegedly shooting from ambush on shore, he must have hidden his boat. It is not in the woodcut. Could Foster's skiff have been a primitive wooden skiff that needed caulking, antedating the early forms of clinker-built guide-boats, which did not need caulking?

Historians must be cautious in equating the first appearance of a certain boat type with the date of the first report. It is unlikely that the reporter saw the boat at the moment of its creation; rather, he probably saw for the first time something already well established. One can safely assume that the skiff Foster carried at age 60 had been in use for some time, since both Emmons and Benedict reported that the use of small boats in the north woods had long been known.

Professor E. Emmons, state geologist, traveled extensively through the north woods from 1836 to 1842 for the survey of the second geological district. He reported that, with scarcely a carrying place, the hunters and fishermen took their boats from Raquette Lake into the headwaters of the Black River.[10]

Professor Emmons's assistant, the civil engineer Farrand N. Benedict, who conducted the topographical survey in the Adirondacks, confirmed these findings. He reported that it had been long known that hunters transported their fish, game, and fur in small boats through the waterways from Lake Champlain to the Black River. "From their accounts it appeared that the carrying places were few and short. . . . My own travels over this route, which were commenced in 1835, verified these statements. . . ."[11] Benedict's mention of carrying places indicates that the boats he referred to were portable, but of what type? With his technical training, Benedict would have called them canoes, if such they were, as he did later in 1840 when he reported on his journey from Cedar River to Blue Mountain Lake. That same year found Professor Emmons at Raquette Lake at the establishment of Beach and Wood where "a supply of light boats are always on hand for fishing or hunting, or for exploring the inlets and neighboring lakes."[12] Though Professor Emmons had no name for these boats and gave no description, he understood their function.

To the early records of small boat travel in the reports of Benedict and Emmons should be added that of Charles Fenno Hoffman, who came to Lake Sanford in 1837. He observed that the hunter, through several links and portages, could float his craft from Lake Sanford to Lake Henderson and from there all the way to the St. Lawrence. We know therefore that the boat was portable. Because Hoffman and his party "pull" through a narrow passage and, upon reaching the lake, are "lying upon their oars" to listen for shouted echoes, we know that the boat is not a canoe but a pulling boat, a rowboat with oars.[13]

In his book *Long Lake,* the Reverend John Todd, the first of a parade of clerical tourists, reported on his three visits to Long Lake, where men had gone to hunt and fish, to survey the land, and to buy and sell it. Todd was distressed that no one had come to care for the souls of the inhabitants. Todd spread the word during his first visit in 1841 that he would hold Sabbath services. When the settlers arrived in little boats

he did not seem surprised at their means of transportation, nor did he claim to be a pioneer discoverer. This seems to indicate that he had seen similar boats before. Were these boats portable? Is it possible that John Todd saw a real portable boat for the first time in 1842 in Saranac, where he embarked for his second visit to Long Lake? There "we procured a little boat," he wrote, "such a one as a man can carry on his head through the woods, from river to river and from lake to lake."[14] But again, Todd's tone is matter of fact, not one of surprise. For the first time we can conjure up a picture: "Such a one as a man can carry on his head. . . ."

In the account of Todd's third visit to Long Lake, in 1843, we see the boat in the characteristic mirror image on the misty lake "looking sometimes twice as large as they were, and sometimes looking double — one boat above the water and a second below it." Todd was the first writer of whom we have knowledge who paid attention to the part these small boats played in the daily lives of the settlers. "They were here alone, shut out from the world," wrote Todd, "their little boats were their horses, and the lake their only path."[15]

Where did these little boats come from? Did the settlers who came to Long Lake just after 1830 bring them from their previous location or did they construct them on the shores of Long Lake after their arrival? Who were the builders? Who brought the patterns and from where? Were these boats crude or had they already an advanced design? Did they have square transoms? The only information Todd gave us was that they were little and that they were rowed.

An act of the legislature of the State of New York incorporating the town of Long Lake was passed May 7, 1837. A few years later the town was surveyed and run into lots by Judge Richards, each lot containing 200 acres. A Mr. Austin was listed among those who had made considerable improvements.[16] In his *Journal of a Surveying Excursion to Raquette Lake & Vicinity,* Mr. A.E. Leavenworth referred to a visit to Long Lake. He arrived the night of August 18, 1851, and spent the night at the beach. The following morning he and his party rowed nine miles and walked five more to "Mr. Austin's at the head of the Long Lake," where they were served breakfast by Mrs. Austin. Referring to Mr. Austin's activities,

Painting by J[ames] C[ameron], presumably at Long Lake. At lower left is a crude skiff, built about 1850. (Adirondack Museum)

Leavenworth wrote in his *Journal*: "In the winter season he builds boats, about one a week & sells them for about $15.00."[17] If it took Mr. Austin only one week to build a boat, then they were of simple construction. A painting that was still in the possession of F.N. Benedict in 1880, and is now in the collection of the Adirondack Museum, shows a rowing boat drawn up on a lakeshore (according to family tradition this was Long Lake). Visible are the stem, one side built up of four strakes, and the hazy impression of one oar. The stern is not shown. The picture is signed and dated at lower center, tentatively deciphered as J.C. [Cameron?] [1852?].

Where did Mr. Austin learn to build boats? According to the Long Lake census report of 1850, a William J. Austin, 36 years old, farmer, was born in Vermont. Lake Champlain to the west and the Connecticut River to the east are Vermont's only extensive waterways. A great-great-grandson, Harold Austin, who in 1978 still resided near Long Lake, could not give us any precise information. William J. Austin left Long Lake sometime after 1850 and appears again on the census report of the town of Moriah, New York, in 1860.

The Albany newspaper man Samuel H. Hammond

journeyed through the Chateaugay woods in 1848. He and his guide, Joe Tucker, carried no boat but relied, instead, on what they would find at the lake shores. At Meacham's Lake, not far from the Upper Saranac, Tucker produced out of the bushes a light "canoe," which he had fashioned the previous spring and hidden there. In these waters the craft could have been an early Saranac boat. It proved fast enough to overtake a swimming deer and light enough to carry around the rapids of Lower Saranac. This is the region where John Todd, six years earlier, procured a little boat such as a man could carry on his head.

At Ragged Lake, where they could find no boat, Hammond's guide said: "We will coast this lake as we have done the rest, and that in a vessel of our own construction."[18] Hammond reported that what they built was a curiosity in its way but that by the exercise of great caution it enabled them to navigate the lake. As long as they remained seated it was steady enough. Hammond called the rivers and the lakes they passed through the highways, the turnpikes, and the railroads of that wild region. He compared the boats they encountered to carriages, stagecoaches, and cars in which everybody must travel.[19]

The truth of the comparison was confirmed by Joel

T. Headley, another preacher and a cousin of Far-rand N. Benedict, who reported on his Adirondack experiences in the *New York Times* in 1858. One evening Headley decided to accompany a young man who had to go for some butter. They crossed the lake in a small boat, then walked across a narrow footpath to the next lake where they picked up another little boat moored at the shore. After crossing the second lake they came to a log hut whence they procured the butter. Upon their return to the Lower Saranac another man was waiting for the boat to get some milk from his cow, pastured in a clearing half a mile down the lake.[20]

The first adequate description we found of the small boats in terms of function was published in the *New York Times* by its editor, Henry J. Raymond. Traveling overland in 1855 with a party to Eagle Lake, he was met there by a fleet of seven boats from Raquette Lake bringing supplies that had been carted in from Lowville in Lewis County over the Carthage Road to North Point. Raymond remarked: "No other boats than these little skiffs are used at all upon these lakes, partly because heavier ones could not be carried, as they are, by hand, and partly because they answer all purposes. . . ."[21] Unhappily, Raymond failed to give details about form or construction.

The earliest specific report we have giving some details about a portable boat was published in the *Spirit of the Times* of February 3, 1844. A sportsman writing under the pen name of "Bob Rackett" came to Raquette Lake in 1843 with a party of friends. Their guide was Higby the Hunter, who had built a boat in the woods out of cedar. Rackett estimated the weight to be about 90 pounds. Higby rowed it up the Fulton Chain and across Raquette Lake during a thunder squall carrying three passengers, a dog, one hundred pounds of provisions, and the sportsmen's duffel. The boat was carried over the portages by means of a yoke rigged across the gunwales. If Higby built the boat in the woods with no other tool than hatchet, drawknife, and hammer, using nails and probably green cedar riven on the spot (we are not told where Higby obtained the cedar), as Rackett reported, the boat must have been rather crude, for even the most skillful craftsman could not do fine matching in the woods. Yet a cedar boat weighing 90

pounds, swift enough to pursue a swimming deer, and carried on a yoke, begins to resemble the description of the future guide-boat, unless Rackett misjudged the weight. What had seemed to him like a cockleshell on a rough lake might have been in reality a heavy boat on the carry.

Another reporter, using the pseudonym "Sporting Naturalist," wrote a series of articles about an expedition to the Eckford Lakes in the summer of 1849 with Mitchell Sabattis as guide. One day found him near the cabin of Mr. Austin on the shore of Long Lake. Mitchell Sabattis had left him a few miles back to get the boat he had built for himself. Upon rejoining the Sporting Naturalist, Sabattis requested his help to pitch the boat, which was, according to the Naturalist, a very light but well-built boat. Here again we wonder what kind of plank boat needed pitching in the summer. We know the craft was a rowboat because Sabattis shipped his oars and took up the silent paddle at the sight of a deer.[22]

The Naturalist estimated the weight of the boat to be between 50 and 60 pounds. This seems incredibly light for those days. In spite of its supposed lightness, however, Sabattis left the boat behind at the first landing on the Raquette River in favor of whatever he might find at the other end of the carry, which proved to be a rather rickety and somewhat antiquated affair. That Sabattis did not carry his own boat to the next launching place raises the suspicion that the correspondent was no expert at guessing weight. Sabattis had practical experience. He may have considered his boat too fragile for the rough waters of Raquette Lake because, after arriving at the next carry, between Forked Lake and Raquette Lake, he again found another boat concealed in the bushes. It was an entirely new, but rather clumsily built, wide skiff, according to the Naturalist. Sabattis may also have wanted to avoid carrying the heavy burden of the boat he built himself.

Witness the account of Benson Lossing who, seeking the headwaters of the Hudson, hired guides at Saranac in 1859. Lossing was surprised to see with what apparent ease his guide, a Penobscot Indian from Maine, carried a boat weighing at least 160 pounds "and with a dog-trot bore it the whole distance, stopping only once. The boat rests upon a yoke . . . fitted to the neck and shoulders, and it is

Heavy Chase Lake "portable boat" with rough planking. (Helen Durant)

thus borne with the ease of the coracle."[23] Lossing was one of the rare Adirondack travelers familiar with the European counterpart of the portable boat, but apparently he did not know its weight. James Hornell gives the weight of a coracle built for a heavy man as 34 pounds; one constructed for an older person wishing to save himself extra exertion weighed 28 pounds, while the average weight of a coracle varied between 26 and 29 pounds.[24]

The observation of T.B. Thorpe, an ardent fisherman who traveled through the Adirondacks the same year as Lossing, came closer to reality. What seemed to him a light skiff on the lakes of the Fulton Chain assumed much heavier proportions on the carries. To Thorpe, the guide's task seemed "as impossible as carrying a man of war, yet [he] brought the ponderous thing along, steadily and gracefully, and set it down with scarcely a perceptible flush on his honest face."[25] Often the guide avoided carrying the "ponderous thing" by leaving it behind, counting on finding another boat at the end of the carry.

The boats mentioned in this chapter were portable rowing boats — skiffs, not canoes. There is a wide gap in our knowledge of their construction and that of the boats that appear later. This poses crucial questions concerning the mystery of forgotten craft. How did a crude carry-boat develop into the exquisite guide-boat? Because many of us have lost the manual skill of the early craftsmen and could not develop or build such a sophisticated craft, we sometimes tend to conclude, too hastily, that they could not have done it either. Although the north woods builder may have had no theoretical knowledge of arithmetic and geometry or of the laws of motion and gravity, science is not the exclusive property of modern man. The noted anthropologist Bronislaw Malinowski reminds us of this fact in his observations of the primitive Malaysians who know instinctively about buoyancy and leverage.[26]

Between the vanished birch canoe, dugouts and other makeshift craft, and the first beginnings of a peculiar form of construction that became known as the Adirondack guide-boat, there is an interval of trial and error, of experiment and failure, of which we cannot yet give a precise account.

It may come as a bit of a shock to some to realize that one of the world's most exquisitely contrived boats, approaching the rowing shell and the violin in delicacy, was built and perfected in the north woods first by unknown woodsmen who had struggled under their burden on the carries, and later by the guides and local carpenters. Fashioning their craft in obscure little shops, the individual builders searched for materials in the nearby forests. They examined and tested the lightness, strength, and variety in the curves of the spruce roots bending from the stump, and uncovered a secret that launched a thousand boats.

Notes

1. Verplanck Colvin, "Portable Boats," in *Transactions of the Albany Institute* (Albany: J. Munsell, 1876), VIII, p. 255. (Read before the Albany Institute on May 1, 1875.)
2. James Hornell, *Water Transport* (Cambridge: At the University Press, 1946), pp. 176, 181, 182.
3. *The History of Herodotus,* Vol. I, p. 160. Translated by George Rawlinson. An Everyman's Library Edition. By permission of E.P. Dutton.

4. James Hornell, *British Coracles and Irish Curraghs* (London: Society for Nautical Research, 1938), p. 6.

5. *Travels of William Bartram,* ed. Mark van Doren (Dover Publications, 1928), p. 363.

6. Meriwether Lewis, *Lewis and Clark Expedition* (Philadelphia and New York: J.B. Lippincott Co., 1961), I, pp. 245-266.

7. Colvin, pp. 254-265.

8. Jeptha R. Simms, *Trappers of New York* (Albany: J. Munsell, 1850), p. 190; Joseph F. Grady, *The Adirondacks* (Little Falls, N.Y.: Press of the Journal & Courier, 1933), pp. 80-85.

9. Simms, p. 212.

10. *The New York Geological and Mineralogical Reports,* 1839, Assembly Document no. 275 (Albany, 1840), p. 228.

11. Letter dated: Dec. 20, 1845, Burlington, Vermont, in *New York State Senate, 69th Session,* Document no. 73 (Albany, 1846), p. 10.

12. *New York State, Report of Geological Survey,* 1841, Assembly Document no. 150, p. 120.

13. Charles Fenno Hoffman, *Wild Scenes in the Forest and Prairie* (New York, 1843; London: Richard Bentley, n.d., ca. 1843), pp. 17-21.

14. John Todd, *Long Lake* (Pittsfield, Mass.: E.P. Little, 1845), pp. 7, 37.

15. *Ibid.*

16. Howard I. Becker, *Early Long Lake Documents* (Rexford, N.Y., 1957). Amos Deane, "An attempt to present the Claims of Long Lake to the Consideration of all those who are in Search of Good Land at a Low Price" (Albany: Joel Munsell, 1846).

17. "Journal of a Surveying Excursion to Raquette Lake & Vicinity, August 1851," by A.E. Leavenworth, microfilm in the Adirondack Museum.

18. Samuel H. Hammond, *Hills, Lakes and Forest Streams* (New York, 1854).

19. Samuel H. Hammond and W.L. Mansfield, *Country Margins and Rambles of a Journalist* (New York: J.C. Derby, 1855), p. 306.

20. *New York Times,* August 9 and 13, 1858.

21. *New York Times,* June 19 and July 14, 1855.

22. *Spirit of the Times,* September 8-December 8, 1849.

23. B.J. Lossing, *The Hudson from the Wilderness to the Sea* (New York: Virtue and Yorston, 1866), pp. 6, 11.

24. James Hornell, *British Coracles,* pp. 29-30.

25. Thomas B. Thorpe, *Harper's New Monthly Magazine,* July 1859.

26. Bronislaw Malinowski, *Magic, Science and Religion and other Essays* (Garden City, N.Y.: Doubleday Anchor Books, 1954), p. 34.

IV/Evolution of the Adirondack Guide-Boat

. . . so my best plan is to make me a little boat big enough to sit in, and carry it . . .

"The Sixth Voyage of Sinbad"[1]

In tracing the development of boats there is a temptation to try to fit each design into a progressive pattern of evolution. But new forms are not necessarily dependent on old forms; changed details can be innovations as the result of availability of new materials. Concerning evolution in boatbuilding, James Hornell wrote in *Water Transport*:

> Some boats have failed to progress far beyond their primary condition . . . others have evolved into water-craft of considerable complexity . . . . Usually the process has been slow and prolonged, but there can be no doubt that, by reason of the exceptional inventive skill of occasional individuals or communities, progress has sometimes been accelerated by what may be considered a sudden and radical mutation—the superimposition of a secondary invention of revolutionary importance upon the primary conception and design.[2]

The origin of the Adirondack guide-boat has never been satisfactorily explained. The boat came into existence somewhere between 1825 and 1835, achieved its extraordinary perfection between 1890 and 1900, and then fell into disuse. It is now primarily found in museums and in the boat houses of the few remaining private camps in the Adirondacks. Where did this boat come from? Was it a development of the Indian's canoe or was it a regional invention?

A long-accepted legend is that the Adirondack guide-boat was invented by Mitchell Sabattis, a full-blooded Abenaki Indian and guide. A procession of travelers brought back from Long Lake in Hamilton County fabulous tales of this legendary woodsman and hunter who killed moose and panthers and bear, played the fiddle, and led the singing in church. Marvels accrued to him until it was only natural to attribute the invention of the guide-boat to him. The tale of Sabattis's accomplishments was widespread before anyone wrote it down. The historian Alfred L. Donaldson had it from Dr. Arpad Gerster who had it from John Holland.[3] Donaldson put it in his book, *A History of the Adirondacks,* and it became gospel.

Referring in the index of his book to the "first Adirondack guide-boat built," Donaldson wrote:

> Nothing of greater historical interest attaches to Long Lake than the fact that the Adirondack guide-boat was evolved there. Its progenitors were Sabattis and one of the Palmers who saw the need of devising something sturdier and swifter than the canoe. Their joint product must have been put in use as early as 1842, for that was the date of Dr. Todd's

Mitchell Sabattis. (Adirondack Museum)

second visit, in recounting which he says: "We procured a little boat, such a one as a man can carry on his head through the woods, from river to river, and from lake to lake." He [Todd] also speaks of the people coming to church in their "little boats," which would indicate that the new model was then in general use.[4]

Donaldson implied that the little boats were guide-boats because in a sentence following our quote, Donaldson said: "It differed in one important respect, however, from the guide-boat of today. It had a square stern. . . ."

There are several inconsistencies in Donaldson's account. Todd made three consecutive visits to Long Lake and preached there in 1841, 1842, and 1843. It was about his first trip in 1841 that Todd wrote: "The Sabbath morning came and we met the little boats. . . and one huge bark canoe."[5] On his second visit to Long Lake in 1842, Todd traveled from Lake Champlain west until he reached Saranac, and it was here, not at Long Lake, that he "procured a little boat. . . ."[6] Todd does not mention a square stern, although he does tell us that the boats were rowed.

Mitchell Sabattis himself gave as his birthdate September 29, 1824.[7] It is not impossible that he built boats at an early age, but it is hardly likely that he was the progenitor of all the little boats "long known as used by hunters" reported in the 1830s by Professor E. Emmons and Farrand N. Benedict. Sabattis lived on the shore of Long Lake not far from the boatbuilder

William Austin, with whom he could have exchanged ideas and patterns. Being an Indian, Sabattis was probably a superb canoe builder, but if he was also the legendary woodsman he was reported to be, he would scarcely have invented a square-ended skiff. This form was impractical in the dense Adirondack woods and was not in the Indian tradition.

We have been unable to track down the source of Donaldson's statement, or of later speculation that the Palmer involved was named Cy.[8] Cyrus H. Palmer, who was a boatbuilder in the latter half of the century, was not born until 1845, according to cemetery records, which show that he died on December 8, 1897, at age 52.

In 1935 Talbot Bissell, a resident of Long Lake from 1888 to 1941, wrote "Their Little Boats," in which he stated: "That the guide-boat was evolved at Long Lake is certain, but there is still some dispute as to who originated it."[9] Mr. Bissell was rightly cautious when he used the verb "evolve." The boat probably evolved simultaneously in different places in the Adirondacks as the builders borrowed and learned from each other.

Leaving myth and legend aside, we must say that no one man invented the carry-boat that eventually evolved into the guide-boat. No one man built "the first" one. For a hundred years before Sabattis, men were traveling this otherwise impassable wilderness "in Bark Canoes, or very light Battoes, . . . which may be easily carried on Men's Shoulders,"[10] as Cadwallader Colden observed as early as 1727 in his report on travel through the wilderness of northern New York. The development from carry-boat to the ultimate guide-boat was slow. Use under many different circumstances and for many different purposes suggested changes and improvements.

If not invented but "evolved," was the guide-boat a highly developed canoe? That was a form with which the trapper was familiar. Though he sometimes made a dugout, we have found no evidence that the white trapper ever built a birch canoe in the Adirondacks nor that the Indian made birch canoes in this region. Most of the Indians came down from the St. Lawrence River on hunting expeditions. They brought their canoes with them, because the north woods lacked the proper birches. In an emergency, the Indian could make a canoe out of spruce bark.

The few Indian hunters and guides living in the Adirondacks before the development of the guide-boat had relatives in the north who visited and may have supplied them with birch canoes.

Moreover, the construction methods of canoe and guide-boat are mutually incompatible. The theory that the guide-boat was invented by an Indian becomes questionable if the student ignores the pleasing outline of the tumblehome stems and concentrates, instead, on the pattern of the roughly five thousand copper tacks and three thousand brass screws. The birch canoe is a brilliant achievement, of great beauty, but it is wholly indigenous: the Indian used the materials the forest provided and fashioned his craft with Stone Age tools. The bark canoe, whether birch, elm, or spruce, began with an outer sheathing made flexible, and then folded and sewn or gummed. Into this preshaped hull the Indian forced a frame of riven wood splints and thwarts. He used no metal fastenings.

In contrast, the guide-boat maker started with the framework: a bottom board, two stems, and ribs fashioned from natural crooks shaped by fine steel tools. The thin planking that covered the frame formed the hull. Though the white man kept the paddle and learned to wield it in the silent Indian manner, he added the more efficient oars, which did not lie within the Indian tradition. The guide-boat is essentially a rowboat whose outward form superficially resembles the canoe-form; she evolved from another species of rowing boat, from another "carry-boat." But which one? The appellation *carry-boat* means nothing more than that the boat could be carried. It gives no clue to construction or antecedents.

Between the "light Battoes" of Colden's 1727 account and the unique form and construction that became the Adirondack guide-boat lies an interval of obscure experimentation. Territories immediately surrounding New York and adjoining states had not produced anything resembling the guide-boat, nor did there seem to be any local industry capable of creating such a complicated craft. In Canada, whose waters mingle with those of New York on three sides, the white man made the longest sustained efforts to build a rowboat that could equal or surpass the canoe. These efforts took many directions, but none seemed to lead to the guide-boat.

To contrive a boat suitable to his needs, and eventually light enough to carry on his back, the Adirondack builder resorted to the ancient shipwright's practice of laying planks upon a frame, but he found new byways and detours. A similar circuitous path can be traced in the development of the dory, whose design was altered by the fishermen who used it, by changes big and infinitely small, until they had achieved the perfect boat for their needs. Whereas it took the dory two centuries to reach perfection, the guide-boat, evolving from unknown antecedents in a rather small area, took much less time. The boat of the hunters developed as a happy amalgam of innovation and useful details borrowed from other craft.

We can imagine the early settlers starting their initial efforts to build a boat with a crude flat bottom and abrupt straight sides, a natural form for a primitive plank boat. E. Roland Robinson reported, at the turn of the century, that, while walking along the shores of meadow or woodland, he sometimes came upon an old boat, "an ancient scow of primitive pattern. The straight lines of her battered sides are not relieved by the slightest curve from bow to stern, from gunwale to bottom . . . ."[11] The Museum has two samples of this form: a square-ended river scow and an amphibious ice punt.

As builders worked to improve stability and ease of movement, the plank keel (or bottom board) gradually narrowed and the sides began to round and swell. Curved ribs became necessary to support the rounding hull. As the bottom became narrower, the side planks likewise had to be narrowed to fit the rib contour. Again, Mr. Robinson reported on finding "the half stripped bones of an old trapping skiff. Though of almost as primitive mold, she is a very different pattern from the scow. Short and narrow, sharp at both ends, her sides of three lapped streaks fastened to a few knees of natural crook . . . the trapper . . . with his long setting pole drove her over submerged logs and coaxed her through intricate passages of the flooded wood."

The basic structure of the guide-boat, from early types to the perfected craft, remained the same: a frame of natural-crook ribs erected on a flat, elliptical bottom. Imperceptibly, the boat assumed a standard form, with only slight variations peculiar to builder and place.

Harvey Moody's boat. Pencil sketch by Thomas Addison Richards, 1853. (Adirondack Museum)

Reporting on the boats he saw on his second trip into the north woods in 1853, Samuel Hammond described them as constructed of spruce or cedar boards a quarter of an inch thick, clapboarded upon knees of the natural crook and carried, bottom upwards, fastened to a yoke that was adjusted to the shoulders.[12] Alfred Billings Street had traveled with a party of friends from the Lower Saranac to Tupper Lake around 1854 when he noticed carrying boats with yokes. In *Woods and Waters,* published in 1860, he wrote:

> Drawn half way up the green bank, near a log hut, were four Saranac boats. These boats are dark-colored, slender as a pike, buoyant as a cork, made gracefully of thin pine, with knees of fir, their weight from ninety to one hundred and twenty pounds. Each has two oars on iron pins, a paddle, a neck-yoke for the "carries". . . .[13]

The date of Street's trip is approximate. His excursion would have been before the end of 1859 because his account concluded with the ascent of Whiteface Mountain, where the guide was Dauphin Thompson from North Elba, who lost his life during John Brown's famous raid at Harper's Ferry in October 1859.[14] Street's own guide on this trip was Harvey Moody,[15] whose brother Cort was also guiding for Street's party. In the library at Saranac Lake is an undated photograph of Fernando Cortez Moody, the

first white child born in Saranac. The photo shows a bearded guide holding an ancient gun. Moody is seated on the bow of an equally ancient boat with heavy stem rising above the bow deck and thick laps clearly showing, yet, unmistakably, a guide-boat prototype with natural-crook ribs, square loom oars on fixed pins, and a riser for the carrying yoke. It resembles the old 1848 "bookcase" boat, which is preserved in the camp of Franklin Brandreth. That boat has a well-worn groove in the gunwale amidships where the yoke rested. The Moody of the photograph is an old man. The boat is not necessarily the one he used for the Street expedition but might have been one he kept for his own use.

In the accounts of Street and Hammond, a recognizable guide-boat appeared as out of nowhere, completely equipped in the ultimate form and manner. If, in one's imagination, the sides of those boats are trimmed a trifle, the clapboard edges smoothed out, and a few pounds taken off the weight, they become guide-boats in their perfected form. The word of a casual tourist and the scribble of a journalist on vacation surprise us with a sudden report of a boat that has been slowly emerging. The fact that the documented appearance is so abrupt does not mean that the boat developed at a leap, but rather, that we lack documentation of its progression.

William H. Boardman, editor and part-owner of the magazine *Railway Age,* and a careful observer of

Fernando Cortez Moody. (Saranac Lake Free Library, Adirondack Collection.)

guide-boat construction, described the boat as it was around 1865:

> The bowline alone was pointed, the gunwale lines tapering inward on nearly a straight line from amidships to a narrow, square stern. They were clinker-built, of thin board, each of whose lower edges lapped over the board next below . . . .[16]

Boardman wrote that the designing of such boats, "fitted with oars and carrying a yoke," was apparently undertaken seriously by different persons after 1860.

Among artist-travelers, Frederick B. Allen was exceptional in catching the salient details of the guide-boat along with the charm and manners of the waterways. His sketches, made during trips to the Adirondacks in 1869 and 1870, show the early types described by Hammond, Street, and Boardman. The boats in those sketches are true prototypes of the later delicate double-enders.[17]

The change from square stern to double-ender occurred around the 1870s. It made no substantial difference below the waterline, where the boats were already virtual double-enders. Removing the transom made handling easier. The beached boat could be pushed out into the lake with greater facility. The

1848 "bookcase boat" in camp of Franklin Brandreth. (Helen Durant)

"The bowline alone was pointed, the gunwale lines nearly straight from amidships to a narrow, square stern. The lower edge of each strake lapped over the board next below." (Every Saturday, Sept. 3, 1870)

guide who paddled like an American Indian, and not like an Eskimo or a South Sea Islander, required a pointed stern for good performance.

Willard Sutton (1865–1960) had been a guide at the Prospect House in Blue Mountain Lake and at The Cedars, the F.C. Durant camp on Forked Lake. When we spoke with him at the Brandreth camp in 1958, he was of the opinion that the square sterns were wrong. "To balance the boat properly," he said, "the man in the boat had to carry ballast to keep the stem up." The square-sterned Carey boat at Brandreth still has stains on the stern planking, showing that the stern rode very low in the water. This was not only because of the extra weight of the transom and the ballast but also because of the overall design of the Carey boat, with its shortened stern stem and greatest width forward.

The use of the square transom in Adirondack boats, similar to that of the Whitehall or the wherry,

is an anomaly yet to be explained. The bateau had already demonstrated the advantage of the pointed stern, so clearly superior for all uses in narrow streams and shoal waters. The Indian had known it all along. The transom stem, made as high and narrow as possible in the early guide-boat to overcome obvious disadvantages, seems an archaic survival from another craft and another place.

With all the conflicting claims about who built the first guide-boat, there is equal confusion as to who effected the change from square stern to double-ender. Could there have been two distinct types of guide-boats in the Adirondacks before 1870? Double-enders had been reported since 1864, when Lucia D. Pychowska wrote in the *Continental Monthly* that she had traveled through the Adirondacks in a faery craft, sharp at both ends.[18] W.H.H. Murray reported in 1869 that the Adirondack boats were on the average some 15 feet long and sharp at both ends.[19]

View from Holland's Beach, Blue Mountain Lake, New York, about 1879. Between 1874 and 1882, square-ended guide-boats and double-enders were found side by side. (Adirondack Museum)

Until the early 1880s, square-ended boats and double-enders were seen side by side. The change is perplexing and could very well hold the secret of the origin of the Adirondack guide-boat. Once the square end was experimentally abandoned—on the intuition of some practical guide, perhaps, or an imaginative builder—the square stern quickly disappeared from the lakes.

Donaldson claims that the only important improvement to guide-boat construction not originated by Caleb Chase of Newcomb was reduction in weight.[20] If we take Donaldson at his word, this would make Chase the innovator of the double-ender. In a letter published in *Forest and Stream* of March 9, 1876, D.W. Mandell, a reader, compared the Chase boats with those of Carey and Stanton of Long Lake. He said that the boats of the latter two builders were "somewhat squarer while those of Chase were alike at both ends." This would make Chase one of the earliest converters to double-ended boats but not necessarily the innovator.

When Henry Stanton went to Boonville in 1879 to assist Dwight Grant, bringing his own patterns with him, square-ended guide-boats were on the decline. We have found no evidence that Dwight Grant ever built one. This was confirmed by his son, Lewis, who also told us that, as a youth (around 1890), he loved to row the *Gypsy* at the Lawrence Camp at Limekiln Lake, "perhaps because it was the only one with a square stern, but I do not think my father built it. There were not many of the old square stern guide-boats on the Fulton Chain in my day." If Mandell was correct in his observation, Stanton must have switched to double-enders between 1876 and 1879,

Kenneth Durant rowing Talbot Bissell's Chase boat at Endion, Long Lake. The mirror image is evidence of the guide-boat's symmetry. (Helen Durant)

the bow and stern of the new model were alike and decked for a foot or so toward the waist.[21]

Some of the early guide-boats were built with the widest beam slightly forward of amidships, imitating the shape of a duck or a codfish. Some had their bow stems slightly higher than the stern. These earlier forms were gradually replaced by true double-enders with the widest beam amidships. Without fittings, bow and stern, port and starboard, were indistinguishable except for the run of the scarph laps, visible only to the expert. These variations did not affect the essential structure.

A further refinement in the construction of guide-boats was the smooth skin of the hull. In the conventional lapstrake or "clapboarded" siding, mentioned by Hammond, the lap of the lower edge of each plank over the plank just below it is clearly visible. Howard I. Chapelle, in his authoritative *Boatbuilding*, described the bevel required on the outside upper edge of each plank in the usual lapstrake construction, and said that each succeeding strake should lie flat upon the under plank. It was clenched with nails or rivets, a construction that was "very light and strong," requiring no caulking. No bevel was needed on the bottom edge of the strake. Each succeeding plank showed its bottom edge, as do the walls of a clapboarded house. The clapboard effect made the lapstrake hull instantly recognizable, even by the most lubberly.[22]

A skilled Adirondack builder, experienced in making small lapstrake boats and accustomed to beveling the outside upper edge of each strake, progressed by a stroke of sheer genius to beveling the inside lower edge of each strake as well and fitting the two bevels together. The rest was easy but daring: he fastened these joined bevels with clinched, tiny copper tacks, instead of the heavier nails or rivets. He was already accustomed to doing something like this when he joined the vertical scarphs of his siding with glue and copper tacks. In applying a similar method to the lengthwise edges of the planks, he not only lightened his boat considerably, but made a smooth surface within and without, thus removing the hitherto most characteristic outward feature of the lapstrake.

If, contrary to the definition of some, we find that technically the guide-boat must be classified as both lapstrake and clinker-built, nevertheless, there is a

Double-ended Grant boat number 11 of 1904 with decks at stem and stern. (Helen Durant)

either through independent innovation or after having seen double-enders made by other builders.

Willard Sutton told us that Henry and Ed Stanton made the first double-enders "that I knew of" and that they had begun to do so "about eighty years ago." That would be about 1878. Mr. Sutton, being 93 years old when we spoke with him in 1958, could not give a precise date, but his memory seemed lively. Generally speaking, most builders started conversion to double-enders around 1875. Boardman said that valid distinction between the two that Dwight Grant rightly insisted upon. The smooth-skin, sawn-rib construction of the guide-boat was not what was popularly visualized as lapstrake. Whatever the siding may have been in earlier forms, sometime after 1860 the smooth skin became an essential characteristic of the guide-boat. It required the most painstaking craftsmanship to cut the bevels and fit the joints so that they would not show and could not be felt.

In the dory and the St. Lawrence River skiff, the laps were often refined and diminished by clever shaping, and as the planks approached the stem, the laps disappeared entirely, but as far as we can determine, only in the guide-boat was the lap invisible over the entire length. In the ingenious and functional development of the beveled guide-boat lap, whether feather-edge or Grant ship-lap, the laps remained but disappeared from view, confusing many. Boardman called these invisible joints "chisel-edged." For this he may be forgiven. The joints remained lapstrake, clenched with thousands of tiny tacks, but because the matching was so perfectly done, the boat was easily and often mistaken as carvel-built. (In carvel construction, the planks meet flush at the seams instead of overlapping.)

The durable joints permitted a thinner siding. Though the smooth-skinned boat became more fragile, it remained strong enough for Adirondack waters, and it was much lighter. Donaldson credits Willie Martin of Saranac Lake with being the first to think of making the guide-boat lighter, but he gives no clue as to how Martin achieved this.[23] Talbot Bissell calls Martin the genius who first tooled lightness into them but he does not tell us, either, how Martin did it.[24] Most guide-boat builders were preoccupied with the problem of weight. Some were more successful than others in solving the problem. (Certainly Dwight Grant succeeded in making his boats considerably lighter over the years without sacrificing strength.)

There are two easily recognizable types of guide-boat. The earliest was the traditional Saranac boat with its incurving tumblehome bow and stern. This boat was made, with certain variations, by all builders on Raquette waters, and as far east as Lake Placid. The somewhat later form, known as the Brown's Tract boat, was found on the Fulton Chain

of Lakes and the Moose River. The latter had some outward rake to the stems, bow and stern. The two models are strikingly dissimilar in profile; at the waterline, however, they are alike. Both models have a conspicuous rise in the sheer, bow and stern, to throw off splashing waves.

A desire for refinement and elegance fortunately did not lead to decadence or superfluous ornamentation. Some boats revealed the builder's preference for the beauty of natural wood under clear varnish, or perhaps a few strips of contrasting hardwood on the decks. But changes in design were changes in form, not in function.

The New Yorker of April 5, 1958, published "A Letter from the North," in which its author, E.B. White, wrote:

> I do not recall ever seeing a properly designed boat that was not also a beautiful boat. Purity of line, loveliness, symmetry—these arrive mysteriously whenever someone who knows and cares creates something that is perfectly fitted to do its work. . . . Nobody styled the orb web of a spider, nobody styled the . . . canoe. Both are beautiful, and for a common reason: each was designed to perform a special task under special conditions.

The same tribute is applicable to the Adirondack guide-boat. It was built by trappers and hunters and guides, and some builders were all three. Chase of Newcomb, Dwight and Lewis Grant of Boonville, Riley and Ben Parsons of Old Forge, Theodore and Willard Hanmer of Saranac Lake are only a few among them. Dwight Grant, the demanding and insistent guide, instructed Dwight Grant the cautious and careful carpenter. No individual held a patent or even thought about patenting his own special contribution to design or construction. No one hesitated to copy or improve the work of others, to follow the best methods or the best patterns available. Father and son worked together. Thus an art was passed from hand to hand and from generation to generation.

When William Boardman tried to describe the guide-boat in its perfected state, he wrote:

> It was a tangle of beautiful, varying curves, the result of lives of study. . . . It has been a slow develop-

ment, with improvements suggested by . . . ingenious woodsmen who generously applauded each
other's successes.[25]

To date, Boardman's statement is the most comprehensive ever published on the origin and development of this specific Adirondack craft.

Notes

1. *Arabian Night Tales* (New York: Walter J. Black, n.d.), p. 418.
2. James Hornell, *Water Transport* (Cambridge: At the University Press, 1946), p. vii.
3. Statements made on August 20, 1919, by John G. Holland at Lake Harris House to Henry S. Harper and Dr. Arpad Gerster. 17 pages. Manuscript in Dr. Gerster's handwriting. Saranac Lake Library.
4. Alfred L. Donaldson, *A History of the Adirondacks* (New York: The Century Co., 1921), II, p. 79. Reprinted by permission of Hawthorn Books Inc.
5. John Todd, *Long Lake* (Pittsfield, Mass.: E.P. Little, 1845), p. 6.
6. *Ibid.*, p. 11.
7. *Shooting and Fishing*, April 26, 1906: "Mitchell Sabattis," by Harry V. Radford.
8. R.B. Miller, *American Forests*, July 1951.
9. Talbot Bissell, "42 Pounds to Portage," *The Skipper* XXVII, no. 1 (January 1967). Original manuscript was titled "Their Little Boats."
10. Cadwallader Colden, *History of the Five Indian Nations* (New York: New Amsterdam Book Co., 1902), I, p. 243.
11. E. Roland Robinson, *Forest and Stream*, October 7, 1899, p. 282.
12. S.H. Hammond, *Wild Northern Scenes; or, Sporting Adventures with the Rifle and the Rod* (New York: Derby & Jackson, 1860), pp. 35–36.
13. Alfred B. Street, *Woods and Waters, or the Saranacs and Racket* (New York: M. Doolady, 1860), p. 27.
14. *Ibid.*, p. 325.
15. *Ibid.*, p. 25.
16. William H. Boardman, *The Lovers of the Woods* (New York: McClure, Phillips & Co., 1901), p. 80.
17. The original F.B. Allen sketches are in the Adirondack Museum.
18. Lucia D. Pychowska, "Sketches of American Life and Scenery" (no. V), *The Continental Monthly*, VI, December 1864, p. 666.
19. *Boston Daily Advertiser*, July 17 and 19, 1869.
20. Donaldson, p. 69.
21. Boardman, p. 78.
22. Howard I. Chapelle, *Boatbuilding* (New York: W.W. Norton & Co., 1941), pp. 449–452.
23. Donaldson, p. 306.
24. Bissell, *op. cit.*
25. Boardman, pp. 78–80.

V/The Guides

By turns we praised the stature of our guides,
Their rival strength and suppleness, their skill
To row, to swim, to shoot, to build a camp,
. . . .
Look to yourselves, ye polished gentlemen!
No city airs or arts pass current here.
Your rank is all reversed: let men of cloth
Bow to the stalwart churls in overalls. . . .

Ralph Waldo Emerson[1]

The early history of the north woods was a turbulent one, which brought successive social and economic changes. Territorial wars with the Indians, the French, and finally, with the British, wiped out many of the Colonial settlements.

Most of the first white settlers came from the valleys of Vermont. Some of these settlers were already acquainted with the New York wilderness, having fought there in 1771 as members of the Green Mountain Boys. This irregular force of the American Continental Army, under command of Ethan Allen, captured Fort Ticonderoga in 1775. Nat Foster, John Cheney, the Moody brothers, and "Old Mountain" Phelps all came from across Lake Champlain.

The settler came to the wilderness a pioneer, planning to clear a piece of land on which to build his shanty and grow a crop. But spring arrived late and winter early. If in the Vermont hills it had been possible to farm some acres at a subsistence level, the New York wilderness proved far less hospitable to the plow. George E. Hoffman reported to Governor William H. Seward in 1840:

> The settler who is enticed by the apparent cheapness of the land . . . must labor for two years at a heavy expense before he receives any apparent return . . . and his surplus produce will not bear the expense of transportation. He then leaves the country for some more favored spot, or else depends upon his success as a hunter.[2]

To supplement his food supply, the settler hunted game. He used the pelts to clothe his family and took the surplus furs to the nearest settlement market to exchange them for those necessities he could not grow, or catch, or make himself. Trips to market took time and perseverance; all travel, if not by water, was over obscure footpaths. Following foot trails during his third visit to Long Lake in 1843, John Todd con-

The Herreshoff manor at Thendara in the Brown's Tract, probably about 1840-1850. (Adirondack Museum)

sidered the journey "fatiguing beyond what language can describe. What must it be then," wrote Todd, "to go in a settler and make your home in these solitudes."[3]

The hunter or trapper did not own the land he worked; he only staked out a certain territory for his exclusive use. His livelihood depended upon special knowledge of the runways of deer and moose, the secret haunts of sable and marten. Priority of occupancy established claim to appropriated territory. This attitude the settler had in common with the native Americans, the Indians, who had no written deed to the land they hunted; they simply claimed certain regions of the woods as their exclusive game preserve, from which they took no more than they needed for subsistence.

Into these remote clearings there came, as early as the middle 1820s, explorers, surveyors and, occasionally, a sportsman. With traditional frontier hospitality the settler gave food and shelter to the wayfaring stranger. If the stranger requested to be led safely through the wilderness, he agreed to assist; survival depended on knowledge of the woods. To supplement his income the hunter gradually took on guiding as an additional vocation. Making profit of necessity, he turned his shanty into a simple inn. The growth of this nascent profession of host-guide was predicted in 1837 by Charles Fenno Hoffman in *Wild Scenes in the Forest and Prairie.*[4]

Before the famous hunter Nat Foster moved out of the Brown's Tract after the shooting incident in 1833, parties of sportsmen from Lewis and Oneida counties received overnight accommodations at the Foster home, to be guided the following morning to the lakes of the Fulton Chain. In the opinion of A.L. Byron-Curtiss, who wrote about the life of Nat Foster, this might be regarded as the beginning of an extensive network of guides maintained till the end of the nineteenth century.[5]

In the Brown's Tract in 1838, the deserted Herreshoff Manor became a combination farm and hostelry owned and operated by Otis Arnold. Similarly, Sam Dunning, a scout and hunter who lived near the inlet to Lake Piseco, "entertained company," which meant that he chose the guests to whom he gave overnight shelter. Facilities were adequate but not always luxurious. Frederick S. Stallknecht and his travel companion, Charles E. Whitehead, came to the north woods in 1858 and stopped at the clearing of the farmer-hunter Bill Helms on Forked Lake where, in a log shanty of two rooms and a garret Helms sheltered his wife and six children, a helping maid, and four hounds. He also entertained there two regular boarders, and "kept hotel."[6]

John Cheney, a professional hunter who supplied venison to the management of the McIntyre Iron Works, had resided in the Adirondack wilderness for about 13 years when he guided for Charles Lanman, who wrote a book about his travels in the United States, published in London in 1859.[7] While hunting with Max Treade near the top of Mount Tahawus, Cheney met Richard Dana, Jr., who preferred world travel to studies at Harvard. The hunters took Dana and his party under their charge. "The edges of this enormous wilderness," wrote Alfred Billings Street in *Woods and Waters,* in which he recounts his Adirondack travels during the early 1850s, "are thinly inhabited by hunters and trappers who pierce its deepest recesses in their light boats and act as guides to visitors in the summer."[8]

Martin Moody, one of the small band that lowered the body of John Brown, the abolitionist, into the grave at North Elba in 1859, was a trapper as well as host at the Mount Morris House near the east shore of Tupper Lake. At one time or another he guided for most of the names in early Adirondack history, among them: the Reverends John Todd and Joel T. Headley, the surveyor Verplanck Colvin, and the guide-book writers E.R. Wallace and S.R. Stoddard. Among his most illustrious patrons were Ralph Waldo Emerson, Alfred Billings Street, professor Louis Agassiz, and James Russell Lowell, "[all] Boston gentlemen whose character and acquirements have given to their shanty [on Follensby] Pond the name of the Philosophers' Camp."[9] (James Russell Lowell originally had named the camp Camp Maple because of the huge maples around it, and Professor Paul F. Jamieson is of the opinion that the name Philosophers' Camp came from the guides.[10])

It is well to remember when we use the word *guide* or *guiding* that there is no more a precise date on which the Adirondack woodsman first began to offer guiding services professionally than there is a date on which the first guide-boat was "invented." For a while the hunter's secondary occupation as host and guide could be practiced on a seasonal basis; he could hunt for the market in winter and take care of the sportsman during the summer. His dual role was reflected in the advertisement of the emporium of Calvin and Byron P. Graves in Boonville which read: "Guide's Clothing and Suits for the Woods a specialty. Highest prices paid for fur."[11] Gradually, however, guiding vacationers became lucrative. When the income from guiding exceeded the profits from trading, the trapper began to consider the sportsman a welcome

patron instead of an intruder. The professional hunter became a professional guide, guardian, and mentor to the amateur sportsman.

The earliest tourists to the north woods, whose primary goal was the rivers and lakes with their bounty of trout, were, for the most part, entirely dependent upon their guides for shelter, sustenance, and transportation. To travel the lakes and streams they needed a boat; to manage the boat they needed the guide. While the hunter-trapper had relied on finding a primitive skiff hidden on the lake shore, as a guide he needed a boat of his own. Without one a woodsman could scarcely qualify as guide in the lake region. During his transition from trapper to full-time guide, the use and purpose of his boat also underwent change, and simultaneously its construction developed and improved. The trapper had been skilled in managing a simple skiff. The guide needed a stable craft to make the tourist feel safe and comfortable. Finally, the guide's boat, with which he earned his living, became the guide-boat, the guide's symbol, and the dominant vehicle of travel for 50 years.

While the guide-boat was made light for the carries, it was also made swift for the pursuit of a swimming deer, and silent for stealthy approach by night. The history of the north woods guide and his boat is intimately linked with fishing and two forms of the hunt, hounding and jacking (or floating), both now illegal.

Hounding, the frontier method of daylight hunting, was a survival from feudal times when owners of large tracts of land were wealthy enough to support bands of retainers. Three groups of hunters were involved: first, the drivers who took the hounds into the hills to set them on fresh deer tracks; then the experienced woodsmen with rifles who crouched at stations where the fleeing deer might pass; and, finally, the guides with their clients ready to intercept by boat any deer taking to water to elude the hounds. If the underbrush around the stations was too thick to permit free view of the runways, they might be abandoned for watch points on slight promontories. The sportsman on the watch point nearest the escaping deer usually had to be restrained by his guide from pulling the trigger too early. The rules of the game demanded that the deer be allowed to swim out into the lake far enough to evade the pursuing hounds.

Hounding an Adirondack deer. The hunt itself was an exciting gamble, the kill at the end a prosaic slaughter. (Forest and Stream, *March 11, 1886)*

Then the guide and his patron in the boat attempted to cut off the deer's escape. Since most Adirondack lakes are irregular in shape, the deer had several advantages. The skill of the oarsman and the swiftness of the boat could be more important than the gun. If the guide's judgment was right and his rowing expert, he could outwit the deer and overtake the frightened animal. Then guide and sportsman together would get hold of the deer by means of a wythed sapling, drown it, or knock the deer dead with an oar. Or the guide, in the bow of the boat, would grasp the deer by the tail while the sportsman shot it through the head. While the hunt itself was an exciting gamble, the kill at the end was a prosaic slaughter.

The Indians used a similar method of hunting when Samuel de Champlain traveled along the north shore of Lake Ontario toward the western edges of Iroquois territory early in the seventeenth century. Instead of hounds, four or five hundred Indians were positioned as beaters, forcing bear and deer out into the open points projecting into the river. Game trying to escape by swimming was pursued and killed by other Indians in canoes.[12]

When an increasing number of tourists began to flock into the woods, hounding became a spectator sport. Its deterioration is evident in an 1872 account of guests at Paul Smiths drawing lots for watch points the night before the hunt.[13]

Jacking was the sportsman's term for hunting deer at night, preferably when the moon was down and clouds shut out the stars. With one guide at the pad-

dle in the stern and another in the bow with rifle, the sportsman sat comfortably amidships, dressed as warmly as possible because he might be sitting motionless for a long time. As soon as dusk set in, the hunt started. A four- to five-foot-long pole was inserted in the bow deck. On top of the pole was the jack light, a piece of bark or tin bent around a wooden base, acting as reflector on one side and as shade on the other side. The source of light could be a torch fashioned of small slivers cut from a sappy pine knot and securely tied together with a narrow ribbon of bark. Sometimes two wide candles were used or two oil lamps behind a glass front. All light was thrown forward, leaving the boat and its occupants in the shade. The silent progress along the lake was described by some as a weird and ghostlike performance. The deer, which came to the shore at night to feed, were bewildered by the unnatural light and froze, thus making easy targets for the huntsmen. This method of hunting lacked the heart-rousing enthusiasm of the chase or the contest of wits between oarsman and deer. To some it was just killing in cold blood.

Alfred B. Street, unskilled in the use of a rifle, enjoyed jacking purely as a spectator. He was interested in the skill with which the guides coordinated each other's movements. The newness of the experience, the picturesqueness of the entire scene, the passing sights and nocturnal sounds delighted him. About all this he gave a romantic description in his book *Woods and Waters.*[14]

Floating for deer in the Adirondacks. A jack lantern, composed of a bit of tin, acted as a reflector on one side and as a shade on the other side. Boat and occupants remained in the shadow while the deer, dazzled by the unnatural light, became an easy target. (Harper's Weekly, *Oct. 24, 1868).*

Though seemingly cruel, hounding and jacking were time-honored sports until they were outlawed in 1897. When the law was enforced in 1902, it restricted the guide's function and limited the special use for which his boat had been designed.

Trolling, like hounding and jacking, demanded skill on the part of the guide. It was impractical to fish the heavily wooded Adirondack lakes and streams from the banks. The fisherman needed a boat with skilled hands at the oar or paddle, and a guide who knew how and where to draw the lure over likely spots and keep it clear of rocks and weeds. While the guide pulled the oars slowly with almost mechanical precision, he kept his eyes on the rod for the first sign of a strike. The fish was hooked as the boat moved over it. It required little exertion or skill on the part of the tourist. All he had to do was haul in the fish.

The majority of the guides followed their new vocation by instinct, having grown up in the woods. They were known after their particular region. Saranac guides were not expected to know the byways of the Fulton Chain of Lakes, though some exceptional guides might be acquainted with more than one region. At the reasonable rate of two or three dollars per day (if the sportsman kept the game), the guide would provide a boat capable of holding two passengers and their gear and carry it over the portages. He knew how to use a gun, how to track deer, how to strip bark from a spruce tree to cover the sides and roof of a shelter, how to make a bed from balsam boughs, and how to prepare trout and venison. But the guide's first and foremost task was to see to the safety of his party, at the risk of his life if need be. Verplanck Colvin recognized his debt to Alvah Dunning, who guided for him during perilous undertakings for the Adirondack Survey. Colvin admitted that on more than one occasion, when overcome by fatigue and hunger, he made up his mind to lie down and perish in the snow, and that he owed his survival to the resolution and endurance of Alvah.[15]

The guide knew how to make shelter and how to fashion a bed from balsam boughs. (Adirondack Museum)

In the 1880s, during the summer seasons, there were probably no fewer than 500 guides working. The aristocrats among them were the independent guides, such as Harvey and Martin Moody, Alvah Dunning, Dwight Grant, John Cheney, Bill Helms, and the famous Abenaki Indian Mitchell Sabattis. They had their private clientele who reserved time well in advance and paid handsomely.

Next in rank were the house guides, attached to private camps. They were paid by the month, ready to serve at any time. Lewis Grant, who for a few months was a house guide at the Miller Camp at Little Moose in 1905, later wrote that, in addition to the housekeeper, the cook, and a waitress, the Millers employed four guides—one for the owner of the camp, one for his wife, and two more to accompany the two sons. Lewis was not kept very busy: the two boys preferred playing with their friends to following their appointed mentor on excursions.

The lowest in rank were the guides who waited at the docks of the large resort hotels. Paid by the hour, they were hired mostly by newly arrived tourists who

had failed to engage beforehand a trusted and favorite woodsman. The inexperienced tourist who wanted to be rowed around the lakes picked the boat that attracted him most. The guide who was its owner came with it; thus, the skill of the guide was unpredictable. A fine-appearing boat, it was hoped, guaranteed a dependable guide. This was generally true, but not always.

The guide was like the captain of a ship. When an outsider failed to recognize that in the wilderness the Adirondack woodsman was at least his equal, there was trouble; Adirondack independence bowed to no one. Lester A. Beardsley, who used the pen name "Piseco," wrote that one of the best guides he ever employed kept his clients' wading boots thoroughly greased. "Once I asked him," wrote Piseco, "to black for me another pair so that I might appear at a dance. I found out just where he drew the line, the first was guide's business, the second lackey's."[16]

The guides commanded the respect of their clients while maintaining a sturdy independence. With fine impartiality they referred to them as "sports," regardless of skill and manners. They treated them with honest familiarity and gave them their full attention. Of Harvey Moody, who was his guide in 1854, Alfred B. Street wrote: "He not only thoroughly understood the region and the habit of its every bird, fish, and animal, but was full of resources in his vocations. As guide he was entirely reliable and always ready. He handled rifle, rod and oar with equal skill, and taught his woodcraft with a cheerful patience."[17] Many a city man felt intimidated by the competence of his guide, because the guide's knowledge of the woods was far superior to his. "*They* are the doctors of the wilderness, and we the low-prized laymen," wrote Emerson.[18] (Though he praised his guides and even counted their daily oar strokes, Emerson failed to give us details about the form or construction of their boats.)

Those who arrived in the north woods at the end of the nineteenth century tend to picture the Adirondack guide as a bearded ancient. We should not forget, however, that Dwight and Francis Grant and Sanford Sperry of Boonville were already experienced woodsmen in 1856 when they were in their early twenties. Harvey Moody was only 22 when, as head guide, he brought the Honorable Miss Amelia Matilda Murray, maid-of-honor to Queen Victoria, and Horatio Seymour, Governor of the State of New York, from Saranac to Boonville in 1855. Gerald Kenwell, born in Indian Lake in 1887, may well have been the youngest guide ever employed. In the spring of 1896, when he was only nine years old, he took his first party into the Moose River region. Among them was Mr. Mert Lewis, then Attorney General of the State of New York.[19]

In spite of its attraction for some, the life of a guide was a hard one. Some aged prematurely. "Many a bronzed fellow presents the appearance of an old man before he has yet reached his prime," according to one correspondent.[20] W.H.H. Murray portrayed the guide Steve Martin as follows:

A tall, sinewy man he was, in height some six feet two, in weight turning perhaps one hundred and seventy pounds, . . . every ounce of superfluous flesh "sweated" off his body by his constant work at the paddle and oars, which gave him a certain gaunt, bony look, to be seen only in men who live the hunter's life and eat the hunter's fare along our fron-

tiers. Yet there was a certain litheness about the form, a springy elasticity . . . a suppleness of motion. . . . His shoulders were brought the least trifle forward, as a boatman's generally are. . . ."[21]

While artists sketched the carries romantically with imposing waterfalls and a smooth path shaded by arched trees, and writers described them graphically as the occasion of much mirth, the carries were no highways. On the more traveled trails the guide might stop occasionally to cut up a fallen tree that obstructed the path, but usually the tree remained where it had dropped. One simply walked around it, hoping to hit the trail again.

If, at times, the carry was a pathway, or at least a line of blazed trees, more often it existed only in the memory of the guide. Woodsmen traveled by signs imperceptible to the eyes of the city men. Speaking of the carry between Little Salmon and Big Salmon near Tupper Lake, H. Perry Smith wrote that it was difficult for anyone but a guide to understand why it was called a carry, except that it was a passage over a strip of land that one could not get through by water.[22]

While traversing the portages, the tourist was expected to carry some of the gear. The guides appreciated consideration from their patrons. When Nessmuk (author and Adirondack traveler George Washington Sears) helped his guide raise the boat, the guide, without comment, took Nessmuk's blanket roll and hung it upon his own shoulders. "It was a kindly thing to do, and like his generous nature," said Nessmuk.[23] Amelia Matilda Murray, walking through the Brown's Tract, filled her Scots plaid with baskets and bundles, and she and her female companion carried it between them. William J. Stillman, being a competent woodsman, carried his own boat when necessary, along with his axe and rifle.

To most travelers, however, the guide remained indispensable. When C.L. Thuber, a potential Adirondack tourist, inquired if the Adirondack boat could be hired without a guide, *Forest and Stream* of June 11, 1874, replied that those familiar with the woods, and pecuniarily responsible, could hire a boat without a guide but that the hotel keepers were "too careful to let a 'greenhorn' go into the woods alone. Both man and boat might be lost."

A young teacher named John MacMullen, who

To most travelers, the guide remained indispensable. (Lewis L. Grant)

ventured forth into the wilderness in 1843 with a youthful companion, left a record of the hazards the absence of a guide presented. Unable to get a light skiff at Long Lake, they started down the Raquette River in a heavy "sloop's yawl." Whatever this craft may have been, it was too heavy to carry more than two or three steps at a time. Launched on the river, it was wrecked in the first rapids. They walked to the next still water and with great effort built a raft, which was soon obstructed by driftwood. From this predicament they were rescued by Indians who built them a spruce bark canoe, which took the better part of two days to complete. It carried the wayfarers, two Indians, and all their baggage and provisions safely through many rapids to the nearest settlement.[24]

Contemporary accounts vividly pictured the helplessness of travelers who failed to make prior arrangements for a guide. The 45 guides employed by

For guests at the resort hotels, boat travel remained an enjoyable adventure and tourists would "do the lakes." (Maitland C. Desormo)

Martin's on the Lower Saranac were not always sufficient to serve the increasing number of the hotel's patrons. Sometimes, having engaged a guide for a week, a party enjoyed its experiences so much that it changed plans and remained in the woods an extra week or so. The tourists contested feverishly for the guide's services, standing guard on the pier to catch the first glimpse of an incoming boat, and watching each other jealously to see that no one took unfair advantage.

For the guests at the great resort hotels, boat travel remained an enjoyable adventure. From the Brown's Tract or from the Prospect House on Blue Mountain Lake, they went to visit friends at Lake Placid or St. Regis. Boating was, indeed, the most convenient way across the wilderness without roads. On such excursions the guide was seldom required to make camp or cook meals, although now and then he might prepare the traditional flapjacks at the noon halt.

By 1874 camping out was no longer necessary if one preferred hotel life, because few wilderness routes were without hotel facilities less than a day's journey apart. By 1890 railroad and steamboat lines were bringing tourists into the north woods. Because of the new nature of travel, the function of the guides gradually changed. Tourists, provided they could find a willing guide, would "do the lakes," covering as much distance as possible. At the end of a day's rowing, the guide would arrange for a hot meal with overnight lodging in a hotel.

Dr. Arpad Gerster felt increasing annoyance on such tours because, in his opinion, the guides showed too great an impatience to reach the next hotel dining room. "Even in the eighties," he wrote, "the Adirondack guide began to change his character. From a woodsman, he was turning into a mere machine for transportation, losing his woodcraft, his leisurely and knowing ways."[25]

The guide, relieved of having to make camp at night, looked forward to a nourishing meal and an indoor bed. Sometimes he had to pay for these amenities himself; at other times the patron paid. In the end the guide inevitably paid dearly with the loss of his skills.

Notes

1. *The Poems of Ralph Waldo Emerson* (London: Humphrey Milford, Oxford University Press, 1914), p. 196.
2. George E. Hoffman, "Report to Governor William H. Seward," in documents accompanying the Governor's message. Senate Document no. 2, December 1840 (Albany, 1840), Part 4, pp. 7-9; and Assembly Document no. 3, December 1840 (Albany, 1840).
3. John Todd, *Long Lake* (Pittsfield, Mass.: E.P. Little, 1845), p. 31.
4. Charles Fenno Hoffman, *Wild Scenes in the Forest and Prairie* (New York, 1843; London: Richard Bentley, n.d. ca. 1843), I, p. 28.
5. A.L. Byron-Curtiss, *The Life and Adventures of Nat Foster* (Utica, N.Y.: Press of Thomas J. Griffith, 1897), pp. 262-263.
6. *Frank Leslie's Illustrated Newspaper,* November 13 and 20, 1858, p. 379.
7. Charles Lanman, *Adventures in the Wilds of the United States,* 2 vols. (London, 1859), I, p. 229.
8. Alfred Billings Street, *Woods and Waters, or The Saranacs and Racket* (New York: M. Doolady, 1860), Introduction.
9. Charles E. Whitehead, *The New York Evening Post,* August 30, 1858.
10. Letter to Helen Durant, February 12, 1979.
11. E.R. Wallace, *Guide to the Adirondacks* (New York: The American News Co.; Syracuse: Waverly Publishing Co., 1875), advertisement at the end of the book, no page number.
12. John Bakeless, *The Eyes of Discovery* (New York: Dover Publications, 1950 and 1961), p. 131.

13. *The Conservationist,* August-September 1955, p. 119, quoting from the *American Sportsman* of 1872.
14. Street, p. 26.
15. *American Angler,* September 22, 1883, p. 186.
16. *Forest and Stream,* May 3, 1883, p. 263.
17. Street, p. 26.
18. *Poems,* p. 196.
19. *Syracuse Herald American,* July 27, 1958.
20. *American Angler,* September 22, 1883.
21. W.H.H. Murray, *Adventures in the Wilderness* (Boston: Fields, Osgood & Co., 1869), pp. 175–176.
22. H. Perry Smith, *The Modern Babes in the Wood Together with Guide to the Adirondacks* by E.R. Wallace (Hartford: Columbian Book Co.; Syracuse, N.Y.: Watson Gill, 1872), p. 198.
23. *Forest and Stream,* December 29, 1881, p. 425.
24. *St. Lawrence Plaindealer* (Canton, N.Y.), August 24, 1881.
25. Arpad Gerster, *Recollections of a New York Surgeon* (New York: Paul B. Hoeber, 1917), p. 276.

VI/Boonville and the Brown's Tract

Boonville has long been a popular point of entrance to the "Hunter's Paradise." The people of that village unite in making welcome and aiding pleasure parties.

E.R. Wallace[1]

Boonville, New York, on the Black River, halfway between Utica to the south and Old Forge to the north, lay on the route to the Brown's Tract and the Fulton Chain of Lakes. It supplied early visitors to this part of the north woods with pack horses and guides, as well as lodging. Later, as tourism in the last quarter of the nineteenth century increased the demand for guide-boats, the guide and carpenter Dwight Grant found it a good place to open a boat shop.

The town derived its name from Gerrit Boon, an agent of Dutch land speculators, who established the first settlement on the Black River in 1793. The Reverend John Taylor, on a missionary tour in 1802, reported that the settlers were mostly poor. A man would acquire a hundred acres of undeveloped land and clear 10 to 20 acres. After building a log hut on it, he would sell the parcel to someone else for a profit, then buy more land and repeat the process. "It is considered here but small affair for a man to sell, take his family and some provisions and go into the woods . . . [and] begin anew . . . they all foresee that in a few years they will have a great plenty of worldly goods."[2] This constant moving on and begin-

ning again was a familiar pattern of the American frontier.

Land speculation flourished and exploitation of the land was widespread. Gerrit Boon planned to make sugar out of the sap of maple trees, which, the Dutch understood, flowed freely all year round. Production of maple sugar would mean trade and might drive the West Indian cane sugar off the world market. Boon's enterprise, however, failed dismally.[3] The early roads leading to and from Boonville resembled trails rather than highways. Washington Irving passed by Boonville in 1803 on his way to Oswegatchie and wrote about his journey: "We found the road dreadfully rugged and miry . . . the stumps and roots of trees stood in every direction . . . we were several times obliged to get out of the waggons [*sic*] and walk as the road was so bad that the horses could scarcely get along. . . . In several parts of the road I had been up to my middle in mud and water."[4] The pioneer of steam navigation, Robert Fulton, may have gone that way in 1811. He had been appointed by the New York Legislature to investigate a direct water route between the Hudson River and the Great Lakes. That scheme was abandoned, but the survey resulted in the opening of the Erie Canal in 1825, and the eight lakes, formerly known as the Middle Branch Moose Lakes, were renamed the Fulton Chain of Lakes.[5]

Boonville had an early, and perhaps deserved, reputation as a tough town. It was to Boonville that Nat Foster retired in 1833 after his trial for shooting an Indian. The Sporting Naturalist, spending the night at Beach's Camp on Raquette Lake in 1849, encountered there "four or five rough-looking fellows from Boonville."[6] And a Southern gentleman who made a circuit of the woods with his slave-valet in attendance found the town a charming prospect, the accommodations poor, and the inhabitants less pleasing.[7] The town's diversions were inviting enough, however, to persuade a party of sportsmen on their way to the Fulton Chain in 1857 to tarry overnight to attend a concert and a ball.[8]

Boonville became a gateway to the north woods first for the trappers and hunters who, at the close of the eighteenth century, followed the Indian's trail up the Middle Branch Moose. Sportsmen from the Mohawk Valley followed the hunters. The inhabitants of Boonville, many of them experienced woodsmen, were friendly, welcoming, and capable of giving the visiting sportsmen good advice about what to take along into the woods, or what to leave behind. Sportsmen found the town a convenient point of departure for their backwoods adventures and the Hurlburt House a pleasant place to start from, reported E.R. Wallace in the 1872 edition of his *Guide to the Adirondacks*. At the end of their journey it was again a convivial place to celebrate success. "The flavor of trout and venison was as natural to the place as fragrance to a rose," declared Wallace.[9]

There were a number of other ways to enter the interior of the north woods, as *Putnam's Monthly* reported in 1854. Coming from Saratoga, Glens Falls, or Lake George, the huntsman could travel some 30 miles over Spruce Mountain to Chester and Schroon Lake, then master another 30 miles of trails through the woods to Long Lake. A second choice was to go from Plattsburgh up the Saranac River to the Saranac Lakes. From there, one could cross over to the Raquette River (carrying boat and gear) and travel up the Raquette River to Long Lake. Another possibility, no less cumbersome, was to start at Lowville in Lewis County, "from which there is a road, or a place for one . . . to Raquette Lake."[10]

Tourists from New York and New England generally preferred the longer, "easier" route by train through Albany and Troy to the steamboat dock at Whitehall, hence by steamboat over Lake Champlain to Port Kent, and from there by coach for six miles to Keeseville. Then one traveled another 56 miles in the coach over a plank road to Martin's at the Lower Saranac, where one's guide stood waiting. In 1869 W.H.H. Murray called this "the shortest, easiest, and beyond all odds the best route to the Adirondacks."[11]

An accessible and popular resort area long before anyone ventured to risk investment in a hotel on the Brown's Tract, the Saranac region offered many facilities to tourists. Between 1849 and 1860, five major hotels had started operation in the Saranac area, of which Martin's on Lower Saranac was "the first hotel in the Adirondacks built solely to attract people of leisure and wealth."[12] For the traveler going from the Saranac Lakes to Raquette Lake there were stopping places for bed and board at easy rowing stages, such as the Raquette Lake House on Tioga Point, Mother Johnson's at Raquette Falls, and Palmer's on Long Lake.[13]

Farther south, livery teams from Saratoga Springs brought sportsmen to the Skidmore Inn, opposite the Hamilton County Court House in Lake Pleasant. On the lake itself one could choose between the Satterlee House and the Lake House. Situated in the south of Hamilton County, Lake Pleasant is now easily accessible by modern highway, but in the mid-1800's, even under the most favorable conditions, the trip would have been an arduous journey. Though an early resort, the town and the lake were removed from the vast waterways that connected the Fulton Chain of Lakes with the Saranac region to the north.

For those sportsmen impatient to reach their woodland haunts, "there is another route still," promised *Putnam's Monthly* of 1854, "and probably the best one. Starting from Boonville . . . going north-easterly across Moose River to Brown's Tract, some thirty miles; then following up a chain of lakes, eight in number. . . . From Eighth Lake you must carry your boat about two miles and then strike the Raquette waters."[14]

Martin's on Lower Saranac, the first hotel in the Adirondacks built solely to attract people of leisure and wealth. (Adirondack Museum)

The Brown's Tract was named after its owner, John Brown, a wealthy merchant from Providence, Rhode Island, who acquired the 210,000 acres in 1798 after former owners had been involved in a complicated series of purchases, mortgages and litigations.[15] It included the lands lying around the headwaters of the Moose River. Popularly regarded for a long time as the whole of the New York wilderness, it constituted only one-seventh of that region. W.H.H. Murray regarded the Brown's Tract as the least interesting part of the Adirondacks because it lacked the intricate meshwork of lakes and lofty mountains and the grandeur of the northern part of the region.[16]

Some reports disparaged the Fulton Chain as a repulsive wasteland, noxious with mosquitoes and midges.[17] The Reverend Joel T. Headley, a prolific writer of keen observation who first visited the north woods in 1844, voiced another opinion. He spoke in glowing terms of his voyage through the eight lakes of the Fulton Chain, all connected by streams and forming a group of surpassing beauty. "[These lakes] are not a mere repetition of the first, but vary in size and shape, with a different frame-work of hills. The change is ever from beauty to beauty. . . . A ride through these eight lakes is an episode in a man's life he can never forget."[18]

General Richard U. Sherman visited the Brown's Tract in 1853 and the Fulton Chain in 1856, this time

with H. Dwight Grant as his guide. The following year, meeting with a group of sportsmen in Utica, Sherman was the prime mover in forming the Brown's Tract Association.[19] The Club built its main lodge on Third Lake of the Fulton Chain and established open camps on Raquette Lake and Big Moose. In 1858 the name was changed to the Northwoods Walton Club to emphasize more clearly the character of the members' annual excursions through the woods to the Fulton Chain.

The journey demanded toil, stamina, and endurance, warned the *Programme* the Waltonians published in 1859. Daily railroad connections went as far as Boonville, but beyond, difficulties awaited the traveler. To reach the hostelry of Otis Arnold, nearly 20 miles distant, the traveler had to follow a difficult bridle path, slog through deep quagmires, climb over boulders, and cross an unbridged raging river. One could go on foot or ride a pack horse. Whichever way one chose, the *Programme* suggested changing off every three hours "to render the journey less wearying than by exclusive riding or walking." Yet, the innate beauty of the woods, the variety and majesty of the surroundings, and the abundance of game promised unlimited adventure.[20]

The *Programme* also gave advice on what kind of bait to bring, assuring the members that they did not have to fish if they did not choose to. They were free to "roam the woods, row the lakes, or rest in camp, sing, hallo, dance, swim or turn summersaults, as they may be in the mood."

Relaxed and frolicsome, the Waltonians soon forgot the ordeal of the way in, the boulders, the swamps, and the arduous corduroy road. They offered to share their trout and mirth with those who found in these enjoyments sufficient recompense for the temporary toil and privations. Although this liberal attitude was characteristic of the club, on one point the instructions were firm: club members must use the services of good guides.

The rough road from Boonville through the Brown's Tract delayed the development of hotels and other facilities in the Fulton Chain until 1871, when the Forge House near First Lake was opened in time for spring fishing. It had "all the Comforts of a First Class Country Hotel," 13 bedrooms, an office, parlor and bar, attic accommodations for the guides, as well as a

*Members of the Northwoods Walton
Club at Third Lake Landing. (Adirondack Museum)*

barn for horses and dog kennels in the rear. Some
of its enthusiastic admirers spoke of the Forge
House as "the gates of paradise—reached through
purgatory."[21] The owner, Cyrus Sanford Sperry,
hoping to supplant the hostelry of Otis Arnold as a
rendezvous for sportsmen, advertised that the hotel
would be accessible "to ladies as well as gentlemen."
He offered "good guides and boats always in
readiness."[22] That first spring the Forge House
welcomed a party of 14, consisting of General Sherman and seven companions plus six guides, headed
by H. Dwight Grant.

The guide and his boat were now more than ever
necessary, as visitors arrived attracted by the prospect
of gliding smoothly through linked waterways, propelled by expert oarsmen. Boonville, which had supplied pack horses when needed, now provided skilled
guides whose concern became the well-being of their
patrons.

A bridge was built where previously there had been
only a ford through the swift waters of the Moose

The Forge House near First Lake. (Adirondack Museum)

River, and by 1875 the road to Arnold's was so much
improved that Wallace reported that ladies could
ride the entire distance on a springboard.[23] Twenty
years later Wallace changed his opinion about the
road, as he recorded in his guide of 1895 that in the
passage of time the excursion had become a serious
undertaking once the traveler had crossed the bridge
over the Moose River. Though ladies could now ride
Phelph's stage, some still preferred pack horses. "The
road to Arnold's has long been noted for its out-
rageous roughness," noted Wallace. Its condition
probably caused the remark by Judge Stone of Lewis
County that "this section presented such a forbidding
aspect it would make a crow shed tears of blood to fly
over it."[24]

By 1885 the gradual disappearance of trout caused
by overfishing threatened the Fulton Chain's reputation as the paradise of fishermen. Under active promotion by H. Dwight Grant, the Boonville Sportsmen's Club raised funds to build a fish hatchery on
Fourth Lake. General Sherman, who had been State
Fish and Game Protector since 1879, increased
substantially the number of state-owned fish hatch-
eries. Dwight Grant's project received encouragement from Sherman as well as the enthusiastic support of the guides, who were interested not only in the
well-being of the tourists but also in the security of
their own profession.

Increased tourism to the central Adirondacks
demanded improved methods of transportation. In
1888 newspaper dispatches reported plans for the
building of a narrow-gauge railroad between Moose
River Settlement and Old Forge Lake on the Fulton
Chain, and construction was begun. However, land-

owners along the way, fearing the danger of fire in their forests presented by the wood-burning locomotives, objected to the undertaking. A compromise was reached: the railroad would end at Minnehaha on the Moose River, five miles below Thendara. From there the side-wheeler *Fawn*, built by Theodore Seeber, would bring the passengers to Old Forge over the Moose River through dams and locks built by Dwight Grant. It was a pleasant boat ride through varied and ever-changing scenery.

Despite its abbreviated length, the railroad, facetiously referred to as "Peg Leg" because of its wooden rails, became celebrated. The *Boonville Herald* of June 27, 1889, announced that:

> . . . arrangements are now complete for making daily trips to Old Forge by means of the Fulton Chain Railroad to Stillwater, and thence by steamboat to Old Forge. The railroad the entire distance was completed last week. . . . Iron rails will take the place of the wooden ones now in use as soon as necessary arrangements can be perfected. . . . A trial has been made of the steamer on Moose River which will connect with the railroad at Minnehaha or Stillwater. . . . It looks very much as if buckboard travelling over the Brown's Tract was a thing of the past. . . .

A month later, on July 25, the Boonville paper jubilantly reported that the facilities for going to the Fulton Chain of Lakes were never better than at present. True, the roadbeds and grades and wooden rails did not permit much speed. On some stretches of the road the passengers had to join the crew in "giving the engine a lift," yet the open car provided a pleasant trip to Minnehaha.

All that summer of 1889 the column "Adirondack Echoes" in the *Boonville Herald* reported a boom in camp and hotel building as well as in fishing and guiding on the Fulton Chain. If there was now and then a note of apprehension, it was muted. For four years Peg Leg carried its miniature locomotive and open-sided passenger car over the seven-mile run. It was the butt of much ridicule, yet, in its brief life, it brought the first wave of day-trippers into the Fulton Chain. Peg Leg was abandoned upon the completion of the Adirondack and St. Lawrence Railroad in 1893. The side-wheeler *Fawn* continued to serve a few years longer as an excursion boat, giving

tourists an Adirondack lake cruise without the expense of a guide and guide-boat.

The days and ways of guides and boats and quiet waters now were clearly threatened by the ease of access to the north woods; still, there was hope that something of the past might prevail. Three items in the *Boonville Herald* of August 1, 1889, reflect the confusion of the times, betraying a speculative enthusiasm for the future and a nostalgia for the past. Alvah Dunning, a renowned guide now old and no longer in demand, is still in the news. He is reported to be suffering from an ugly cut on his hand. With entrepreneurs and speculators busily developing the Adirondacks, building more camps, hotels, and railroads to bring more tourists, the paper reports an amazing rise in land prices throughout the north woods. But, in another item the *Herald* says:

> Those who go to the Adirondacks miss the greatest of all the attractions if they do not camp in the regular unadulterated woods' style and partake of the life that their forefathers indulged in years ago when the primitive state of affairs precluded them from having all the "fixins" of the present day.

In 1892 the railroads linked Thendara on the Fulton Chain with Herkimer, bypassing Boonville. The town's attention was diverted to a new field of oil and natural gas, which soon petered out, and to building a brewery, which burned down twice.[25]

In 1893 the Adirondack and St. Lawrence Railroad became the Adirondack Division of the New York Central Railroad. Later a spur was added from Thendara to Old Forge. Visitors who had never undergone the hardships of the former devious routes through the mountains now came pouring into the region by the trainload.

Joseph F. Grady observed:

> Swift as the sunrise, a new era dawned upon the Adirondacks, and puzzled old guides found themselves viewing askance the railroad and its heterogeneous human influx. To them, the new order came as a mixed blessing, as a revolution that spelled the doom of the good old days.[26]

The swelling flood of day-trippers, content to gaze at the scenery without effort, diminished the attraction of the Fulton Chain for those who enjoyed the wilderness for its sylvan beauty without the benefit of modern conveniences. It also threatened the cherished privacy and isolation of the Waltonians who, again under the leadership of General Sherman, took flight to a more inaccessible region.

For a while the increasing tourism would demand an increased supply of guide-boats. Foreseeing this in 1879, H. Dwight Grant rented space from the Rice Brothers in Boonville and began to build the exquisite guide-boat. In 1881 he opened his own shop on Post Street.

Notes

1. E.R. Wallace, *Descriptive Guide to the Adirondacks* (Syracuse, N.Y.: Watson Gill, 1894), p. 57.
2. "Journal of the Rev. John Taylor's Missionary Tour through the Mohawk & Black River Countries in 1802," *The Documentary History of the State of New York*, ed. E.B. O'Callaghan, M.D. (Albany: Weed, Parsons & Co., Public Printers, 1850), III, p. 1149.
3. W. Chapman White, *Adirondack Country* (New York: Duell, Sloan & Pearce, 1954), p. 75.
4. Washington Irving, *Journals and Notebooks*, ed. N. Wright (Madison, Milwaukee, London: University of Wisconsin Press, 1969), I, pp. 18-20.
5. Joseph F. Grady, *The Adirondacks* (Little Falls, N.Y.: Press of the Journal & Courier Co., 1933), p. 58.
6. *Spirit of the Times*, November 24, 1849, p. 475.
7. *Spirit of the Times*, April 9, 1853, p. 87.
8. Scope [C.M. Scholefield?], "Wildwood Notes," *Utica Morning Herald*, October 7, 1857.
9. *The Modern Babes in the Wood* by H. Perry Smith to which is added *Descriptive Guide to the Adirondacks* by E.R. Wallace (Hartford: Columbian Book Company; Syracuse, N.Y.: Watson Gill, 1872), p. 248. [What Wallace calls the Hurlburt House was probably Hulbert's Hotel.]
10. [Farrand N. Benedict?], "The Wilds of Northern New York," *Putnam's Monthly*, September 1854, p. 269.
11. W.H.H. Murray, *Adventures in the Wilderness* (Boston: Fields, Osgood & Co., 1869), p. 42.
12. Alfred L. Donaldson, *A History of the Adirondacks* (New York: The Century Co., 1921), I, p. 298. Reprinted by permission of Hawthorn Books.
13. Murray, pp. 44-48.
14. [Benedict?] in *Putnam's Monthly*, September 1854, p. 269.
15. Donaldson, I, pp. 88-135.
16. Murray, p. 9.
17. Wallace, 1872, p. 252.
18. Joel T. Headley, *The Adirondack; or Life in the Woods* (New York: Baker & Scribner, 1849), pp. 234-236.
19. For biographical data on General Richard U. Sherman, see: *History of the Mohawk Valley Gateway to the West*, ed. Nelson Greene (Chicago: S.J. Clarke Publishing Co., 1925), III, p. 10.
20. *Programme, Northwoods Walton Club* (Utica: Roberts, Printers, 1859).
21. S.R. Stoddard, *The Adirondacks Illustrated* (Glens Falls, N.Y.: published by the author, 1881), p. 225.
22. Handbill advertising the Forge House, 1871. Original in the archives of the Adirondack Museum.
23. Wallace, 1875, pp. 14-15.
24. *Ibid.*, 1895, pp. 59-60.
25. *Boonville Herald*, July 4 and August 8, 1889; June 26, 1890; January 8, 1891.
26. Grady, p. 247.

VII/The Grants of Boonville

Father and son worked together. Thus an art is passed on.
The Viking Ships by Brøgger and Shetelig[1]

After Gerrit Boon established the first settlement on the Black River in 1793, H. Dwight Grant's ancestors were among the first homesteaders of the Town of Boonville.[2] Elisha Grant, Sr., and his family migrated from Lee, Massachusetts, in 1797. One of their four sons, Elisha, Jr., born in 1774, in 1805 became the first Constable and Collector of Boonville. His son, Nelson Grant, born in 1804, farmed near Boonville. He was the town's Supervisor from 1847 to 1851; and his grandson, Lewis, credits him with naming the Bisby Lakes.

> He [my grandfather] had a man working for him by the name of Bisby, one of those fellows that would wear a coonskin cap all summer. . . . he was no woodsman and he would get my grandfather to go fishing with him. They went to Woodhull Lake . . . and they saw some ducks leave the lake and fly over the hilltop, and it looked as if they dropped down into the water there. So they went to the top of the hill, and could see a chain of lakes, and went over there and fished . . . and grandfather, as a joke, thought it would be good to call them Bisby Lakes and they still go by that name.[3]

Nelson's eldest son, Charles, born in 1831, was a surveyor. He built the first log camp (as opposed to the usual open camps) on the north shore of Third Lake of the Fulton Chain. It was a one-and-a-half-story log structure that became a favorite meeting point for fishermen. Early in the morning of April 8, 1868, as he broke his way from Boonville toward his camp through deep, crusted snow, exhaustion overcame Charles Grant. He sat down to rest in the freezing temperature and never rose.

Henry Dwight Grant, the second of Nelson's 10 children, was born on the farm in 1833. As a lad, living on the edge of the woods, Dwight took off to hunt and fish whenever he could be spared from farm chores; in the winter he made successful trips into the woods with his gun and a few traps. He knew where to find game. He knew where to find a boat and how to maneuver it expertly and silently. When he was 17 he tramped the woods with his father from Boonville to the Limekiln Falls and made a raft to float down the South Branch to Moose River Settlement, fishing and camping along the way. At the age of 21 he was known as a trustworthy and well-informed woodsman. In 1856, at the age of 23, he guided General Sherman through the Fulton Chain of Lakes.

As a young man, Grant rowed or paddled heavy flat-bottomed skiffs or dugouts borrowed from neighbors or found by the lake shore. In these he followed the Brown's Tract to the Bisby Lakes, the Moose River, and the Fulton Chain of Lakes, then went on to the waters of the Raquette and sometimes

H. Dwight Grant, guide, boatbuilder, legislator. (Mrs. Maude Gillespie)

all the way to the Saranacs. But for continuous and extended travel in a country where economic necessity did not permit much leisure, Grant needed a work boat of his own, light enough to carry over land, yet swift and maneuverable in the water. He witnessed the arrival of the first so-called Saranac boats on the Fulton Chain, circa 1860, the old square-sterned models, which became, for a while, standard equipment for guides throughout the woods.

In the versatile manner of his day, Grant combined many skills and trades. He was a farmer, carpenter, millwright, sawyer, and guide. Although the woods soon lured him away from farming, he does not seem to have been a professional trapper or hunter, as were many of his contemporaries. One fall, though, before the Civil War, he joined Otis Arnold (who kept the hostelry on the old Herreshoff Manor) and Arnold's sons on a camping trip to the head of Fourth Lake, where they hunted and fished with good success.

While gathering fish from a weir they had constructed at the outlet of Fifth Lake, they were interrupted by rival woodsmen, the Johnson brothers, who camped at the foot of Fourth Lake. The Arnolds had good luck that fall and the Johnsons did not Both were hunting for the commercial markets. There was an argument about who had prior rights to the territory. Guns appeared on both sides, but no shots were fired. The Johnsons left; Grant and the Arnolds remained at their camp until late in the season — so late, in fact, that their boats, loaded with game and fish, ran into ice at the foot of Fourth Lake. Hiding boats and catch on the shore at Cold Springs about a mile above the foot of the lake, they walked through the woods back to Old Forge and the Arnold house to wait until the ice got thick enough to walk on. The second evening after their return, one of the Johnsons knocked at the Arnolds' door and announced that his brother had drowned. Dwight Grant, with the Arnolds, helped recover the body. That ended the feud between the Johnsons and the Arnolds.[4] Lewis Grant said that his father had always thought that the Johnson boy drowned on his way to see what the Arnolds had left in their cache at Cold Springs.

When hunting pelts and meat for the market was no longer profitable, lumbering became Dwight Grant's winter occupation. He constructed and ran the water-powered sawmill on Mile Brook shown on an 1857 town map of Boonville.[5]

In 1862 he enlisted in the Union Army, won promotion to first lieutenant in Company I, 117th Regiment, New York Volunteers, and was captured at the Battle of Drury's Bluff in Virginia on May 16, 1864. He escaped, was recaptured, and spent seven months in Confederate prisons. Mustered out in September 1865, he returned to Boonville and the woods he loved.

The following year Dwight built and ran a water-powered sawmill for his uncle, Albert C. Grant, on Woodhull Creek, near the town of Forestport, New York. The mill is gone but Grant's Mill, named after the owner, not the builder, remains on the map. Dwight also built camps on the Fulton Chain of Lakes. To get out the lumber he restored the mill at Old Forge, built around 1817 by the son-in-law of John Brown of Providence. Dwight's slick, a four-inch chisel with offset handle made by a blacksmith at Old

Forge for Grant's use in framing heavy timbers for his log buildings, is now in the Adirondack Museum.

In 1871 Grant was listed on the register of the Forge House on First Lake of the Fulton Chain as head guide for General Sherman's party. In 1873 Dwight Grant moved his family into the town of Boonville. About that time he built a simple camp on the north shore of Fourth Lake for Lewis H. Lawrence of Utica, at a point known as Fair View, where the Waltonians had once maintained an open log cabin. Young Mr. Lawrence had camped there a few summers and, liking the spot, began a program of improvements. Over a period of years, with the skilled help of Dwight Grant, the little structure was transformed into a pretentious summer home of unique design, with stables, dog kennels, guide's quarters, and miscellaneous other out-buildings. "With its expansive level of well-kept lawn . . . it loomed as a show place during the last quarter of the [nineteenth] century," wrote Joseph F. Grady in *The Adirondacks*. Today the place is called Lawrence Point.

Dwight Grant became the caretaker and head guide at the Lawrence establishment in 1874, beginning 23 years in an employment well suited to his vocation and tastes. The care of an Adirondack camp was a ceaseless round of repairs, alterations, and additions. The growth of families and the accretion of guests required more rooms, more boats and boathouses, and with them, enlarged quarters for the guides and other retainers. Grant's employment gave full scope to his varied skills and ingenuity as a carpenter. Nor was he permitted to forget his craft as a guide. Fishing and hunting expeditions with the family and their guests often meant carrying heavy boats and equally heavy pack baskets and gear.

The restless young Lawrence, moreover, was not content with all the comforts he had on Fourth Lake. With Grant's aid he built three other camps on Limekiln, Moss (then Morse), and Seventh Lakes. Roaming from one camp to another, Lawrence was always accompanied by a staff of attendants carrying the necessary trappings for his enjoyment and comfort in the woods. Dwight's son, Lewis, named after Mr. Lawrence, remembered with pleasure his boyhood days at the Lawrence camps, especially the square-sterned *Gypsy* he was allowed to row, and the vegetable garden, which his father fertilized with

suckers. "If the mink or foxes did not dig them [the suckers] before they rotted, there would be a nice garden in the fall," wrote Lewis.

The elder Mr. Lawrence, who had amassed a fortune through business ventures, mainly railroading and lumbering, did not visit his son's sumptuous camp on Fourth Lake until 1879, when he was already 72 years old. Discovering how much he enjoyed it, he returned as often as time and business permitted. Seven years later, feeble and ailing, he undertook another visit, hoping the woods would restore his health. Against the advice of his physicians and accompanied by a doctor and nurses, he traveled to Boonville by railroad and from there by cushioned buckboard to the Moose River Settlement. Grady describes the trip:

> There a specially designed armchair . . . and a group of stalwart guides were waiting to carry him over the thirteen rough miles of the Brown's Tract road to the Forge Pond . . . [where] the party took to boats and arrived without mishap at the Lawrence camp.

One of the guides was Dwight Grant. The hoped-for recovery did not materialize. The old man died in the woods in September of 1886.

Dwight Grant had been five years with the Lawrence camps before he decided to do something about guide-boats other than rowing and carrying them. He was 46 years old and had spent a good part of his years on the water and on the carries. He knew how boats handled with oars and with paddles; he knew how they behaved in high winds and in the shallows; and he knew that, however easily they handled in the water, they remained a heavy burden on the carries. As a guide he felt the need for a lighter, steadier boat; as a carpenter he believed that he could make one. Moreover, Dwight Grant needed an occupation for the winter months. Lewis wrote that he was a great reader, but only on evenings and Sundays. He needed something to do throughout the day, "as father could not sit around doing nothing and enjoy life. . . ." And so he turned to guide-boat building.

As a boatbuilder Dwight Grant was a relative latecomer. Henry and George Stanton of Long Lake, Caleb Chase of Newcomb, Theodore Hanmer of Saranac Lake, and many others had already established their reputations before Dwight Grant

*The Grant home and boat shop in Boonville, New York.
(Helen Durant)*

started his new career. We have more documentation
of the Grant boats than of those of earlier builders,
however. The Grant boat shop in Boonville, with its
carefully kept records and its tools, was still intact
when we met Dwight's son, Lewis, in 1958. Brought
alive in conversations and correspondence with
Lewis, it provided the basis for later chapters on the
construction of the guide-boat.

About the new venture, Lewis Grant wrote:

My father had Henry Stanton come to Boonville in
1879 and again in 1880 . . . to get him started in
making guide-boats and they worked in a shop at the
Rice Brothers sash and blind mill on Post Street . . .
before my father built his shop in 1881 so you see,
Henry Stanton was the man that learned my father
how to build his first guide-boat.[6]

The Stanton brothers, Henry and George, were the
sons of William Henry Stanton, a chair-maker, who
came to Long Lake from the Champlain Valley in
1849. William Henry, Jr., was born in 1844 and
George in 1847. As Long Lake history has it, they
learned boatbuilding from Cyrus H. Palmer, who was
about their own age. Some say that the Stantons had
valuable assistance from one Herbert Salisbury, an
elusive character about whom little is known (*see also*
John Gardner's remarks in Appendix C).

Willard Sutton told us that this Herbert Salisbury
was a pattern-maker from Syracuse who had established himself in Long Lake, where he "trued up the
Long Lake guide-boat patterns to make them better
running." Though Sutton could not remember the
exact date when Salisbury settled in Long Lake, his

account did not sound like hearsay, but was told in
the tone of "I knew him well."

Whether Dwight Grant himself built any guide-
boats that first season is uncertain, as he was also a
member of the Albany Assembly that year. Lewis
Grant speculated that his father had Stanton down
that year primarily to talk things over, to make patterns, and to get out spruce stumps to season over the
next year. He thought that they probably did not actually build boats until the winter of 1880-81.

We lack complete data on the boats built during
those two winters. An old account book, which was
still in the possession of Lewis Grant in 1959, showed
that Dwight Grant sold nine boats in the winter and
spring of 1880-81. All were presumably built with the
assistance of Henry Stanton, though some may have
been completed after the latter's return to Long
Lake. They were all sold before Dwight Grant built
his own shop in the fall of 1881. The quality of Grant's
earliest product is attested to by the fact that of the
nine boats built, seven were sold to well-known
guides.

Most of the boats were built on advance orders,
and Dwight Grant kept a record of the names of the
buyers. But Lewis Grant wrote us:

My father had all the names of the people he sold his
boats to in his books but they did not get down on the
tally boards . . . all but the first one of his books
were thrown out or destroyed while I was superintendent of the Adirondack League Club, from
1906-1916.[7]

Prices ranged from $40 for a 12-foot boat to $58 for
a 16-foot boat. Lewis Grant wrote on March 14, 1959:
"A lot of Father's first made boats had wooden seats
and just a plain, straight deck, not a circular deck,
and those things made the difference in the price of
the boat." The earliest Grant boat we have seen in a
photograph is one with a 13-foot bottom board, built
in 1882, shown lying on the dock of the Taylor Camp
at Little Moose Lake. Dwight Grant sold it for $48.
Three other boats of the same length, built the same
year, were down in the books for $60 each. The dif-
ference in price probably means there were plain
wooden seats in the cheaper boat and caned seats and
circle decks (*see* Gardner Plate X, Appendix C) in the
other three boats. Caned seats were lighter than solid
wooden ones. The circle decks with firm spruce back-

Camp of Lewis H. Taylor at Little Moose Lake, built in 1881 under supervision of H. Dwight Grant. In foreground is a boat built by H. Dwight Grant in 1882 with straight deck—transverse boards. (Lewis L. Grant)

ing were stronger than straight decks and did not add extra weight. They soon became standard with all builders.

In the fall and winter of 1881–82, Grant built his own shop, 20 by 30 feet, behind the Grant home on Post Street in Boonville. There, on January 21, 1882, he started building guide-boats with the help of Lester Fox, Robert Bartlett, Gus Syphert, and Theodore Seeber.[8] About three months later the new shop had turned out one sailboat and 21 guide-boats, a production not equaled until the peak year of 1891. The sailboat was for Mr. L.H. Taylor, for whom Grant later built a camp on Little Moose. Of the 21 guide-boats, 11 were bought by guides, five by summer visitors, three by Boonville men, one by Grant's eldest son, Sidney, and one by Grant's carpenter, Theodore Seeber.

Prices ranged from $53 to $70 according to the size of the boat. Seeber paid only $20 for an 18-foot boat, presumably a shell that he finished on his own time, while Gus Syphert acquired a 16-foot boat also at a low price, probably by some similar arrangement.

The Adirondack traveler and author Nessmuk, a man of small stature, was a devotee of very small canoes. He did not like guide-boats very much and found them cranky. Nessmuk had been bragging that he could cruise his smallest canoe across Lake Ontario. That was too much for Gus Syphert who, in addition to working in the Grant shop, was also an expert guide. He dared Nessmuk to pit his 12-pound

Rushton canoe against a 60-pound Grant guide-boat, betting $100 that he himself would finish the trip from Moose River to Paul Smiths on St. Regis Lake and return to the Forge House by a roundabout way at least 48 hours ahead of Nessmuk. The unequal contest never came off. Nessmuk beat a hasty retreat, asserting that the "canoe would be of no more value to the North Woods guide than a bread-tray." Nessmuk argued that, as long as speed was the prime factor, the guide-boats were not likely to be superseded, but he found them tiresome to ride in.[9]

The surviving records for 1881–82 list only the boats that were sold at the Grant shop and therefore do not include a boat sent to the state fair at Utica in September 1882, which took "first premium." The official catalog of the New York State Fair listed Entry 2113 as "Adirondack Guide Boat by H. Dwight Grant, of Boonville, New York."[10]

Entry 2113 was built under the influence of Henry Stanton. Painted white and appropriately named the *Ghost*, the boat was 16 feet 4 inches overall and was characteristic of the Long Lake models of its day, somewhat in the manner of the Saranac tumblehome. Ribs, decks, and siding were heavier than in Grant's later models. The laps of the planking were visible and feather-edged. The strakes were fastened with iron screws. The decks were perhaps somewhat longer than those of the conventional Long Lake boats, with a more sweeping curve along the gunwale, and there was more than ordinary room in the stern seat. Though it lacked the rake of bow and stern characteristic of the later Grant models, it was a craft of delicate beauty.

A photograph of the *Ghost* taken at Bisby Lake in 1965 shows a stern seat back rest with a four-piece frame. Later, Grant made his back rests with steamed bow frames, thereby lightening this necessary accessory that generally went over the carries with the boat. The back rest of the middle seat, shown in the photograph, is an anachronism. It was probably added to the boat at a later date because Grant did not make such back rests when he built the *Ghost* in 1882. Though he appears to have considered the middle back rest as a nonessential luxury, he made it as light as possible, just in case it had to be carried.

Through the sale of the *Ghost* to Mr. A.E. Touzaline, a member of the Bisby Club, Dwight

The Ghost *was built by H. Dwight Grant in 1881/82. The stern seat back rest has a four-piece frame. The back rest of the middle seat with its steamed bow frame was probably added at a later date, since Grant did not make such back rests in 1882. (Helen Durant)*

Grant recovered part of the expenses for its journey to the Utica Fair. Grant never exhibited another boat; crating and shipping charges, plus wages for a man to look after the boat, were too high. Grant's boats needed no promotion: they sold themselves as fast as he could build them.

The *Ghost* remained at Bisby Lake for many years. Mr. Touzaline presented the boat to his friend George H. Maurice, with whom he shared a cottage at Bisby. It remained in the family for several generations, an important document in guide-boat history.

The *Ghost* now rests safely at the Adirondack Museum, a gift from Charles F. Maurice. The remarkably good condition of such an old boat is a tribute to the ingenuity and fine workmanship of the master-builder Dwight Grant.

Learning that four Grant boats had been ferried to the Moose River in the spring of 1883, the *Boonville Herald* of May 3 reported that the demand for them was large. By then the boats were almost exclusively used by guides, who found them light and swift. "These boats . . . cannot be improved for hunting and fishing purposes," said the *Herald*.

It is unlikely that many guide-boats were built during the season of 1882-83. That was the winter Dwight Grant enlarged his boat shop to build the *Hunter*, the first steamboat on the Fulton Chain of Lakes. It was 35 feet long, with an eight-foot beam, and was hauled from Boonville to Old Forge in the spring of 1883. Its future captain was Jonathan Meeker, brother of Jane Meeker, whom Dwight Grant had married in 1858. To five-year-old Lewis, "it looked as if the shop was all steamboat, with no place to work." Dwight Grant made a further contribution to steamboat travel when, between 1888 and 1889, he took time off from the shop to build the dams and locks on the Moose River, which made the

The Ghost *on Bisby Lake in 1965. The rower is Charles F. Maurice. (Helen Durant)*

water navigable for the double-decked side-wheeler *Fawn*, built at Old Forge by Theodore Seeber.

While building the *Hunter* and taking care of the Lawrence camp as well, Grant found time to superintend the building of a camp on Little Moose for Mr. L.H. Taylor, for whom he had built a sailboat the previous year. Thomas Griffin looked after the actual building and got out 13,000 feet of spruce logs for walls, for which Grant paid him $65. Griffin hauled the spruce to the mill at Old Forge, where Grant got out 5,594 board feet of lumber and charged Mr. Taylor $25.16 for the sawing. Lewis Grant added, "I bet it was good spruce lumber. They did not pick any poor trees in those days." For all beams, windows, doors, lumber, hardware, and furnishings purchased from Boonville stores for this camp, and a guide-boat, Dwight Grant charged Mr. Taylor a total of $750.18. This included a fee of $2.00 to Will Sperry for making rustic camp furniture. Adirondack "luxury" did not come so high in those days.

Each year, as soon as the ice went out of the lakes, usually in April or May, Dwight Grant returned to his duties at the Lawrence camp, leaving his sons, with perhaps a carpenter or two, to finish decks, seats, and oars and the painting and varnishing of the boats.

All boats built during the winter of 1883–84 and after were tallied on a series of slender, fine-grained, half-inch pine panels (*see* Appendix A). Dwight Grant noted dimensions, weight, number of ribs, and other details, and frequently added the names of the purchasers. These tally boards, now preserved in the Adirondack Museum, offer a comprehensive record of progress in design and production for 23 years. The tallies were interrupted in 1906 when Dwight Grant retired, but they were resumed by Lewis Grant in 1917.

The first tally board showed 13 boats completed by the spring of 1884 and the same number in 1885. Production increased to 15 in 1886 and fell to 11 in 1887. With Dwight Grant and six carpenters at work in 1891, output reached a peak of 25 boats. Dwight Grant and Lester Fox built the boats; the five other carpenters made ribs, oars, paddles, yokes, and decks, and did the sanding, varnishing, and painting. Gus Syphert, a snowshoe-maker, caned the seats and back rests.

For the 23 years from 1883–84 to 1905–06, the tallies account for 327 boats. To these must be added 31 boats built from 1879 to 1882, nine with Henry Stanton at the Rice Brothers' mill, and 22 in the new shop on Post Street, before Grant used tally boards. This adds up to 358 guide-boats, an average of over 14 per year for 25 years. Dwight Grant estimated that it took 21 days of 10 hours each to make a 16-foot boat with three cane seats, one cane back rest, one pair of oars, a paddle, and a yoke. The best carpenter in Boonville in the 1880s was paid $2 for a 10-hour day.

Paradoxically, as the need for guides lessened, the demand for guide-boats increased. The tallies of the Grant shop reveal that a camp owner might buy two or more boats in a single season. The frequency with which certain guides and caretakers returned as purchasers indicated that some of the boats were resold.

Will Commerford, a Brown's Tract guide, bought a number of boats. He and some other guides would get jobs late in the summer season taking sportsmen through the Fulton Chain, Raquette Lake, Forked Lake, Long Lake, and from there to the Saranacs. They would then sell their boats to Saranac guides and return to Thendara by train. After using the boats all summer in their guiding, they sold them for more than they paid for them.

In 1903, for his camp at Bisby Lake, William P. Hall of New York City bought from Grant a standard 14½-foot guide-boat and an 18-foot family boat. They were equipped with gratings to protect bottom and siding against the ladies' sharp heels. The family boat was a gentleman's pleasure craft, elegantly finished in natural wood on the inside, painted dark blue on the outside, and furnished with caned seats and curving backs of the St. Lawrence skiff type. Only Grant's workmanlike discipline could be trusted to refrain from further tendency to opulence and ostentation. Hall also bought a 12-foot "Raider" that year. Lewis Grant explained:

> . . . Father called all guide-boats with bottom boards twelve feet or less Raiders, as they were used mostly by one or two men to make a raid on a distant, hard-to-get-to lake . . . or river springhole and get some real fishing.[11]

In 1906 Mr. Hall bought two more boats. These had 13½-foot bottoms, a length that became popular with sportsmen. They were painted a conservative

Grant guide-boat on Lawrence dock. Note back rests that differ from later Grant models. Grant built guide-boats for L.H. Lawrence in 1885, 1887, 1891, and 1892, and may have sold many more to the Lawrence guides. (Lewis L. Grant)

Dwight Grant guide-boat number 11 of 1904 at the Hubbell Camp on Big Moose. The false grating protects the bottom and siding from the sharp heels of the ladies' shoes. (Helen Durant)

dark green on the inside, blue on the outside. The gratings were omitted. No doubt they were found to be an unnecessary clutter — or the ladies at the Hall camp had been persuaded to lower their heels. At this time Grant was also asked to furnish two extra neck-yokes, a sign that the older Hall boats still traveled the carries.

In 1897 Dwight Grant resigned as supervisor of the Lawrence camp to become manager of the Adirondack League Lodge at Little Moose. He remained there until 1900, when he was appointed superintendent of all the camps in the vast League preserve. Their main lodges were at Bisby, Little Moose, and Honnedaga, and there were many smaller camps and private cottages.

Eight guide-boats were finished in the Boonville shop in 1906, the year poor health compelled Dwight Grant to retire. His elder son, Floyd, did most of the carpentry. When Lewis succeeded his father as superintendent of the Adirondack League Club in January 1906, the shop closed down. Lewis could not spare the time from his League duties to continue building boats and Floyd did not want to carry on alone. He went to Schenectady to work for General Electric. Dwight Grant died in May 1911 at the age of 78. The progressive improvements Dwight Grant made in guide-boat design will be discussed in later chapters.

Guide-boats on the Fulton Chain. Because the railroad brought an invasion of steamboat trippers, the end of independent guiding occurred there sooner than at Blue Mountain Lake. (Fynmore Studios)

Grant reduced the average weight of his 16-foot boats to approximately 75 pounds. Some of Grant's admirers overstated the revolutionary nature of his achievement. Joseph F. Grady said that Grant's boats were "thirty to sixty pounds lighter than any former models,"[12] but this would hold only if he had in mind the boats reported by Lossing in 1859 and by Boardman in 1865 as weighing between 120 and 160 pounds. Much weight had been taken off in the intervening years by other shipbuilders, such as Chase of Newcomb, and Willie Martin of Saranac, before Grant even tried his hand at boatbuilding. Dwight Grant, a meticulous workman not given to overstatement, would be the first to repudiate exaggerations. His son Lewis said: "I will go along with thirty pounds or a little more but think sixty pounds is a lot too much."

Dwight Grant had seen as well as any other woodsman, probably better than most, the approaching disappearance of the independent guide. Because the railway brought an invasion of steamboat trippers and canoeists to the Fulton Chain, the end came there sooner than to Blue Mountain Lake, Long Lake, or Saranac Lake. Grant put his roots in

deep and, like a good forest tree, bent with the wind. He had become a guide in the middle of the nineteenth century when the guide's monopoly over woodland travel was unchallenged. He had built the first steamboat for the Fulton Chain of Lakes even though his colleagues protested. He had built locks and dams for steamboat penetration at Thendara. With wise foresight he had secured congenial summer employment as caretaker at the Lawrence camp and so escaped the necessity of looking for arduous, occasional jobs the tourist trade had to offer.

While others complained about the preserves and the posted lands, Dwight Grant moved from the private camp into the greater security of the Adirondack League Club, whose vast acres preserved not only game and solitude but also the art of the guides and the guide-boat. And for the guides and sportsmen in those protected recesses, he built boats.

Dwight Grant's social and civic duties reflected his high standing in the community. He was vice-president of the Public Library, a member of the Board of Education, and he served for several terms on the Board of Supervisors of Boonville. In 1879 he was elected to the State Assembly at Albany, served on the County Committee of the Republican Party, and was an active member of the Boonville Sportsmen's Club. He served as vice-president, and later as a member on the executive committee of the Brown's Tract Guides Association, which had been organized in the Grant shop in 1898. When, a year later, Governor Theodore Roosevelt invited the Association to Albany to discuss conservation measures, Dwight Grant was one of the delegates. Artemus M. Church, first secretary-treasurer of the Association, told Lewis Grant that they let his father do most of the talking.

In the words of Joseph Grady:

Dwight Grant was an outstanding woodsman, easily one of the most versatile and accomplished of his time. . . . He was a man of scholarly and distinguished appearance, a thoughtful, effective speaker, profoundly versed in the affairs of the forest. . . . At Albany he gained the immediate confidence and respect of his associates. . . . By exerting his influence in behalf of conservation of the State's wildlife, he effected a notable revision in the game laws. As "Honorable Dwight Grant" he continued to follow his multiple vocations . . . frankly declaring that he cherished his good name as a guide more than his title of Honorable.[13]

As a member of the Sportsmen's Club, Dwight Grant promoted projects for the benefit of sportsmen and the guides dependent upon them. At Albany, he supported measures to the same end, and when the time for restraint arrived, he was ready to oppose jacking and hounding, which had been the preferred ways of hunting in his youth.

William H. Boardman was president of the Adirondack League Club when Mr. and Mrs. Grant were managers of the Mountain Lodge at Little Moose Lake. The friendship between Boardman and Grant can be recognized in Boardman's book *The Lovers of the Woods*, a semifictional but carefully authentic picture of Adirondack life. There is good reason to believe that the fictional "John," described with such warmth and appreciation, is a composite of several woodsmen, but mostly a portrait of Dwight Grant. Boardman's John relates that he was taken prisoner in the Battle of Drury's Bluff, where Grant was captured when General Beauregard defeated General Butler.[14]

Another detail in Boardman's book points to Grant: A lively extrovert named Colonel Warren, after long absence from the woods, arrives in low health and spirits. John, who for 20 years has been the Colonel's guide, prescribes a little tamarack tea every night and morning. The Colonel will have none of it and demands a more pleasant remedy: John's specialty, the mountain ash cocktail.[15]

Lewis Grant thought that his father had never actually guided for Boardman but that they became good friends at Mountain Lodge, where there were many opportunities for reminiscing and chatting. "Mr. Boardman was surely telling about Father in his book, in regards Drury's Bluff and the mountain ash cocktail," said Lewis. "Father would crush the inner bark of the ash in liquor. It gave the drink a sharp tang." Lewis had not heard of anyone else making a mountain ash cocktail in 50 years.

Boardman especially liked Dwight Grant's boats for fishing on Bisby waters. In *Lovers of the Woods* he pays tribute to Grant as a boatbuilder, referring twice to Grant boats: one, an 11-foot carry-boat in which the "bow and stern were alike,"[16] might have been the one Boardman bought from Grant in 1891. Its measurements are carefully entered on the tally board for that year: 11-foot bottom, weighing with all equipment 55 pounds. Sixty years later Boardman's friend George H. Maurice remembered that boat. "Boardman called it a Raider, good for sneaking off to little known ponds in search of trout."[17] The fictional John had such a raiding craft. Dwight Grant may have brought the term back from the Civil War.

A description of a second Grant boat purchased by Boardman reflects his esteem for the builder:

A fourteen-foot ship that weighs only sixty pounds and carries a thousand pounds of load over a rough water; which is safe; . . . which never leaks; and which lasts, with ordinary good care, for twenty years, needs to be made by a man who knows how . . . .[18]

Grant had built such a boat, 15 feet long, for Boardman in 1889. For all Boardman's admiration for the master craftsman, he underestimated the endurance of a Grant boat. Almost a century after it left the Boonville shop in 1882, the *Ghost*, the boat that was exhibited in Utica, was found sound and tight at Bisby Lake. In 1965 Kenneth Durant rowed it on that Lake and could report that, after more than 80 years

H. Dwight Grant's Ghost. *Notice tumblehome bow.*
(Helen Durant)

of regular use, it did not leak a drop. It was true and clean in the water and sweetly responsive to the slightest stroke of the oars.

The distinguished guide-boat builder Theodore Hanmer of Saranac Lake said that it takes a woodsman to build a woodsman's boat.[19] Dwight Grant had preeminently this first qualification, to which he brought other requisites of skill and ingenuity. Thirty years of experience rowing a guide-boat, slogging through mud with a boat on his back, straddling fallen trunks, his shoulders protesting, made him calculate design and dimensions with the utmost finesse.

Another guide-boat built by Dwight Grant deserves mention. Built in 1884, it was "launched on the Fulton Chain of Lakes in April 1885 at the time of the passage of the Forest Preserve Bill," noted the *Boonville Herald* on July 11, 1935, in its report of the Central Adirondack Anniversary Pageant. This boat had seen continuous service "during the past fifty years. . . . From 1895 to 1900 it was owned and used by President Benjamin Harrison." The boat passed in review at Old Forge with Mrs. Benjamin Harrison seated in the stern.

Grant was a great boatbuilder, a skilled guide, a leader in his community, and a legislator. Yet, as

Lewis Grant told us, "When Father and some other man took a ride in one of the first automobiles to reach Boonville, they got stuck on a sandy hill. Father's conclusion was that they are all right for a rich man's plaything, but they won't amount to much." Ironically, Grant himself was a maker of a simple but beautiful utilitarian work boat that outlived its usefulness and became an expensive luxury, a rich man's plaything.

Lewis Lawrence Grant was born in Boonville, New York, in 1878, the year his father was elected to the Assembly in Albany. His boyhood was divided between life in the boat shop and trips with his father into the woods. Lewis's Boonville memories were mostly of winter, when he did the house chores, shoveled snow, and started the morning fires in the

Lewis Grant in his boatshop, Boonville, New York, 1958.
(Helen Durant)

shop. He kept out of the way of his father's busy carpenters, retreating to the paint room overhead, where he had a corner for "kid stuff," making sleds and toboggans from the thin sides of great circular cheese boxes.

When he was 13 his father gave him a guide-boat, number 13 on the tally board for 1892. When we mentioned the boat 65 years later, Lewis told of happy vacations on Fourth Lake of the Fulton Chain where he often went fishing with his mother.

In 1895, when he was 17, Lewis started work in his father's boat shop, putting on decks, shaping ribs, and making oars, paddles, and seat frames. Soon, he progressed to fastening shaped strakes to the frames, assisting his brother Floyd, who had learned the difficult art of "getting out the siding."

Lewis was never a guide, except for one brief spell in 1905 when for 56 days he guided at Little Moose Lake for the sons of Mr. Charles Miller, a lawyer from New York City. The next year he took his father's place as superintendent of the Adirondack League Club. It was harder work than guiding young boys, but "twice the money per day with expenses and [it was] the year round," said Lewis.

Lewis's mother had never felt as comfortable with the city people as did her gregarious husband and son. After Dwight's death she lived alone in Boonville, but when her health failed at the age of 80, she needed her son to look after her. Lewis resigned from his post with the Adirondack League Club in 1916 and returned to Boonville. He reopened the shop on Post Street, wired it for electricity, installed some machinery, and pulled out the remaining supply of spruce roots, long ago gathered by his father.

During the first few years after he reopened the shop, Lewis briefly employed some assistants, notably his father's chief carpenter, Lester Fox, who received as wages 30 cents an hour. The caning of seats was farmed out. After 1920, Lewis's account book showed no expenses for outside labor; he had learned to do his own caning.

Lewis was a good carpenter and built guide-boats to his father's patterns. The tally boards show that he built a total of 19 guide-boats between 1917 and 1923 before he used up most of his father's root stock. In 1921 his charges for boats, including federal tax, ran from $155 to $207, according to size and finish. In

1882 his father's prices for similar boats, without tax, had been between $48 and $70.

From the names on the tally boards of 1883 to 1885, we know that 17 of the first 19 purchasers of Dwight Grant's boats during that period were guides. Of the 19 guide-boats that Lewis Grant built between 1917 and 1923, 17 were sold to the Adirondack League for their clubhouses or to individual club members; one boat was sold to Lewis's neighbor; none were sold to guides.

Root stock became scarce and prices rose, but for a few more years Lewis was able to supply a dwindling market among League members. In 1934 Lewis built his last guide-boat. He gathered what remained on hand of his father's root stock and managed to buy more to make the ribs for a 13½-foot boat. Meanwhile, he was creating a good business in flat-bottomed boats of pine, which were gradually supplanting the more costly and fragile guide-boats. Flat-bottomed boats had long been used at Bisby Lake, where fly fishermen preferred their stability and children of League members enjoyed romping around in them. Many such boats were left the year round at neighboring ponds for convenience. "In the old days," Lewis recalled, "when the guides saw a flat-bottomed boat, they would say: 'There's a Bisby guide-boat.'"[20]

Along with boats, Lewis made paddles and oars,

The Grant camp on Fourth Lake of the Fulton Chain. Lewis Grant created a good business in flat-bottomed boats of pine. (Lewis L. Grant)

for which he created some ingenious labor-saving machinery. "Father never saw this," he would say, throwing the switch to start an oar-shaping device. New times demanded new ways and new materials. After 1940 he acquired marine plywood and began to make car-top boats. He would have continued the search for lightness as long as guides backed boats over the carries, but when motor roads paralleled the water courses, and outboard motors supplanted oars, lightness was no longer essential. In 1951 he built a car-top boat, "especially light," for his own fishing expeditions. It was 12 feet long and weighed 95 pounds. The 12-foot guide-boat he built in 1921 weighed 59 pounds complete with oars, seats, and yoke.

In the League clubs and on some private preserves, such as those on Bisby Lake and Brandreth Lake, extra care was taken to prolong the life of the existing guide-boats. Lewis Grant kept busy patching, repairing, and refinishing, as did Willard Hanmer at Saranac Lake. "In 1957 I repaired four boats from Bisby Lake which were built by my father over fifty years before and were still in good shape," wrote Lewis.[21] The same year he patched a boat built by his father in 1886 for Henry Covey of Big Moose, listed as number 14 on the tally board for that year.

The lives of Dwight and Lewis Grant spanned the history of the guide-boat. Dwight, born in 1833, witnessed the disappearance of the dugout and the Indian canoe. In 1934, one hundred years after his father's birth, Lewis built his last guide-boat. He saw it transformed from the guide's crude work boat to a luxury product for leisure class enjoyment, saw it preserved in private enclaves, and, ultimately, saw it become a museum piece. After Lewis Grant visited the Adirondack Museum in 1959, he wrote: "We saw no. 3, 1905 guide-boat [the *Virginia*] that my brother Floyd and I built for Mr. Jeffress and will say that they know how to take care of a boat as it still looks like a new boat."

When we first met Lewis Grant in 1958, he was sitting in a rocking chair on the porch of his home in front of the boat shop his father built in 1881. He was a little man, not much over five feet tall, and was then already 80 years old but alert and vivacious, eager to give us as much information as possible. When he noticed that words alone were not enough, he would

Lewis Grant would take us to his boat shop and demonstrate the making of certain details. (Helen Durant)

rise and say: "Come on, I'll show you." Then he would lead us to the shop and would demonstrate the making of certain details of construction.

There were gratifying moments during our study there, such as finding the stern of an old boat and finding the old man's memory so reliable. Such incidents inspired confidence in Lewis Grant as our guide to his father's boat shop practices, and confidence in the ability of Dwight Grant to build a boat, which, as he promised, "will always retain its original shape."[22] We owe much to the scrupulous care, precision, and historical sense with which Lewis explained the operations of the boat shop in patient conversations and voluminous letters, supplemented by detailed sketches and construction models. No effort was too much for him. When already 81 years old, he wrote us:

You will have to come to see me this summer and we will start right from digging out the spruce stump to get the ribs, to building the boat, step by step, as with what I have in the shop, I can show you more about guide-boat building, in three or four hours, than I could write you in a month. You have to see how things are done to really understand plans or drawings.[23]

In spite of the rich documentation, written descriptions by two master builders, notes on conversations, the tally boards, the complete shop patterns, and the boat itself, there are obscure spots that make it difficult to get the building of the boat into narrative, to reconstruct the ways and atmosphere of a shop in which a guide-boat was last built over 40 years ago.

The contents of the Post Street boat shop, the tools of Dwight and Lewis Grant, many construction samples made especially for us, plus an extensive diary kept by Lewis, are all preserved in the Adirondack Museum. Lewis was a gentle man and generous with his contributions. This was his tribute to a greatly honored father.

Lewis also spoke with great affection and warmth about his mother, but his sense of history had been wounded when, out of an urge for order and neatness, she cleaned out the attic after Dwight Grant's death and burned records and documents he had so carefully accumulated.

Lewis wanted to have the story of the Post Street shop told right, he said, "for Father's sake," and no pains were too great to assist us. Speaking of Dwight Grant's career and the many years he spent at the Lawrence camp and the Adirondack League Club, Lewis emphasized how much his father enjoyed fishing and hunting. "He loved the woods," said Lewis with great simplicity.

Lewis Grant died in Boonville on September 27, 1960. He was 82 years old.

Notes

1. A.W. Brøgger and Haakon Shetelig, *The Viking Ships* (Oslo, Norway: Dreyers Forlag; Los Angeles: Knud K. Mogensen Publishing, 1951), p. 74.
2. Unless otherwise noted, the material in this chapter has been compiled from a series of letters from and conversations with Lewis L. Grant; from the tally boards of the Grant shop; from a list of purchasers of Grant boats annotated by Lewis Grant; from Joseph F. Grady, *The Adirondacks* (Little Falls, N.Y.: Press of the Journal & Courier Co., 1933), especially the chapter on transportation; and from the *Boonville Herald.*
3. Letter, October 17, 1958.
4. Letter, April 15, 1959.
5. Map in Erwin Library, Boonville, N.Y.
6. Letter, January 17, 1958.
7. Letter, March 14, 1959.
8. The name is variously spelled Seeber or Seber. Lewis Grant spelled it both ways. When we asked him which was correct, he wrote on August 6, 1960: "I just went and looked for the right way of spelling [from his father's pay books], it should be Seiber." We will continue to use the most commonly used spelling, Seeber.
9. *Forest and Stream,* August 10, September 28, and October 19, 1882.
10. Letter from New York State Library, Albany, February 24, 1959.
11. Letter, March 14, 1959.
12. Grady, p. 187.
13. *Ibid.,* pp. 212-214.
14. William H. Boardman. *The Lovers of the Woods* (New York: McClure, Phillips & Co., 1901), p. 227.
15. *Ibid.,* pp. 118-119.
16. *Ibid.,* p. 78.
17. Letter, November 4, 1958.
18. Boardman, p. 81.
19. *North Country Life,* Spring 1957, p. 23.
20. Letter, February 6, 1959.
21. Letter, August 30, 1959.
22. H. Dwight Grant, 1890 pamphlet, Adirondack Museum.
23. Letter, May 12, 1959.

VIII/Warren Cole

The affection which we have for the companions of our solitude is very strong.

W.C. Prime[1]

The Grants left us the most complete record of guide-boat construction, but in other areas of the north woods there were other builders equally important. One of the most renowned guides and guide-boat builders in Long Lake was Warren Cole. He was born in the region of the Saranac Lakes in 1854. His grandfather, Michael Charbonneau, came down to Tupper Lake from Canada around 1840. His name was soon anglicized to Cole. According to family tradition, Michael was a nephew of the guide and hunter Toussaint Charbonneau, whose Indian wife, Sacajawea, played an important part in the Lewis and Clark expedition.[2] Grandfather Cole was a true pioneer. The summer after he came to the Tupper settlement, he trudged back through the forest to the Champlain Valley, cutting and stacking wild hay as he went. He returned the next winter with a herd of cattle, which he drove across frozen Tupper Lake and fed on the salvaged hay.[3]

Warren Cole's father, Augustus, was killed in the 1864 battle of Drury's Bluff, the same battle in which the Confederates captured Dwight Grant.[4] In the familiar Adirondack pattern, young Warren worked at lumber jobs on the Raquette River but soon went deeper into the woods near Long Lake, where his uncles ran a boat shop and were guides. Warren assisted them in both occupations.

In 1881 Warren Cole was involved in a shooting incident. A would-be guide, using the name Parker, allegedly molested a lady on a journey between Forked Lake and Long Lake. Parker fled but was tracked and finally apprehended by Warren Cole in Canada and returned to the States. Because Cole at the time was Long Lake's constable, he had to keep the accused overnight, pending an investigation. He shackled the prisoner to his own wrist; nevertheless, Parker managed to escape again. When Cole found him launching a boat for his getaway and Parker refused to surrender, Cole shot him.

Nessmuk came to the support of Warren Cole and the reputation of Adirondack guides. ". . . the man Charles Parker was not a guide," Nessmuk wrote, "and was not so considered by the guides. The constable at Long Lake is a genuine guide [who] saw at once the importance of bringing him [Parker] to punishment."[6] Apparently Parker was really Frank Cook, who had been arrested in Highgate, Vermont, in 1873 on charges of adultery, but escaped. In 1878 he had been sent to jail for intoxication.

T.S. Morell, who made numerous trips through the Adirondacks and reported on them in the *American Angler* under the pseudonym "Old Izaak," wrote that he considered the shooting of Parker a daring deed, which rid the woods of one of the worst

Warren Cole, 1854-1922. (Wright F. Cole)

boats at the Sportsmen's Show in Madison Square Garden in New York City, in 1899; the same year he was elected vice-president of the Adirondack Guides' Association.[9]

Guide-boats were rated cranky, tippy, or steady, relative terms largely dependent upon the experience and behavior of the occupants. The boats of Warren Cole were considered steady. It was said of them that they would roll but would not turn over. Something in the swell of the ribs checked the roll before water came over the gunwale. As a result, Cole boats were favored by the inexperienced guests at lake-shore boarding houses and by camp-owning families with children who were learning to row. Capacious and staunchly built, his boats were not noted for speed, but they were widely appreciated for their stability and fine workmanship.

Across from the Cole boat shop, on the opposite shore of Long Lake, was the Endion property, in those days a summer hotel. It was purchased around 1888 by James Bissell of Newcomb, who had married Lena Talbot of Olmstedville. Their son, Talbot, was only four years old when Cole bought the Lapell boat

characters. "We notet [*sic*] the place where he was shot; handled the rifle, and admired the man who killed him. This deed has made the north woods as safe for ladies as our city. . . ."[7]

During the winter of 1889 Warren Cole repaired guide-boats at The Cedars, Frederick C. Durant's private camp on Forked Lake, and during the following winter at Durant's Prospect House on Blue Mountain Lake.[8]

After 20 years of experience as a carpenter in Alvah Cole's boat shop and as a guide on the lakes and carries, Warren Cole, in 1892, bought the shop of Orren Lapell on the shore of Long Lake. There, during the winters, he built boats for 16 years. Spring, summer, and fall, he guided. Warren Cole was a latecomer among Long Lake boatbuilders. The boat shops of, among others, Reuben Carey, Henry and George Stanton, Wallace Emerson, and the Palmers were already well established. Cole exhibited one of his

Warren Cole (right) *exhibits his guide-boat at the Sportsmen's Show at Madison Square Garden, New York City, in 1899. (Wright F. Cole)*

Warren Cole's boat shop at Long Lake, New York. (Wright F. Cole)

shop in 1892. As a growing youth, during the long winter months, Talbot would cross the frozen lake on foot to spend hours and days watching Cole at work.

Talbot Bissell never lost his love for guide-boats. He later wrote down his childhood memories of Cole in his shop. He thought of Cole as the greatest of them all in honest workmanship. The following comes from his article, "Their Little Boats."

> Enter his shop from the biting cold of an Adirondack winter day and you feel suddenly enveloped in a fluid warmth flowing out from the great iron stove in the corner. Enveloped, too, in a strange odor one will smell nowhere else in the world — a satisfying mixture of fragrant cedar shavings, resinous spruce, fruity black cherry, shellac, paint and wood-smoke all combined in an unforgettable sense of well-being. . . .
>
> Along one side of the shop stands a curious framework — "stocks," on which the boat is assembled. Pivoted at either end, it can be turned in any position needed in the course of putting the endless parts of the boat together.
>
> Along the wall hang dozens of patterns — brown and glistening from age and handling. . . . In racks near the ceiling, great wide boards of thin white cedar are drying in the warmth. They have been drying for years. . . . In a corner of the shop is a rack of knee-planks — grotesque curved boards possibly five feet long and an inch thick. These, too, have been seasoned since the day they were grubbed out of frozen ground. . . .[10]

This manuscript, which recounts with such vivid enjoyment the atmosphere and scents of the shop, the sight of the many hand tools of razor-edge sharpness, and the successive steps in building a guide-boat, was written in 1935. Lost for many years, it was rediscovered and subsequently published in *The Skipper* of January 1967 under the title "42 Pounds to Portage."

Warren Cole used primarily white pine for the siding of his guide-boats. (Though the annual report of 1895 made by the Forest Commission in Albany said that in 1893 spruce was the leading merchantable species of the New York forest because the white pine had been taken many years ago, good pines could still be found in the interior of the woods.) At Long Lake, about 1901, Cole came upon a great pine, near the Long Lake West road, measuring six feet across the base. He bought it for ten dollars. The lumbermen told him he was wasting his money on an unmanageable monster; the butt log was too large for any local mill. Cole split it in half with wedges. From the two half butts and five additional 16-foot logs, all quarter-sawn, came several thousand feet of clear planks, which lasted Cole to the end of his boatbuilding career.

Machinery was of little use in the construction of a guide-boat. The nearest thing to a power tool in the Cole shop was an antiquated foot-treadle jigsaw with which he reduced the ungainly planks the local saw-mill had cut from the root stumps to delicate ribs. Mr. Bissell wrote in his article:

> His heavy shoulders, stooped from a life time of toil at bench and oar and axe, are hunched over his work, his deep blue eyes guiding the dancing blade along the pencilled lines.

Complete with accessories, a Cole boat weighed approximately 60 pounds and took roughly 175 man-hours to complete, not counting the time Cole spent in the woods looking for the right timber and grubbing out the root crooks. "Gleaming in the spring sunshine," Mr. Bissell observed, "[the boat stood] a thing of delicate beauty." Talbot Bissell's son, Thomas, who still lives at Endion, cherishes a fine example of an early Cole guide-boat purchased by Lena Bissell from Warren Cole in 1900.

Kenneth Durant rowing his Warren Cole boat on Blue Mountain Lake, July 1959. His passenger is John Gardner. (Helen Durant)

Cole's early boats followed the conventional Long Lake patterns, with feather-edged laps and tumble-home stems, like those Henry Stanton had taken to Dwight Grant in Boonville in 1879. About 1905, Cole changed his stem pattern to make it almost vertical. (Dwight Grant and Riley Parsons had made their change somewhat earlier.) A slight lengthening of the sheer plank relieved his boats of a blunt-nosed appearance, and this change, though not as marked as in the Brown's Tract models, immediately established a new profile on Long Lake. By advancing the stem slightly without changing the underwater line, Cole added grace and elegance to his boats. During his career Cole built about 225 boats. Most of them were in the 16-foot class, but he would build heavier freight boats and smaller hunting craft to order.

Nicknamed the Old Blue Giant, Warren Cole was a tall man. In 1905 he built himself a boat to fit his own arms and legs. It was designed for faster rowing than his usual sturdy model, with greater length for capacity, yet it was light-weight for ease on the carries. When Cole rowed it up to the dock at The Cedars on Forked Lake, Kenneth Durant noticed its sleek lines and persuaded Cole to part with it. Wright Cole remembered the night his father returned home

without his boat and allowed that Mr. Durant now had it. Durant regularly used and enjoyed Cole's boat from 1905 through 1960, when it was given to the Adirondack Museum in tribute to the north woods guide-boat builders.[11]

Originally, the boat was fitted with the conventional steel rowlock pins and sockets. These were eventually replaced with new brass rowlocks. The present bow and stern seats are those made in the Cole shop, though they have been re-caned. The original yoke and middle seat have been lost. The present middle seat appears to be one from a boat formerly owned by Ethel Durant and built by Farrand Austin, who made fine boats of excellent design. The back rest of the Austin middle seat fits into two slots and is held in position by rigid wooden rods. Thus it is always in an upright position, but it compels the stern passenger to step over it in walking toward the bow of the boat to get out.

In 1909 failing eyesight compelled Warren Cole to give up boatbuilding. He retired to farming in Vermont and later joined his son, Wright, at carpentry in Poughkeepsie, New York. Every fall father and son returned to the north woods. Warren Cole died there on November 20, 1922, while hunting deer.

Notes

1. William C. Prime, *I go a-fishing* (New York and London: Harper & Brothers Publishers, 1902), p. 131.
2. Conversations with Wright Cole on May 20, 1959, provided much of the information for this chapter.
3. *Tupper Lake Free Press and Herald,* March 10, 1960.
4. *Ibid.,* December 7, 1967.
5. Conversations with Wright Cole, 1959.
6. *Forest and Stream,* August 18, 1881, p. 48.
7. *American Angler,* June 9, 1883, p. 355.
8. Wright Cole, letter, April 2, 1959. Harrison Durant, letter, March 4, 1965.
9. *Forest and Stream,* February 4, 1899, p. 85.
10. Unless otherwise noted, all direct quotes about Warren Cole's Long Lake boat shop are from Talbot Bissell's "Their Little Boats," published in *The Skipper,* January 1967, under the title, "42 Pounds to Portage."
11. Boat no. 57-192.2 at Adirondack Museum.

IX/Pleasure Boating: The Competitors

Thirty years of experience has demonstrated to the Adirondack Guide that no other boat manufactured can begin to compete with them for durability, speed, lightness, capacity and ability to ride through rough water in safety.

H. Dwight Grant[1]

Though railroads, steamboats, and Concord coaches had made the woods and lakes more accessible to tourists at the end of the nineteenth century and seemed to threaten the guide and his profession, at least temporarily they provided new uses for the guide's boat. In contrast to the early sportsman on a brief vacation and constantly on the move, private camp owners and summer residents on the club preserves were more relaxed, content, for the most part, to remain within the comfortable seclusion of their main lodges. Their guides were called upon for occasional excursions to nearby streams and ponds over short and easy carries. Since many of these camps and lodges could be reached only by water, a boat remained a necessity.

On the private docks the fleet of guide-boats increased as camp owners, their families and friends began to learn the ways of oar and paddle. It was not unusual to have a boat for each member of the family, with extra boats for guests and retainers. In addition, it was convenient to have a spare boat by the shore of a favored pond and to keep a larger boat for family outings or to carry freight.

Sportsmen who wished to carry their own boats through the woods generally preferred a shorter and lighter guide-boat. The seven short boats with 13½-foot bottoms built by Dwight Grant in 1897 averaged 6½ pounds lighter than the work boats generally used by the guides. The change in function of the guide-boat, from work boat to pleasure craft, was further evident in the conspicuous increase of even smaller boats, ones with bottoms 12 feet and less. They were not suitable for a long pull with a heavy load, though an occasional guide might find it profitable to keep such a small skiff in addition to his regular work boat.

The distinction between the guide-boat's two functions was early recognized by Caleb Chase, who had begun building boats in Newcomb, New York, in 1852. On his business card he identified himself as a "Builder of Guiding and Pleasure Boats." It seems that the difference between these two terms merely represents two aspects of the same boat, and not a difference in construction.

Among the Adirondack vacationers were many who had no experience whatsoever in handling the native guide-boat and who feared its cranky behavior; nevertheless, they wanted to save themselves the expense of a guide. These tourists were tempted by offers from competing boatbuilders outside the Adirondacks who promised craft "safer" than the guide-boat.

Paper boats became the rage. In 1871, Waters, Balch & Company, of Troy, New York, advocated paper boats on the Adirondack model.[2] In 1874 N.H. Bishop paddled his 58-pound paper canoe from Troy to the Gulf of Mexico.[3] Circa 1880 Dr. Arpad Gerster, who had a taste for innovations, sailed a paper canoe on the Harlem River. (He does not seem to have taken it to his camp on Raquette Lake.) Between 1888 and 1890 Dr. Gerster also acquired a folding canvas boat (no. 61.12.2 of the Adirondack Museum collection) and an 11-foot strip-built boat (no. 56.61.3 of the collection), which he had made "ad hoc" (i.e., the strip-built boat) for his solitary excursions in the Adirondacks, to avoid being nudged along by hurrying guides.[4] Verplanck Colvin, who earlier had invented an "envelope boat," assembled and launched it on the shore of Ampersand Pond in 1873 to the great amusement of the guides, who kept their own boats. In 1875 a folding canvas boat produced by Osgood in Battle Creek, Michigan, became available. It was considerably cheaper than a guide-boat.

The guide-boat was not compact enough, complained the editor of *Forest and Stream* in the August 26, 1875, issue. He wanted something that could be folded into a small package and toted about like a valise. That was exactly what the Hegeman Company offered in Wallace's *Guide to the Adirondacks* of 1875. The English clergyman E.L. Berton offered another perilous innovation—his self-folding boat, also mentioned in *Forest and Stream* of August 26, 1875.

Wallace, who in 1878 lent his patronage to Rushton of Canton, New York, recommending his lapstrake bent-frame boat as the complete answer to the sportsmen's needs, "less tottlish and less cramped" than other cranky boats, himself achieved a somewhat tottlish balance between rival craft by tempering his enthusiasm for Rushton with a footnote in his 1894 edition stating that the boats manufactured at Long Lake, Saranac Lake, and other points in the Adirondacks "remain unsurpassed for use in that region."[5]

Joyner of Glens Falls, Rushton of Canton, Everson

of Williamsburg, New York, and other small-craft builders outside the Adirondacks in the 1880s were riding the wooden canoe boom, a vogue from England inspired by John MacGregor, the Scottish canoeist, traveler, and philanthropist, and by his disciple, Baden Powell. In 1865 MacGregor had started on a long cruise through Europe in his *Rob Roy*. In 1866 he published a record of his trip, *A Thousand Miles in the Rob Roy Canoe,* which made MacGregor and his canoe famous. Rushton began to build *Rob Roy* canoes and won wide publicity in 1882 with the *Sairy Gamp,* the first of several tiny canoes he built for Messmuk. Everson made the first of the *Shadow* canoes, which were an adaptation of Baden Powell's *Nautilus,* modified for American waters.

Rushton, who had reduced the weight of his canoes by sacrificing capacity, began to offer roomier, modified St. Lawrence skiffs in addition to large cruising and sailing canoes of the *Rob Roy* type. In his 1881 catalog he listed, among others, two small boats, 12 and 13 feet, especially designed for guides, hunters, and trappers, to carry two persons and baggage with safety "on small lakes in any ordinary weather." The guides, however, would not accept any limitation. Their professional work boat, however fragile looking, if properly handled could ride out any storm on the average freshwater lake, carrying a load of 500 pounds.

Rushton even tried to argue the superiority of machine-made ribs over the hand-shaped natural-crook frames used in the traditional guide-boat. "The stems are bent," announced Rushton in the same catalog, "thereby obtaining a more perfect shape, better material and less weight than could be had by using natural crooks." An undated catalog declared that the guide-boat "is not a boat which we could recommend for the use of women and children, although many use them."[6]

In the 1882 edition of *The Adirondacks Illustrated,* S.R. Stoddard noted that Joyner had been making boats in his Glens Falls factory that better met the requirements of the wilderness, especially in the qualities of lightness and steadiness, "which those who have attempted to navigate the regular boat [the Long Lake guide-boat] must have wished for. Joyner's light sporting boat . . . must eventually take the place of the cranky craft so generally used in the

Prospect House, Blue Mountain Lake, New York. (Helen Durant)

wilderness. . . ."[7] That same year F.C. Durant bought for the Prospect House at Blue Mountain Lake a fleet of 82 Joyner rowboats, said to be larger and steadier than the ordinary traveling boat of the Adirondacks.[8]

In the decade 1880 to 1890, the Thousand Islands competed with the Adirondacks for the tourist trade. In 1888 Bain & Company of Clayton, New York, emerged as the St. Lawrence River Skiff, Canoe and Steam Launch Company. They conducted an aggressive sales campaign far beyond the Thousand Islands region into Lake George and the Adirondacks. While the guide-boat was not practical for the long stretches of the great St. Lawrence River, the St. Lawrence skiff, though not portable, had its uses within the confines of the larger Adirondack lakes; some migration was inevitable. Tourists and sportsmen who preferred a steady boat, easy to row yet elegant in appearance, might choose a St. Lawrence skiff in natural wood with piano finish. The popularity of these skiffs inspired still more imitation. "Our largest boats," stated the Rushton catalog of 1891, "would resemble the St. Lawrence skiff, only they have finer lines and are finer built." The resemblance was superficial. Rushton's boats were built on 2½-inch oak keels on edge. The classic St. Lawrence skiff had an elliptical bottom board like the guide-boat.

Joyner manufactured a sectional boat in two nesting pieces "similar to Alexandria Bay or St. Lawrence River boats."[9] Two of Dwight Grant's carpenters, Theodore Seeber and Riley Parsons, had opened their own boat shop in Old Forge in 1890, where they built guide-boats on the Grant pattern. Now they, too, added the "heavier St. Lawrence boats" to their line.

In 1885 Stoddard resumed his allegiance to the famous Long Lake boats; nevertheless, he frequently suggested that the novice was better off in something other than the guide-boat. In 1891 he noted in his guidebook that the Algonquin Hotel in Saranac Lake offered its guests a choice of boats: comfortably large and steady, or of the cranky Adirondack build. The Cascade Lake House offered large, comfortable boats for the timid, and light guiding boats for the hunter and fisherman. In 1899 Stoddard announced that the Prospect House at Blue Mountain Lake supplied "broad boats of the Champlain type for safety, and narrow Adirondack skiffs for hunting and fishing."

We need not pay too much attention to the allegations and infidelities of a day when guidebook texts and advertising were so conveniently married. In exchange for advertising, Stoddard, Wallace, and the rest of the travel writers over the years had tempted the amateur with strange craft, none of which ever threatened to displace the guide-boat in the affection of the guides. Only the dilettantes of the woods could be impressed by the advertised novelties.

With so many imitations of the guide-boat and other small craft plying the waters of the Adirondacks, the 1892 travel brochure entitled *The Adirondack Mountains* pointed with unusual discrimination to the distinguishing features of the Adirondack guide-boat, which has a "smooth skin built over ribs of natural curvature."[10] This was precisely the characteristic emphasized by Dwight Grant in the pamphlet he had published in 1890 to advertise his guide-boat.

Asserting the superiority of the native craft over all imitations, Dwight Grant claimed a place for the Adirondack guide-boat in the new and expanding market of the amateur oarsman.

Notes

1. H. Dwight Grant, 1890 pamphlet, Adirondack Museum.
2. *Annual Illustrated Catalogue and Oarsman's Manual for 1871* (Troy, N.Y.: Waters, Balch & Co.), p. 97.
3. N.H. Bishop, *Voyage of the Paper Canoe* (Boston: Lee and Shepard, 1878).
4. Arpad Gerster, *Recollections of a New York Surgeon* (New York: Paul B. Hoeber, 1917), pp. 204, 276, 277; and *Medical Pickwick*, II, no. 10 (October 1916), p. 368.
5. E.R. Wallace, *Descriptive Guide to the Adirondacks* (Syracuse, N.Y.: Watson Gill, 1894), p. 487.
6. Rushton catalog, undated, in library of St. Lawrence University.
7. S.R. Stoddard, *The Adirondacks Illustrated* (Glens Falls, N.Y.: published by the author, 1882), p. 116.
8. Kenneth Durant, letter, November 22, 1959; Stoddard, 1883, p. 201; testimonial by F.C. Durant in Joyner catalog, 1890.
9. Joyner catalog, 1884.
10. *The Adirondack Mountains*, Four Track Series (New York: Central Railroad and Hudson River Railroad Co., 1892), pp. 26–27.

X/Changing Ways

The genius of change has possession of the land; we cannot control it.

Verplanck Colvin[1]

The supremacy and solitude of the white trapper was short-lived. He had guarded his trap lines, secret fishing domain, and squatter's cabin in what he considered the free forest. In the 1820s he became host and guide to the few surveyors and an occasional adventurous sportsman. By the 1850s, however, land speculators, lumbermen, and a fresh wave of settlers began to arrive. The woodsman found his ancient haunts invaded by pioneers of improvement and his shanty resting on someone's private estate. As the methods of transportation improved during the 1870s and 1880s, the tourists began to overrun the woods, becoming the dominant economic factor. Clubs and leagues, which had bought large tracts of land to secure exclusive hunting and fishing privileges for their members, began to post their holdings. What some called progress was not to the taste of all. The serious sportsman who came to hunt and enjoy the solitude regretted the influx of tourists. As early as 1858, Charles E. Whitehead was disillusioned by the sight of debris left behind by other campers—deer antlers, bits of rope, broken bottles, and names carved on blazed trees.[2]

The movement to the woods for recreation and pleasure was a manifestation of nineteenth century romanticism, based upon an American economy that produced a leisure class with the means to escape the heat and turmoil of the big cities. As the opening of the north woods progressed, these wealthy city residents yearned for the primitive woods and a simple way of life, yet they did not feel comfortable in the wilderness without all the trappings of their city civilization. They began by building four walls around what was once an open shanty and transformed it into a lodge. Then they added guest houses, a boathouse, wine cellars, ice houses, and quarters for their retainers. At times their opulence became so oppressive that they needed to retreat from it to simpler camps deeper in the woods.

With its simple woodland camps on Raquette Lake and Big Moose surrounded by luxury camps, the Northwoods Walton Club was gradually driven out of existence. Because many of its members were prominent businessmen and legislators, their annual egressions from the woods were viewed, according to Joseph F. Grady, "somewhat in the nature of an exploring party returning to civilization with graphic accounts of a newly discovered continent."[3]

These accounts by news and magazine writers and the swelling flood of tourists denied them the pleasure of solitude in the company of a select group of like-minded sportsmen. Intending to recapture a measure

Paul Smiths on the Lower St. Regis. (Adirondack Museum)

of privacy, General Sherman in 1878 organized the Bisby Club, which comprised mostly the members of the defunct Northwoods Walton Club. Though the tract of land they purchased at Bisby Lake was only a few miles south of Old Forge, its inaccessibility protected the isolation and privacy the club members sought.

In his 1879 report on the topographical survey of the Adirondack region, Verplanck Colvin noted that the rapidity with which certain changes took place as the wilderness was opened to travelers had something almost startling about it. To facilitate travel through the woods and to shorten the climbs to the mountain summits, new trails were blazed, Colvin reported. Everywhere he went, the ubiquitous tourist followed. Bark and log huts became insufficient; hotels sprang up as if by magic. With the old trails and accompanying miseries thrown aside, the romance, too, was gone forever, lamented Colvin. Still, he tried to put a good face upon the penetration of the forest:

> Changes have opened to travel many of the most interesting nooks among our mountains. . . . Save to the hermit of the forest, whose semi-savage life cannot always be maintained, these changes are rather changes for the better. . . .[4]

The eye of the beholder adjusted to new perspectives. The semi-savage hermits who stood in the way of change were "hardy trappers" only a few years earlier in 1874, lauded by Colvin when they led him to countless lakes and ponds they had discovered.

Colvin's assistant, Fred Mather, arrived at Blue Mountain Lake Village in June of 1882. He spent the night at the Prospect House, which provided its guests with electricity, running water, and steam heat in every room. A hydraulic elevator served the upper floors. Mather was appalled at the luxury:

> We remained overnight at the Prospect House whose size and style astonished one who expected backwoods simplicity. . . . It can accommodate six hundred guests [with] all the pomp and circumstance of a city house. . . .[5]

At Paul Smiths on the Lower St. Regis, another great resort hotel, the fishermen and hunters who arrived for tea in their fancy hunting costumes reappeared in broadcloth and linen for supper, noted A. Judd Northrup, who made many trips through the north woods. "At the piano is seated a lady in elegant summer costume . . . the rich tones rise and swell and sink and die away in music [and] turning the sheets as she plays, stand men in faultless attire." Yet, Northrup enjoyed watching the gaiety, the fashion, and the social life when, after sunset, the boats filled with ladies, gentlemen, and children pushed out on the lake, "each boat rowed by a strong oarsman who

Heavily traveled routes offered this service; otherwise, the boat went on the guide's back. (Saranac Lake Free Library)

knows how to row a genuine Adirondack boat with swiftness and handle it with safety."[6]

By the 1890s railroad and steamboat travel were available from Utica to Malone, spanning the two ends of the north woods. Increased hotel facilities reached from Old Forge to the Saranacs. Drawing-room cars from New York were hauled into the Saranac Lake region over the Chateaugay Railroad, which connected with the Delaware and Hudson Railroad.[7]

The new ways of travel also affected the guides. Over the larger carries, now cleared of most obstructions, boats and passenger gear were transported on wagons drawn by horses or oxen. Crossing the two-mile carry between Upper St. Regis and Big Clear Pond, Northrup found the walk easy and agreeable. So easy was it, in fact, that a party of two gentlemen and two handsome ladies, accompanied by their children and the guides, was setting off on the walk over the carry with light, tripping steps, as if walking down the lawn at home, wrote Northrup.[8]

The conditions that lightened the burden on the guide's back also increased his pay somewhat. Raymond Spears, a correspondent for *Forest and Stream*, reported in 1900 that an old-time guide told him that he now earned four dollars a day instead of two and a half, lived and ate better, and that, except for trips to branch camps, he no longer had to tote such heavy packs; a horse did it.[9]

Contemporary accounts began to refer to the guides as shrewd rascals and lazy extortionists. It is true that some of the time a guide would favor one of his special patrons. T.S. Morell ("Old Izaak") acknowledged in 1884 that he had received a letter from Mitchell Sabattis announcing the discovery of a lake probably never seen before, full of the finest trout, known only to Sabattis and his son Isaac. They would "keep the secret for the benefit of their patrons and friends; and . . . take every precaution to prevent other guides from following their trail." Two years earlier, in the spring of 1882, Sabattis had guided Morell and his party from Clear Pond to "another" lake for trout fishing. "There was no road or trail; our path was through the virgin forest. . . . Mitchell led the way . . . he only knew the route." The lake had a name, but Sabattis did not want it mentioned; otherwise visiting sportsmen would clean it out.[10]

The so-called secrecy of the guide was, in fact, often a simplified form of conservation. He gave his patron a chance at catching a big fish and shooting a deer. Fish and venison provided their meals in the woods. The sportsman took the antlers home as a trophy; the guide kept the pelts. When the tourist season was over, the woodsman needed the rest of the game for subsistence.

The new tourism changed the function of the guides. Now hired primarily to row pleasure parties around the lakes, they became servants, reduced to the role of water rickshaw boys, to an often selfish and ostentatious clientele. Their ranks were diluted by inexperienced men and boys, some of whom were, perhaps, spoiled by the lavish presents heaped upon them by their wealthy patrons to curry their favor, until they refused to work for those unwilling to pay more than the going wages. The change was not in the old and trustworthy guides, but in the multitude and class of people that thronged the woods and in their relationship to the guides. During the month of August there were more excursionists than at any other time, wrote Thaddeus Norris in 1877, "some of them the most pretentious hunters you ever laid eyes on. I'll bet [they] could not tell a buck from an old stump . . . [yet] walked about with bowie-knives stuck in [their] belts."[11]

W.H.H. Murray called the new class of tourists a motley crowd. He understood that these lavish spenders and the arrival of women tourists with their special needs had, to a certain extent, a demoralizing effect upon the guides, but he regretted that the guides had become a convenient scapegoat for ignorant sportsmen.[12] One only had to stay away from the fashionable hotels to find the guide who had not forgotten his woodcraft and remained helpful, loyal, and trustworthy.

In an attempt to stem the tide of change and to check some of the evils that were springing up here and there, the legitimate guides, who were pessimistic about their future in the woods, in 1891 formed the Adirondack Guides' Association. Its membership numbered 626 men.[13] They agreed to observe uniform rates and the game laws, among other rules. Dr. Frank E. Kendall, the honorary president, addressed the eighth annual meeting of the Association at Saranac Lake on January 23, 1901, with these words:

> In the early days . . . the Adirondacks were visited by people who loved the woods and came solely to hunt and fish. One of the first arrangements to be made was to find an able-bodied man . . . fearless but discreet . . . whose very presence gave one an unexplainable confidence. Such a man was then and is now known as a guide. . . .[14]

When the 1897 law against hounding and jacking was enforced in 1902, the guide-boat lost one of its primary functions; nevertheless, the guide's work boat continued under its own momentum as a valued pleasure craft. While many guides lost their jobs, those who became boatbuilders prospered for a while and continued to improve the boat. The guide developed new skills and found still other occupations.

Two historians of the Adirondacks have linked the guide-boat with a passing era, overlapping the nineteenth and twentieth centuries. In the preface to *History of the Adirondacks,* published in 1921, Alfred L. Donaldson wrote:

> The great uprooting agencies of all that has vanished . . . have been the automobile and the splendid roads. . . . They have driven . . . the guide and his boat into the last trenches of their usefulness. They have changed a great wild spot with a few parks, into a great park with a few wild spots.[15]

Thirty years later, in *Township 34,* Harold K. Hochschild reported the process completed:

> The guide-boat is following the guide out of the present into the past . . . the tourists who in the 1870s, 1880s and 1890s travelled through the Adirondacks with guides were adventurous members of the wealthy families. . . . The canoeists who now range the Adirondack waters . . . are drawn largely from social groups which could not afford to visit the region when it was only a rich man's paradise. . . . The amateur woodsman . . . has gained in independence and economy. The guide is no longer needed to play nurse.[16]

The records of the Conservation Department

campsite at the Forked Lake outlet for the summer of 1948 showed that 580 canoes passed through. If any guide-boats passed, they may have been noticed as curiosities, but they were not recorded.[17]

Though guide-boats are now seldom seen on public waters, they are carefully preserved at the few remaining private camps and clubs, such as Bisby, where motorboats are not suffered on the lake. There, guide-boats are preserved with the care others lavish on old books. They come in silently from the lake and ride up the floating dock, the traditional dull thump at the bow followed by the rumble of the hull over dock planking and the pleasant rattle of oars as they are stowed in the resonant hull, before the boats are carefully stored on the racks in the boat house.

Wrought by plain men with simple tools, the mystery of carpentry become art, the gallant guide-boat, robbed of its birthright by public campsites, outboard motors, boat-trailers and motels, survives, nevertheless, as a welcome and generous reminder of a past way of life.

Notes

1. Verplanck Colvin, *Seventh Annual Report on the Progress of the Topographical Survey of the Adirondack Region of New York State for the Year 1879,* Assembly Document no. 87, March 7, 1879 (Albany: Weed, Parsons & Co., 1880), pp. 7–9.
2. *New York Evening Post,* August 30, 1858.
3. Joseph F. Grady, *The Adirondacks* (Little Falls, N.Y. : Press of the Journal & Courier Co., 1933), p. 127.
4. Colvin, pp. 7–9.
5. *Forest and Stream,* July 6, 1882.
6. Ansel Judd Northrup, *Camps and Tramps in the Adirondacks* (Syracuse, 1880), p. 111.
7. S.R. Stoddard, *The Adirondacks Illustrated* (Glens Falls, N.Y.: published by the author, 1888), p. 238.
8. Northrup, p. 116.
9. *Forest and Stream,* June 6, 1900.
10. *American Angler,* February 9, 1884, and June 17 and 24, 1882.
11. *American Angler,* Memorial Edition, 1877.
12. *New York Tribune,* October 23, 1869.
13. William Chapman White, *Adirondack Country* (New York: Duell, Sloan & Pearce, 1954), p. 160.
14. *Forest and Stream,* February 2, 1901.
15. Alfred L. Donaldson, *A History of the Adirondacks* (New York: The Century Co., 1921), I, p. viii. Reprinted by permission of Hawthorn Books.
16. Harold K. Hochschild, *Township 34* (New York, 1952. Privately printed), p. 384.
17. *Ibid.*

II

The Guide-Boat:
Its Construction and Handling

XI/Four American Work Boats

After all not to create only, or found only,
But to bring perhaps from afar what is already founded,
To give it our own identity, average, limitless, free. . . .

Walt Whitman[1]

Visitors to the Adirondack Museum may wonder why a Maine wherry, a bateau, and a dory are exhibited among a group of Adirondack guide-boats in a wilderness museum. The surprised visitor will discover, if he pauses to study, a kinship among these four American work boats. They are more closely related than they might appear to be to the casual observer.[2]

Their basic similarity is not in the hull form but in the construction, which John Gardner calls "dory construction," after the most widely known of the craft that employ it. Four main characteristics of dory construction can be singled out:

(1) Construction starts with a bottom board tapered at the ends (instead of a keel). The bottom boards of the guide-boat, the wherry, and some of the dories are only one board wide. Other dories and the bateau have a wider bottom requiring several boards cleated together. In many cases the bottom board is slightly rockered fore and aft, that is, it curves up at the ends. The bateau is pointed at both ends. Dories, wherries, and the early guide-boats had square sterns. In all cases the bottom board serves to locate, place, and secure the natural-crook frames; it establishes the size of the boat and its shape to some extent.

(2) The ribs (or frames), including stem and stern, originally sawn from natural crooks (or knees), are made up in matched pairs, one on each side of the boat, with feet meeting or overlapping on the bottom board. When fastened in position on the bottom board, these frames determine the shape of the hull. They serve the same function as molds, required in other modes of construction.

(3) Planking is clinker or lapstrake. In conjunction with the natural-crook frames, it produces an exceptionally strong hull fabric requiring little internal bracing.

(4) The garboard plank, the one lying next to the bottom board, is wider at the ends than in the middle, sometimes as much as two or three times as wide. This makes it possible to have straighter planking lines for the strakes above. When such a garboard shape is laid out on a flat width of planking stock, the upper edge will be straight or nearly so while the lower edge will be curved, more or less concave depending upon width and rocker of the bottom.

Closely related to this basic construction are certain characteristic hull lines. All four boats are slack-bilged double-enders, or virtual double-enders. Like the early square-sterned guide-boats, with their

73

Detail of Das Weihe Häuschen, *by Albrecht Dürer, which supports the European ancestry of American small craft. (British Museum, London)*

small, high-tucked transoms well above the water, the wherry and the dory were double-enders at the waterline. They can all be launched stern first, a procedure not advisable for an ordinary square-sterned boat with a low, wide transom.

The origins of American small craft are intricate puzzles in cultural diffusion with many pieces missing. The many points of structural likeness cannot be merely coincidental. The basic construction shared by the boats under consideration was not a native American invention or development. Without question the construction goes back to European antecedents, at least as far as the boat portrayed by Albrecht Dürer in his watercolor *Das Weihe Häuschen*.[3].

Though the four boats all share the same basic construction, they diverge markedly in their secondary specializations, which developed in America in response to local needs. As far as these secondary characteristics go, there is some basis for the claim that these four boats are of native American origin. In *The Dory Book* John Gardner has treated this point extensively in the section entitled "Search for Beginnings."[4]

The migration of boat types does not require importation of actual boats; it happens almost imperceptibly through the minds of men who build and travel. The first white men to arrive in America brought with them both the small boats they had used on the European continent and the skill to adapt

them to new waters. During early settlement and exploration, coastal and inland waters teemed with small boats essential to travel in the days before roads.

Bateaux. The white man's early and most substantial contribution to the fleet of small boats in northeastern waters was the bateau. The bateaux that Peter Kalm saw on the Hudson above Albany in 1749 were 18 to 24 feet long, sharp at both ends with some sheer, flat-bottomed, and constructed of boards of white pine. Kalm remarked that he saw no boat here like those in Sweden or other parts of Europe.[5] From this we may draw the conclusion that the bateau was a type new to this traveled European. We have scarcely an inkling where and how the bateau first appeared. The French name and a resemblance to certain ancient and modern fishing types, a structural likeness to the dory and the American wherry (both mystery ships in their own right)—these are tempting clues but they do not add much light. The picture is confused by the survival of various nondescript types under the same name.

The first "flat bateau" on record carried a crew of eight soldiers and a sergeant up the St. Lawrence River from Montreal to Lake Ontario and back in June of 1671. Concerning the "batteaux" built by the French Jesuits for their escape down the St. Lawrence from the mission at Onondaga, New York, in 1657, John Gardner wrote us:

I very much doubt if they "invented" their bateau on the spot, but that more likely they built it after memories of boats they had previously known in France. Reliable contemporary description of the Onondaga boat indicates that if it was not quite the same as later bateaux, it was not much different, either.[6]

In the protracted campaigns on the upper New York lakes and the St. Lawrence River during the eighteenth century, thousands of bateaux were employed. Logistical problems, encountered everywhere, found solution in an equation of three variables: draft, capacity, and portability. On the Mohawk and the upper waters of the Hudson, and to a considerable extent on Lake George and Lake Champlain, the bateau represented the least common denominator. If not too heavily laden, it floated over the shallow rifts; if not too heavily built, it could be borne or dragged over the carries. It had the further virtue of being easily constructed from broad planks, available everywhere. Bateaux were rowed, poled, or paddled as conditions dictated. On the lakes they were rowed, in streams and shallow waters they were usually poled. Paddles were used least often.

We know something of bateau construction thanks to the recovery and preservation by the Adirondack Museum of bottoms and frames raised from the silt of Lake George. After 200 years of submersion and erosion, these remains tell us that design and workmanship were surprisingly good for boats built under wartime pressures in frontier settlements in the middle of the eighteenth century. Though the lapstrake planking is rough and unplaned (just as it left the water-powered gang-saw), the laps are neatly and accurately beveled. The preserved remains reveal a sturdy yet relatively light-weight construction, combining clinker planking with natural-crook frames, which produced a flexible, springy hull structure able to sustain severe shocks and twisting strains. John Gardner is of the opinion that their secondary characteristics show that these eighteenth-century bateaux were most certainly developed independently on this side of the ocean. Basic features of construction were just as certainly derived from earlier European craft.

The *New York Times* of June 27, 1965, reported that the hulk raised from Lake George might be one

Bateau raised from Lake George, New York, 1965. (Richard K. Dean)

from the fleet of General Samuel Abercromby, who, after his unsuccessful attempt to dislodge the French from Fort Carillon (now Fort Ticonderoga) in 1758, ordered hundreds of craft filled with stones and scuttled to preserve them for future use.[7]

In comparison to the bateau so important to military operations during the French and Indian Wars and the American Revolution, the nineteenth-century lumberman's bateau had a narrower bottom and sides more flaring and quite straight from bottom knuckle to gunwale. The increase in side flare was facilitated by the availability of wide white pine boards, the same material that, in abundant and cheap supply at the time, produced the Bank dory with its straight, raking sides as a replacement for colonial wherries in the fisheries. A natural outcome of the flaring sides of the bateau was the long raking

Log-driving bateaux on the Ausable River, New York. (New York State Conservation Commission)

ends, which became extreme in some of the river bateaux.

Log driving, made possible by the river bateau, commenced on the Upper Hudson about 1813.[8] In Maine it reached its climax during the 1840s and 1850s. In *Maine, A History*, Mrs. Fannie Hardy Eckstorm called them "boats of a new sort":

> They [the bateaux] must be large cargo carriers yet of very shallow draft; they must be staunch and seaworthy, yet so light that men could carry them for miles on their shoulders; and they must be incredibly quick, for work on rough water. No one knows the story of the evolution of the bateau, but she seems to be a dory, modified to meet the stationary wave of rough water rather than the heaving wave of the sea. Her origin is unknown. . . .[9]

Henry David Thoreau came upon a bateau factory in Old Town, Maine, during the 1890s and described a type modified for special uses as: "light and shapely vessels, calculated for rapid and rocky streams, and to be carried over long portages on men's shoulders. . . . They are made very slight, only two boards to the side . . . of the cleanest and widest white pine. . . ."[10]

One of the last remaining river-driving bateaux of the New York north woods included in the boat collection of the Adirondack Museum is a local variant of the lumberman's bateau, which in Maine and elsewhere was often built with longer, more raking ends.[11] Although it is much heavier, the Adirondack bateau reveals strikingly its kinship with the Bank dory. The river drive demanded strength to endure pounding on rocks and the crush of tumbling logs. Thus, the frames of this bateau are $1\frac{1}{2}$ inches square at the top, swelling to a molded depth of 5 inches at the bottom knuckle; the planking is $\frac{7}{8}$ inch thick and the stems are over 4 inches square. Such dimensions are massive compared with the delicate scantlings of the guide-boat, yet fundamentally the two boats are closely alike in construction.

Detail of bateau at the Adirondack Museum. (Helen Durant)

Maine salmon wherry. (Mrs. Nellie Hart)

Maine salmon wherry used by Captain Robie Ames first in the salmon fishery, later for lobstering, Penobscot Bay. The builder was Captain Elisha Griffin. The boat is now at Mystic Seaport; a replica is at the Adirondack Museum. (Adirondack Museum)

Wherries. Presumably the Maine salmon wherry of the Lower Penobscot Bay is an archaic survival of a type common and widely built in colonial America, like the river bateau. We do not know which came first, wherry or bateau, nor how they were related, except in structure. With its natural-crook frames of cedar roots and lapped planking, the salmon wherry requires a minimum of internal bracing, no inwales, no floor boards, and only one fixed thwart.

Salmon wherries are made full forward, to support a man kneeling in the bow, hauling at a laden net.

They are deep, slack-bilged work boats that handle best with a load in them. The stern trims higher than the bow. They are fine sea boats, pull easily and can be launched stern-first into the surf.

Captain Robie Ames of Lincolnville, Maine, rowed his wherry to his lobster pots until the summer of 1959, when he was in his late seventies. Formerly he had used it in the salmon fisheries, for which it was built in 1892 by Captain Elisha Griffin. Its length overall is 13 feet 5 inches, with a 4-foot, 6-inch beam and a depth amidships of 22 inches. The bottom board is 12½ inches wide in the middle, tapering to the width of stem and stern post at the ends. It has a slight rocker. Frames are sawn to shape from root crooks, identified by the Smithsonian Institution as northern white cedar. The planking is of the same wood, lapped and copper-fastened, seven strakes to the side.

This Lincolnville wherry is a rare survival of a type once common on the northern New England coast, possibly the predominant small work boat there a hundred and fifty years ago. It was replaced by boats less costly and easier to build. In a few places in Maine and Nova Scotia the wherry survived because local fishermen, who demanded the best in a boat, had the time in winter and the skill to build their own.

The woods and the ocean were never very far apart; the rivers led back from the shore and the coastal craft moved inland, but it is improbable that an actual New England wherry was ever used in the Adirondack woods. Aware of the relationship between the wherry and other American work boats, Kenneth Durant and John Gardner persuaded the Adirondack Museum to purchase Captain Ames's wherry for comparative study. The boat now on display at the Museum is a replica of this wherry; the original has been added to the collection of Mystic Seaport in Connecticut.

Dories. It seems possible that the dory may have begun life as a simplified wherry, built easily and inexpensively from wide white pine planks abundantly available at the beginning of the nineteenth century. The most famous dory-type of all, the straight-sided

Bank dory under construction for Mystic Seaport at Lunenburg, Nova Scotia, 1970. (Mystic Seaport)

The guide-boat began and developed as a work boat. Lithograph by Verplanck Colvin showing Mount Haystack from Upper Ausable Inlet.

Grand Banker, is practically a snub-nosed and bob-tailed river bateau. It is a virtual double-ender with a narrow, raking tombstone stern, a simplification of the wherry transom. It was largely their simple, quick construction that enabled cheap mass-produced dories to replace all other small craft, including the wherry, in the nineteenth-century North Atlantic fisheries.

Guide-boats. Leaving aside weight, finish, and some secondary features of shape, the Adirondack guide-boat is the most recent member of a distinct group of American work boats. Origins and interrelations within the group remain unexplained, but the kinship is unmistakable.

The guide-boat began and developed as a work boat. When no other means of transportation existed through much of the Adirondack wilderness, these slim craft carried rough freight, such as packing cases, barrels of kerosene, and cook stoves.

The early lapstrake, square-sterned boats, built before the 1860s, were much like light, slimmed-out wherries. Their slack bilge and the slight curve, as the sides rose from the bottom, also recalled the wherries. Though the guide-boat, with its delicately molded

strakes, was far from a wide-board construction, it nevertheless resembled the bateau with its natural-crook spruce frame, set on a tapered, flat bottom. The early appearance and persistence of a square transom, similar to that of the wherry, is yet to be explained; the bateau had demonstrated the advantages of the pointed stern, so clearly superior for all uses in narrow streams and shoal waters. After the 1860s, when the guide-boat became a double-ender, its profile might recall an Indian's birch canoe, but this casual resemblance was not even skin deep.

The bottom board that is characteristic of the guide-boat, tapering at the ends, fits into a notch under the foot of the spruce stem. Notched stems are also characteristic of the wherry and the colonial bateau but are not found in the dory. As in most dories, and in some colonial bateaux, the bottom board is beveled on its under edge to the angle of the frames and the garboard extends down over it.

The pattern of the guide-boat's garboard resembles that of the dory: hollow curved along its under edge to fit the oval of the bottom board, widened at the ends to straighten the run of the planks above. In its avoidance of internal bracing the guide-boat also resembles the dory, whose stiff frames and lapped planking permit the removal of thwarts for nesting on the decks of fishing schooners.

The unremitting pressure to produce ever lighter boats must have influenced guide-boat lines in ways not immediately apparent. Perhaps if weight considerations had not been paramount, the guide-boat might have acquired a more powerful hull, like the Rangeley or St. Lawrence River skiff.

The turning of the soft points of the tiny copper tacks used to fasten the planks to the frames was done with a clenching iron, which is a "clinking" iron to any Scotsman. Although the noise of this operation was light compared to the clinking that resounded in many an older boat shop, the guide-boat was as much clinker-built as a Gloucester dory or a Maine salmon wherry.

During the one hundred years, more or less, in which the guide-boat was perfected and then fell into disuse, several thousand must have been built and used. In them the guides carried visitors from all over the globe through one of the most widely visited vacation and sporting regions in this country. An object of sheer utility (and in watercraft, function and beauty are inseparable), the boat became an eye-catching thing. Surviving specimens of this extraordinary craft are of great intrinsic interest to all those who love boats and respect fine carpentry. To examine a guide-boat is to wonder at the precision and patience, the skill and inventiveness of the guides and woodsmen who fabricated these frail strips of wood into a harmonious structure of beauty, utility, and lasting strength.

Notes

1. Walt Whitman, "Song of the Exposition" in The Inner Sanctum Edition of the Poetry and Prose of Walt Whitman, ed. Louis Untermeyer (New York: Simon and Schuster, 1949), p. 222.
2. Unless otherwise noted, the material in this chapter has been compiled from research notes by Kenneth Durant; correspondence with many sources, but primarily with Howard I. Chapelle and John Gardner; and from articles by John Gardner published in the Maine Coast Fisherman and Outdoor Maine during 1959–1960.
3. British Museum, London.
4. John Gardner, The Dory Book (Camden, Maine: International Marine Publishing Co., 1978).
5. Peter Kalm, Travels in North America, ed. Adolph B. Benson, 1770 (New York: Dover Publications Inc.), I, pp. 333–371.
6. Letter, July 21, 1978.
7. Benson John Lossing, Pictorial Field Book of the Revolution, 2 vols. (New York: Harper and Brothers, 1859), I, pp. 98 and 191, engravings of bateaux.
8. Sixth Annual Report of the Forest, Fish and Game Commission of the State of New York (Albany, N.Y.: James B. Lyon, State Printer, 1901), p. 255.
9. Fannie Hardy Eckstorm, "Lumbering in Maine," in Maine, A History, by Louis C. Hatch (Somersworth: New Hampshire Publishing Company, 1974), p. 691.
10. Henry David Thoreau, The Maine Woods (Boston and New York: Houghton Mifflin and Co., 1898; Cambridge: The Riverside Press), p. 4.
11. Adirondack Museum, no. 57.157.1.

XII/General Characteristics of the Adirondack Guide-Boat

It was a dainty, graceful, and seaworthy boat. . . .

W.H. Boardman[1]

During the early stages of its development in the nineteenth century, as hunters and trappers became full-time guides, the Adirondack skiff was referred to by travel writers as a boat-canoe, a bateau, a shallop, a cockle-shell, and a faery boat. The guide simply called it his boat. Its appropriate and definitive name, the *Adirondack guide-boat*, came relatively late. How can we define the guide's boat? What are its special characteristics?

After many discussions, Robert Bruce Inverarity, the director of the Adirondack Museum at the time, wrote to Kenneth Durant on October 12, 1959:

> . . . you must simply formulate what definition you wish to use . . . regardless of whether I or any one else agree . . . what you are attempting to do is to get down on paper what you have discovered in your own terms of reference. . . .

We have settled on the following definition:
The Adirondack guide-boat is a narrow wooden boat, pointed at both ends, with short decks at bow and stern, to be carried by one man. The skin is smooth inside and out. Until about 1860 the boats were made with square sterns, high-tucked wineglass transoms, and decks forward only. Before the perfection of the smooth skin, the lower edge of each plank protruded somewhat, like house clapboards.[2]

During the period 1890-1900, the standard working boat of the professional guide, used for sport and travel, averaged 15 to 16 feet overall, with an inside beam between 36 and 39 inches. Its weight, complete with all accessories, averaged 70 to 75 pounds.

Larger, heavier boats known as family boats, church boats, freight boats, or tote boats, though of similar construction, are not considered to fall under the definition of a "guide-boat." They were essential equipment at many waterbound camps but never acquired a definitive name. They resemble the smaller guide-boat in all respects except one: they are too heavy to be carried by one man and therefore have no yoke and no yoke cleats.[3]

The components of a guide-boat are as follows:[4]

Bottom board. This is a single, narrow, elliptical board, ½ to ¾ inch thick, pointed at both ends, with a slight rocker. Its midship width varies greatly but is commonly close to 8 inches. Some boats were built with the greatest width forward of amidships in the traditional shape known as duck-shape, or cod's-head-and-mackerel-tail. The narrow bottom board is sometimes mistakenly spoken of as a keel, but the guide-boat is essentially flat-bottomed, without keel. Some boats are found with a thickening piece,

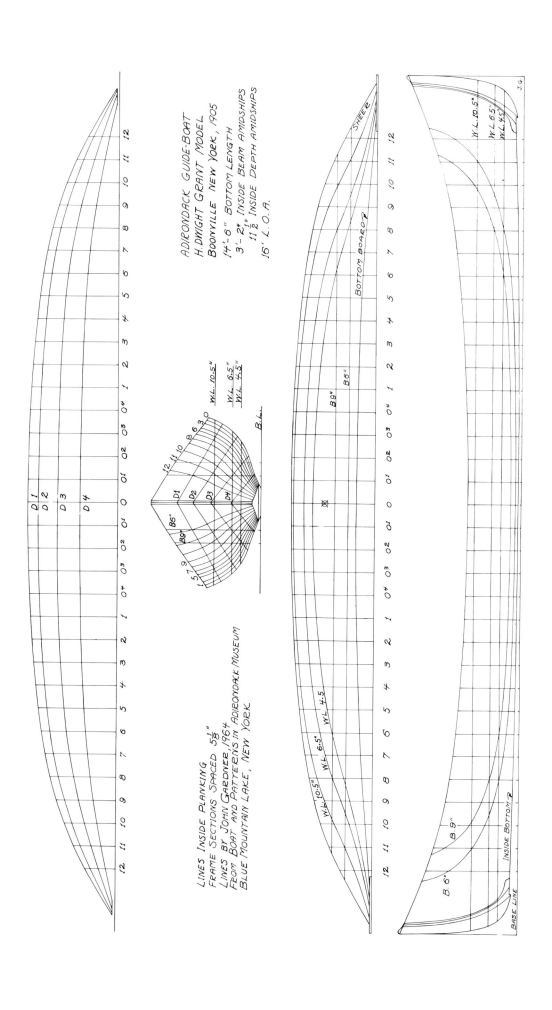

ADIRONDACK GUIDE-BOAT
H. DWIGHT GRANT MODEL
BOONVILLE, NEW YORK, 1905
14'-6" BOTTOM LENGTH
3'-2" INSIDE BEAM AMIDSHIPS
11½" INSIDE DEPTH AMIDSHIPS
16' L.O.A.

LINES INSIDE PLANKING
FRAME SECTIONS SPACED 5⅛"
LINES BY JOHN GARDNER, 1964
FROM BOAT AND PATTERNS IN ADIRONDACK MUSEUM
BLUE MOUNTAIN LAKE, NEW YORK

W.L. 10.5"
W.L. 6.5"
W.L. 4.5"

B.L.

D1
D2
D3
D4

B6"
B9"

12 11 10 8 6 3 0

SHEER

BOTTOM BOARD

B9"

B6"

INSIDE BOTTOM

B.9"

B.6"

BASE LINE

W.L. 10.5"
W.L. 6.5"
W.L. 4.5"

W.L. 10.5"
W.L. 6.5"
W.L. 4.5

D1
D2
D3
D4

J.G.

resembling a keel, laid along the bottom board to add strength or increase stability.

Stems. In common nautical terminology, stem refers to the fore-part of a boat and is sometimes synonymous with bow or prow. The double-ended guide-boat, however, has stems at both ends, frequently identical, and the term applies to both. The stems are curving pieces of natural crook (usually spruce) fastened to each end of the bottom board, rabbeted to receive the plank ends (hood ends). The shape of the stem varies according to local tradition and the fancy of the builder, from the protruding underbody or ram bow in the boats of William Vassar at Bloomingdale, through the various tumblehome forms of Saranac and Long Lake boats, to the outward rake of the Brown's Tract boats built by Grant at Boonville and Parsons at Old Forge. Subtle variations in stem pattern, difficult to measure or describe, are best portrayed in profile photographs.

Ribs. These are also known as frames, knees, or timbers. Ribs are sawn to patterns from natural crooks of spruce stump roots. A flat section of the rib, known as the foot, extends across the bottom board where it is screw-fastened close against the foot of the opposite, identical rib. Curving upward in one piece from the knuckle (chine), the ribs support the planking and determine the shape of the hull. Bottom board, stem, and ribs are the basic frame on which the planking is fastened.

Ribs cut to pattern from natural crooks are a characteristic feature of guide-boat construction, easily distinguished from the pliable ribs, steamed and bent into shape, in canoes and other boats. The essential difference is that bent ribs are made to conform to a predetermined hull shape, whereas the stiff guide-boat ribs, cut to pattern, determine the form of the flexible planking.

In many guide-boats one or more pairs of ribs in the narrow sections at bow and stern lack feet and are therefore not fastened directly to the bottom board. These are known as scribe ribs and are put in after the planking is on.

Across the narrow width of the rib, which lies against the planking, ribs are said to be sided $5/16$ inch plus or minus. The fore and aft sides of the rib, which curve in one plane only, have a molded dimension of $3/4$ inch. Fore and aft spacing of the ribs varies be-

tween 4 and 6 inches from rib center to rib center, although it may be greater for boats longer than 16 feet.

Planks. These are also referred to as planking, streaks, strakes, siding, and rounds of siding. Although the term *plank* is generally associated with larger dimensions, it is also used to describe the thin sides of small boats. Guide-boat planking varies in thickness from $3/16$ inch to $1/4$ inch, and in width from $2\frac{1}{2}$ to 4 inches. The number of the planks to a side varies from six to ten; eight is most common. For reasons of economy and strength, guide-boat planks seldom run in one piece from stem to stem, but are made up of two or more sections, spliced end to end in beveled joints (scarphs) to bring the grain of the wood in line with the curve of the sheer. On the inside of the boat, scarph joints are generally hidden under ribs; on the outside they are marked by a vertical line of tack-heads across the plank.

Guide-boat construction is a refinement of lapstrake or clinker-built construction. The beveled lower edge of each plank laps over a corresponding bevel along the upper edge of the plank below it. Adjoining bevels are fastened by a double row of clenched copper tacks, making a watertight joint between paper-thin, feather-edged planks. This is characteristic of all guide-boats.

In the perfected guide-boat the beveled laps (seams) are so finely fitted as to make a smooth skin within and without. Because the edges of the laps (lands) do not show like house clapboards as they do in the usual lapstrake construction, the guide-boat is often mistaken for carvel, or smooth-edge, construction. Guide-boats were never carvel-built. The laps may be hard to see on a heavily painted boat; under varnish, the line of flat copper tack heads holding the laps may be seen along the edge of each seam. The thickness of planking is not to be judged from the thin edge visible at the gunwale. The top plank, called the sheer plank, is reinforced by the wale and is often thinner than the planks below it.

There are two forms of lap: the traditional feather-edge of Saranac and Raquette builders who planed the bevel down to a vanishing, knife-edge sharpness, and the square-edge rabbeted lap (a modified ship-lap) of Grant in Boonville and Parsons in Old Forge. The rabbeted lap was made with planes of special design, which left a square edge of .028 inch thick the length of the plank to fit into a corresponding recessed shoulder in the adjoining plank. Both laps produce the characteristic smooth skin and they are easily distinguished on a finished boat.

Gunwales. Also called wales or gunnels, the gunwales run from stem to stern on the outside of the boat, flush with the top edge of the sheer plank. The rowlock plates are fastened to the wales, which are beveled to hold the oar blades at right angles to the surface of the water at the beginning and end of each stroke.

Decks. These show great variety in form and construction and may serve as clues to the identity of the maker. The earliest decks appear to have been straight, flat boards laid across from wale to wale at bow and stern. Square-sterned boats had no decks at the stern. Some decks are set within the sheer planks. Another form is made of two boards, running fore and aft, with a narrow strip covering the joint between them. To throw off water, deck surfaces are given a slight camber (arching, convexity), and some have a narrow raised frame (coaming) along the inboard edge. When this inboard edge is rounded toward the stem in a shallow, concave curve, the deck is called a circle deck.

Cleats. These are slender risers fastened to the ribs to support the three seats. Another pair, the yoke cleats (or risers) at the sheer amidships, with rounded notches to hold the neck yoke, are the distinctive mark of the guide-boat. The common type of yoke cleat extends forward to serve as a handhold for the man under the yoke.

Seats. Bow and stern seats are lightly fastened to their respective cleats. The middle seat is removable. Early seats were flat boards, generally supplanted later by woven cane seats, which were lighter. Standard equipment includes a small caned back rest for the stern seat. A back rest for the middle seat is optional. Grant and some early builders made stern back rests with steam-bent bow frames. The more usual type has a four-piece frame joined with mortise and tenon.

Oars. The loom, the part of the oar shaft inboard of the rowlock, is traditionally square. Grant diminished weight by making the loom octagonal. The shaft circumference can be further reduced to round or oval. It terminates in a flat blade supported by a spine. For a 16-foot boat, oars are customarily 8 feet long. The distance from the rowlock to the end of the handle is somewhat more than half the boat's beam, so that the handles cross at midstroke. This is one of the guide-boat's most distinctive characteristics, seldom mentioned and frequently unobserved. The oars overlap on the inboard ends and are therefore rowed with the rower's arms crossed, one oar handle over the other.

Paddle. One paddle is standard equipment with every boat. Patterns vary according to the fancy of the builder and the desires of the customer. Paddles are expendable, easily broken or lost. Original paddles are seldom found with the boat.

Neck-yoke. A wooden yoke, hand-carved of one piece to fit the bearer's shoulders, is essential equipment with every guide-boat.

Rowlocks. Also called a rollok or oarlock, each rowlock is a pair of flat, rounded plates (horns), mounted on a steel or bronze pin, about ½ inch in diameter, which swivels in a socket on a metal strap screwed to the outside of the gunwale. A variant oar pin has internal ball bearings, which save the inconvenience of exposed lubrication and give better wear with less noise. The square oar loom is held in place between the horns by a ³⁄₁₆-inch pin passing from one horn to the other through the loom. Two pairs of rowlock straps with sockets are provided at two rowing stations, bow and middle seats. Some very short boats have only one pair of sockets, midway between bow and amidships. Such boats, double-enders, are rowed in one direction from the bow, in the opposite direction from the middle.

Shoe irons. These are metal bands, about ½ inch wide, brass or iron, along the outside of the bottom board, covering the edge of the garboard. Some builders add a third strip down the center of the bottom board. Willard Hanmer made some of these shoes of hardwood.

Stem band. This is a narrow band of metal protecting the thin, exposed edges of the stems. A widened flat section curves over the lower end of the stem.

Stem caps. These are added by some builders (Grant, Parsons) to protect the end of the stem that protrudes through the deck. They are not on all boats. Grant caps have small limber holes to let out any water that might be caught under the sheer of the decks when the boat is turned over.

Rings. For painter or tow line, a ring is attached at the top of the bow stem, sometimes bow and stern.

Foot plates. There are three plates of thin brass or copper, bent over the ribs (also called stretchers, although they are not used as such), at each rowing station. They protect bottom, sides, and ribs against heavy boots. Small plates of brass or copper protect the inside of the sheer plank against the ends of the yoke.

Fastenings. Ribs are fastened to the bottom board and planking is fastened to ribs and stems with screws. Beveled planking laps are fastened with two rows of clenched tacks, one row driven from the outside along the thin edge of the bevel and clenched inside into the thicker wood; on the opposite edge of the lap a parallel, staggered row is driven from the inside and clenched outside. Earliest boats are fastened with iron screws and tacks. Brass screws and copper tacks were used when they became available. Number, spacing, and size of tacks and screws vary with the judgment of the builder. Invariable are the two rows of tacks fastening the seams.

In summary, the following are the characteristics of the classic Adirondack guide-boat generally in use between 1890 and 1900:

(1) It is a narrow wooden boat, pointed at both ends, with sawn ribs of natural crook erected on a flat, elliptical bottom board.

(2) It has a smooth skin inside and out: beveled lap seams fastened with two rows of clenched copper tacks, one row driven from without and a parallel, staggered row driven from within.

(3) It is portable by one man, as indicated by notched yoke cleats.

(4) The middle seat is removable. There are no fixed thwarts or cross braces.

(5) The oar looms are square, shaved on the corners to octagonal. The handles cross at mid-stroke.

The presence of all these elements may be assumed to identify a guide-boat. The absence of any makes identity questionable. Some early variants have been mentioned in this chapter; boats being built today reflect the introduction of new materials, such as laminated ribs and epoxy fastenings.

The single most revealing feature is the notched yoke cleats of the one-man portable boat, since all guide-boats have them. Although old guide-boats may have lost theirs, because the cleats are fragile and expendable, their original presence is generally detectable. Since yoke cleats are not unusual in other boats, they alone do not identify a guide-boat, however.

Notes

1. William H. Boardman, *The Lovers of the Woods* (New York: McClure, Phillips & Co., 1901), p. 79.
2. Boat no. 61-68 at Adirondack Museum.
3. Boat no. 63-128 at Adirondack Museum.
4. Working in the isolation of the north woods, remote from boat yards and the traditional speech of shipwrights, the Adirondack builder used terms closely connected with house carpentry. He called the keel a bottom board; the ribs were interchangeably frames, timbers, knees, or futtocks. He used the term rake instead of rocker. The sheer of the gunwale as well as the outward slant of stem and stern were also referred to as rake.

XIII/Spruce

First the experts chose their tree in the forest, their main concern being the good nature of the timber.

Sir Westcott Abell[1]

At the end of the summer of 1846, Henry David Thoreau made his first visit to the back woods of Maine. Aware of how new America was and how unevenly settled and explored, Thoreau reminded us in his book *The Maine Woods* that we lived mostly on the shores of the continent. We hardly knew where the rivers came from or realized that the timbers from which our houses were built grew only a short while ago in the forests where the Indian still hunted. "New York," wrote Thoreau, "has her wilderness within her own borders; and though the sailors of Europe are familiar with the soundings of her Hudson . . . an Indian is still needed to guide her scientific men to its headwaters in the Adirondack country."[2]

Oak was traditionally an important part of English shipbuilding, used for both frame and siding. For a large ship, like the 1370-ton *Agamemnon* built in 1781, two thousand average oaks might be felled. "Oak bends easily," John Gardner wrote us, "better than most woods, which makes it an easy wood to plank with, especially for hulls that have hard curves. I think the main reason why English mechanics hung on to oak for planking was because they were used to working with it, and bending it, and that a considerable part of their skill would have been

lost if they had turned to unfamiliar planking wood."[3]

But the supply of oak in England was dwindling. When James I ordered a survey of the royal forests in 1608, only some 350,000 trees were found, and of these, less than half were fit for ship timbers. Oak was also being used increasingly for domestic purposes, and more forest land was being brought under tillage as the population grew. Tilled land brought more profit than woodland, since an oak tree took some hundred years to reach the size needed for the building of warships.

When in 1677 Parliament voted to build new ships, it took much labor and searching to get the lumber. In the next century, oak was imported from Africa. Elm was brought from the Baltic, Africa, and America, and the English also began to import larch, teak, and mahogany from many different sources.[4]

Oak did not grow in the Adirondacks proper because of the high altitude, and the oak being imported to England from Canada in the 1700s was found to be subject to early decay. American larch was the wood that the English hoped might replace their dwindling supply of ship timber. Called tamarack in the Adirondacks and hackmatack by the

Maine farmers (coming closer to the Indian name), it was sold for its roots to boatbuilders in Boston and elsewhere.

In 1840, in a birch canoe paddled by his Indian guide, Ebenezer Emmons traveled down the crooked streams that lead to Raquette Lake, looking for profitable resources. (As he passed through the lakes he named them the Eckford Chain, in honor of the eminent shipbuilder Henry Eckford, and the winding stream at the head of the lakes the Marion River, in honor of Eckford's wife.) He reported that the Marion River passed through a deep marsh, of which the most valuable product was the larch or tamarack, whose largest roots "are adapted in all respects to form the substantial part of vessels."[5] The tamarack along the Marion River was never put to profitable use. In the 1890s an invasion of saw flies killed the larger trees, while annual flooding of the low ground, caused by the dam that maintained Raquette Lake at a proper level for steamboat travel, killed the young ones. Occasional flooding does not kill a tree, but water standing above the normal level for considerable periods at a season of the year when tree growth is going on, causes havoc.[6]

Adirondack woodsmen in need of boat timber passed by the tamarack because they had a better tree: the spruce.[7] Knowledge of the properties of trees was basic to the livelihood of Indian and pioneer. They knew how to make good use of the products their environment provided, and their use of this tree is a case in point.

Sieur de Dièreville, a French traveler, found spruce beer among the settlers of Nova Scotia in 1699. It was a strong decoction brewed from spruce tips and put into a cask with yeast and molasses. When it had fermented two to three days, the lightly colored liquor tasted not unpleasant.[8] British troops, advancing against Ticonderoga in 1776, recovered from scurvy by drinking plenty of spruce beer,[9] while at the other end of Lake Champlain, colonial rebels were fortified with a gill of rum and as much spruce beer as they could drink every day because the lake water was considered unhealthy.[10]

In *The Last of the Mohicans*, James Fenimore Cooper wrote:

'Come friend,' said Hawkeye, drawing out a keg from beneath a cover of leaves . . . addressing the stranger who sat at his elbow . . . 'try a little spruce; 'twill . . . quicken the life in your bosom.'[11]

Nicolas Denys, the French explorer and naturalist, watched the Indians in Acadia grub out long tendrils of spruce root, which they fashioned into strong thread (*watap*) for sewing seams in birch bark. Women and children chewed the gum of the fir until it became a salve, which they applied by aid of fire all along the seams.[12] (This, Denys thought, accounted for the fine teeth of Indian women. He intended to recommend gum chewing to the ladies of France.)

For an Indian or a white man in a hurry, huge sheets of spruce bark would make a tolerable canoe. John MacMullen, stranded near the Raquette River in 1843, observed the construction of one by the Indians who had come to his rescue. When the canoe was completed, it was turned upside down and one of the Indians knelt before it and appeared to kiss the bottom. MacMullen thought that he was witnessing an aboriginal ritual. The Indian, however, was sucking the canoe bottom to check for air holes. Finding one, he tore a small corner off a rag, placed it on the hole, took a wad of chewed spruce gum from his mouth, and laid it upon the rag. With a small burning stick he melted the gum so that it went through the rag into the hole, filling and closing it securely. MacMullen mused upon the expert discrimination with which woodsmen used the materials the forest provided. The bark was used for canoe siding, spruce-root tendrils to sew the seams, spruce gum for pitching, and rifted cedar slats for floors and thwarts. Fat pine splinters served as hunting torches. "Understanding perfectly the peculiar qualities of different trees and profiting by them all," MacMullen wrote, "the trees are as closets from which they take whatever they need."[13] William Boardman made a similar comment upon the manner in which his Adirondack guide improvised shelter. "Like a shop foreman [he] knows exactly where each tool is and where the raw material is stored."[14]

The sportsman or guide traveling through the woods used spruce for practically everything. Needing roof and siding for a shanty, he would reach high with an axe and, with alternate slanting cuts, girdle the spruce in two rings 12 to 15 feet apart, make a perpendicular incision from girdle to girdle, and strip off the bark with a forked stick. In this way he could

THE HOTEL.

Indiscriminate use of bark often caused campsites to be surrounded by desolate stands of girdled trees. (Harper's New Monthly Magazine, *July 1859*)

tear off pieces 12 to 15 feet long and 6 to 8 feet wide. It killed the tree but the woodsman kept dry. In 1655 the Onondagas had made a spruce bark roof for their wilderness chapel. This suggested to Father Dublon that the way to heaven might be found as well under a roof of bark as under an arched ceiling of gold or silver.[15] The first of the luxury camps on Raquette Lake in 1878, that of Dr. Thomas C. Durant on Long Point, had spruce bark roofs.

Though the lodges and shanties with their bark roofs looked picturesque enough, indiscriminate use of the trees often left camping sites surrounded by desolate stands of girdled trees. Having come upon such a sight near Stone (also called Spectacle) Pond, Alfred B. Street wrote: "We found one of our American ruins, a delapidated log hut, with a dead clearing around it, dotted with dark stumps and strewed with half-burned logs."[16] This waste became so flagrant that in 1886 conservation authorities outlawed peeling or girdling trees of their bark for covering camps or shanties. "For such purposes the tree must be felled, and all bark removed therefrom before another tree is cut down."[17]

While along the Marion River and in the inundated lowlands the tamaracks were left to rot, lumbermen in the Adirondacks also concentrated on the spruce. Eastern spruce (which includes red,

white, and black spruce) is described by the Forest Products Laboratory as "moderately light in weight . . . [with] moderate shrinkage, and moderately strong, stiff, tough and hard." The Adirondack boatbuilder learned that the sum of these qualities made a superlative wood for his purpose, but he had competition from the commercial sawmills. Boardman's fictional guide John in *The Lovers of the Woods,* speaking to Colonel Warren with good-humored irony, called spruce the curse of the woods, as it made men greedy. After the lumbermen had cut all the big trees, they returned in a few years for pulpwood. John compared the lumbermen with bass who first eat the minnies, then the trout, and then each other. "Bass and lumbermen and hedgehogs all go to the same place when they die, but they are too dinged slow a-dying."[18]

In 1893 over 240 million board feet of Adirondack spruce went through the mills, and the choppers came back for 92 million feet of pulpwood. This consumption of timber continued for over a decade. The paper mills were insatiable. Amid this rapacity the Adirondack boatbuilder looked only for a small, neglected part of the tree: the stump the lumbermen left behind.

A tamarack tree sends out its principal roots at almost right angles to the trunk, but the Adirondack

In 1893 over 240 million board feet of Adirondack spruce went through the sawmills. The Adirondack boatbuilder used only a small, neglected part of the spruce: the stump the lumbermen left behind. (Adirondack Museum)

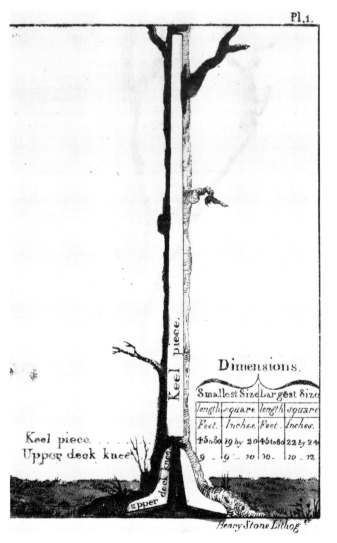

Pl.1.

Keel piece.

Dimensions.

Smallest Size Largest Size

length square length square

Feet. Inches. Feet. Inches.

45 to 50 | 19 by 20 | 45 to 60 | 22 by 24
9 | 9 | 10 | 10 | 10 | 12

Keel piece.
Upper deck knee

upper deck knee

Henry Stone Lithog

spruce sets its thirsty roots deep in the rocky soil. The boatbuilder's first concern was for the excellence of the crooks: therefore he chose primarily the stumps of the red spruce, which is unexcelled for its strength, and its larger knee stock is better suited to the laying out of patterns with the flow of the grain. Spruce is the strongest and toughest wood for its weight in the northeastern forests, pound for pound stiffer than steel. The strongest part of the tree is in the knee, where the tough resilience of the swaying trunk passes, intensified, into the grain and curve of the root: the grain of the stump turns naturally at various degrees of curvature.

In ship construction, where a curved member strays from the line of grain, wood weakens and will crack under strain. Shipwrights had always searched for wooden crooks with a natural curve conforming to the desired pattern of rib and stem. Such curved pieces in old shipbuilding days were called "compass timbers" and were found in trees of irregular growth, or where limb or root bent from the trunk. The massive bulk of spruce root as it departed from the stump afforded the Adirondack builder a wide choice of natural curves.

A 16-foot Grant boat had 36 ribs, no more than $5/16$ of an inch thick, made from 13 different patterns. Such slender ribs depended on the strength of natural crooks, in a variety of curves. The delicate yielding

Ship timbers or compass timbers. (Timber Merchant's Guide *by Peter Guillet, 1823*)

A 16-foot Grant boat had 36 ribs made from 13 different patterns and required a variety of natural crooks. (Helen Durant)

strength of spruce ribs made possible a boat of exquisite proportions; the "light shell of wood after the canoe form," which Samuel Hearne dreamed of but never attained.[19]

Pine was better for bottom boards, and some builders preferred cedar for planking, but only spruce could make ribs and stems, mainstays of guide-boat construction. As English shipwrights had desired the hedgerow oak, the Adirondack boat-builder wanted rock-grown spruce. Oak timbers made the ships of the line; spruce crooks made the guide-boat.

The guide-boat was a complex of rounding surfaces subject to peculiar strains, which required a cunning variety of support. In addition to the usual stresses of navigation, the push and pull of wind and waves, the powerful leverage of the oars, and the burden of cargo, the guide-boat had to endure an added wrench when turned bottom up, with its entire weight resting upon a yoke supported on the gunwales amidships without any cross-bracing. In this position it had to take the jolts of a rough carry. To survive these strains, with a shell of portable weight, the boat required an exceptionally strong frame. The springy roots of the spruce provided not only the adaptable curves of the boat but also its ability to endure sudden shock and prolonged vibrations.

Some builders experimented with other woods. Rushton, who built in Canton, New York, outside the spruce forest, used oak for stems and bottom board, red elm for the ribs, cedar for the siding, and spruce or ash for decks and seats.[20] His boats were not superior because of it. Willard Hanmer of Saranac Lake found tamarack too heavy and full of pitch. He

tried cedar and discovered that the roots grew underground in twisted webs, unsuitable for boat timber.[21] "Lightness, strength and elasticity are the distinguishing qualities of spruce," said J.S. Springer, writing in 1851 about the characteristics of the American forest trees.[22] Carpenters, too, favored spruce for the side rails of their ladders, on which life and limb depended.

Adirondack spruce butts, free of knots and even-grained, with their resilient toughness that withstood vibration, lent sonority to concert harps and were used for the sounding boards of pianos, violin bellies, and organ pipes. Larousse terms the European fir, first cousin to the American spruce, *bois de resonance.* The producers of the Baldwin piano boasted of "singing spruce from the Adirondacks."[23] Clear butt logs used for these sounding boards were known in the southern part of the Adirondacks as "fiddle-butts."[24] Lest their sonority be damaged by wetting, these butts were not river-driven but hauled out dry on sleds or wagons. High prices invited illicit trade; in the 1890s trespassing choppers entered the woods stealthily and wrapped the spruce trunks with blankets of burlap to muffle the reverberation of axe blows.[25]

Sonority, the evidence of good quality and highly desirable in musical instruments, had certain disadvantages in a guide-boat. Parchment-thin siding, stretched drum-tight upon a resonant frame, exaggerated the slightest noise. The click of oars in rowlocks, the rattle of loose gear, were amplified over and under water, alarming deer and trout. These reverberations and echoes were the price paid for resilience and light weight. Resonance was evidence of a boat in good condition. A guide-boat without resonance was a sodden hull, passing into decay. The guide compensated for the boat's noise by taking certain precautions and handling it with superior skill. To subdue the sibilant scratch of reeds and lily pads against a vibrant hull, the night hunter filled his boat with damp sphagnum moss or asked his passengers to wrap their boots in burlap.

Spruce frames made the guide-boat possible and subtly influenced its form. "Not enough attention has been given in the past to the influence of available materials on the evolution of design," in the opinion of John Gardner.[26] In an age of plywood, plastic, and light metals, the carpenter's dependence upon the qualities of wood is often forgotten. The inner structure or the direction and nature of the grain affected and determined his use of tools and limited, but also inspired, his design. Spruce gave to the Adirondack builder what he needed, and he built accordingly. If there had been no spruce, the early woodsman would have found a different tree and another way to build a boat light enough and strong enough for his needs.

The guide-boat served all the purposes, and more, of the bark canoe that it replaced, yet the boat of thin wooden planks fastened with tacks and screws is very different from the shell of birch rind sewn with root strands and caulked with gum. When he ran out of spruce crooks, Lewis Grant stopped making guide-boats, but boat shops in more favorable locations were able to continue as long as guide-boats were needed. Had the demand for guide-boats outlasted the supply of crooks, ingenious and adaptable woodsmen would have learned to work with new materials in new ways to meet the same purposes.

For all its virtue, spruce is a firebrand. The dead tops flame with an explosive roar. It is unsafe for kindling wood, crackling with incendiary sparks. Menace lurks in the spruce duff, a punky compost of resinous, decayed needles that can smolder beneath an extinguished campfire — silent, invisible, smokeless. Though the surface coals may be thoroughly quenched, underground embers can spread fire creeping through the duff, to burst into flames many feet away, sometimes after several days.[27]

In all other ways spruce is a good tree with many uses. It has profited the lumberman, sheltered travelers and hunters, and provided material for the fiddle, the bark canoe, and the morning newspaper. It gave its gum to youthful jaws and its balm to bruised limbs. Under the stress of wind against its bushy top, the tall swaying trunk may break midway or tear out its tenacious roots with a great upheaval of earth, yet no one ever saw a sound tree break where the roots bend from the stump. The guide-boat began at the root of the spruce.

Notes

1. Westcott Abell, *The Shipwright's Trade* (Jamaica, New York: Caravan Book Service, 1962), pp. 2–3.
2. Henry David Thoreau, *The Maine Woods* (Boston and New York: Houghton Mifflin and Co., 1898; Cambridge: The Riverside Press), p. 110.
3. Letter, April 24, 1960.
4. Abell, pp. 92–94.
5. *Annual Report Second Geological District,* New York State Assembly Document no. 150, 1841, p. 119.
6. *Sixth Annual Report of the Forest, Fish and Game Commission of the State of New York* (Albany: James B. Lyon, State Printer, 1901), p. 174.
7. Unless otherwise noted, material on the characteristics of spruce has been compiled from *Wood Handbook,* no. 72, U.S. Dept. of Agriculture, Forest Products Laboratory (U.S. Government Printing Office); and *Annual Report of the Forest Commission* (Albany, 1895).
8. Sieur de Dièreville, *Relations of the Voyage to Port Royal in Acadia or New France,* trans., Mrs. Clarence Webster; ed., John Clarence Webster (Toronto: The Champlain Society, 1933), p. 91.
9. Thomas Anburey, *Travels through the Interior Part of America* (Boston and New York: Houghton Mifflin Co.; Cambridge: The Riverside Press, 1923), I, pp. 81–82.
10. *Boston Gazette,* September 25, 1775. Extract of a letter from an officer in the army at Ticonderoga to a friend, August 25, 1775.
11. J. Fenimore Cooper, *The Last of the Mohicans* (New York: Stringer & Townshend, 1856), p. 70.

12. Nicolas Denys, *The Description and Natural History of the Coasts of North America,* trans. W.F. Ganong (Paris, 1672; Toronto: The Champlain Society, 1908), II, pp. 422-424.

13. *St. Lawrence Plaindealer* (Canton, N.Y.), August 24, 1881.

14. William H. Boardman, *The Lovers of the Woods* (New York: McClure, Phillips & Co., 1901), p. 59.

15. *Jesuit Relations,* ed. R.G. Thwaites, XLII, pp. 123-125.

16. Alfred B. Street, *Woods and Waters, or The Saranacs and Racket* (New York: H. Doolady, 1860), p. 64.

17. *First Annual Report of the Forest Commission of the State of New York* for the year 1885, Assembly Document no. 103 (Albany: The Argus Co., Printers, 1886), p. 72; *Harper's Monthly Magazine,* July 1859, p. 170.

18. Boardman, pp. 147-148.

19. *Journals of Samuel Hearne and Philip Turnor* (1774-1792), ed. J.B. Tyrell (Toronto: The Champlain Society, 1934), p. 188.

20. Rushton catalog, 1881, p. 5.

21. Willard Hanmer, conversations on tape, Adirondack Museum.

22. J.S. Springer, *Forest Life and Forest Trees* (New York: Harper and Brothers, 1851), p. 32.

23. *New York State Conservationist,* February-March, 1960, p. 38; Lyon & Healy, Harp Salon, letter, 1960; *Saturday Review of Literature,* December 12, 1964, advertisement.

24. William F. Fox, *Adirondack Black Spruce* from the *Annual Report of the Forest Commission for 1894* (Albany: James B. Lyon, printer, 1895), p. 7.

25. *Annual Report of the New York Forest Commission for the year ending Dec. 31, 1890,* p. 51.

26. Letter, April 24, 1960.

27. *First Annual Report of the Forest Commission of the State of New York* for the year 1885, Assembly Document no. 103 (Albany: The Argus Co., Printers, 1886), pp. 20, 102.

XIV/The Search for Spruce Crooks

There are so many things one would like to know . . . who thought of using the root of the Adirondack spruce . . . in which the grain of the wood follows the curve of the rib?

Talbot Bissell[1]

Though the white man's boat was shaped with plane and chisel and fastened with a multitude of small screws and tiny tacks, inside the hull the product of the forest, the spruce, provided a framework of natural-grown ribs.

The ability to find the right spruce crooks was as important to the guide-boat craftsman as technical skill. With an image in his mind of the boat he intended to make, a builder studied the crooks hidden in tree stumps. He chose those that matched most nearly the curves of the craft he envisioned. In turn, the stumps and roots he found determined to a degree his final design. He was instructed in this practice by his double heritage as both a woodsman and a shipwright.

While occupied in the forests or on the streams, the woodsman noticed useful things unobserved by the casual traveler. He was drawn to odd shapes: the curves and knots in a tree; the bend of ash for sled runners; forks in sticks for sling shots; crotches for saddles, gun racks, and harnesses; and crooks for boat ribs. These were not easily found and when noticed, not quickly forgotten. He collected what he needed and remembered the rest. When he wanted something, he knew where to find it.

The itinerant pioneer preacher Joseph Craig once stopped short in his exhortation to a large congregation in the woods of the Cumberland. Still gazing devoutly to heaven, he suddenly pointed his finger to a branch and exclaimed, "Brethren, behold up yonder a first rate crotch for a pack-saddle."[2]

For the shipwright, finding trees with the right grain and the right curves and reverse curves needed for ship timbers is an ancient art, the result of long practice and experience.

In 1672 Nicolas Denys went on frequent explorations with French fishermen along the coast of Acadia in Nova Scotia. Between voyages they hid their boats by sinking them under rocks in freshwater ponds, as was done with the bateau the Museum recovered from Lake George. To repair their boats and build new ones, they needed natural-grown crooks. Denys reported that the ribs difficult to find were those with reverse curves; nevertheless, he obtained plenty of them.[3] Denys did not tell us what he found or where, but we know that Acadia abounded in tamarack and spruce, and that spruce crooks were preferred.

For the building of four bateaux at Albany Fort in 1780–81, carpenters of the Hudson's Bay Company collected "poplar crooks for timbers."[4] By 1826 the

93

The Hanmer boat shop, Saranac Lake. Dealing in small dimensions, the Adirondack boatbuilder brought the spruce crooks to his shop. Either there or at the local sawmill they were ripped into regular 2-inch planks. (Adirondack Museum)

Company's ship-carpenters, most of whom hailed from the Orkney Islands, had evolved the famous York boats for the fur trade. The building of these boats was no haphazard business. The York boatbuilder took his axe-men into the woods, seeking suitable spruce from the roots of which the bow and stern pieces would be cut.[5]

The York boat, which in profile somewhat resembled a Viking ship, with prominent stem and stern posts, was a form of enlarged Orkney Island skiff. The York boat was originally built by shipwrights from the Orkney Islands, located at the northernmost tip of Scotland. Descendants of Picts and the later Norse conquerors, they had inherited their knowledge from Norwegian farmers who, for centuries, had built boats in the inland pine forests. Tying five or more boats together, these early builders rowed or sailed them down the long fjords and sold them to saltwater fishermen living on the coast of Norway.[6] These boats, such as the four-oared (*faering*) Hardanger type in the Adirondack Museum (No. 63. 89. 1), were constructed with natural crooks found in the woods of Norway.[7]

The American Navy found the right curves in the live oak, a heavily branched evergreen with close-grained wood resistant to rot. It is a fast-growing tree, often attaining a height of 60 feet and a diameter of more than 4 feet. With its size and irregular shape, the live oak provided the components needed for

American warships: "great timbers" of considerable strength for the hulls, and many compass timbers of curved and irregular shapes for knees, transoms, and the like.

The first Act of Congress of the United States concerning the construction of ships was passed on March 27, 1794. As soon as the money was made available by Congress, axe-men and carpenters from Connecticut, under the guidance of John T. Morgan, master shipwright from Boston, went into Georgia woods with their molds. Within two months a cargo of live oak timbers reached Philadelphia for the construction of the frigate *United States.* She was launched in May of 1797. Her sister ship the *Constellation* was launched in September of that year at Baltimore and the *Constitution* in October at Boston.[8]

Adirondack builders did not have to carry their patterns into the forests. Having fixed upon spruce for their frames, they found a plentiful supply all around them, and dealing in smaller dimensions than the shipbuilders, they could bring the crooks to the shops. They could afford to be fastidious in their selection in order to achieve excellence. "Careful choice of crooks," wrote Lewis Grant, "enabled my father to reduce dimensions in the frames and so lighten the boats."[9] But it took a trained eye.

Spruce was subject to hidden decay. Warren Cole's son, Wright, recalled the care with which his father chose crook timber on their expeditions around Long Lake. Wright Cole would shout his discovery of a likely tree, only to have his father reject it because of twisted grain or because he was suspicious of an invisible "heart rot." When they found a promising tree they felled it; only then were they certain of the soundness of the stump.

Getting the stump out of the ground was hard work. Men who had gathered hackmatack roots in the swamplands of Maine would recall with satisfaction the generous nature of that tree, which sent its roots along the surface and was easily dug out. With ocean shipping nearby, gathering crooks was a profitable sideline for the Maine farmers. There was no easy profit to be made in the Adirondacks, however, where the spruce roots grew deep into the rocky soil.

Because nothing else suited his needs, the guide-boat maker accepted the arduous task of grubbing out spruce stumps as part of his job. Lewis Grant told us how it was done in his father's time, before chain saws or heavy earth movers had been invented. "They had two-man cross-cut saws when I was born in 1878," said Lewis, "but father had a one-man cross-cut saw and he sometimes used a very light charge of dynamite under the stump to blow out dirt and stones but not enough to harm the lumber." Cleared of earth, the roots were cut loose and the freed stump was turned over and sawed partway between the roots. Wedges were driven into the saw cuts and the root sections separated with heavy sledge blows. With good judgment and some luck, the result was four pieces of stump, each with a heavy root attached. The root and the stump of each section were trimmed to make two flat surfaces in one plane that would support the section on the carriage at the sawmill, where it was ripped into regular two-inch planks (or flitches) and left to season for a year or more.

Hauled out over the tote roads in heavy lumber wagons, these unwieldy pieces of irregular shape and intractable disposition were not welcomed by the sawyer. The early up-and-down saws, cutting on the down-stroke, tended to keep the resilient roots from bouncing out of control. A band saw was fairly safe, but under a high-speed circular blade, the stumps could be dangerously erratic.

Spruce stands were not easily found around Boonville, an older settlement. Dwight Grant got some of his best crooks from an old bull spruce in an open field within two miles of the village, but mostly he followed the loggers into the cuttings to find good stumps near a tote road so that he could get them out with wheeled vehicles.[10] It was easier to judge quality in a stump than in a standing tree. The cut revealed any defect at the heart. Stumps, moreover, could be had for the taking (which was dear enough, considering the time spent searching for them and the labor of getting them out) in 1879 when Dwight Grant began building guide-boats.

Though the cross-cut saw was already an ancient and useful tool, the American lumberman, until the end of the nineteenth century, clung to the more versatile axe, with which he and his forefathers had cleared the wilderness with such dexterity. The axe left stumps waist-high, with an ample length of straight grain above the crook, precisely what the boatbuilder needed.

The work of gathering boat timber became increasingly difficult, however. After the establishment of the Adirondack Forest Preserve in 1885, the State was prohibited from selling a single tree or stump. Nearly all land in and around the village of Long Lake, for example, was owned either by the State or by nonresident lumbermen, who would not sell any timber in small quantities. The Forest Commission in 1890 had spoken not unsympathetically of the plight of the Long Lake villagers. Living in the very heart of the woods, they were unable to get lumber for their most pressing needs. "Small trespasses have been committed on State lands to obtain timber for fire wood, barns, houses and . . . the construction of Adirondack skiffs, which are a necessity and the only means of conveyance in that wilderness. . . . The inhabitants, being somewhat desperate, felt justified in obtaining their wood and lumber where it was most convenient, without regard for ownership."[11]

When the Forest Commission found it necessary in 1900 to urge the lumbermen, in the interest of conservation, to cut "no more than six inches above the cut of the root swelling,"[12] and the private preserves and the State began to restrict the free forest, the choppers exchanged the axe for the cross-cut saw and later for the chain saw. The new tools, together with the rising price of spruce butts, caused the loggers to cut close to the ground. These conservation measures affected more than the lumbermen.

Lewis Grant wrote us:

Lewis L. Grant. In his father's time, lumbermen left waist-high spruce stumps, but in his own later years, it was too difficult to get out spruce crooks. (Helen Durant)

In my father's time of boat building . . . they cut the stump waist high, but since I built guide-boats . . . the lumbermen cut the tree within six inches or a foot off the ground and that stump will not make boat ribs. . . . Now I would have to find a good tree, buy it, fall it, dig the stump and sell the balance of the tree if I could. . . It is too much for me at my age [Lewis was now 80] to get them out.[13]

In Lewis Grant's diary we found this entry for November 13, 1956: "Floyde Gallagher [superintendent of the Bisby Club] brought me a spruce root for boat ribs, but it was all in one piece and I could not handle it that way so he took it back to Bisby and is going to try to saw it into planks with his chain saw." The anachronistic marks of Gallagher's chain saw can be seen on two root planks in the Adirondack Museum. The root planks Gallagher brought to Lewis supplied crooks for repairs to the boats of the Adirondack League Club and its members who depended upon Lewis to keep their fleet in good order.

Even with modern tools and a highly mechanized shop, Willard Hanmer saw the digging of spruce roots as an onerous test of eye and hand: "Everything has to fit perfectly and that is not possible with power tools alone. . . . No machine can go out . . . and pick the best tree, or haul up giant roots that will work as ribs."[14] When Hanmer built his last boat at Saranac Lake in 1962, he had a plentiful supply of spruce roots on hand, thanks to a friendly arrangement with a private lumbering operation nearby, which left a few trees cut high for his use. Hanmer ripped out the crook planks in his own sawmill.

Although natural spruce crooks of good quality remained more readily available to the builders near the forests than to builders in the tidewater, who had to depend upon commercial supplies of hackmatack, the problem of finding crooks and getting them out was increased for the Adirondack boatbuilder, because he not only had high standards of quality but needed quantity as well. The guide-boat contained proportionately more ribs than other craft.

Purists insist that the guide-boat must be built with ribs of the natural crook. It is difficult in this age — if not impossible — to find suitable trees; digging out the roots is a task to be dreaded. That, and reducing the stumps to workable planks, might well give the backyard builder pause. Sawyers, long out of practice in dealing with such hazardous pieces, would be reluctant to handle them. Even if the amateur builder could solve all these problems, he would have to wait patiently a year or two to let his root stock season properly.

However, the determined and enterprising builder should not be discouraged. New times demand new ways. Even the oldest builders learned to replace iron screws with newfangled machine-made tacks and small pointed screws. When, toward the end of the nineteenth century, natural crooks were no longer available in sufficient quantities for the Bank dories, the builders found a way to clip two straight pieces together at the knuckle to make a sturdy frame.

In 1830, when natural crooks for the building of whaleboats became scarce, New Bedford builders wondered what they should do for knees. Captain Caleb Anthony, who was then running the packet ship *Iago* between the United States and Le Havre, France, asked Zachariah Hillman, a boatbuilder in New Bedford, why he did not use bent knees as

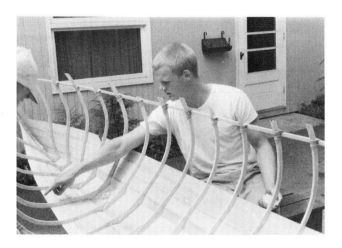

For his second guide-boat, built in 1965, Laurence Babcock used laminated ribs. (Helen Durant)

craftsmen such as Carl Hathaway of Saranac Lake and Harold Austin of Long Lake, whose great-great-grandfather was the William J. Austin known to have built boats in Long Lake in the 1850s. Both Hathaway and Harold Austin build their boats on the old, traditional patterns, though they sometimes mix the patterns of several builders to comply with the demands of their customers. The builder with zeal and imagination will not be stopped by the scarcity of a single part. Laurence Babcock of Post Mills, Vermont, made his guide-boat ribs out of laminated strips of wood, comparable to the sawn spruce ones. The lack of natural crooks has been an incentive for renewed ingeniousness. (*See* John Gardner's chapter, "Modern Materials and Tools.")

In the strength of the slender, resilient spruce crooks lies the secret of lines at once gracious and austere, the delicate charm and surprise of the reverse curve. Eyes and hands of a succession of builders, working within severe functional requirements, happily found the right materials to bring their carpentry to a fine art.

builders did in France. There, they split the wood where they wanted it bent, using iron to keep the parts in place.[15]

Today, guide-boats are still being built, sometimes out of whim and daring, or on special order, by

Notes

1. Talbot Bissell, "42 Pounds to Portage," in *The Skipper* XXVII, no. 1 (January 1967).
2. Harriette Simpson Arnow, *Seedtime on the Cumberland* (New York: Macmillan Co., 1960), p. 214.
3. Nicholas Denys, *The Description and Natural History of the Coasts of North America,* trans. W.F. Ganong (Paris, 1672; Toronto: The Champlain Society, 1908), pp. 340, 378.
4. *The Beaver,* Summer 1956, p. 52.
5. *Ibid.,* March, 1949; Howard I. Chapelle, "Arctic Pioneer Craft," unpublished article written for the Encyclopedia Arctica, Stefansson Collection, Baker Library, Hanover, New Hampshire.
6. A.W. Brøgger and Haakon Shetelig, *The Viking Ships* (Oslo, Norway: Dreyers Forlag; Los Angeles: Knud K. Mogensen Publishing, 1951), pp. 73-74.
7. Boat no. 2583 at Adirondack Museum.
8. Bess Glenn, "Cathcart's Journal and the Search for Naval Timbers," *American Neptune,* July 1943, pp. 239-241.
9. Letter, September 7, 1958.
10. Lewis Grant, letter, March 14, 1958.
11. *Forest, Fish and Game Commission of the State of New York, Report for 1890* State Document no. 84, p. 50.
12. *Sixth Annual Report of the Forest, Fish and Game Commission of the State of New York* (Albany: James B. Lyon, State Printer, 1901), p. 227.
13. Letters, January 9, 1958, and March 14, 1959.
14. *North Country Life,* Spring 1957.
15. A. Howard Clark, "Documents," in *American Neptune,* October 1943, p. 351.

XV/Patterns

I tell this tale, which is stricter true,
Just by way of convincing you
How very little, since things was made
things have altered in the shipwright's trade.

Rudyard Kipling[1]

The shaping of ship components has been the study of centuries and a craft secret since ancient shipbuilders first developed aids to construction. The creativity that shaped their patterns they called the mystery of their craft. They were familiar with the inherent qualities of the materials they used, knew the capacity of their tools, and possessed the skills to use them. They were inclined to preserve the aura of mystery and magic surrounding the art that they acquired with so much effort.

Among the Abenaki Indians who live scattered along the eastern and southern shores of the Gaspé Peninsula and (except for the St. John's River region) throughout the Maritime Provinces, there is a legend that the first canoe was made by their mythical hero Gluska'be, who used the form of a bird's breast as his pattern. Mateo, the mythical figure representing the human creator, when asked how *he* learned to build canoes, replied *"KES'KAMZIT,"* referring to the magic good luck that comes suddenly to an individual. This magic power, acquired as the result of a wish, must be kept a secret, however. To reveal it is to lose it forever.[2]

André Bourg of Terrebonne Parish, Louisiana, who shaped exquisite pirogues of cypress, said that all he did was chop away the wood he did not need; the pirogue was in the log all the time. Arthur van Pelt, who watched Bourg make a pirogue, wrote that, though Bourg used no calipers, "two long curving strips of wood, probably used for a century by his ancestors, gave him the lines that determined the overall shape and sheer of the little craft."[3]

The contours of a boat cannot be reduced to simple linear measurements; the builder needs a model to work by. To reproduce a satisfactory canoe the Penobscot and Malecite Indians recorded a few measurements on notched sticks. The Malecites used three sticks: one to measure the gunwale and position the thwarts, one for the length of the thwarts, and a third one to indicate the length of the canoe and the height of the gunwale at the individual thwart stations.[4] The main purpose of the notched sticks was to establish *proportions* rather than to fix dimensions. This, too, was the nature of the specifications recorded on H. Dwight Grant's tally boards, which derive their name from such notched sticks.

98

Measuring sticks were also used by the New England dory builders. After visiting the Hiram Lowell & Son dory shop in Amesbury, Massachusetts, operated by the same family since 1793, John Gardner reported: "Ralph Lowell told me that they had a bunch of sticks somewhere around the shop with the principal dimensions of the different standard dories marked on them; one stick for each dory."[5]

When hand-line fishing off the Grand Banks was at its peak and standardized dories were produced in quantity, every segment of the boat, except planking and gunwales (which could be sawn to length as the boat was being erected), was made from a master pattern.[6] "I saw a pile, two foot high, of half bottom patterns [at the Lowell dory shop]," continued Gardner, "some of them worn and black with age."

John Gardner believes that patterns were not used in the building of colonial bateaux because their shape was so simple and because it would have been convenient to vary the different boats somewhat to suit the available lumber, especially the natural-crook frames and the different widths and lengths of the planks.[7]

Thomas Agry, the shipwright in charge of building a fleet of two hundred bateaux for the invasion of Canada in 1775, was apparently unfamiliar with the navigational problems of Maine's upper Kennebec River, so that he and his carpenters "did not fully understand the requirements." When Benedict Arnold, who was familiar with watercraft of many sorts, arrived to inspect this fleet, flung together in 18 days, he was heard to comment sharply to himself: "Completed, yes; but many of them smaller than the directions given, and badly, very badly built."[8] This seems to imply that they had received directions but no patterns.

Good patterns are imperative for a good boat; they must be exact; they must be formed and adapted with an understanding eye to need and environment. Their function is two-fold: to aid the carpenter in fashioning intricate forms so that all segments of a boat when put in place may fit exactly and respond and interact properly, and to perpetuate a proven design.

It was said of Reuben Carey, an experienced woodsman and boatbuilder who had been caretaker for many years at the Brandreth camps, that his boats

lost favor because he could not be depended upon to build the same boat twice.[9] Dwight Grant did not encourage drastic departures from basic shapes. With his boat's every timber turning into a different form, Grant's ability, year after year, to build boats so closely alike in beauty and performance, was a recurrent marvel. "Father took great pains with his patterns," Lewis said.

The Adirondack guide-boat shop with a relatively small yearly production used far more patterns than the dory shops. The need to control weight and balance did not permit improvisation; in the complicated structure of the guide-boat, nothing could be left to chance. After building boats during the winter, the Adirondack builder-guide carefully stored his patterns when he resumed his summer vocation, confident that when the lakes froze over he could make the same boat again.

Lewis Grant, who had stopped building guide-boats in 1923 when his father's supply of spruce crooks ran out, built one more small guide-boat in 1934, for which he managed to scrape together sufficient ribs and planking. His diary entry for February 28 of that year reads: "Spent most of the day cleaning up shop and getting ready to build a guide-boat," and three days later: "Cleaned up boat patterns." With his father's carefully preserved patterns, Lewis could begin again after an interval of 11 years. Except for half an inch additional height in the stem, his last boat (sold to Ray Schweinsberg, who had a camp on Third Lake) was an exact duplicate of boat number 3 on Dwight Grant's tally board for 1903, built for William P. Hall, president of the Adirondack League Club from 1911 to 1922.

When we asked Lewis if he could build a guide-boat without patterns, he replied without hesitation: "No, but I could make a boat like that," pointing to a crude, ill-shapen craft on the floor of the shop, waiting for repair. He had great contempt for its form and workmanship. After the Adirondack Museum acquired this boat (the so-called Hough boat) for historical and study reasons, Lewis referred to it again in a letter: "That square end, round bottom, clap-board boat was far from being a guide-boat and was poor workmanship. No guide I ever knew would own it."[10] And again, estimating the relative merits of two boatbuilding brothers, Lewis wrote: "Both were

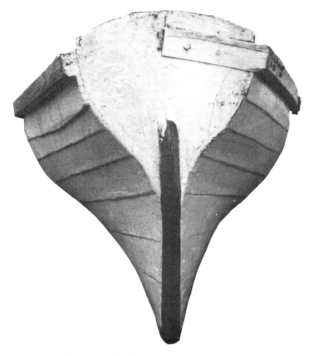

A Chase Lake boat known as the Hough boat. Lewis Grant considered this boat poor workmanship and said he could build such a boat without patterns. (Helen Durant)

The Hanmer boat shop, Saranac Lake. The patterns that primarily influenced the ultimate design of the guide-boat were the contour of the bottom board, the rocker of the bottom board, and the shape of the stem and ribs. (Adirondack Museum)

fine men, but one would say 'that's good enough.' The other brother would not stand for it: he wanted the workmanship to be first class."[11] Guide-boat building was a proud term not lightly bestowed on bad carpentry.

Early boatbuilders sometimes shaped the hull with "a cod's head and mackerel tail," beguiled by the illusion that a wide forward section eased the boat's progress through the water. In certain wherries this form was useful for the raising of nets, but it did not facilitate a boat's progress. Nevertheless, the illusion persisted and found its way into some of the Adirondack boat shops. Guide-boat number 5 on Grant's tally board of 1895 was built on the cod-head principle to suit the whim of the guide Frank Williams, who later, however, bought two more boats from Grant built on more conventional lines.

On all except the 1895 Williams boat, Dwight Grant placed his widest beam precisely amidships. Because this made the boat a true double-ender, it permitted Grant to use quarter patterns for his bottom board (*see* Gardner Plate VIII, Appendix C). Warren Cole of Long Lake also used quarter pat-

terns. The Hanmers of Saranac Lake used whole patterns for their bottom board, which held their boats more closely to a few standard sizes.

The patterns that primarily influenced the ultimate design of the guide-boat were those for the contour of the bottom board, the rocker of the bottom board, and the shape of the stem and the ribs. The bottom board pattern established the form of the boat. The outline at the sheer approximated the outline of the bottom but was modified by the flare of the ribs. On this bottom board were erected the permanent ribs to which the hull was fastened; no molds were needed.

"We had bottom board patterns for short, regular and long guide-boats," said Lewis Grant during a conversation in 1959, "with just the right slight curve on the outside of the bottom to get the right shape boat." Bevel lines, to accommodate the angle of the ribs at each station, were drawn on the quarter pattern for every other rib, starting with the center rib (the 0 rib) and continuing with rib numbers 2, 4, 6, and so on.

14-foot bottom board: 31 pairs of ribs, of which 7 pairs are center no. 0s; 32 spaces, each 5¼ inches

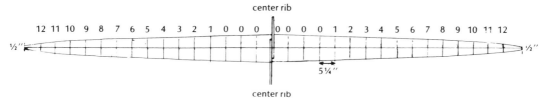

center rib

12 11 10 9 8 7 6 5 4 3 2 1 0 0 0 | 0 0 0 0 1 2 3 4 5 6 7 8 9 10 11 12

½″   ½″

5¼″

center rib

As most of my father's boats with 7 pair of no. 0 center ribs had 13½-foot or 14-foot bottom boards, I have made the rough drawing to cover a 14-foot bottom board. However, the length of the bottom board makes the difference in the spacing of the ribs. With a 12-foot bottom board, using 31 pairs of ribs, the rib lines on the bottom board would be 4½ inches apart. On a 13-foot bottom board they would be 4⅞ inches apart, and on a 14-foot bottom board they would be 5¼ inches apart. We have patterns for bottom boards for short, regular, and long guide-boats. Just the right slight curve on the outside line of the bottom board has to be right to get the right shape boat, and Father took a lot of pains in making these patterns.

The above is the plan of a 14-foot bottom board, ½ inch thick, with 7 pairs of center ribs 8 inches wide inside at center, which makes a boat 15½ feet from tip to tip of stems of a Grant boat. The lines show the spacing of the ribs as per tally boards, and they have to be put on both sides of the bottom board, on the inside to show where to put the ribs and on the outside to show where to put the screws to hold the ribs to the bottom board. Then the bevel has to be made on the outside of the bottom board, full length, before any ribs can be put on. The bottom board bevel has to conform with each rib where that rib is attached to the bottom board.

L L Grant

In most guide-boats the bottom board runs flat for a short distance amidships and then curves slightly upward bow and stern. This curve, called rocker, is important for easy maneuvering of the boat. In short, quick turns, with the oarsman pushing one oar and pulling the other, the boat should pivot on the flat with minimum resistance at bow and stern. To give the bottom board the desired rocker, it is mounted on a stock plank, a 2 x 6 plank on edge, supported by three adjustable stanchions bolted to the floor with iron braces. The stock plank is slightly concave on its upper surface, rising approximately an inch from the low point at center to the higher ends. After ribs and stems have been attached, the bottom board is forced into the concavity of the stock plank and firmly screwed to it. Adjustable stanchions hanging from a

In most guide-boats, the bottom board runs flat for a short distance amidships and then curves slightly upward at the bow and stern. (Helen Durant)

sliding carriage on the ceiling above come down to hold the tops of the stems.

The stock plank was approximately 18 inches shorter than the corresponding bottom board so that, after it was forced into the concavity, the bottom board overhung the plank at each end by about 9 inches. The pattern of the rocker tended to straighten out toward the end of the plank. This caused the bottom line at bow and stern to become straight again but with a slight upward tilt, tangent to the end of the rocker curve. The bottom board was slightly tapered on the underside at the very end to make it fit neatly into the notch of the stem foot.

Dwight Grant used three stock planks for three different sizes of boat. When our study of guide-boat construction in Boonville began in 1958, Lewis Grant had long since made his last guide-boat, but he still had the 9-foot and 11-foot stock planks. The 13-foot stock plank had been put to other uses, so that we could not measure its exact contour. In 1959, aided by parts of the original stock stanchions and an old photograph, Lewis made a drawing from memory of a 14-foot bottom board on his father's 13-foot stock plank. Construction and mechanism were no doubt as he showed them. Detailed dimensions show some discrepancies, but then Lewis had not worked on a boat that size for 36 years. He shows the molded width of the stock plank as $5\frac{1}{8}$ inches in the middle, and 6 inches at the ends. This results in a rocker of $\frac{7}{8}$ inch as marked on the drawing, but we must remember that this drawing is a reconstruction.

We have tracings of the original 9-foot and 11-foot stock planks and from these, together with measurements of the *Virginia,* a boat with a $14\frac{1}{2}$-foot bottom, built on the original 13-foot stock plank in 1905, we made our own approximation of the curve of the missing 13-foot stock plank, shown on Gardner Plate VIII, Appendix C. Still, even this reconstruction has to be accepted with some reservation. Due to age and wear, the boat measured showed some distortions from its original form. We feel, however, that Gardner's drawing of the stock plank is a reliable approximation of the missing piece. It shows a rocker of $1\frac{1}{16}$ inches.

Traditionally, specifications for length refer to the length of the bottom board (or keel) rather than to the length of the boat. Keel length is measured from the heel of the stem post to the base of the transom.

The rake of the stems makes the length overall (LOA), measured between the tops of the metal-capped stems mounted on the rockered bottom board, considerably longer than the keel length. The builders of York boats on Hudson's Bay used a similar measuring system, as did the dory builders in New England. In Grant boats the difference is usually 18 inches.

It may be confusing to hear an Adirondack boat-builder speak of two stems, bow and stern, though well he may, since they are identical, being cut from the same pattern, which gives the contours, the rabbet, and the bearding lines. The pattern also indicates the spot where the foot of the stem fits over the bottom board. A series of horizontal lines at half-inch intervals indicates the desired height of the stem, which, for a boat 16 feet overall, was generally $23\frac{1}{2}$ inches. A separate template gives the curve of the rabbet and bearding lines and the depth of the cut where the stem receives the planking, for convenience in scribing onto the new stem.

We did not learn from Lewis Grant the precise base line from which the height of the stem was measured. The horizontal cross lines were already on the pattern when Lewis went to work in his father's shop in 1895. To Grant's carpenters, the origin of these lines was not important. They had been marked on the pattern by Dwight Grant and they served their purpose. We took the height of the stem from them for Gardner's drawing, Plate VI. With patterned stems fitted to patterned bottom board of given length and width, the overall linear dimensions resulted.

The exact form of a canoe depends largely upon the flexibility and elasticity of the bark and upon the judgment of the builder rather than upon a precise pattern of predetermined lines. It should be apparent that the canoe's shape is also controlled by the form given the ribs when they are bent before assembly. Their bent shape fixes the amount of round, or rounded-V, given to the bottom athwartships. "No fixed rules appear to exist; the eye and judgment of the builder are his only guides," said Adney and Chapelle, co-authors of *The Bark Canoes and Skin Boats of North America.*[12]

For all its obvious kinship with the dory, the guide-boat was the more sophisticated craft. The gunwale of the straight-sided dory followed the contour of the bottom board. In the guide-boat the

H. Dwight Grant Guide-Boats. First the ½-inch white pine bottom board is made and spaced for ribs, and right bevel is put on edge of bottom board to conform with back of each rib at heel of rib. Then bottom board is put on two sawhorses and ribs and stems are attached to bottom board by two screws through bottom board into the foot of each rib and stem. Then boat frame is put on stock and bottom board is fastened to stock with three two-inch no. 8 screws through a small block, as shown in drawing below. Stems are lined up with bottom board by placing T-square on bottom board at center of boat. When in correct line-up, stems are fastened to drop irons on ceiling carriage, with a screw and washer.

Batt is placed at top of ribs from stem to stem. Starting at center rib, ribs are spaced on batt the same as on bottom board and attached to batt at top of rib. Since backs of ribs are square with sides of ribs, number 7, 8, 9, 10, 11, and 12 ribs have to be trimmed with a spokeshave, on the boat end side of the rib, until it is in line with siding that is to be attached to each of those ribs. Now you are ready to start putting on siding, and the boat stays in this high position until "4 rounds," half the siding is on the boat, then stock is dropped to low position and the balance of siding and wale is put on the boat. Then the boat is taken off the stock and weighed.

L. L. Grant

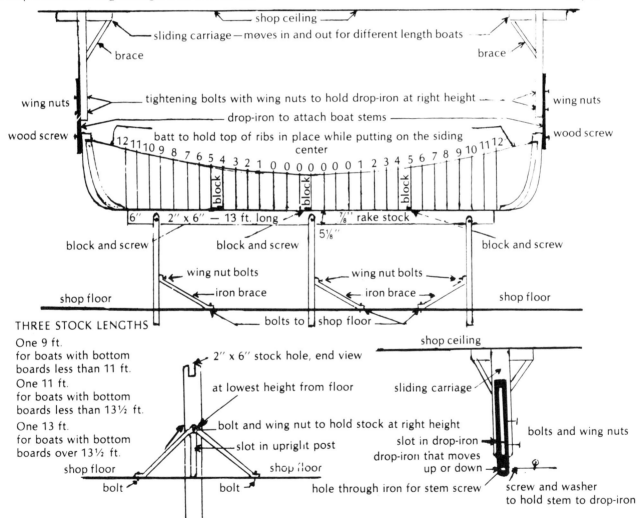

THREE STOCK LENGTHS

One 9 ft.
for boats with bottom
boards less than 11 ft.
One 11 ft.
for boats with bottom
boards less than 13½ ft.
One 13 ft.
for boats with bottom
boards over 13½ ft.

The 9 ft. stock was used on 2 uprights

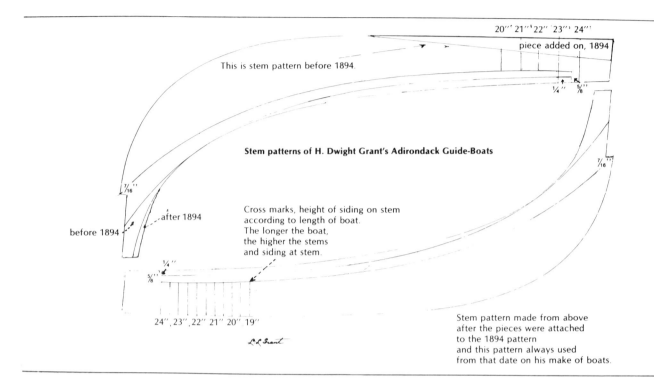

20''' 21'''²22''' 23''' 24'''

piece added on, 1894

¼'' ⁵⁄₈''

This is stem pattern before 1894.

⁷⁄₁₆''

Stem patterns of H. Dwight Grant's Adirondack Guide-Boats

⁷⁄₁₆''

after 1894

Cross marks, height of siding on stem
according to length of boat.
The longer the boat,
the higher the stems
and siding at stem.

before 1894

¼''

⁵⁄₈''

24'' 23'' 22'' 21'' 20'' 19''

Stem pattern made from above
after the pieces were attached
to the 1894 pattern
and this pattern always used
from that date on his make of boats.

contour of the gunwale did not follow so closely the contour of the bottom board. Between bottom and gunwale intervened the swell and the reverse curves of the ribs. When the builder shaped these timbers with an eye for fair form, he declared his hydrodynamic purpose. In the progression of curves, from bottom to wale, imagination had free reign: ". ... these bends of tymber are ye greatest art wᶜʰ belong to the Master Builder and have soe much of variety in them as you can have imaginations . . . ," wrote Sir Anthony Deane in 1670.[13]

Guide-boat rib patterns were not patented or found in any book; they were special to each builder. They established the form of the hull as do molds in other types of craft. For his guide-boat ribs, Grant used 13 different patterns cut from half-inch clear pine. He numbered his center pattern and the corresponding center rib 0. From amidships, on one side toward the bow and on the other side toward the stern, patterns and corresponding ribs were numbered 1 to 12. Whether Grant learned this way of numbering from Henry Stanton or from some other source, it was no Adirondack invention but a system of great antiquity. Howard I. Chapelle wrote us: "It was the old practice to mark the center frame, or ship

mold, '0'. The after frames were numbered 1, 2, 3, etc., to the stern. The fore frames were marked A, B, C, etc. . . . ."[14] For true double-enders like the guide-boat, where both sets of ribs were exactly alike, it was not necessary to distinguish between the two sets of frames.

For each of the 11 ribs numbered 0 through 10, the patterns in the Grant shop were in two parts, one for the upper part of the rib where it formed the side of the boat, and another one for the foot straddling the bottom board. The pattern for the upper part of the rib gave the shape against the planking from the knuckle through the sheer; the contour of the parallel inner line was scribed from the outer one. The second part of the rib pattern started slightly above the knuckle and continued through the foot. Contoured slightly on both sides, a rib widened at the knuckle, the point of greatest stress, then tapered slightly as the foot crossed the bottom board. Rib and foot patterns, the same for boats of all sizes, were made long enough to fit the depth and the bottom width of the largest boat (*see* Gardner Plate III). For ribs numbers 11 and 12, the footless scribe ribs, only the outer contour was required; Dwight Grant shaped these on the two edges of a single pattern board.

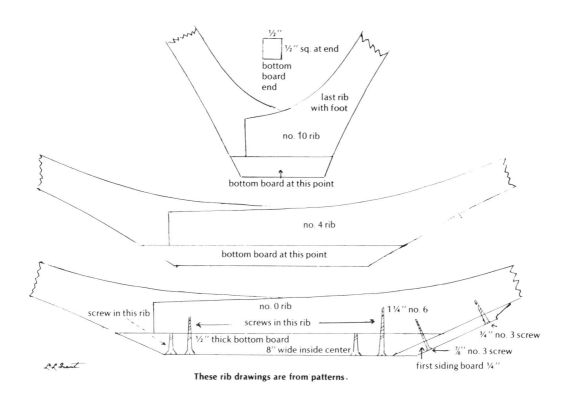

1/2"
1/2" sq. at end
bottom
board
end

last rib
with foot

no. 10 rib

bottom board at this point

no. 4 rib

bottom board at this point

screw in this rib
no. 0 rib
screws in this rib
1 1/4" no. 6
1/2" thick bottom board
8" wide inside center
1/4" no. 3 screw
7/8" no. 3 screw
first siding board 1/4"

These rib drawings are from patterns.

The concave curve of the sheer, the beam, and the LOA remained unpatterned and unmeasured. The beam took care of itself, a function of rib and bottom board pattern, inner tension of the wood and builder's fancy; LOA was determined by the length of the bottom board and the rake of the stems. The boat grew under the carpenter's hand, true to the established pattern. Like Bourg's pirogue, it was there all the time: in the ribs, cut to pattern, numbered and stacked in a bin.

The pattern for the garboard, or bottom strake, was of great importance. Its shape was determined by the rib patterns, the stem rabbet, and the elliptical form of the bottom board (*see* Gardner Plate VIII). The garboard strake twisted almost 64 degrees in its half length, from nearly flat as it left the bottom board amidships to a nearly vertical plane where it joined the stem. It was difficult to lay out the necessary shape in flat stock to achieve the required twist and curve to join the elliptical form of the

rockered bottom. But with the help of a pattern, the experienced builder could fit the garboard under the bevel of the bottom board and then cut the edges flush. Grant wanted his garboard straight along the upper edge so he could line up the strakes above it. While his garboard was cut precisely to pattern, the seven remaining strake patterns were used only to rough out the boards to be scribed on the bottom edge and lined at the top as they went on the boat.

There were many more patterns, templates, and gauges for other segments of the boat and its accessories. The Adirondack Museum has over 70 items needed for the construction of one Grant guide-boat, and even that number may be incomplete. Although Lewis Grant made his last guide-boat in 1934, the contents of the Grant shop did not come to the Museum until 1960, after his death. In the interval many small items may have been lost.

In spite of the variety of patterns peculiar to builders and locality, their boats were not always easy to identify. From across the water, only an expert could tell boats of one Long Lake builder from those of another. The tumblehome stems of Long Lake boats seemed less pronounced than Saranac stems, while Bloomingdale boats had ram bows.

When the Brown's Tract boats (those made by Grant and the Parsonses) began to appear on Raquette waters, their rake shocked those accustomed to the Saranac profile. To young Kenneth Durant on Forked Lake, they seemed like intruders that acted like guide-boats but did not look like them. It was 50 years before he heard of Dwight Grant. The guides and the camp owners on Bisby Lake and Little Moose felt the same way about the Saranac boats with their tumblehome stems. Such was the force of habit.

Among related craft, the Adirondack guide-boat developed last and had the most limited geographical range, where its highly specialized uses survived only briefly. Perhaps it was for this reason that the guide-boat showed the least deviation from standard shape. Patterns passed from father to son, were bought or borrowed, copied, adapted, and amended.

When Dwight Grant sent for Henry Stanton in 1879, he must have been familiar with the Stanton model and possibly had already tried his hand at copying rib and stem posts. We may assume that Henry Stanton rowed his own guide-boat from Long Lake to Boonville via the Fulton Chain of Lakes and that he brought his boat patterns with him. We know that Grant's early boats had the feather-edged lap of the Long Lake and Saranac models. Soon after building the *Ghost* in 1882, Dwight Grant created his special plane and introduced his square-edge ship-lap, which replaced the traditional feather edge. This made the seams of his planking almost invisible, a unique contribution that passed generally unnoticed. Grant also found that he could abandon the so-called tumblehome stem pattern of the Long Lake models without damage to function and with great improvement in appearance. The Grant boats represented the peak in construction. They were "all guide-boat," without archaic features.

When Riley Parsons and Theodore Seeber opened their boat shop in Old Forge in 1890, they took with them not only years of experience from Grant's Boonville shop but also his rib patterns and a copy of his special lap plane. Soon thereafter they began to

accentuate Grant's raking stem. As Lewis Grant wrote us:

> They got the rib shapes from one of my father's boats. They also put the tip of the stems out an inch or a little more than Father's last model, so they would not look just like the Grant guide-boat. I just repaired a very old Seeber and Parsons guide-boat and father's first rib patterns fit that boat.[15]

After his father's death in 1906, Lewis Grant introduced some machinery into the shop but "did not make any changes in patterns of the guide-boats my father made," he wrote us, "and have not seen any improvements anyone else has made."[16]

During the early 1880s Dwight Grant began to extend the outward curve of his boat ribs. "I was very young at the time," wrote Lewis Grant, "and only remember what I heard my father tell about the change. . . . Father's last rib patterns show a lot of difference from his first ones. He kept the curve of the rib going outward."[17] These changes required new patterns for each rib.

When we suggested that the wide bearing and the resulting new flare at the bow, which permitted a heavier load in a rough sea, might have made a slower boat, Lewis replied that his father made guide-boats, not racing boats. This is consistent with the title page of Dwight Grant's 1890 pamphlet, which offers not speed, but "light weight, buoyancy and easy running."[18]

The stern seat of a guide-boat is in a narrow space close against the deck; the bow seat is placed farther amidships, at a wider station for better leverage of the oars (*see* Gardner Plate XIII). When Dwight Grant extended the outward curve of the ribs, it incidentally increased the dimensions of bow and stern seats. "You have noticed what a lot more room there is on his stern seat. His boats are wider there than any other guide-boat I ever saw. The same difference is at the bow," wrote Lewis.[19] These ample dimensions can be seen in the *Ghost*.

The flare at the bow, combined with the tumblehome stem carried over from Henry Stanton's pattern, made a blunt-nosed appearance, which Lewis called "podgy." In 1894 Dwight Grant tacked a small wedge on the upper half of that stem pattern, which created the silhouette that became so con-

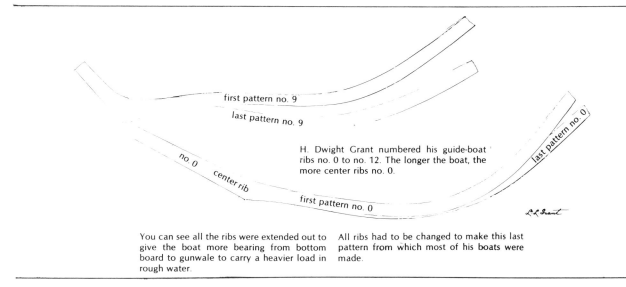

first pattern no. 9

last pattern no. 9

no. 0

center rib

first pattern no. 0

last pattern no. 0

last pattern no. 0

H. Dwight Grant numbered his guide-boat ribs no. 0 to no. 12. The longer the boat, the more center ribs no. 0.

You can see all the ribs were extended out to give the boat more bearing from bottom board to gunwale to carry a heavier load in rough water.

All ribs had to be changed to make this last pattern from which most of his boats were made.

spicuous in the Brown's Tract region. It gave the Grant boats the appearance of a sharp rake, bow and stern. This was mostly an optical illusion because the slight modification added less than an inch to the fore-and-aft width of the tops of the stems in a 16-foot boat.

A tendency to take spray and splash from the waves slapping over the bow in a brisk head wind was an uncomfortable feature of many guide-boats. To overcome this inconvenience, Dwight Grant increased the stem height slightly at the bow. Notations on the tally boards show the stem changes in progress. From 1896 on, Grant made bow and stern the same height. Thus all his boats became true double-enders in all dimensions.

Lewis Grant thought that his father had changed the stem just for looks. This may have been the purpose, but the change affected the shape and performance of the Grant boat more than the son thought. Though the new rake was only slightly beyond the vertical, it was an eye-catching departure from the tumblehome. It carried the rabbet line at the stem outward almost ¾ of an inch at the top of the garboard, but more than 3 inches at the sheer. The extended plank ends changed the shape of the hull below the load line and even more above.

Theoretically, it would seem that the use of patterns would produce identical boats, but since guide-boats are handmade, machine uniformity cannot be expected. Subtle deviations in adjustment of the patterns and in hand-shaping the parts within the norms set by the patterns are to be expected. Wood has hidden inner qualities; the tension of the sheer batten contends with the resistance of the ribs; ribs respond differently to pressure; there are variable atmospheric conditions and influences during construction. What pleases the eye of one builder may

Far left: Cut-off stern of Grant boat number 5 of 1902. Left: Grant boat number 14 of 1886. (Helen Durant)

not please another. For that matter, the same builder may not be pleased alike on two different days.

By a happy chance in 1964 there could be seen side by side on a dock at Bisby Lake two guide-boats built in 1921, one after the other (numbers 2 and 3), by Lewis Grant from the same materials and to the same patterns. Under their varnish both boats, excellently preserved, showed every detail of construction. On the tally boards all measurements were the same. The boats might have been called identical twins, yet, when the shells were taken from the stocks, one weighed 43 pounds and the other 45. This was within the range of tolerance allowed by Dwight Grant, who knew that closer conformity was not to be expected. Inspection of the boats revealed small differences between them discernible only with fine calibration. Even more interesting were small discrepancies within each boat, slight irregularities in construction, not easily seen and probably without any effect on the boat's performance.

The construction of a guide-boat is a succession of overlapping processes that do not always follow a strict chronological order. In the following chapters we shall describe the various phases of this assembly.

Notes

1. Portion of "The Sailor" from the poem "A Truthful Song," copyright 1910 by Rudyard Kipling. From the book *Rudyard Kipling's Verse: Definitive Edition.* Reprinted by permission of Doubleday & Company, Inc.
2. Wilson D. Wallis and Ruth Sawtell Wallis, *The Micmac Indians of Eastern Canada* (Minneapolis: University of Minnesota Press, 1955), pp. 42, 153, 162, 330.
3. Arthur van Pelt, "Louisiana," in *Wildfowling in the Mississippi Flyway,* ed. Eugene V. Connett (Toronto, New York, London: D. Van Nostrand Co., 1949), pp. 327-328.
4. E.T. Adney and H.I. Chapelle, *The Bark Canoes and Skin Boats of North America* (Washington, D.C.: Smithsonian Institution, 1964), p. 37; Frank G. Speck, *Penobscot Man* (Philadelphia: University of Pennsylvania Press, 1940), pp. 63-64.
5. Letter, March 8, 1964.
6. Howard I. Chapelle, *American Small Sailing Craft* (New York: W.W. Norton & Co., 1951), pp. 87-88.
7. Letter, March 15, 1964.
8. Justin H. Smith, *Our Struggle for the Fourteenth Colony* (New York and London: G.P. Putnam's Sons, The Knickerbocker Press, 1907), I, p. 525.
9. Fox B. Conner, letter, September 8, 1958.
10. Letter, September 7, 1958.
11. Letter, June 7, 1959. Grant was referring to Ben and Ira Parsons, sons of Riley Parsons, who had been a carpenter in Dwight Grant's Boonville shop.
12. Adney and Chapelle, p. 52.
13. Westcott Abell, *The Shipwright's Trade* (Jamaica, New York: Caravan Book Service, 1962), p. 60. Anthony Deane ms. in Pepysian Library, no. 2910, Magdalene College, Cambridge.
14. Howard I. Chapelle, letter, June 9, 1959.
15. Letter, June 7, 1959.
16. Letter, September 7, 1958.
17. Letter, August 29, 1958.
18. Dwight Grant, 1890 pamphlet, Adirondack Museum.
19. Letter, August 29, 1958.

XVI/The Frame

Small and light as these boats are, they will sustain three men and all they really need in the way of baggage. . . .

W. H. H. Murray[1]

About 1890 the *Boonville Herald and Adirondack Steam Print* ran off a four-page pamphlet with the comprehensive title:

The · Famous · Adirondack · Guide · Boats,
Models of
Beauty. Fine Workmanship. Good Material and
Moderate Prices.
Light Weight, Buoyant, Good Sea Boats and Easy Running.

H. D. GRANT, Manufacturer, Boonville, N. Y.

Lewis recalled setting the plate for a blueprint illustration at the end of the pamphlet in a sunny window of Grant's Post Street home when he himself was a boy. That picture shows two of Grant's early guide-boats on the dock of the Lawrence Camp on Fourth Lake of the Fulton Chain. Consistent with Lewis's guess that the date was 1890 is an entry in the *Boonville Herald* of January 8, 1891, which repeats the title of the pamphlet and notes that the Honorable H.D. Grant manufactures boats that are not excelled.

Grant's pamphlet is a unique document, a careful, succinct account of the structure of a guide-boat by one of its foremost builders. It is not a technical manual for carpenters, nor a "how-to" for amateurs. It gives no sophisticated architectural lines or offset tables. Omitting details of the intricate process, it describes the basic structure of the guide-boat and the materials used. It is written in simple and vigorous language that any carpenter can understand. Our study of Grant's account will be supplemented by the tally boards, reproduced in Appendix A, on which this meticulous builder entered the dimensions of every boat made in his shop, and by the explanations and sketches supplied in letters and conversations with his son, assistant, and successor, Lewis L. Grant.

Dwight Grant describes how the process of construction begins in his own shop:

First a bottom board of one-half inch pine, from 6 to 9 inches wide in the middle, tapered to five-eights inch to each end. To this is fastened the bow and stern stems and knees, five inches apart through the body of the boat. . . .[2]

Though ribs and stems could be cut in advance, the construction of all guide-boats, from the earliest known prototypes, began with a bottom board taper-

Blueprint from Dwight Grant's 1890 pamphlet showing Grant boats on Lawrence dock, Fourth Lake.

ing to both ends. Even the early square-sterned models tended to become double-enders below the waterline. The bottom board supports the frame of spruce ribs, which serves both to give shape to the sides and to support the planking. "This mode of construction is simpler and easier than the widely used method of employing movable building molds and battens," according to John Gardner, who says that in some respects the guide-boat was a most difficult boat to build and in others it was, fortunately, quite easy.

Dwight Grant began his struggle to hold down the boat's weight by using ½-inch pine plank for his bottom board. This was somewhat less than customary. Warren Cole of Long Lake preferred ¾-inch bottoms; Rushton of Canton made them ⅝ inch; Hanmer of Saranac Lake gave his 16-foot boats a ¾-inch bottom, increasing this thickness somewhat where the bottom board joined the stems, a point he considered vulnerable. Some other builders did the same. Merlin Austin of Long Lake made his bottom board ½ inch thick at the center, increasing it to ¾ inch at both ends.

Though ½-inch pine seems fragile for such an important segment of the guide-boat, the bottom board is reinforced and protected by the feet of the ribs, which cross it in adjacent pairs at approximately 5-inch intervals, depending upon the size of the boat. These tough spruce knees are the real floor of the boat, taking all the traffic. The bottom board is further armored underneath by iron shoes, which take the wear and tear every time the boat is pulled out of the water. Their effectiveness is shown by the need for replacement every few years.

In 1890 Dwight Grant recorded the widest point of his bottom board as 6 to 9 inches. Apparently he did

some experimenting. From his tally boards we can see that the early bottom boards, through 1891, were generally between 7 and 8 inches amidships. Beginning in 1892, they were usually 8½ inches for boats in the neighborhood of 16 feet LOA, but there were exceptions: Boat number 9 of 1904 was only 7½ inches amidships, while the *Virginia*, built in 1905, was 8¾ inches amidships, as were two other boats built that same year.

Some tolerance was permitted in the tapering as well. Grant's pamphlet gives ⅝ inch for the tapered ends. John Gardner's Plate VIII (Appendix C), made from measurements of the *Virginia*, shows the quarter pattern for the bottom board ending in ¼ inch, which makes a ½-inch end.

While the flat bottom of the dory was made from wide boards, cleated together and cut to shape on the outside edges, the bottom board of a guide-boat could always be made in one piece. The centerlines were marked lengthwise and crosswise on the roughed-out ½-inch pine plank, and Grant's quarter pattern, indicating contours, was laid out in the four positions defined by the centerlines and adjusted to the desired width and length of the boat.

The pattern was traced on both sides of the bottom board: on the upper surface to space the ribs, and on the under side to place the screws that would fasten the knees. The back of Grant's pattern had marks at every other rib station, from the forward rib 10 to the center ribs and all the way to rib 10 aft. These lines indicated the proper bevel angle for the under edge of the bottom board at that station, which was also the angle of the outer edge of the rib where it joined the bottom board. This angle became gradually more acute as it approached bow and stern.

John Gardner explained to us the customary method for cutting a changing bevel on a long, curved member. The carpenter set his bevel square to the bevel lines on the pattern to get the proper angle at each station. He then cut away sufficient wood to conform to the blade of the bevel square, and marked the exact *spot* where the bevel had been measured with a heavy pencil line. When he had cut and marked all the spots, a fair batten of suitable flexibility was "run" through this series of spots and temporarily tacked in place with small brads in order that a fair line could be drawn connecting the spots. The edge was then planed so that later the garboard would fit securely against rib and bottom board.

Grant's pamphlet continues:

> The stems and knees are made from natural crooks of the spruce roots, a strong and durable timber, the grain of the timber running with the model of the knee, knees five-sixteenth by three-fourth inches, rounded on inside edge.

Already cut from Grant's pattern, the stems were the first sections to be attached to the bottom board. They were notched $\frac{7}{16}$ of an inch deep at the bottom, so that they would not protrude below the $\frac{1}{2}$-inch bottom board, and fastened with two screws. Lewis explained to us that the bottom board was then lightly hand-dressed with a plane to make a flush joint.

The stems were rabbeted at the sides to take the ends of the planking. This rabbet went down to the forward under-edge of the bottom board, as shown in Lewis Grant's sketch (page 112).

The carpenter was not put through the trouble of measuring for height at the stem; this was determined for various lengths of boats by the series of horizontal cross lines on the pattern at half-inch intervals from 19 inches to 24 inches. The carpenter had only to transfer the required height from the pattern to the rabbet on the stem. This located the place where the end of the sheer batten would be fastened and, ultimately, the top of the sheer plank. For boats of 16 feet LOA, the indicated height at the stems was generally 23½ inches.

The modern reader must remember that once the Adirondack boatbuilder brought his stump pieces and planking into the shop, all shaping went by hand and eye. He had no bench saw or sander, no machinery for steam-bending or forcing parts into

The stems are rabbeted at the sides to take the ends of the planking. They are notched at the bottom to make a flush joint with the bottom board. (Helen Durant)

place. The tough spruce-root crooks had to be worked into rib shapes and stems entirely by hand. They had to fit and stay there. This required a skill beyond the capacity of many expert carpenters.

In Warren Cole's shop in Long Lake, the spruce crooks for the ribs were rough-shaped, double thick, on a foot-treadle jigsaw. This same tool worked a small circular saw, which split the crooks into two equal pieces, making twin pairs of the same grain and tension for opposite sides of the boat. This, however, was an advanced technique. Dwight Grant, who cut his ribs four thick, brought them to the Rice Brothers' mill in Boonville, where they were cut into single pairs with a band saw.

In shaping a rib, the two patterns were applied to the roughed-out rib plank, overlapped and registered at the point of the knuckle in such a way that the grain of the wood followed the shape of the rib. There was a slight tolerance for adjusting the two patterns to make a single rib. Customarily the ribs were shaped, numbered, and stored in a bin or cradle before boat construction began.

When Dwight Grant's pamphlet describes "knees five-sixteenth by three-fourth inches, rounded on inside edge," this means, in more technical terms, that the ribs are *sided* $\frac{5}{16}$ of an inch and *molded* $\frac{3}{4}$ of an inch. "When father got to making lighter boats," wrote Lewis Grant, "he would only use the best of a tree root for the ribs . . . and made them about $\frac{3}{16}$"

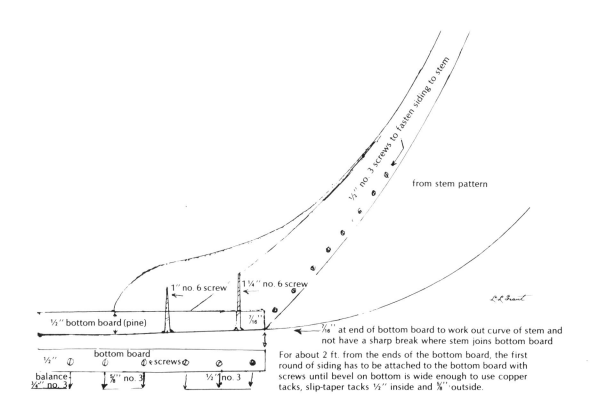

½" no. 3 screws to fasten siding to stem

from stem pattern

1" no. 6 screw

1¼" no. 6 screw

½" bottom board (pine)

⁷⁄₁₆"

⁷⁄₁₆" at end of bottom board to work out curve of stem and not have a sharp break where stem joins bottom board

bottom board

½"   ← screws

balance ¾" no. 3   ⅝" no. 3   ½" no. 3

For about 2 ft. from the ends of the bottom board, the first round of siding has to be attached to the bottom board with screws until bevel on bottom is wide enough to use copper tacks, slip-taper tacks ½" inside and ⅝" outside.

thinner than the first boats [built on the Stanton pattern] . . . in a 16-foot boat with sixty-six ribs [this] made an appreciable difference in weight. . . ."[3] When measuring the *Virginia*, John Gardner noticed that the short foot on the number 10 rib at either end of the boat was slightly heavier: molded ⅞ of an inch.[4]

The number of ribs differed with the length of the boat. Only the 10-foot-bottom boats were built with one pair of center (0) ribs, and few boats were that short. The 11-foot bottom usually carried three pairs of 0 ribs. Grant's favored length, the 14 to 14½-foot bottom, had from seven to nine pairs of 0 ribs and sometimes even an extra pair of number 1 ribs. With the 12 numbered pairs on each side, this made from

Customarily the numbered ribs are stored in a bin or cradle. (Helen Durant)

Hanmer kept his bottom board on edge. Lines on bottom board indicate centers of ribs. (Adirondack Museum)

62 to 66 ribs per boat. Regardless of the number of ribs, the 13 basic rib patterns and the single pattern for the two stems provided the shape of the boat.

Grant's pamphlet gives 5 inches for the spacing of the ribs. On the margin of a draft for this chapter, Lewis Grant wrote that this should be *about* 5 inches, as it varies with the length of the boat and from boat to boat.

While Hanmer mounted a jig on sawhorses to hold his bottom board on edge so that he had easy access to both sides of it, Grant put his bottom board flat on a set of sawhorses. With the spacing lines drawn and the bevel finished, the foot of the number 10 rib was laid against the lines and held flush with the bevel by a special clamp consisting of an iron hairpin tong tightened with a sliding ring like a barbecue broiler. The jaws of the clamp were covered with leather to protect the ribs. (Warren Cole used a similar clamp covered with wood. Theodore Hanmer contrived a clamp made from an old steel trap, later improved by his son Willard.[5] It took two men to set the long clamp used by Dwight Grant. Lewis, when he worked alone in the shop after his father's death, devised a system of double clamps that enabled him to set the ribs without help.)

With the rib firmly held in place, the builder could turn the bottom board upside down, make holes where the lines indicated the places for the screws,

and fasten the foot through the bottom board with two #6 screws. Then the opposite number 10 rib was laid against its mate, clamped, and screwed firm. Overlapping ribs were fastened with the port ribs forward. After the first rib and its mate had been fastened, the next port rib was clamped in place and the process repeated to the far end of the boat. (Hanmer apparently drilled the screw holes before he clamped on the rib feet. Warren Cole and George Smith of Long Lake fastened the rib feet together in pairs before putting them on the bottom board.)

The heels of the ribs must follow the curve laid by the quarter pattern of the bottom board. Their

The boat shop of George Smith, Long Lake, New York. (Helen Durant)

The Hanmer boat shop. The heels of the ribs must follow the curve of the bottom board; the feet become shorter as the bottom board narrows. (Adirondack Museum)

precise location depends upon the accuracy with which the carpenter fairs the curve. In Grant boats, on an 8-inch-wide bottom, the 0 rib feet extend 7 inches across the bottom board. The feet become shorter as the bottom board narrows, but the proportion of the length of the feet to the width of the bottom board, which varies with builders, must be maintained. At the Adirondack Museum there is an unidentified guide-boat (possibly built by George Smith of Long Lake, who learned boatbuilding from Cy Palmer, according to Cy's grandson Hale Palmer[6]) with knees crossing the bottom board all the way and butting against the opposite garboard.

The footless scribe-ribs are fastened to the hull in the narrow spaces by bow and stern after the planking is on. (Helen Durant)

Rib feet details. Typical sections from: (1) George W. Smith guide-boat; (2) John Blanchard guide-boat. (Thomas Warrington)

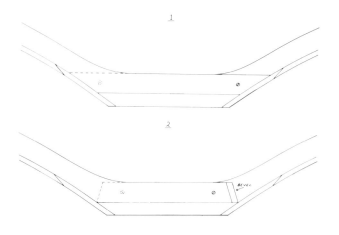

The bottom board crossed by firmly fastened pairs of ribs, plus the stems, constituted the basic framework of the guide-boat and would always retain its original shape. (The footless ribs numbers 11 and 12, the so-called scribe-ribs, were fastened to the hull in the narrow spaces by bow and stern after the planking was on.) This framework was then placed on the adjustable stock plank. The bottom board was forced into the plank's concavity, to give it the desired rocker, and fastened with three 2-inch, #8 screws.

Both stems, their height already determined by the horizontal lines transferred from the stem pattern, were lined up with the depth at center, and then they were fastened with a screw and washer to the drop iron on the ceiling carriage of the stock assembly shown in Grant's sketches in the preceding chapter.

Grant's pamphlet continues:

A light batt is then fastened to the upper end of each stem, running along on the outside of the knees on each side of the frame, the batt being fastened to each knee at the proper height to give the top of the boat the desired rake and hold the knees in place until the siding is put on.

Dwight's Grant's abbreviated statement of an exceedingly complicated procedure needs further explanation:

It would be difficult, even for the best of carpenters, to have the tops of all 62 to 66 slender ribs in perfect line. Unequal clamp pressure or the inherent characteristics of the wood as well as the limitations of hand and eye could cause slight irregularities at the sheer line, which defined the position of the top of the sheer plank. The ribs were adjusted with the help of a sheer batten (the Grants called it a "batt"), a thin flexible strip of wood of uniform dimensions. The trained eye and skill of the master boatbuilder were needed to apply it properly.

The spruce ribs, sawn out of the crook of the root, were tough and pliable. As they stood, each alone, free, and parallel with each other except for a slight inclination imparted by the curve of the bottom board's rocker, they could be moved at the top, most easily sideways, but they could also be bent slightly in or out. The sheer batten, placed around the ribs from stem to stem, brought each into line. Ribs too far out of line were replaced at this point.

The method of fastening the sheer batten prescribed by Dwight Grant and employed in most other boat shops was not followed by all boatbuilders. In Boston-built Whitehall boats, the battens were fastened tightly in the rabbet of the stem but were merely tied aft with a cord.[7] In the shop of Cyrus Palmer at Long Lake, the sheer batten extended between the last ribs at each end and did not reach the stems, as we can see from an old photograph of a guide-boat on the stocks. One end of the sheer batten stops short at the last rib; the other end is not clearly shown.

In the Hanmer shop the sheer batten was placed *above* the height of the gunwale so that it could remain in place until the sheer plank was mounted.

The boat shop of Cyrus Palmer. (Adirondack Museum)

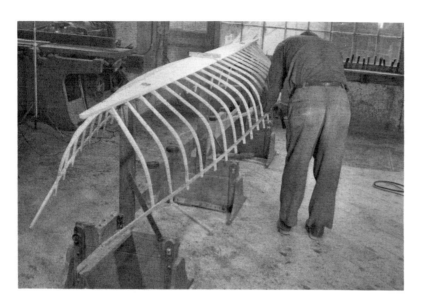

In the Hanmer shop the sheer batten was placed above the height of the gunwales. (Adirondack Museum)

Since Hanmer did his planking with the boat upside down on the stocks, the batten was stayed by slender sticks running down to a lengthwise plank on the floor under the stock plank. Hanmer left shop instructions with the following emphatic warning:

> Use stay lathes . . . to avoid flat spots or angles and also to allow for spreading at center without leaving bulge in waling, etc. THIS IS VERY IMPORTANT.

The Grant and Palmer shops, where planking was done with the boat right side up, had no such provisions for bracing.

In the Grant shop, according to Lewis, the sheer batten was fastened first to the center 0 rib at the height given for that boat on the tally board, before being brought around to the stems. Only by working in this manner was it possible to get both ends alike. After the ends were fastened to the stems at the height where ultimately the upper edge of the sheer plank and gunwale would come, the batten was shifted up and down between the fixed points, sighted (the Grants said "gunned"), to seek a true curve, a fair line, from the center 0 rib where the sheer ran straight, through an ascending curve to the tops of the stems. Beam and curve at each rib station were fixed by the fair sweep of the batten according to the builder's eye and fancy. As William Sutherland remarked in 1711: "You must observe first to pitch upon the Fashion of your foremost and aftermost Timber, which upwards

chiefly depends upon Fancy; for some choose to work more hollow, and some less. . . ."[8] The builder was not fettered by his pattern but was encouraged by his "notion," which devised the pattern. He held free rein in fairing the sheer line.

Though it may be possible to define a fair line in mathematical terms, certainly the Adirondack boatbuilder did not know enough mathematics to do it. What, then, is a fair line? During one of our conversations, Lewis Grant said that you have to use your eyes to see that the batten has the right true curve. The emphasis is shifted from absolute patterns to the realm of aesthetics, from dimensions and tools to the master's eye. It has always been so. The shape of the hollowed log and the form of the canoe came from the eye of the ancient builder long before patterns or architect's lines were available.

The batten, with its own inner will, has no allegiance to patterns. It wants a curve, the curve inherent in the materials under bending stress. The carpenter is rewarded for all previous pains, as he has in hand the perfect tool for his purpose. The shape of the bottom board pattern so carefully designed, the strength and resilience of the spruce-root crooks so laboriously dug out and so cunningly shaped in their variety of bends and reverse curves, all join to aid the master's eye. For a moment he, too, ignores the patterns and uses Fancy to build his boat.

John Gardner, who is not only an eminent historian of small boats but a practical boatbuilder as well, gives a more technical explanation of the fair line:

The fair line in boat building derives, I am sure, from an important characteristic of wood. . . . When a long strip of uniform dimensions is bent, it tends to assume a curve that is symmetrical and flowing, that is gradual and even. . . . Wooden battens are indispensable tools in the boat builder's trade. By means of their use he is able to lay out fair curves, or test curves for fairness. . . . The boat builder gradually trains his "eye" to see fairness or unfairness in curves with an acuteness that the unskilled can't approach, yet he still must fall back on battens to give him true, that is fair, curves in many places.[9]

Raising or lowering the sheer batten in the process of adjustment affected the beam at center. This is why Dwight Grant did not consider the beam an essential dimension to be entered on the tally board. While overall length was closely determined by the length of the bottom board, the beam was more elastic. It was more important to adjust the sheer batten to the right true curve and at the same time remove any irregularities in the ribs than to fix a predetermined beam. Depth at quarter was determined by the sheer batten in its appointed curve.

Had there been only one 0 rib and the batten permitted to follow its natural curve to the stems, the boats would have had the melon-slice form so dear to careless artists. The guide-boat, however, has seven or nine identical center ribs, almost in a straight line, and here the batten, holding the ribs in precise position, follows this almost straight line. Then, almost imperceptibly, it starts to curve toward the stems. From rib number 1 through rib number 10 it is al-lowed to take more nearly its own inner curve, a curve adjusted no doubt by many earlier battens with which the carpenter faired the lines of his patterns. Few artists have caught the straight flow of the guide-boat at midsection. Winslow Homer did not see it. Frederick Allen has a hint of it in his upturned boat and suggests it elsewhere.[10]

Of all the writers, William H. Boardman showed that he knew the boat best when he spoke of the gunwale lines swelling sharply out from the bow, running to amidships in a gradually softening curve, becoming nearly but not quite straight.[11] This straight midsection, rising to the sheer, may be one of the rare traces of aboriginal influence in the guide-boat. It is the form of the spruce bark canoe, which, unlike the more pliable birch, is shaped by two gores or folds at the quarters. Between these sharp bends the stiff bark tends to run straight, as can be seen also in the elm bark canoe at the Peabody Museum in Salem, Massachusetts.

When the right true curve had been found and the eye of the master satisfied, all ribs were fastened to the batten at the proper places. But the edge of the bottom board is an ellipse curving in toward the stems, and the sheer is another ellipse modified by the shape of the ribs and by the flare of the ribs at the quarter. Whatever the curve, the back of each rib had to fit it. Since the back of the rib is square with the side of the rib, the edge toward the ends of the boat from rib center had to be trimmed with a spokeshave until it was in line with the planking. "Now," said Lewis Grant, "we are ready to start putting on the siding."

Notes

1. W.H.H. Murray, *Adventures in the Wilderness* (Boston: Fields, Osgood & Co., 1869).
2. Dwight Grant, 1890 pamphlet, Adirondack Museum.
3. Letter, September 7, 1958.
4. Letter, May 2, 1959.
5. *The Conservationist,* June/July 1948, p. 7.
6. A.K. Bostock, letter, July 20, 1963.
7. Charlton L. Smith, *The Rudder,* August 1943.
8. Westcott Abell, *The Shipwright's Trade* (Jamaica, New York: Caravan Book Service, 1962), p. 76.
9. Letter, January 23, 1964.
10. Kenneth Durant, ed., *Guide-Boat Days and Ways* (Blue Mountain Lake, N.Y.: The Adirondack Museum, 1963), pp. 106, 152, 172, 214.
11. William H. Boardman, *The Lovers of the Woods* (New York: McClure, Phillips & Co., 1901), p. 78.

XVII/Planking

Planking . . . unless it be carefully done, will undeniably mar all the other good Properties belonging to any Ship.

William Sutherland[1]

The perfection and delicacy of guide-boat planking is something to humble a boatbuilder's pride, in the words of John Gardner. In making a guide-boat the chief skill, if not the lion's share of the labor, was in the planking. For this the boatbuilder needed a special aptitude as well as infinite care and patience.

By one of the quirks of nautical terminology, anything that goes on the side of a boat, even though it be only an eighth of an inch thick, is a plank. Dwight Grant and other Adirondack builders called their planks "siding." Two opposite strakes, port and starboard, were "a round of siding."

For his siding Dwight Grant began by using Adirondack pine, a light and hardy timber. "If you got a good tree," wrote Lewis, "there was none better, but a lot of it was shaky and there was too much waste."[2] Dwight changed to Great Lakes white pine, which had narrow sap wood. Some Adirondack boatbuilders used white cedar for siding, but he thought it spongy and puffy when thoroughly wet, thereby destroying the symmetry of the boat. Dwight Grant paid a premium for the privilege of pulling down stacks at the lumber yard so that he could pick out the best 4- and 6-inch planks, straight-grained and ab-solutely free from shakes and knots. Lewis remembered one plank, 4 inches thick, 28 inches wide, and 18 feet long, "without sap." In those days 4-inch planks were really 4 inches thick.

The chosen planks were quarter-sawn into boards ¼ inch thick and 4 to 6 inches wide. Dwight Grant preferred a cut not completely edge-grained but rather with the annual rings at a slant; if a split developed, it was a beveled fissure that could be made watertight with a few clenched tacks.

Before planking could begin on a 16-foot Grant boat, nine pairs of 0 ribs and 10 pairs of numbered ribs were fastened to the bottom board, at approximately 5-inch intervals with the sheer battens sweeping through the tops of the ribs from stem to stern on both sides. Where the planking would bend in toward bow and stern, following the tapered curves of the bottom and sheer, the backs of the ribs were beveled for a snug fit.

In the Grant shop this framework, with the bottom board screwed tightly into the rockered stock plank and the stems stayed to the stanchions overhead, remained in an upright position throughout construction. Planking began at the bottom, so the stock plank was raised to its highest position to give easy access. After four rounds of siding had been applied, the stems were loosened from the carriage overhead and the stock dropped in stages to a lower position so that the rest of the strakes could be put on. Then the boat was taken off the stock.

In Warren Cole's shop at Long Lake, the stock plank was hung on iron pivots that permitted the framework to be turned to any convenient position during construction. Planking at Rushton's in Canton, New York, was done with the boat upside down on fixed stocks.

When Lewis Grant spoke about planking, he made it clear that there were two distinctly separate operations. The first, and most difficult, was getting out the siding. Once the planks were properly rounded and hollowed, lined up with the preceding strakes, and both edges cut with the special Grant plane, the second operation, putting the siding on, merely involved fitting the edges together and fastening the strakes at seams and ribs. If properly got out, the strakes had to fit and, apparently, any carpenter could fasten them to the boat.

In the 1880s Dwight Grant got out the siding and Lester Fox, one of Boonville's best carpenters, put it on the boat. Then Dwight Grant taught Fox how to get it out and the elder son, Floyd Grant, put it on the boat. In 1895, when Floyd had learned how to get it out, Lewis put it on. Finally, when left alone to run the shop, Lewis got it out and put it on. Four men learned how to do it but none recorded their procedure or told us exactly how getting out the siding was done. Dwight Grant gave us no clue when he wrote in his pamphlet:

> The bottom board having been bevelled to the model of each knee, the first round of siding is then put on by being fastened to the knees and bottom board with screws one and one-fourth inches apart and two screws in each round into all of the knees and four screws where it is fastened to the stem.

This notation tells us nothing about the art of planking. This was not modesty or concealment: probably Grant found it unnecessary to explain what he did seemingly without effort. When Lewis Grant was at a loss for words to explain something, he would show us, but only the steps, not the essential manner,

the secret way of the hands. There is a point beyond which the creative man cannot communicate his skills. And so, the process of planking remains, to some extent, the last secret in the boatbuilding trade. The skill and know-how is passed along, but plankers do not write books. John Gardner thinks that an entire book, and not a small one at that, would be required to treat planking adequately. In a number of letters he explained:

> In the guide-boat we find a distinctive hull and a unique style of planking, yet, the perennial planking problems present themselves and must be dealt with in the same general way as they are handled for other boats. . . . It takes a *planker* to plank most hulls properly.
>
> In my opinion the hardest part of the Grant planking operation, by far, was shaping the planks for round and hollow, nevertheless maintaining the highly critical thickness tolerance. The ultimate refinement was Grant's lap cut to uniform exactitude with the special plane he had devised for it.
>
> Generally it is possible to smooth the outside surface of the boat to fairness with plane and sandpaper after the planking is on and fastened, but not in the guide-boat. Its planks are too thin. All shaping of the planks must be done at the bench so that when the planking goes on it is finished and lies perfectly smooth and fair throughout. This may not seem such a tall order to those who have not planked a boat, but a planker will know what is required, and few of my acquaintances in the trade would qualify. Lining the planks is indeed an operation of a higher order, requiring special judgment and a trained eye.[3]

Strakes on a Grant boat (in addition to the garboard there were usually seven) were normally of two pieces to a side. The garboard, the fourth, and the seventh strake were in two equal lengths, spliced amidships; the second, third, fifth, and sixth strakes were made of one long and one short piece and put on in a staggered pattern. Each side of the top strake, or sheer plank, was usually in three pieces. "By using this spliced siding," said Lewis Grant, "you get no cross grain in the length, and can use narrower lumber. Father used quarter-sawed white pine, ¼ inch thick and 4½ to 6 inches wide."

The first two strakes are slightly concave on their outer side and correspondingly convex within. As the

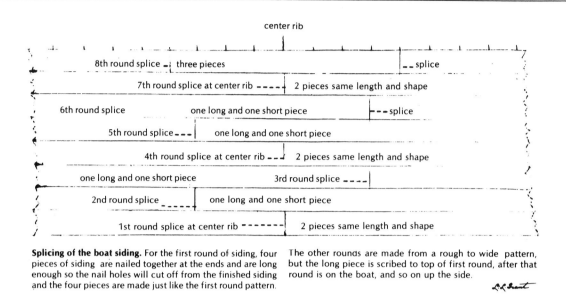

center rib

8th round splice --; three pieces   -- splice

7th round splice at center rib - - - -| 2 pieces same length and shape

6th round splice   one long and one short piece |- - -splice

5th round splice - - -| one long and one short piece

4th round splice at center rib - - -| 2 pieces same length and shape

one long and one short piece   3rd round splice - - - -|

2nd round splice - - - - -| one long and one short piece

1st round splice at center rib - - - - - - -| 2 pieces same length and shape

Splicing of the boat siding. For the first round of siding, four pieces of siding are nailed together at the ends and are long enough so the nail holes will cut off from the finished siding and the four pieces are made just like the first round pattern. The other rounds are made from a rough to wide pattern, but the long piece is scribed to top of first round, after that round is on the boat, and so on up the side.

frame swells and turns upward, this reverses to an outward convexity and inward concavity. For this delicate shaping Dwight Grant made his own planes with concave and convex surfaces. The carpenter was confronted here with a subtle twist, requiring perfect fit and satin surface, within and without. No deviation was possible, nothing scanted, nothing skimped, no faulty joints to be smoothed with sander, no cracks to be concealed with paint or putty. If the work was three-dimensional, the concept included a fourth dimension: the inner tensile quality of wood under the shaping tools and later stresses of the boat in motion. Out of long experience with this task, Lewis Grant could say with pardonable pride:

> All so-called carpenters cannot do that and make a perfect joint. To concave and convex the siding to $\frac{3}{16}$ of an inch was a piece of work that one of the best house-building carpenters in Boonville could not learn to do right. He could work to a straight line but not to a true curve on this fine work. . . .[4]

The first round of siding to be put on was the garboard. Though the Grant shop had patterns for all eight strakes, only the garboards were cut precisely to pattern to fit the double curve of the bevel, tapered and rockered, on the lower edge of the bottom board. The upper edge of the garboard was beveled with Grant's plane to receive the second strake and the sur-

face slightly hollowed to the shape of the ribs, diminishing to flat as it entered the stem rabbet (*see* Gardner Plate VI). The four pieces to make the two garboards were got out in matched pairs laid flat together and nailed at the ends, long enough so that the nail holes could be cut off the finished planks. In this way the pieces for the two sides would be got out as one, and thus would finish to exactly the same shape and width. Made to fit perfectly, they were then fastened to the bottom board and frames.

To make the upper edge as straight as possible, the garboard was widened at both ends, fishtailed dory-fashion, so that it could be almost an extension of the flat bottom board amidships and from there twist nearly 64 degrees to lie flat against the vertical stem (*see* Gardner Plate VIII). The unusual sheer of the guide-boat and the fullness of the bottom board amidships combine to make the space to be planked only slightly wider at the stems than amidships. The flaring ends of the garboard, aided by a slight widening at the ends of all planks, enabled Grant to avoid the problem of "diminish" encountered in many small boats, where the space at the stem is likely to be less than amidships. He was able to achieve a relatively even width of planks above the garboard and avoid the costly use of wide stock.

The distance between the upper edge of the garboard and the top of the sheer batten (ultimately to be the top of the gunwale) was marked off on the sides of the ribs in seven equal intervals at center, stems, and quarters. A batten, run through each set of these marks, was clamped in place and adjusted up and down for fairness. This gave a line for the planks across all ribs. These planking lines, marked on the ribs ahead of time, were normally transferred to the upper edge of the sections of the planking stock when they were clamped on the ribs, the bottom edge being scribed from the upper edge of the plank below.

The pieces for the second strake were first cut roughly to shape, using patterns wider than the finished plank. The longer piece was temporarily clamped in place, slightly overlapping the top edge of the garboard so that its shape could be scribed between the ribs with a pencil line. This lined the bottom edge for planing and beveling to fit the lap on the upper edge of the garboard. While this piece was still clamped in place, the marks on the ribs indicating the width of the second strake were transferred to it. A batten was run through these marks to line out the top edge after the section of plank had been removed from the boat to guide shaping and beveling at the bench. The same procedure was followed for the shorter section, as well as for the rest of the strakes.

As planking proceeded up the sides, strake by strake, the lines setting off the plank spacing would be rechecked using the fairing batten. Here again the batten was adjusted to suit the builder's eye, utilizing, and depending on, the batten's inherent tendency to bend uniformly in fair, continuous, sweeping curves. With the batten as an indispensable aid, the planker sought to establish a fair curve or sweep through a series of points previously determined. By sighting the sweep of the batten, the planker was guided in making slight adjustments in both the points and the batten, until correspondence of both in a fair curve, pleasing to the builder's eye, was achieved.

The extent to which Dwight Grant and his assistants used the marks and the fair batten to line their planks is conjectural. Probably it depended upon individual skills and work habits, and on experience. The spaces marked at the individual stations with the help of the fair batten were useful but not imperative; they were aids to construction rather than positive controls. John Gardner's opinion is that

after a few boats, three marks for the line would be enough. The builder's eye, the inner requirements of the wood, the natural curve of the batten, could compel some deviation at any time. Deliberation, renewed sighting, and compromise ensued.

> . . . it is not just a matter of getting even widths, it is also a matter of insuring fair planking lines. The two, while connected and influencing each other, are not the same thing . . . it would be possible to have even widths with utterly unfair planking lines. While even widths are desirable, they must yield to fair planking lines, and in order to get the latter, it is generally necessary to make slight concessions in the former.[5]

Measurements of completed boats reveal that plank widths, though they appear regular, do not everywhere correspond to the original space marks.

In a succession of simple operations, by virtue of his flexible material, the guide-boat builder transferred incommensurable curves on a bent plank to flat wood. The process is known as spiling and is vastly more intricate on boats with less yielding planks. The spiling batten was unknown in Adirondack boat shops. The ease and advantage won for the builder here were paid for at high price, however, with the care and skill required to work his fragile planks.

If the guide-boat builder escaped the difficulties of diminish and spiling, the peculiar nature of his boat presented other problems. The delicacy of $\frac{3}{16}$-inch pine or cedar permitted scant tolerances in shaping planks hollow or round on either side and sometimes both in a single strake. Here, however, there was another boon peculiar to the guide-boat. The closely spaced, stiff ribs presented the planker with the boat's form in full-size model. The framework of stem, ribs, and bottom board, assembled on the stock plank, anticipated the boat. It awaited its smooth skin of pliant wood. The task was to make the planks fit.

The curves of a boat cannot be converted to a flat surface by any geometry known to the average carpenter. The guide-boat builder worked with materials of infinite variety subject to irregularities, resistance, and atmospheric influence. Sawn spruce crooks could be erratic. Nothing was predictable. A bit of uneven grain or a moment of inattention could produce mutations sure to be exaggerated in the repetition from plank to plank. A deformed rib could not be permitted to push the planking out or to pull it in, making dips or bumps. The builder had to keep a balanced proportion between the stiffness of the plank and the tension of the rib. Pull or pressure over a span of 10 inches (with ribs spaced 5 inches) was never allowed to exceed the capacity of the plank to resist distortion. The ribs were elastic but the planks were very thin. Two soft ribs or two hard ribs in succession could do serious damage. They had to be replaced before planking began.

Even a slight adjustment of rib contours during the planking must have affected to some extent the line of the sheer batten. A hard rib pushed in would raise the batten at that station; a soft rib pulled out would lower it correspondingly. Though these effects would be almost imperceptible, there could be some derangement of the sheer line. "Therefore," said Lewis Grant, "we would gun it again." If necessary the batten was shifted and the sheer line already marked on the ribs was changed.

When the top plank (or sheer plank) was mounted, the batten had to be removed. The shell was then taken off the stock and weighed on the steel yard. Lewis Grant told us that his father knew within two pounds, plus or minus, what any hull should weigh as it came off the stock. Any deviation of more than two pounds had to be explained.

> Where my father decreased the weight of his boats was in the decks, ribs and siding. . . . His first few boats were on the Stanton patterns and if you had looked closely at that 1882 boat [the *Ghost*] you would have seen that the siding, ribs and decks were

heavier than the three [boats] which were built a few years later. . . . When Father got to making the lighter boat, the first siding board at bottom was ¼ inch, the next board up was ¼ inch on the lower edge and tapered to ³⁄₁₆ inch on the top edge, and all the rest of the boards up were ³⁄₁₆ inch thick. There was no doubt 25 lbs. in weight saved right there.[6]

L. Francis Herreshoff considered the boatbuilder (as distinguished from the ship carpenter) an artist, the demands of whose craft were of a superior order because his creations must stand shrinking and swelling when left soaking in the water. In the opinion of Herreshoff, the boatbuilder can easily do cabinetwork and excel the cabinetworker, but the cabinetworker cannot do strong, light boat work. Herreshoff wrote that older boatbuilders could set up the midship section mold on top of the keel with the stem at one end and the sternboard at the other and plank a rowboat mostly by eye. This could only be done, said Herreshoff, with a lapstrake boat where each plank, as it was sprung into place, was fastened to the previous plank with rivets or clenched nails. Herreshoff noted:

> Before 1900 many of the sections along our New England coast had slightly different methods of building. . . . About this time the small boat was beautifully built and every part, model, construction and internal arrangement was for some specific reason the result of much experience, and, as often happens, out of perfect adaptation to use came beauty.[7]

Notes

1. Westcott Abell, *The Shipwright's Trade* (Jamaica, New York: Caravan Book Service, 1962), p. 77.
2. Letter, November 17, 1958.
3. Letters, August 18, September 9 and 15, 1964.
4. Letter, October 17, 1958.
5. Letter, August 23, 1964.
6. Letter, September 7, 1958.
7. *The Rudder,* October 1947. "The Common Sense of Yacht Design" by L. Francis Herreshoff. Copyright 1947, Fawcett Publications, by permission of C.B.S. Publications.

XVIII/The Grant Lap and Plane

Each round of siding lays two and one half inches surface in width and [they] are joined to each other by an improved bevelled lap . . . cut by a tool made for the purpose, cutting all places alike thereby fitting as perfect as the bark to a tree.

H. Dwight Grant[1]

James Beetle, who began building whaleboats in New Bedford in 1827 and claimed to have built over two thousand of them, was bothered by the noise of waves slapping against the under edges of planks in conventional clinker-built craft. He wrote that the clinkering noise the lap boat made in a calm increased with the wind and the sea. The crashing sound it made in a swell frequently scared the whale away.[2] Beetle's remedy was to build a smooth-skin whaleboat. (Beetle's observation of the behavior of whales was sounder than his etymology. He thought that the term "clinker" came from the peculiar noise the boat made going over the water. If he had listened to the sound of clenching hammers in his own boat shop, he might have heard the echo of an ancient word.)

Early boats of the north woods hunters were also made with noisy overlapping planks and for this reason were inferior to the Indian's silent birch canoe. In the mature guide-boat, the planking lap was not accidental, but a studied and critical part of its structure. Only by lapping could a plank as thin as $3/16$ inch be made watertight. Moreover, riveted laps added greatly to the strength and stiffness of the sides.

At the height of the sailing canoe vogue in the United States during the 1880s, there was a great argument over the merits of smooth-skin construction versus lapstrake. W.P. Stephens made an unsuccessful effort to introduce a type of smooth-skin construction known as ribband carvel, used in England for canoes and in Massachusetts and Connecticut for whaleboats, but Americans were strongly prejudiced in favor of lapstrake.[3] In 1886, however, a smooth-skin canoe, the *Pecowsic,* built by F. Joyner of Glens Falls, won the international race on the St. Lawrence River. This was enough to turn sentiment in favor of the smooth skin.

Since trout and deer are as wary as whales, the huntsman and boatbuilder set about removing the defect of the noisy lapstrake. In conventional lapstrake only one edge, the outside upper edge of each plank, was beveled, just enough to fit the angle of the flat inner surface of the overlapping plank above it. Dory builders beveled the edges of both planks for a closer fit, and where the planks approached the stem, the bevels were cut deeper to make a smooth inner and outer surface. Knowing no more than that, the Adirondack boatbuilder needed only imagination to realize that a bevel on both planks would make a smooth skin, but to do that with a plank ³⁄₁₆ inch thick required daring and skill. The outer edge of this thin plank had to be diminished to a vanishing feather edge, not to the sixteenth of an inch W.P. Stephens had suggested and found difficult enough. A feather edge was hard to cut precisely, free-hand, and hard to fit with perfect tightness on the curving side of the boat. Inherent in the material is a limitation: no matter how fine the grain and no matter how sharp the tool, wood cannot be brought down to razor sharpness without danger of its shredding or splintering at the edge when two planks are fastened together with the double row of tiny clenched tacks. The ability of the Adirondack boat-builder to fashion this joint successfully is a mark of extraordinary skill. Under the hand of an expert, the two bevels fit perfectly, and with sanding and painting, the surface appears and feels satin smooth.

Dwight Grant learned to make a feather edge from Henry Stanton of Long Lake. Seeking something better, he designed a rabbet plane and had it cast at the Boonville foundry. It cut a minute, firm, square outer edge on the bevel and a corresponding inner recessed shoulder. Guided by a narrow ridge, called a fence, on the side of the 6-inch steel sole, Grant's plane, sliding along the square-planed edge of the plank, cut a bevel ²¹⁄₃₂ inch wide, leaving a flat outer edge .028 inch thick. On the adjoining plank, it cut a matching shoulder, called the gain, of the same dimensions. These bevels were then butted one against the other as in a scarph joint. Grant dared to execute this on a ³⁄₁₆-inch curved and convex plank and thus combined craft and science in the tradition of the great masters.

Grant designed his plane with a steel sole on a wooden stock in the manner of the old-fashioned molding planes of which he had a fine set (now in the Museum, together with the wooden model for the plane casting and the first experimental plane with a wooden sole). The iron blade of the plane, beveled only on the lower edge, was set slightly askew for a slanting slice (as a man will hold his razor for a close shave). The iron of the plane was held in place by a hardwood edge. Shavings discharged through an opening on the left side of the stock. The depth of the cut was controlled by a shoulder, also called a stop, along the sole opposite the fence. Sole, shoulder, and

Lewis Grant cuts the Grant ship-lap with a specially designed rabbet plane. (Helen Durant)

fence were of one piece of polished steel. Dimensions of cut and angle of bevel were cast into solid metal and could not be varied.

"Father had two lapping planes that were just alike," wrote Lewis Grant. "One he . . . set . . . to take off a thicker shaving starting the lap; the other [he] set to a very fine shaving to finish the lap."[4] Kept very sharp and properly controlled, Grant's plane made a firm, smooth-skin seam, cutting all places alike, beveled face against beveled face, fine, straight outer edge against matching shoulder. Thin planks, hollow and round or straight, molded to the boat's form, fitted the curve of the frame "as perfect as the bark to a tree."

In his *Catalogue and Price List* for 1884, Joyner presented himself as the builder of smooth-skin lapstrake and gave a description of his method. Although the stock Joyner used was heavier than Grant's, their laps seemed to be essentially the same. In 1885 Joyner advertised himself in Stoddard's *The Adirondacks Illustrated* as "the inventor of smooth lap streak joint in hulls."[5] We do not know where Joyner built boats before he established his shop in Glens Falls. His catalogues do not show guide-boats.

In 1882 he sold a large livery fleet to the Prospect

House at Blue Mountain Lake, but those were not guide-boats. We know of no link between Grant and Joyner and no precise evidence of priority in use of the lap. Lewis Grant said that he never heard his father mention Joyner. We have found no evidence that Joyner invented the smooth-skin lap. He may have improved upon it, or he may have introduced this lap to canoe building outside the Adirondacks.

Dwight Grant did not make any claims to invention. The special plane he designed was merely "a tool made for the purpose," and the purpose was to join the boat seams with "an improved bevelled lap," which overcame the disadvantages of the feather lap.

It is not known where Grant derived the idea for his special ship-lap, nor precisely when he began to use it. The *Ghost,* built in 1882, is feather-edged; a boat he built in 1886, originally owned by Henry Covey of Big Moose, and brought to Lewis Grant for repair in 1959, was found to have the new Grant lap. That narrows the date down to within four years.

When Grant's carpenters, Theodore Seeber and Riley Parsons, set up their own shop in Old Forge in 1890, they brought with them a copy of Grant's plane and achieved with it boat planking of amazing fineness. Grant's ship-lap does not seem to have been attempted elsewhere. Outside of Boonville and Old Forge, so far as we know, all Adirondack shops joined their smooth-skin planks with facing feather-edged bevels, which allowed for some adjustment and smoothing by plane and sandpaper after the planks

were fastened to the boat. The Grant lap, resulting in superlative achievement and refinement, imposed severe demands upon the carpenters getting out the siding. Nevertheless, respect for Grant's ship-lap should not diminish our admiration for the skill needed to plank with a feather edge.

Working in Grant's method the carpenter had to make the ship-lap as perfect as humanly possible before the planking was fastened to the boat. If a lap did not come together just right, the plank was taken back to the bench for slight replaning, which could result in a plank slightly narrower in places than first intended. John Gardner describes another kind of adjustment:

> Say that a plank, when put on, did not correspond by as much as one-sixteenth, or possibly even as much as one-eighth [inch] to the curve of the plank below it. If this discrepancy was gradually distributed over the whole length of the plank (say the ends touched but it gaped open the one-sixteenth or the one-eighth in the middle, and there were no humps, lumps, or short holes in either of the mating edges), then the top plank could probably be sprung down ("edge-set" in shop parlance) to give a tight, touching fit throughout. In this case the slight shoulder on the Grant lap would perform an important function. It would catch and prevent any part of the edge from slipping by and going too far. Of course, wherever the lap was pushed together it would mate perfectly, for the special plane insures uniformity.[6]

Notes

1. H. Dwight Grant, 1890 pamphlet, Adirondack Museum.
2. "Beetle Whale Boats," *American Neptune,* October 1943, p. 352.
3. W.P. Stephens, *Canoe and Boat Building* (New York: Forest and Stream Publishing Co., 1889), p. 28.
4. Letter, August 6, 1960.
5. S.R. Stoddard, *The Adirondacks Illustrated* (Glens Falls, N.Y.: published by the author, 1885), p. 252.
6. Letter, September 20, 1964.

XIX/Sny and Scarph

Snying is observed to make the working of Ships Bow very difficult.

William Sutherland[1]

Viking ships and the smaller Viking boats, double-enders with an almost straight run through the midsection of the ship, share with the guide-boat the abrupt upward turn of garboard and sheer at bow and stern. This form answered the need for a bulwark against the entrance of waves into a pulling boat where the use of oars required a relatively low freeboard. This characteristic sharp rise the Norseman called *sny*.

In *Boats and Boatmen* T.C. Lethbridge shows graphically with a child's folded paper boat the relationship between beam and bow. Widening the beam elevates the bow, and vice versa.[2] Carried to an imaginary extreme, which the paper boat would not permit, a further widening amidships with a lengthwise contraction at the sheer might draw the stems back into the tumblehome pattern of Saranac and Long Lake boats.

Sny makes difficulties for the builder and can make planking expensive. As William Sutherland wrote:

> All the Plank, which births up any Ship's Bow, must be converted from principal compass Timber. For altho' Plank may be easily bent flat-ways, yet take what Method you please, it cannot be near so well bent edge-ways, because of the great Disproportion between the Breadth and Thickness.[3]

The problems that beset the great oak ships of the line in England were experienced in miniature five centuries later three thousand miles to the west. There was no boat in which this disproportion was so marked as the guide-boat, where the sny sometimes required planks 6 inches broad at bow and stern, with only $3/16$-inch thickness, increasing the danger of edge-set. Dwight Grant was merely paraphrasing Sutherland when he said that guide-boat planking must be made from "solid timber, not warped nor sprung on but made to fit."[4]

What Sutherland called compass timber Dwight Grant called solid timber. It must be grown timber, that is, with the grain conforming to the curve of the sny. This would call for a straight plank with an upward curve at the end, but trees do not grow that way. Sutherland continued: "no Piece should be molded streighter than its Growth or natural Grain. . . ."[5]

To get the upward sweep of sheer at bow and stern, the Norsemen resorted to a device that they were not the first to use. They called it a *scarph*, a lengthwise splice in planking. A boat built around A.D. 600, long buried in Kvalsund, Norway, and excavated in 1920, embodied important advances in Norse shipbuilding, among which was the use of narrow planks of several pieces spliced end-to-end, instead of the broad, whole strakes used earlier.

Presumably experience had taught them that it was superstition to believe that broad, whole strakes without ekings were so strong. It is soon to be recognised among boat builders that the ship will have much more elasticity at sea with a hull made out of many boards joined together,

wrote A.W. Brøgger and H. Shetelig in *The Viking Ships*.[6] When the Norse builders mastered the use of scarphed strakes, their joined planks were freed from the limitations of straight lumber and thus were able to follow the soaring curve of stems at bow and stern. Compare the relatively flat sheer of the Nydam boat of the fourth century, built of straight wide planks, with the curves of the Kvalsund stems, already lifted beyond practical requirements. These were further developed in the highly scarphed and fancifully embellished prow of the Oseberg ship (about A.D. 800), achieving Venetian elegance.[7]

The small Norwegian double-ender (*faering*) in the Adirondack Museum shows a high sheer achieved through the use of a garboard in three pieces, and three wide strakes, all spliced. As mentioned earlier, the Viking form came to the North American continent through the Orkney Island carpenters, who built high-stemmed York boats for the Hudson's Bay Company. These few analogies in form and construction do not imply any direct relationship between the guide-boat and Norwegian craft. Their builders simply faced similar problems. The challenge of sny and scarph were met in every Adirondack boat shop, though these terms were rarely heard there.

In spite of ample precedents to the contrary, the fetish of single-length strakes lingered on. In his 1889 manual for amateur builders, W.P. Stephens said that small-boat strakes should be "in single lengths if possible."[8] Stephens could indulge this prejudice because his early cruising canoes, derived from Eskimo kayaks via MacGregor's *Rob Roy,* were short with little sheer. For the guide-boat, which had to pull heavy loads across a windy lake, a high prow was desirable. To use a long plank with such a sharp curve at the end not only would have been a costly waste of wide stock but also would have caused a weakness in structure. Edge-setting or warping were not safe, guide-boat planks could not endure steaming. Splicing was necessary and so taken for granted

that Dwight Grant did not even mention it in his pamphlet.

By a slight shift of the grain in line with the sny, two pieces, or sometimes three, precisely scarphed, became stronger than a single piece in which grain did not follow curve. Much depended upon the skill of the carpenter in making two identical bevels with accurately fitting flat surfaces (the "fayed" surfaces in boat shop parlance), holding the two pieces end to end in perfect alignment.

Hervey Garrett Smith wrote in *Boat Carpentry:*

> The simple plank scarf requires more skill to make than a timber scarf, for a mechanically perfect joint must be made if it is to have any value at all . . . both surfaces must be exactly alike—square with the edge and face of the plank, with the same angle of cut, and in absolutely perfect contact. . . .[9]

In the north woods neither skill nor patience was lacking. The scarphs were made with careful precision with the broad and slightly rounded blade of a paring chisel.[10] John Gardner remarked that, in spite of the common prejudice among boatbuilders against short lengths of plank, the spliced planks of the guide-boat never showed structural weakness, and that one reason for this was the careful manner in which the scarphs were made.[11]

The chisel used in the Grant shop had a slightly rounded blade, 2 inches wide and 8 inches long, and a

Grant's chisel for making scarphs. (Helen Durant)

Lewis Grant cutting a scarph. The right hand pushes the chisel; the left hand is held flat upon the blade. (Helen Durant)

wooden handle in a socket. This was the most cherished tool in the shop, kept in a secret drawer to guard against borrowers. The plank to be scarphed was scored lightly with a sharp penknife across its width where the scarph was to begin and on the under side where the splice was to end. The length of Grant's scarphs was 1¹⁷⁄₃₂ inches (*see* Gardner Plate IX). Pushed gently by hand, never struck, the keen blade of the chisel began to slice at the score, taking fine shavings. The builder's right hand pushed while his left lay flat upon the blade with exquisite tactile guidance. The slight knife score on the under side made a fine square edge to the scarf. The joining plank was beveled correspondingly for precise fit. The edge of the scarphed end of the under plank was brought flush with the forward side of the rib. A slight cement of white lead and varnish was applied. The upper plank was laid on while it was firmly fitted into the bevel of the plank below it, and fastened in the usual fashion with three screws that passed through both members of the scarph into the rib. The after end of the scarph was fastened with seven copper tacks, clenched inside. Reinforcing this splice held firmly against the rib were the lengthwise clenched seams with the two adjoining planks. A splice secured in this manner in no way weakened the planking. By permitting adjustment of the grain, the splice greatly strengthened the strake. It took care to make it right.

Lewis Grant made a diagram of the pattern of scarphs on his father's boats, showing the joints staggered from garboard to sheer (*see* Chapter XVIII). They remind one of the Egyptian boats described by Herodotus, which were built by "arranging the planks like bricks, and attaching them by tier to a

number of long stakes or poles till the hull is complete. . . ."¹²

The first, fourth, and seventh strakes on a Grant boat were in two pieces each side, spliced on the center rib; the second, third, fifth, and sixth strakes were each in one long and one short piece, spliced on the second, third, or fourth rib from the center, according to the length of the boat, with the short pieces at alternating ends. Because of the sharp upward curve of Grant's boats at the two quarters, the sheer plank was made in three equal pieces. In this arrangement all splices at the same station were separated by two whole planks, called passing strakes. This is the norm according to the diagram supplied by Lewis Grant. In some Grant boats, even some built by Lewis himself, the seventh strake is in three pieces with two scarphs. On the Waldheim boat (number 12 on the 1890 tally board), strakes 7 and 8 are in three pieces with two scarphs each. This arrangement is also seen on boats 2 and 3 from the 1921 tally board.

In the finest handwork, practice does not always conform to rule. The craftsman must meet exigencies. The scarphs of the 16-foot Grant boat *Virginia* do not follow the usual pattern. The third, fourth, and seventh strakes are each in three pieces instead of two as in Lewis Grant's diagram. When this discrepancy was pointed out to Lewis, he offered an intimate view of boat shop ways and ingenuity. The *Virginia* was built in the early months of 1905 when Dwight Grant was already ailing. Floyd and Lewis had taken over the shop. Lewis explained:

My brother Floyd made the siding for the *Virginia* . . . and if the splices are as you say, this is unusual. However the two pieces of the first round

Detail of Big Fish Eat Little Fish *by Peter Bruegel the Elder, 1556. Ancient boat shop practice prescribed that the outside lap of the scarphs should always point aft. In this engraving the scarphs are lapped the wrong way. This error is discomfiting to an observant boatman.* (Graphic Worlds of Peter Bruegel the Elder, by H. Arthur Klein, Dover, 1963)

on each side had to be made of 6″ stock . . . and the two end pieces for the three-piece 8th round each side, had to be made of 6″ stock and we must have been running low of 6″ stock . . . . Floyd made these rounds in three pieces, each side, out of 4″ and 5″ stock. . . to save the 6″ stock. . . . In making three pieces . . . you get a better straight grain . . . and it should make a very little better boat, but it took quite a little more time to make a three piece round each side, than it did a two piece round, each side. . . .[13]

The saving of wide-stock lumber for places where it was essential was offset by increased labor time.

Lewis thought that after 1916, when he resumed boatbuilding in Boonville, he had always made the scarphs as shown in his diagram; nevertheless, we found that in a 16-foot boat he built in 1921, the seventh strake was in three pieces, no doubt for good practical reasons.[14]

The Oseberg ship, with its fine lines and elaborate decoration, has been called the showpiece of the Viking finds. More than a thousand years after it was buried as the grave ship of a young queen, experts argue about certain anomalous arrangements of the scarphs at bow and stern. One conclusion is that "it was undoubtedly the size and availability of the materials which obliged the builder to dispose joins in their present position,"[15] a practical opinion with which Lewis Grant would have agreed.

Ancient boat shop practice prescribed that the outside lap of the scarph should always point aft, with the flow of passing water. The Viking boats were built this way, with some exceptions. The small Norse boat in the Museum was made thus. On Indian canoes the bark was overlapped with the exposed edges toward the stern so as not to reduce speed.[16] The direction of the scarph was, indeed, the only indication of bow and stern in the shell of a Grant double-ender before the seats and yoke cleats were installed. It felt right to the boatman and was believed to discourage entrance of water through the lap and to prevent the point of a scarph from catching on a nail head or splinter in the dock or on some sharp twig when the boat was hauled ashore. There is some question whether this arrangement of scarph laps in the guide-boat was not more of a tradition, satisfying a sense of fitness, than a practical requirement. A well-made scarph is imperceptible to the touch under varnish or paint on a smooth-skin guide-boat. There is no vulnerable protrusion to catch on anything. Moreover, although the guide-boat is pulled bow first onto the dock or shore, it is launched stern first, against the lay of the scarphs. No damage seems to result.

Though the direction of the scarphs was important in the flexible planking of a Viking boat, which might encounter floating ice slivers in a fjord, and perhaps equally necessary to the loosely folded bark canoe, in the guide-boat it seems to have been only habit. But the tradition, however inconsequential, is strongly felt. A well-known drawing by Peter Bruegel the Elder, *Big Fish Eat Little Fish*, shows a dorylike boat in the foreground, with a sharp sheer at the bow that clearly calls for scarphs in the planking.[17] The drawing shows that the scarphs are there but they are lapped the wrong way. This may be an error of the artist or of the engraver, but it makes an observant boatman uncomfortable.

At the Hubbell Camp on Big Moose there is a fine boat built in the Grant shop (number 11 on the 1904 tally). The scarph of the fourth strake on the center rib laps in the wrong direction. It is not as conspicuous as on the Bruegel boat, and it definitely does not affect quality or performance of that boat, but it is there against Grant's rules and for no explainable reason. One almost welcomes human error in the midst of such perfection.

Notes

1. Westcott Abell, *The Shipwright's Trade* (Jamaica, New York: Caravan Book Service, 1962), p. 81.
2. T.C. Lethbridge, *Boats and Boatmen* (London, New York: Thames and Hudson, 1952), p. 11.
3. Abell, p. 81.
4. H. Dwight Grant, 1890 pamphlet, Adirondack Museum.
5. Abell, p. 77.
6. A.W. Brøgger and Haakon Shetelig, *The Viking Ships* (Oslo, Norway: Dreyers Forlag; Los Angeles: Knud K. Mogensen Publishing, 1951), p. 55.
7. *Ibid.*, pp. 54, 56, 57, 85, 87, 96.
8. W.P. Stephens, *Canoe and Boat Building* (New York: Forest and Stream Publishing Co., 1889), p. 116.
9. Hervey Garrett Smith, *Boat Carpentry*, 2nd ed. (Princeton, N.J.: D. Van Nostrand Co., 1955), pp. 94-96.
10. Henry C. Mercer, *Ancient Carpenters' Tools* (Doylestown, Pennsylvania: The Bucks County Historical Society, 1951), p. 166.
11. John Gardner, *Outdoor Maine*, September 1960.
12. *The History of Herodotus*, Vol. I, p. 160. Translated by George Rawlinson. An Everyman's Library Edition. By permission of E.P. Dutton.
13. Letter, August 6, 1960.
14. Boat number 2 on 1921 tally board, observed at the Maurice dock on Bisby Lake.
15. Brøgger and Shetelig, p. 198.
16. Terence T. Quirke, *Canoes the World Over* (Urbana, Illinois: University of Illinois Press, 1952), p. 98.
17. No. B 139 M 128, 1556. Original in the Albertina, Vienna.

XX/Tacks and Screws

In meane time did Calypso wimbles bring. He bor'd, closde, naild, and
ordered every thing.

Homer, *The Odyssey*[1]

Natural-crook ribs and overlapping seams, common to all guide-boats, clearly have European antecedents. A guide-boat under construction strikingly resembles in miniature a large wooden vessel on the ways, a New England schooner or an earlier British frigate. The seams are traditional Viking lapstrake. Feather-edge or Grant's square-edge ship-lap hides construction under a smooth skin but does not change the essential nature of the craft. Small screws and tiny tacks are only refinements of treenails and spikes reduced to delicate dimensions. Though the number is astonishing (about two thousand flat-head screws and four thousand tacks in a 16-foot guide-boat), there is nothing indigenous to America in these familiar devices. In one respect only were guide-boat fastenings unique: the double row of tacks at the edge of the bevel, one row driven from the outside in, and a parallel row, staggered, from the inside out, are unlike any fastening used in boat shops of Europe or America.

When Nicolas Denys watched the Indians sewing the seams of their birch canoes in New Brunswick sometime before 1650, he noticed that they overlapped the two edges, one over the other, and sewed them with spruce roots. To prevent splitting in a row of close stitches in line with the grain of the bark, they first pierced holes in the bark with a straight thrust of a tapered punch made of splintered turkey leg (or other sharp-pointed bone), which severed the fibers instead of pushing them aside. The bark shell was lined with slats of cedar split to the length they wished and as thin as they pleased.[2]

In the eighteenth century when the Hudson's Bay fur traders arrived, they brought steel hatchets, crooked knives, and steel canoe awls. Triangular or square in cross section, the corners of the canoe awl cut the fibers in the manner of the bone piercer, which it replaced.[3] Square or triangular awls were not confined to the North American fur trade. The Chinese and Japanese used similar tools. In 1703 Joseph Moxon, an early historian of carpentry, described an awl with a square blade "which enters the wood better than a round blade because it breaks the grain." In 1846 Charles Holzapffel mentioned an awl "sharpened with three facets as a tapering, triangular prism."[4] These tools were pushed straight into the bark or thin wood, never turned or twisted.

All carpenters knew the danger of boring holes too close to the margin of thin wood. Early American shingle makers, working with bristle oak, devised a special tool that pushed a chisel point across the grain to avoid separating the fibers. Dory makers used a flat, chisel-pointed nail that cut the fibers as it entered the wood. When a dory nail was to be driven close to the edge of thin wood, the hole was precut with a chisel-pointed awl.[5]

Indian and white man used similar tools. They knew as well as the Homeric Greeks had known how to split cedar into the long, thin slats seen by Nicolas Denys in the early seventeenth century, and they knew the risks in using this fissile material. Wood so easily riven could quickly split along a line of tacks. The tissue-thin feather edge in a guide-boat lap was even more fragile than canoe bark and in like danger of splitting along the row of tacks. The Grant bevel, at its edge, was only .028 inch, a hazardous thinness for cedar or pine. Where the point of the tack entered, within $\frac{2}{16}$ inch of the beveled edge, the wood was no more than $\frac{1}{16}$ inch thick, and on a feather edge it could be even less; the joined bevels amounted to no more than $\frac{3}{16}$ inch. Preparing a row of tack holes along such a tenuous edge, the Adirondack boat-builder ran the same risks as the squaw sewing birch rind. Accordingly, to pierce holes for their tacks, the Adirondack boatbuilders used an awl, minutely pointed and diamond-shaped in cross-section, with two sharp cutting edges. The sharp edge was pressed against the grain "until you felt it snap," said Carl Hathaway, guide-boat builder of Saranac Lake. Once the two frail bevels were firmly clenched, face to face, the plank regained its full strength.

In spite of the intensive mechanization of his boat shop in Saranac Lake, Willard Hanmer continued to use the diamond-shaped hand awl, but some Adirondack boat shops in later years replaced the hand awl with a spiral ratchet drill with a very fine bit. After Lewis Grant had installed electricity, he used a high-speed drill with a reduction bit to drill the tack holes. The fiber-cutting properties of the modern high-speed drill appear to have originated from the primitive bow drill and the pump drill, which employed a wraparound thong to twirl a spindle. Chinese shipbuilders used a device like that and it was known to the Eskimos and the Penobscot Indians.[6]

The north woods builder making a wooden boat potentially more fragile than birch bark found that he could hold his feathered laps safely with two rows of tacks: inside, three heads in line on every seam be-

tween the ribs, and outside, heads in groups of four, interrupted by the brass screws holding the planks to the ribs. On a guide-boat in natural wood, the copper heads and clenched points gleam through the varnish in a pattern of pleasant repetition. Though it varies slightly with different makers, the pattern is essentially the same and suggests faintly the stitching on a bark canoe.

The resemblance to Indian stitching and the use of similar tools will not support a theory of derivation. The most that can be said in the light of present knowledge (and much remains to be learned) is that two groups of boatbuilders of disparate origins, living in close proximity though working in different materials, found the solution to similar problems by similar means.

On the frontier and in the backwoods, culture and technology developed unevenly, never in precise chronology. Where sawn planks and metal fastenings were not to be had, resourceful pioneers contrived portable lapstrake boats of riven cedar, fastened with thongs of rawhide or split spruce roots.

Within the period that concerns our boat, the expedient of riven planks was scarcely necessary. Settlements providing sawn boards and hardware were accessible to most Adirondack waters. Before 1825 sawmills encircled the periphery of the north woods (and before the mills there were saw pits). Boonville and Plattsburgh both had their first sawmills in 1769. Within the north woods the first sawmill in Essex was erected in 1784; Lake Pleasant had one in 1795; Saranac and Ausable in 1806; Minerva in 1807; and Indian Lake in 1849.[7]

The Adirondack guide-boat could not have developed as it did without the proximity of sawmills and hardware stores where small screws and tacks could be obtained. The early, crude, hand-wrought nails were avoided by the cabinet maker, who preferred to glue, dovetail, or peg together his furniture.[8] The small boat maker would gladly have done the same had modern glues, such as epoxy, with their waterproof bonding power, been available. Craft in guide-boat form have recently been constructed using epoxies. These have only a single row of tacks to hold the bevels together while the adhesive sets. The classic guide-boat, however, came before epoxy and before marine plywood. Intricate skill made up for the lack of such useful materials. The

Tacks set in pre-drilled holes, ready for clenching.
(Adirondack Museum)

guide-boat maker joined his seams with a thin layer of white lead or varnish for waterproofing and fastened them with a multitude of small tacks.

From documented records it is clear that the construction of the guide-boat improved with the development of machine-made tacks and screws. A tackmaking machine had been invented in 1810, and machine-made pointed screws were available in 1846.[9] The portable boats seen at Saranac Lake and Long Lake, mentioned by various writers from 1830 to 1845, may have been fastened with primitive blunt-pointed screws or entirely with nails like those found in the so-called "bookcase" boat (1848) at Brandreth Lake. Copper tacks, available soon after 1810, were only a reduced version of the clench nails well known in the boat trade. The first iron cut nails were too brittle to clench, and hand-forged nails continued to be used for boat work[10] until ca. 1870, when machine-cut clenchable nails became available. Yet hand-forged nails were not practical in a guide-boat, considering the quantity required.

The first screws and clench tacks were made of iron

and were of surprising durability. Iron screws used to fasten the *Ghost* in 1882 still held the boat firm and seaworthy in 1965. Replacement of iron screws and tacks with brass and copper tacks proceeded irregularly in different places and with different builders. Dwight Grant appears to have used both screws and tacks of iron, except on varnished boats where he used brass. Lewis Grant wrote us:

> . . . I think my father used iron tacks on the first boats he built at the Rice Brothers' mill and perhaps a few years in his shop . . . he never used any iron tacks on guide-boats that I can remember, but one day when my brother Floyd and I were building boats, I said to Floyd, I wonder why father bought all those small iron tacks that are in the cupboard and Floyd said that father had to use iron tacks when he started building guide-boats as he could not get copper tacks in those days. I was only a year old when Father started building guide-boats but my brother Floyd was 13 and he sure knew.[11]

Though they were available elsewhere, copper tacks may not have been for sale in Boonville in 1879. The trouble with iron screws became acute in any repair job: rusted threads made them difficult to remove without damaging the wood. After repairing several boats fastened with iron screws, Lewis decided never to use them below the waterline.

Piercing holes and setting several thousand tacks was a tedious job. Adirondack shops used a great variety of arrangements to facilitate the work. In the Grant shop the boat was built right side up on adjustable stocks that could be raised or lowered. Grant started his planking with the stocks in high position where the clenching hand could reach through the ribs. Warren Cole fastened his framework to a rockered plank-on-edge, which revolved between two upright posts. Cy Palmer appears to have planked his boats bottom side up, as did Rushton at Canton, New York, and Hanmer at Saranac Lake. The Hanmer stock tipped to give the clencher better access to the inside of the hull. Whatever the arrangements of the stocks, however, the Adirondack style of fastening with a double row of tacks to be clenched inside and out required that the hull be kept clear of any temporary molds or other obstructions to allow the free use of hammer and clenching iron.

Someone had to stick four thousand tiny tacks into each 16-foot guide-boat, and little fingers could be

Willard Hanmer clenching tacks. (Adirondack Museum)

deft at this, whether induced by beguilement or bribery. So in many Adirondack boat shops, children stuck the tiny copper tacks into the holes pierced for them, and the carpenter clenched them later. The granddaughter of Caleb Chase of Newcomb said she was paid five cents for each row of tacks once around the boat.[12] Wright Cole and Leslie Palmer, sons of Long Lake guide-boat builders, had similar memories. Willard Hanmer said, "When you got into trouble at school, when you got home you would have more tacks to stick."[13]

"I never stuck many tacks in boat siding when I was a boy going to school," wrote Lewis Grant. "Perhaps a few when Father and I were alone in the shop. The year he built 25 guide-boats [1890–1891] he had six men working for him and he did not want me to get in the way."[14] (Young Lewis had other responsibilities: he did the house chores, shoveled the winter walks free of snow, and got the shop fire going in the morning.) Lewis continued:

> After I left the Club and came home to take care of Mother I wired the shop for electricity, and I would put the holes in the siding in the daylight and stick

the tacks in the evening when the holes showed up fine with the lights. Mother liked to stick tacks for me and we were in the shop one evening in March, 1921, and it was snowing and glowing and Mother stuck the tacks and I clenched and headed them. She was 84 years old at the time and happy to think that she could help me on boat work.

A deft stroke of the setting hammer brought the tack heads level with the wood without a dent. Simultaneously, in the other hand, a clenching iron turned the point of the tack away from the thin edge of the bevel, to curl across the grain back into the thicker wood. Skillfully done, this operation left the flat copper head and the clenched point flush with the smooth skin of the hull. With sanding and varnish, heads and points were clearly visible yet impalpable to the touch.

Dwight Grant wanted only $\frac{1}{16}$ inch for the clench. On $\frac{3}{16}$-inch planking he used $\frac{1}{4}$-inch copper tacks (2-ounce tacks, they were called, referring to the weight per thousand).[15] When upper strakes were less than $\frac{3}{16}$ inch, he used $1\frac{1}{2}$-ounce tacks, $\frac{3}{16}$ inch long. Those were very small tacks to hold boat seams firmly fastened through many years of repeated exposure to sun, wind, rain, and pounding waves.

At bow and stern the boat curved to a point where it was impossible to wield the setting hammer. Here, for a short distance from the stem, both rows of tacks had to be driven from the outside. Along the midship section, the garboard was fastened to the bottom board bevel with three $\frac{5}{8}$-inch tacks from the outside in each rib space, clenched on the bottom; two $\frac{1}{2}$-inch tacks were driven through the bottom and clenched on the plank. At about two feet from the stem (at rib number 7 on a 16-foot boat), the upward twist of the garboard and the corresponding angle of the bevel made it impossible to use clench fastenings. From there on, the garboard was fastened with screws into the edge of the bottom board.

The arrangement of tacks and screws was uniform on Grant boats: four tacks from without and three from within on each seam between the ribs, and the screws in regular order on each rib. In his later boats Dwight Grant used three screws on each rib, but this was not always the case. Lewis Grant, in 1960, repaired boat number 14 on the 1886 tally board, built originally for Henry Covey of Big Moose. He wrote:

I thought that Father always put that center screw in the ⁹⁄₁₆" siding but [this] boat tells me that he did not. Of course Jim's boat is 74 years old . . . but I think it would have been in better condition if it had that center screw when built. I have repaired a lot of my father's boats that were old but this is the oldest and the first one I ever repaired that had only two screws in the ⁹⁄₁₆" siding, so Father must have started to use the center screws . . . soon after that boat was built as was done on account of the siding being so thin.[16]

Great accuracy was required in drilling the screw holes to ensure that they came precisely in the middle of the ⅜-inch-wide rib. Lines were drawn across the bottom board to guide the #6 screws into the rib feet. A clamp was placed at the top of each rib to prevent splitting when the screw was put through the wale and sheer plank. On painted boats these screws in the wale were countersunk and puttied; on varnished boats the brass heads were set almost flush with the wood, only slightly countersunk. Willard Hanmer was very particular in having all the slots in the screw heads parallel.

A count of tacks and screws and their sizes for the guide-boat and accessories can be found in Appendix D.

The total number of tacks and screws in boats of the same size would vary only slightly, depending upon the number of scarphs and possible irregularities. Dwight Grant and his sons, by prudent arrangement, employed the minimum of fastenings in the smallest practical sizes.

Notes

1. *Chapman's Homer, The Odyssey* & *The Lesser Homerica*, ed. Allardyce Nicoll, Bollingen Series XLI (Pantheon Books, 1956), II, p. 96. By permission of the Princeton University Press.
2. Nicolas Denys, *The Description and Natural History of the Coasts of North America*, trans. W.F. Ganong (Paris, 1672; Toronto: The Champlain Society, 1908), I, pp. 420–422; II, p. 421.
3. E.T. Adney and H.I. Chapelle, *The Bark Canoes and Skin Boats of North America* (Washington, D.C.: Smithsonian Institution, 1964), pp. 21, 29.
4. Charles Holzapffel, *Turning and Mechanical Manipulations* (London, 1846), II, p. 539, as quoted in H.C. Mercer, *Ancient Carpenters' Tools*, 2nd ed. (Doylestown, Pennsylvania: The Bucks County Historical Society, 1951), pp. 176–77, 210; Joseph Moxon, as quoted in Mercer, p. 176.
5. John Gardner, letter, August 1, 1965.
6. Mercer, pp. 211–213.
7. *Sixth Annual Report of the Forest, Fish and Game Commission of the State of New York* (Albany: James B. Lyon, State Printer, 1901), pp. 285–306.
8. Mercer, p. 235.
9. W.W. Cross & Co., letter, August 11, 1959.
10. Mercer, p. 238.
11. Letter, May 12, 1959.
12. Leslie Rist, letter, May 26, 1958.
13. Willard Hanmer, tape recording, Adirondack Museum.
14. Letter, March 14, 1959.
15. W.W. Cross & Co., letter, September 1, 1965.
16. Letter, March 14, 1960.

XXI/Gunwale, Decks, Accessories, and Hardware

Our boats weigh one hundred and ten pounds each; the tackle and furniture of each consists of two oars, a scull and a yoke wherewith to carry it across portages . . . .

F.S. Stallknecht[1]

The gunwale was one continuous piece running from stem to stern on either side of the boat, outside the sheer plank and flush with its top edge. It was wider at the center, diminishing toward bow and stern. The thickness of the gunwale increased from the top to the bottom edge to conform to the flare of the boat's siding. This increasing thickness at the bottom edge was also necessary so that the outer surface of the wale would hold the oarlock straps at right angles to the bottom board and therefore to the surface of the water (*see* Gardner Plates IX and XI). The height of the gunwale amidships varied according to the length of the boat and the height of the ends of the sheer plank in the stem rabbet. In the Grant shop it was noted on the tally boards as "depth center." For most of the regular Grant boats the gunwale height was from 11 to 11¾ inches. On a short, 9-foot-bottom boat, such as number 6 on Grant's tally board for 1894, it was only 10¾ inches at center.

Dwight Grant used oak and sometimes cherry or white ash for his gunwales. On a few short boats, where lightness was required, he used spruce. The wales were bent after soaking them in burlap sacking kept wet with hot water.

Dwight Grant stated in his 1890 pamphlet that his deck circles were made of "red elm backed by natural crooks of spruce root for carlin and decked with pine, oak or walnut." Only in the design of decks did the guide-boat builder ever indulge in ornamentation. He might use contrasting grains and colors in the wood, or vary the shape of the covering piece that overlaid the joint in the deck planks. Such modest ornamentation became a signature by which the builder was recognized.

Decks were set into the top of and flush with the gunwale and the sheer strake. In the Grant shop the red elm deck circles that finished the inner, curved edge of the decks were bent in a steam box. To throw off water, deck surfaces were given a slight camber or sometimes a narrow raised frame along the inboard edge (*see* Gardner Plates X and XI).

In Grant boats each deck was strongly reinforced from underneath by two cross beams about 1 by ½ inch, put in square with the top of the siding and butted against the wales through notches in the sheer planks. They were needed to stiffen the end structure and to carry the weight of the guide sitting astride the bow deck while taking on passengers (*see* Gardner Plates X and XI).

Guide-boat carlins are two-piece, curved members

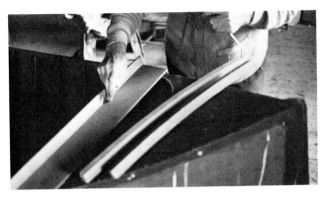

Lewis Grant uses a device for scribing the deck curve. (Helen Durant)

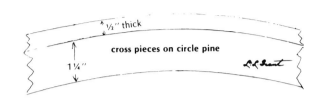

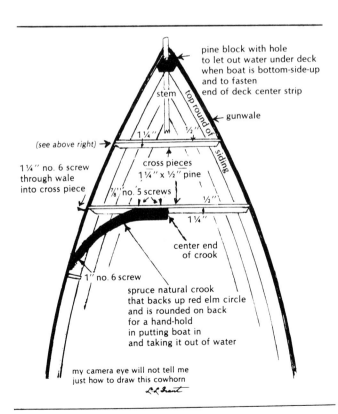

that lie under the curved edge of the deck. The two pieces join on the deck beam that is farther from the stem, and are faced by the deck circles. The shape of the carlin is not adapted to the support of the deck; rather, it braces the sides from wale to wale. When the guide launched the boat from a slanting dock or a shelving beach, he straddled the deck and held it steady with his knees, but his weight was forward of the carlin. When the guide vaulted in over the deck,

as the bow took to water, his outstretched hands grasped the gunwale. This put considerable strain on the boat at that point. In the earliest guide-boats, when decks were planked transversely, these planks served as bracing thwarts. When the circle deck was adopted, with fore and aft planking, it was necessary to supply some cross bracing. Grant's carlins are these braces, curved to admit the rower's back, or to make room for the knees and arms of forward-facing fishermen.

Grant's carlins were sturdy natural-spruce crooks, wider at the bottom than at the top edge, placed under the rim of the deck behind the deck circles where the hand grasped them to lift the bow out of the water (*see* Gardner Plates X and XI). Two men, carrying a boat between them for a short distance, without removing oars or other gear, could hold on to the edges of the decks. Grant made his carlins rounded and smooth for a comfortable grip. Hanmer cut a large oval in his decks for the hand hold.

Early boats may have a hole in the bow deck to hold the staff of a jack light or, on festive occasions, a flag staff. Lewis Grant said that his father drilled a hole for the jack staff only if the customer asked him to, but he thought that often the guides themselves drilled the hole.

To let out water that accumulated under the deck when the boat was turned upside down, a limber hole was bored through the deck, which drained through a corresponding hole in the stem cap. The block under the stem end of the deck had a large limber hole, ½ inch by ⅜ inch, cut from top to bottom through the side that fits against the inner face of the

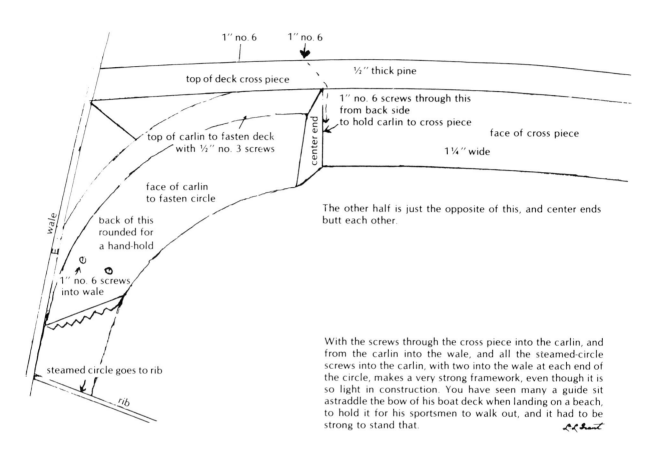

1″ no. 6   1″ no. 6

½″ thick pine

top of deck cross piece

1″ no. 6 screws through this
from back side
to hold carlin to cross piece

center end

face of cross piece

top of carlin to fasten deck
with ½″ no. 3 screws

1¼″ wide

face of carlin
to fasten circle

The other half is just the opposite of this, and center ends
butt each other.

back of this
rounded for
a hand-hold

wale

1″ no. 6 screws
into wale

With the screws through the cross piece into the carlin, and
from the carlin into the wale, and all the steamed-circle
screws into the carlin, with two into the wale at each end of
the circle, makes a very strong framework, even though it is
so light in construction. You have seen many a guide sit
astraddle the bow of his boat deck when landing on a beach,
to hold it for his sportsmen to walk out, and it had to be
strong to stand that.   *L. L. Grant*

steamed circle goes to rib

rib

stem, as shown in Grant's sketch. After the decks
were installed with their supporting members, the
boat was structurally complete.

Although some early travel writers reported that
the guides carried the boats on their heads, this must
have been appearance rather than reality. The classic
guide-boat was borne on a shoulder yoke. In the hazy
photo of Cortez Moody with his boat (page 21), there
appears to be a block fastened against the sheer plank
to support a yoke.[2] Yoke cleats were mounted inside
the gunwale. Projections on either side of the yoke fit
into the slots of the yoke cleat, slightly ahead of the
center rib.

*Hanmer cut a large oval in his decks for the
hand hold. (Adirondack Museum)*

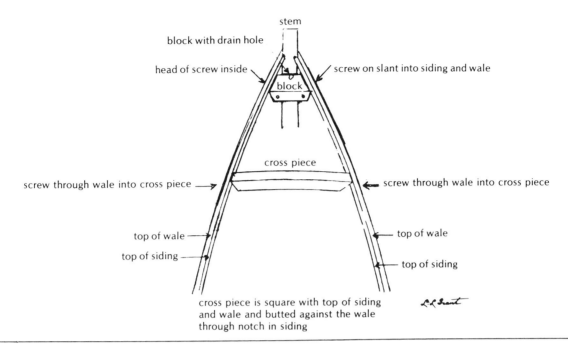

stem

block with drain hole

head of screw inside

screw on slant into siding and wale

block

cross piece

screw through wale into cross piece →

← screw through wale into cross piece

top of wale

top of wale

top of siding

top of siding

cross piece is square with top of siding
and wale and butted against the wale
through notch in siding

The extended arms of the yoke cleats governed the up-and-down movement of the boat on the carry and controlled side-sway. Typically the forward section of the yoke cleat spanned a distance from the slot of about four rib spaces toward the stem while the aft section spanned about two rib spaces from the slot toward the stern. This inequality was most important for carrying the boat. The extended arms equalized the weight of the boat to make an almost perfect balance with a slight downward pressure at the stern. The exact proportion for the fore and aft yoke cleat pieces varied with the builder.

In the Warren Cole boat that Kenneth Durant acquired in 1905, the yoke cleat ran four rib spaces forward of the slot at center and one rib space aft. This can be clearly seen in the photo of the Warren Cole boat exhibited at the Madison Square Garden Sportsmen's Show in 1899. Caleb Chase and others around Long Lake and Saranac used this same pattern. Although evidence at hand is not altogether conclusive, it appears that Dwight Grant did not like such uneven arms on the yoke cleat. Judging from photographs, he was not a tall man like Warren Cole. Three rib spaces forward was probably all the forward reach he needed or could manage comfortably.

Dwight Grant had begun to lengthen the after arm before 1890,[3] using a cleat spanning three rib spaces forward and two aft. The yoke cleat on the *Virginia,* built in 1905, spanned three rib spaces forward and three aft; a boat built by Lewis Grant in 1922 had the same yoke cleat arrangement. Because he had to place the balancing notch forward of the center rib, in order to use arms of equal length, Grant was forced to make the after arm slightly the longer of the two by perhaps an inch and a half.

Kenneth Durant wrote to John Gardner:

At first I thought that the cleats on the *Virginia* had been removed for painting and replaced afterwards, however, this cannot have happened because the yoke will fit on the ribs only in the position in which they are now. I cannot explain it. . . .[4]

And again Durant wrote:

The yoke cleat on the *Virginia* looks wrong; it *is* wrong . . . but who am I to tell a Grant how to shape the cleats? . . . The evidence accumulates that Floyd made no mistake; that he shaped yoke cleats according to the Grant pattern of that day . . . so what is wrong with the cleat on the *Virginia?* . . . It is too long on the after end . . . it is wrong by Dwight Grant's own standard which thought to reduce all superfluous wood. . . . You do not need all that wood abaft the notch to support the boat.[5]

Grant boat number 11 of 1904, with seat risers. He made the arms of the yoke cleat of even length. (Helen Durant)

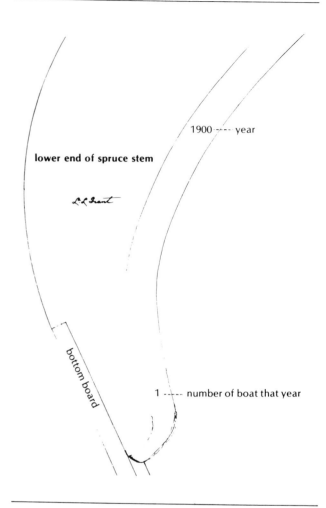

lower end of spruce stem

1900 ---- year

bottom board

1 --- number of boat that year

Grant's yoke cleats were molded to reduce weight. Later, Lewis Grant made his cleats half round on a square base, somewhat heavier than his father's. "The guides were no longer carrying the boats," Lewis explained. The date and number of a Grant boat can be found on the inner side of the yoke cleat and on the lower end of the stems. Sometimes, one seat and the yoke as well would carry the number.

Neck yokes were carved by hand from a single piece of wood. Grant used pine, cedar, or basswood. Sometimes they were fashioned from a small cedar log, the curve of the trunk forming the top of the yoke, the underside shaved thin. Thus the natural grain was used to combine strength and lightness. The Museum has a specially curved shave made by Warren Cole for shaping neck yokes as well as a partially completed yoke made by Lewis Grant.

"All my first class boats," wrote Dwight Grant in his pamphlet, "are furnished with three cane seats and one cane back rest for the stern seat. The frames are made to fit the boat and are strung with heavy binding cane." Dimensions and construction details can be read from John Gardner's Plate XIII.

It was ever the boast of its builder that the guide-boat had no fixed thwarts. Bow and stern seats with light frames made of white ash or elm, and caned, were fastened with round-headed screws to slender risers. The middle seat was adjustable to the arms and legs of the rower and could be removed to make way for the guide's head and yoke on the carries, or to give room to stow a load of duffel. Earlier flat board seats were replaced by caned seats not merely to make the boats more luxurious. Caned seats were lighter and had a slight give: they kept the rower in place.

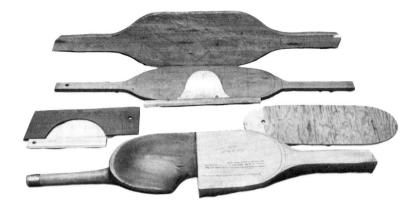

Left: *Neck yokes are carved from a single piece of wood. (Helen Durant)* Below: *Back rest of Warren Cole boat. In a properly constructed back rest, the side pieces extend above the cross bar. When the oars are raised without unshipping, these points catch the blades. (Adirondack Museum)*

The customary back rests were formed of two light side pieces supporting an arched top, and a shorter lower brace, with cane stretched between. The side pieces generally extended above the top crossbar in two conspicuous points, or ears, which had a useful function: when the rower in the middle seat wished to raise his oars from the water without unshipping, he would catch the blades within those points. This is impossible with the one-piece bow frame that Dwight Grant created with steam box and clamps. Parsons of Old Forge copied Grant's design, but we have not observed it elsewhere in the north woods. Kenneth Durant considered the bow frame design defective and could only assume that Dwight Grant always unshipped his oars before launching or landing.

Some builders supplied a removable back rest for the middle seat for the comfort of the middle seat passenger, who always sat facing aft to keep his or her

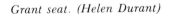

Grant seat. (Helen Durant)

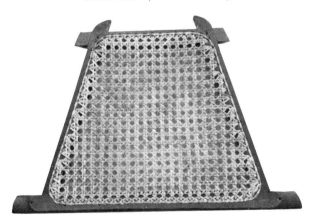

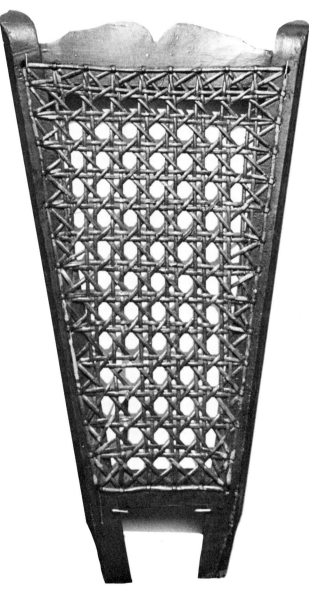

Lewis Grant fashions an oar; Kenneth Durant watches. (Helen Durant)

legs out of the rower's way. These backs were considered excess weight on long journeys, so the middle seat passenger used a pack basket or some other piece of luggage to lean against. Lewis Grant confirmed that his father sometimes made a light, narrow back that could be propped between the yoke and the seat.

One of the earliest discoveries by boatmen was that in some waters the bottom is too deep to be reached with a pole. Paddles were invented very early. Pictures of Egyptian boats in antiquity show paddles in use, not only for moving the boat, but also for steering. True rowing may not have evolved until the sides of boats rose too high for effective use of paddles.[6]

Paddles were fairly simple to make. The Indians had established a useful pattern, which was copied or varied to suit special needs or the fancy of the builder. Although the guide-boat was primarily a pulling boat, the paddle was essential equipment.

For the oars, the chief propulsion tool of the guide-boat, the Indians supplied no precedent. In its simplest form the oar is merely a blade with a shaft and a handle, which propel the boat by pulling against the water over a fulcrum. The well-made guide-boat oar is almost as complex and ingenious in design as the boat it propels.

The oars had to be properly balanced to exert the utmost propulsive force with the least exertion. They had to be strong to hold the boat in the rapids or to make a dash after a swimming buck. Like the boat, the oars had to be light because they were carried over the portages. The noise they made in the rowlocks when the oarsman rowed vigorously had to be silenced through gentle strokes when he approached a trout hole.

Oars were hand-shaved from planks cut from the butt log of soft maple. Though eight feet long, when properly fashioned they balanced so perfectly that they had an unbelievable lightness in the hand. Yet, they stood the steady pulling of the strongest man.

Few who have handled guide-boats inspect the intricacy of the oar design. The handle, nicely finished to fit the grasp of the fingers, slightly tapered for a firm hold, abruptly enters the heaviest part of the oar: the butt of the loom, which continues through the oarpin into the shaft. The octagonal shape of the loom is gradually rounded before the shank widens into the flat of the blade. The shaft is flexible and springy to take up the stress of the long pull and to ease the shock of the stroke on the sensitive craft. The strength and flexibility of the shaft, the size of the blade, the position of the fulcrum, and the force extended by the rower are all factors in a finely balanced equation. Just as the boat itself is sufficiently stable to perform all its necessary functions but will

Shaping an oar handle. (Helen Durant)

The blade of the oar maintains a raised spine on each side for stiffening. (Helen Durant)

upset if carelessly managed, so the slender, pliant oar is capable of powerful leverage and swift maneuver but will break if misused.

The round in the lower end of the shaft flattens gradually at the blade but continues into a raised spine on each side of the blade for stiffening. The spine disappears gradually as the blade widens. The loom is shaped so that its angled surfaces fit smoothly within the rowlock horn.

Customarily, oars for a guide-boat of 15 feet or longer were about 8 feet long and weighed about 7 pounds. Two oars could be made from a single piece of wood 2 inches by 6 inches by 12 feet. The pattern was in the shape of a finished oar. Dwight Grant had his oars roughed out somewhat larger than his pattern at the local mill. They were then run over the jointer and planed down. Final planing was done by hand at the Grant shop. The thickness was determined by a gauge at the point on the shaft where the oarpin would be attached. A string, stretched along the centerline of the pattern, fastened with tacks 3 inches from each end, showed any warp either way, by divergence from the surface or from the centerline. For the small Raiders the guide might demand a lighter oar, about 7 feet 4 inches long, made of spruce.

After Dwight Grant's death, Lewis designed a mechanical oar-blade shaper. A special device held the oar while moving the face of the blade across the edge of the teeth of a 7-inch circular saw driven by an electric motor. Cutting with a grinding action, the saw teeth shaped the concave face of the blade where it joined the reinforcement of the extended shaft. Lewis also devised another shaper to cut the corners from the square-roughed looms and shafts to make them octagonal (thereby reducing weight).

The Adirondack Museum has the hand shave with which Lewis shaped oars and paddles in the early days. It was made by a blacksmith from a file, the usual source of high-carbon steel for handmade cutting tools in those days.

Dwight Grant's 1890 pamphlet continued:

The bottom board is protected by two shoes of five eighth inch band iron put on with screws and counter-sunk at each end under a solid brass nickel-plated stemband, reaching from bottom to top of stem.

Lewis Grant invented a special device to hold the oar while moving the face of the blade across the edge of the teeth of a seven-inch circular saw. (Helen Durant)

The shoes protected the edge of the bottom board where it joined the garboard. On Grant boats two shoe irons were customary, but on an occasional boat Grant seems to have added a third band in the middle of the bottom board, because in 1958 Lewis wrote that one of his father's boats, in the shop for repair, had three galvanized iron shoes.[7] Later Lewis wrote that his father used ⅝-inch black band iron on his first

nickel-plated brass stemcaps ¾ inch wide and ⅛ inch thick

hole in stemcap to let water out of boat after it has been washed out and is bottom-side-up

center deck piece

stemcap

screw

screw

decking

screw

wale

painter ring and staple

last round of siding

nickel-plated brass stemband

finishing nail to hold stemband to stem

spruce stem

finishing nail

groove in stem for siding

Grant boat number 11 of 1904 with three bands of metal shoes. (Helen Durant)

boats but that ultimately he was able to obtain ½-inch galvanized band iron, which was narrower but thicker and better.[8] Iron shoes were used on painted boats in the Grant shop; varnished boats had brass shoes. While the wood of planking and frame endured all ordinary use, the protective metal strips were expendable and needed occasional replacement.

According to Talbot Bissell, the shoe irons on Warren Cole's boats were thin ribbons of wrought iron, ¾ inch wide. These strips had to be hammered on an anvil until they became slightly bow-shaped to fit the curve of the bottom board. Then holes were drilled for the screws, one every three inches, and the screws countersunk.[9]

Grant's stembands had a groove in the back that fitted over the stem (*see* Gardner Plate XIV). Flat at both ends, they ran down the thin cutwater and out along the bottom board until the flat end covered the wrought iron shoe of the bottom board. Many builders omitted a stem cap, letting the top of the stemband finish at the line of the gunwale with a ring for the painter.

The design of the caps with which some builders covered the tops of the stems often became a signature of the builder. Grant's stem caps were nickel-plated. They were unique in having a hole drilled through. When the boat was turned over, water that might have caught under the sheer of the deck could drain out there. Lewis Grant did not remember how early his father began to use this type of stem cap, but he reported in 1959 that one of his father's boats still at White Lake (Sullivan County, New York) did not have stem caps.[10] It was boat number 13 on the tally board for 1888. Lewis thought that it had been sold to one Bill Dart, but the tally board for that year does not give the names of the purchasers. Lewis also mentioned that his father's former carpenters, Parsons and Seeber, used stem caps but of a very light metal bent over the tops of the stems.

A supplier of boat hardware, R.A. Moore, of Kensington, Connecticut, issued a catalog in 1883 showing stembands in three patterns named respectively for three guide-boat builders: Fred W. Rice and William A. Martin, both of Saranac, and H. Dwight Grant of Boonville. An 1892 edition of the Moore catalog, which Lewis Grant once showed us, said that the Grant stemband had a V back and was the lightest of all.

Grant's rowlocks consisted of steel or bronze pins, about ½ inch in diameter, attached to horns that swiveled against the sides of the oar looms. The pins fitted into sockets on metal straps screwed to the outside of the gunwales. Two sets of sockets were provided to allow the oars to be used at two different stations. Lewis Grant wrote us:

> . . . you will see from the picture you took of the boat [the *Ghost*] that it did not have a stem cap but from an old record I think it had the first set of oarlocks my father got from Mr. Moore. . . .[11]

Dwight Grant had told Mr. Moore, who frequently came up the Fulton Chain for fishing trips, that he was not quite satisfied with the rowlocks provided by

the Boonville Foundry. He showed Mr. Moore exactly what he wanted and after that Mr. Moore made most of the rowlocks used by Dwight Grant. "I have never seen any made on this pattern since Mr. Moore's death that would compare in workmanship," said Lewis.

Three foot-plates of thin brass or copper were bent over the ribs, not as braces for the rower, but to protect the ribs and the bottom board against the friction of the rower's boots. Small plates of brass or copper protected the inside of the sheer plank against the ends of the yoke.

Grant's pamphlet does not mention the final finish given each boat before the accessories and the hardware were put on. Every hull had a good sanding and three coats of paint or spar varnish. The varnished boats were good to look at and displayed to advantage the builder's art and the pattern of tacks and screws. They also required more upkeep than the painted boats. Fishermen and hunters generally preferred an inconspicuous color. Dark blue boats, like the one in Winslow Homer's watercolor *The Blue Boat,* were popular. The traditional finish at Long Lake was black outside and green inside; it was invisible at night and minimized glare on sunny days.

Dwight Grant's first boats, said Lewis, were painted a dark blue outside and a dark brown inside, which some of the guides referred to as "Brown's Tract mud." Most of Grant's customers preferred navy blue outside and tile green inside, with decks and wales black. Lewis Grant did not know the proportion of varnished boats to painted boats made in his father's shop.

The completed guide-boat represented experience, skill, artistry, and weeks of hard work. Builders such as Dwight Grant took justifiable pride in their boats. In his reminiscences written for *Guide-Boat Days and Ways,* Willard Hanmer concluded:

> When spring comes . . . I am usually glad when the last boat is completed, but then . . . after the hunting season, I always have an urge to start building boats again. There seems to be a feeling of confidence in one's ability, not to be afraid to tackle any kind of a job in woodworking, once you have learned to build an Adirondack guide-boat.[12]

Notes

1. Frederick S. Stallknecht, *Frank Leslie's Illustrated Newspaper,* November 13 and 20, 1858.
2. Photo, Cortez Moody, in Saranac Lake Free Library, Saranac Lake, New York.
3. Photo at back of Dwight Grant's 1890 pamphlet, Adirondack Museum.
4. Letter, January 1, 1964.
5. Letter, January 7, 1964.
6. T.C. Lethbridge, *Boats and Boatmen* (London and New York: Thames and Hudson, 1952), pp. 104, 123, 149.
7. Letter, September 7, 1958.
8. Letter, February 21, 1960.
9. Talbot Bissell, "42 Pounds to Portage," in *The Skipper* XXVII, no. 1 (January 1967).
10. Letter, August 30, 1959.
11. Letter, June 28, 1959.
12. Kenneth Durant, ed., *Guide-Boat Days and Ways* (Blue Mountain Lake, N.Y.: Adirondack Museum, 1963), pp. 236-237.

XXII/Modern Materials and Tools
by John Gardner

No doubt Dwight Grant would have grabbed at epoxy and other modern materials to cut weight.

Kenneth Durant[1]

When Kenneth Durant first undertook his study of the guide-boat in the late 1950s, he was convinced, he told me, that the guide-boat had about reached the end of its active career on the water. He surmised that very soon no more guide-boats would be built, because all of the old builders would have passed on, and the essential authentic materials would no longer be obtainable, except at prohibitive cost. In particular, large spruce stumps, from which guide-boat stems and natural-crook frames had been obtained, were rarely to be found any more, and when they were, digging them out of the ground and sawing them by hand was far too expensive an operation for present-day commercial builders to undertake. As Durant saw it, then, the guide-boat had become, or was about to become, a museum piece, an historic artifact. And while of great local interest in the Adirondacks, as well as wider general interest from the standpoint of small craft design because of its exquisite construction, the guide-boat, as a boat, was finished.

What ensued, Durant had not anticipated. In part as a result of his interest, and the wider interest and publicity issuing from his research, there occurred during the following decade a modest yet viable guide-boat revival among small craft amateurs, spread over a rather wide area of the country. New guide-boats have been built from plans supplied by Durant and with his encouragement in Vermont, Wisconsin, and Maine. Articles about guide-boats and guide-boat construction have appeared in boating publications. And in the last few years guide-boats have figured prominently in two major annual small craft events, the Small Craft Workshop at Mystic Seaport and the Thousand Islands Antique Boat Show at Clayton, New York. And locally, in the Adirondacks, at least two native builders, Carl Hathaway of Saranac Lake and Harold Austin at Blue Mountain Lake, have been producing guide-boats for sale, albeit in a small way. The anticipated demise of the guide-boat, as a boat, did not occur.

To a large extent guide-boat construction is relatively simple, straightforward, and within the capabilities of nonprofessional builders, yet at the same time, to build a guide-boat exactly as they were once built a century ago would be difficult, if not next to impossible, as a first-time project for most amateurs.

In the first place, spruce stumps of a size and quality necessary to make guide-boat stems and ribs are simply not to be had now, except in rare instances. Indeed, it appeared for a time that with the supply of stump crooks cut off, guide-boat construction must come to an end, as Durant predicted.

Second, classic planking operations require skill and precision of a special order. Guide-boat stems, ribs, bottoms, garboards, decks, seats, and so forth — all the principal hull members, excepting the planking or "siding" above the garboards — are readily shaped from patterns and assembled according to standard, easily followed procedures. No special skills are required beyond careful workmanship and some facility with hand tools. But hollowing and rounding the delicate planks and beveling and fitting the laps is something else. This is not to say that planking skill cannot be acquired in time. Many wintertime builders, who plied the waterways in summer as guides, became creditable plankers, leaving behind exquisite boats to prove it, but it took time and practice to acquire the exacting skill, if not a special aptitude. First-time builders can hardly expect to do a superior planking job of the classic sort.

The two main obstacles to guide-boat construction by beginners, then, are lack of spruce stumps and the difficulty of classic planking methods. An entirely acceptable substitute for stump crooks is available in the form of glued laminations of thin spruce strips. And instead of the difficult, classic method of planking, easier procedures can be used that employ glued strips, as well as narrower and more numerous planks with glued laps. Well within the grasp of the nonprofessional, new methods achieve first-rate results, judged by both appearance and utility. Modern plastic adhesives made this possible, as was demonstrated to Kenneth Durant's satisfaction, no less, over 10 years ago.

Well-made laminated stems and ribs are somewhat stiffer and stronger than ribs of the same dimensions cut from natural crooks, but as the latter were quite adequate, no particular advantage would be gained by changing to laminations if stump crooks were plentiful and cheap. Glued strip planking, however, as well as planking with glued laps, has distinct advantages, most notable of which is permanent watertightness, which classic guide-boats did not have. Their tendency to dry out and spring leaks would be a serious shortcoming in a modern boat, intended to be transported over the road on the top of a car or on a trailer. When Tom Fulk's guide-boat planked with epoxy-glued strips was launched on Blue Mountain Lake in 1968 after a cartop ride from Wisconsin under hot sun and through fast-moving air, not a drop showed anywhere inside, something not likely, as Kenneth Durant observed, "with the best-made copper fastened guide-boat."[2]

Other present-day advantages supporting the adoption of glued-strip planking and planking with glued laps are economy and the ready availability of materials.

For the ultra-thin $\frac{3}{16}$-inch plank of the classic nineteenth century guide-boats, the best old-growth northern white pine, quarter-sawn from large logs, was the preferred material, difficult to obtain even then, and ever so much more difficult to obtain now, even without considering present-day costs.

For strip planking, less expensive and more readily available pine lumber not entirely free of knots and other defects, including edge sap, can be used, as the inferior parts are readily avoided and rejected when stripping up the boards on the circular saw. Short lengths can be used by glue splicing. Select quarter-sawn lumber is not required. Further, with glued-strip construction, as well as with glued laps, the several thousand small copper tacks formerly needed for fastening the plank laps are eliminated, together with the tedious labor of "sticking" the tacks and clenching them.

In spite of all this, some purists do not look kindly on the use of glued laminations or glued-strip planking in guide-boat construction. There is no reasonable justification for this rejection from a functional and utilitarian standpoint. Boats built with glue can be just as strong, just as light, and just as handsome, with exactly the same form and finish, as the best of the classics. If boats so built were painted as guides formerly painted their boats, it would be next to impossible to tell a well-built, strip-planked boat without scraping away some of the paint. On varnished boats the absence of rows of tacks along the plank laps would be the most obvious difference.

Should plastic adhesives be objected to as not being traditional, it may be countered that neither were small wood screws traditional when guide-boat builders first adopted them more than one hundred years ago, yet without thousands of small wood screws, the classic guide-boat could not have been built. And as for waterproof adhesives, early guide-boat builders used the best adhesive available to them for cementing their planking laps, namely the "best Brooklyn lead, thinned with spar composition."[3]

The evolution of the guide-boat — beginning in the first quarter of the nineteenth century with crude, heavy clinker hunting skiffs with transom sterns — was a gradual process of improvement and change, which continued until what we know as the classic guide-boat was achieved at the century's end. Now that a new period in small craft boating has opened with a revival of the guide-boat for recreational use, a resumption of the evolutionary process is in order.

None of the excellent performance qualities of the guide-boat need suffer from the use of plastic adhesives in its construction. No changes of any consequence are required in the basic hull form; in fact, no changes whatever in classic shape need result.

The application of modern thermoplastic adhesives to guide-boat construction was first proposed in 1965. In January of that year Kenneth Durant wrote me: "I have just discovered a Vermont boy, 20 years old, who last summer made a most creditable guide-boat. So far as I can learn, he had no guidance except an old boat he found in the woods and took apart to see how it was made. He made his ribs of plywood, otherwise orthodox construction. . . . Would you be willing to share with him your ideas about advanced g-b construction — lamination, glues, etc.? He plans to make another boat next summer."[4]

Laurence Babcock, a Middlebury College junior, had done what Durant had thought impossible and what Lewis Grant said he himself could not do. At 90 pounds stripped, the boat he had constructed was too

heavy, and it was much too cranky, with a bottom board only six inches wide, but after rowing it, Durant pronounced it "a beautiful boat, very easy to row, pulling straight and true."[5]

In line with Durant's suggestion, I made up two sample Grant-pattern number 7 ribs cut from a curved laminated blank formed from spruce strips $\frac{1}{16}$ inch thick, bent and tightly clamped on a curved form after epoxy glue had been applied between the strips. On receipt of the two samples, Durant replied: "I am greatly impressed by your ribs. You have demonstrated your ability to make a rib as strong, and I believe as light, as ever the old tree did herself. And handsome too."[6] Babcock was likewise impressed, for as soon as he saw the sample ribs, he decided on laminated ribs for his next boat.[7] And on laminated stems as well. Since then others have used laminated ribs and stems, and they have proved thoroughly reliable. As for appearance, when properly made, the glue lines between the laminations are virtually invisible after varnishing — one has to look close to see them.

Babcock's second guide-boat, completed during the summer of 1965, not only had epoxy-glued laminated ribs and stems, but epoxy glue was also used in lieu of metal fastenings for the planking laps, the wale strips, and the rowlock plates. Because of the additional stiffness of the laminated ribs, Babcock reduced the siding from $\frac{5}{16}$ inch to $\frac{1}{4}$ inch, and increased their spacing from Grant's $5\frac{1}{8}$ inches on centers to $6\frac{1}{4}$ inches and to 7 inches toward the ends of the boat. By so doing he decreased the number of ribs from the standard 33 pairs to 23 pairs. Additional savings in weight were achieved by reducing

Laurence Babcock in the first guide-boat he built in 1965. (Helen Durant)

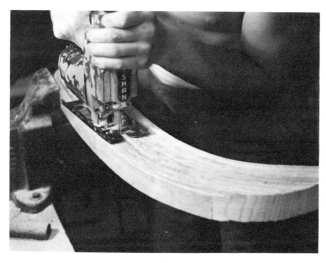

Laurence Babcock working the laminated stem of his guide-boat. (Helen Durant)

Babcock's press for laminating ribs. (Helen Durant)

the thickness of the two top strakes of Sitka spruce to ⅛ inch with a light, thin wale of Idaho pine. The net result of these various reductions was a boat several pounds lighter than the standard 16-foot boat.

After a searching examination of Babcock's new boat, ending with a row, the ultimate test, Durant pronounced it excellent in all respects, a remarkable achievement. Subsequent use has substantiated this judgment.

Babcock's achievement was reported in detail in an article published in the October 1965 issue of the *National Fisherman,* an article of which Durant thought highly enough to distribute 20 copies to selected con-

tacts.[8] Babcock's accomplishment reported in this article provided some objective confirmation of assertions concerning the promising potential of wood-plastic composite construction for boatbuilding set forth in a series of four articles published earlier in the year in the *National Fisherman.* These articles broke new ground by giving widespread dissemination for the first time to a novel technology of wood-plastic composites and its application to boatbuilding, based on pioneering experimentation by Dr. Lindsay Lord, N.A., Professor Charles Bouc, John Koopman, and others. Since then, various methods of composite wood-plastic construction have been developed and widely adapted by boatbuilders, of which probably the best known and most widely used at this time is the WEST system developed by the Gougeon Brothers of Bay City, Michigan.

Among those who read these articles in the *National Fisherman,* including the account of Bab-

Laurence Babcock carrying his guide-boat. (Helen Durant)

Cutting laminated curved blanks to produce two ribs constituting an opposing pair. (Helen Durant)

cock's guide-boat, was Thomas A. Fulk of Bessemer, Michigan, a forest ranger with the U.S. Forest Service. He had previously built several boats on his own, and had once worked for a considerable time in a boat shop. On H.I. Chapelle's suggestion, he wrote Durant asking for guide-boat lines, stating that he wished to build a guide-boat not only out of admiration for the type itself, but also because he was especially interested in light construction methods. His request made a good impression on Durant, who agreed to assist him by furnishing lines, as well as patterns for the stems, ribs, bottom board, and garboard, the latter of which Fulk changed somewhat.

Fulk laminated his ribs on gluing forms made to the exact shape of the inside contour of each rib. In all, 13 separate gluing forms were required. Spruce strips $\frac{1}{16}$ inch by $\frac{3}{4}$ inch in width were laminated to produce curved blanks from which two ribs constituting an opposing pair were obtained. Fulk followed Babcock's example by finishing his ribs $\frac{1}{4}$ inch thick, but later stated that if he were doing it again, he would side them the original $\frac{5}{16}$ inch to give more thickness to receive the plank fastenings. Unlike Babcock, Fulk stayed close to the standard Grant rib spacing, using $5\frac{1}{4}$ inches from center to center.

Fulk's major innovation was to plank above the garboard with strips $1\frac{1}{8}$ inches wide, the first time a guide-boat was strip-planked, as far as is known. In Fulk's words it was the "perfect answer." The edges of the strips were shaped with a molding head attachment for a table saw operating at relatively low speed. A high-speed router or shaper would have done the job better.[9] On one edge a standing 90° angle V was cut, on the other a like hollow V, so that the one would fit into the other. As the strips were applied to

the side of the boat, they were edge-glued but not glued to the ribs. Instead, a single bronze annular nail, #14 gauge and $\frac{3}{4}$ inch long, was driven through the center of the strip into each rib through previously drilled pilot holes about 70 percent of nail diameter, and the heads of the nails were countersunk ever so slightly, so that the final light sanding of the hull after planking would bring them just flush with the surface. For fastening the strips, Fulk also experimented with $\frac{3}{4}$-inch bronze staples of #19 gauge wire driven by a pneumatic stapling gun; he found this a workable system, but expensive considering the cost of stapling equipment. Fulk finished the outside of his boat with three coats of white epoxy paint, while the inside had three coats of marine varnish.

Fulk offered only one criticism of this strip planking technique, and that a very minor one. While the outside of the hull sanded perfectly fair and smooth with no seams or strips in evidence after painting, inside on the hollow curves, some of the strips showed slightly flat—enough, that is, to be recognizable as strips. These strips were $1\frac{1}{8}$ inches wide. With narrower strips the effect would have been less obvious; possibly it would have disappeared entirely.

The structure of Fulk's boat—with its glued-strip planking securely nailed to the closely spaced, laminated ribs—may well be stronger, and even much stronger, than necessary. There are glued-strip boats and canoes now being built without any internal ribbing, which seem to be standing up adequately in service. After two seasons of hard use in which heavy loads were carried in rough water, Fulk's boat was in top condition when Durant tested it at Blue Mountain Lake in October 1968. Not a drop of water showed inside after the long ride from Wisconsin, and it was on that occasion that Durant bestowed his highest accolade: Fulk's boat "felt right under the pants." For Durant, who had been rowing guide-boats for more than 60 years, a boat in the water had to "feel right" when you rowed it. Strip planking passed the test.[10]

A decade later, writing in the January 1979 issue of the *National Fisherman*, Fulk reported that his guide-boat was still basically in as good shape as when first built, and that he expected it to last another 40 years, at least. Except for three small, two-inch checks confined to the outer surface of the hull, the planking was like new. Fulk attributed this to his use of thoroughly seasoned, edge-grain pine for planking strips. Inside, where the oarsman's feet chafe in rowing, there is some wear because Fulk failed to install the brass foot-plates with which guide-boats were usually equipped. Also, if the ring nails with which the planking strips were fastened to the ribs had been sunk slightly below the finished surface, refinishing would be easier. If he were doing the job again, Fulk states, he would countersink the heads a bit more. Fulk changed from an epoxy paint to two coats of polyurethane white solely because of the superior brushing qualities of the latter. The epoxy-glued ribs and stems have retained their shape and show no signs of delamination. Although the boat has not had the protracted hard use that guide's work boats once received, it has absorbed, without noticeable damage, the repeated impacts and stressful flexing incident to car-top transport. In a word, 10 years of use have demonstrated that Fulk's building methods utilizing modern materials can produce a boat of lasting strength and structural integrity.

Both laminated ribs and stems as well as strip planking require gluing, and if the boat is to be varnished, the glue must be colorless and nonstaining. Of course it goes without saying that it must be waterproof as well. The only glues now available that meet these essential requirements are some of the epoxy formulations and Aerolite 306, a British urea resin. In addition, these particular plastic adhesives are gap-filling when joints don't fit perfectly, and they require only enough clamping pressure in gluing to ensure firm contact of the meeting surfaces until the glue sets. If the boat is to be painted, resorcinol resin glues may be used, but such glues are staining and

also require more accurately fitted joints, more clamping pressure, and a gluing temperature of 70° Fahrenheit or higher.

The spruce strips for making the laminated ribs should be about $\frac{1}{16}$ inch thick; they may be used just as they come from the circular saw without planing, provided the cut is not too rough and ragged. Slight roughness makes for a stronger glue joint, provided the gluing surfaces are not so rough as to result in an uneven glue line.

One way to make a jig or form for gluing the rib blanks is to mark the curved inside shape of the rib on a piece of $\frac{3}{4}$-inch plywood. Next saw out a number of short pieces of 2-inch-thick plank, two or three inches wide, to fit the inside of this curve, and fasten them securely to the plywood with screws from the under side, making a curved bending form raised above the plywood base to which it is attached and standing at right angles to it. Glue is applied to the strips that are to form the laminated rib blank, and the bundle of strips, resting on its side on the plywood base, is bent around the curved form and hauled tight with C-clamps. Several blocks with hollow curves to fit the outside of the curved strip assembly are used with the C-clamps to distribute and equalize the pressure on the outside of the strips. Clamps and clamping pressure must be ample to squeeze the laminations close enough to obtain the tight glue lines throughout that are essential for strength and appearance. Parts of the gluing form that may come in contact with glue squeezed from the strip assembly should be liberally coated with paste wax, which acts as a release agent; otherwise, when the glue hardens, the rib blank will adhere to the bending form.

This is an outline of the basic procedure, although many minor variations will produce the same results. Fulk's strips, as already mentioned, were only $\frac{3}{4}$ inch wide, and he used wedges instead of clamps to apply gluing pressure.

Variations of the planking process, with glued-strip planking or with planks of different widths or with modified laps, offer a wide range for individual choice. A high-speed router or shaper is recommended for beveling the laps as well as the mating edges of the planking strips. Using a router and a simple jig, Larry Babcock found he could put a perfect Grant lap on a strake in a few minutes, regardless of cross grain; the same operation had taken hours with a hand plane, and sometimes planks were spoiled because of the difficult grain.[11]

If care is taken in fitting and gluing accurately formed planking laps with shouldered edges like the Grant lap, the joints will be practically invisible after a light sanding and several coats of varnish. Small ring nails, or even small wood screws, can be used according to Fulk's method to fasten the planking strips to the ribs, but fine bronze brads would probably be adequate, and if these are set in slightly and the holes filled, they should hardly be visible after finishing.

Because there are no tacks to interfere, the outer surface of the planked hull is easily made perfectly fair and smooth by judicious sanding prior to painting or varnishing.

Inside, much can be done to relieve any appearance of flatness in some of the strips by scraping carefully between the ribs with a sharp hand scraper with a blade that has been slightly rounded to conform to the inner curves of the hull. This was the method employed by Willard Hanmer, who omitted hollowing the inside of his planks in order to simplify and speed up construction. If narrower planks, say half width, are used on the rounded portion of the hull midway between the garboard and the sheer, hollowing the inside is hardly necessary. A few passes with a sharp scraper should be sufficient. With glued-up construction, additional planks present no problem, as they would in classic tack-fastened construction. When laps are cut with a router and glued, the additional labor entailed by increasing the number of planks is insignificant.

Strip planking admits of many variations. The method worked out and successfully used by Fulk is a good one to start from. Garboards of the traditional sort are required for a secure, watertight connection with the bottom board. For his garboards Fulk adopted the Grant pattern but slightly altered the run of the upper edge to minimize edge set in the first of the strips above it.

Because of the unusual shape of the classic guideboat hull, low freeboard amidships and upswept sheer at the ends, the width of the side surface varies but little from end to end and throughout the boat. The shape of the garboard is lined out to absorb differences in width, so that the space above will be of uniform width throughout. When this is the case, parallel-sided strips without taper can be used. A sheer plank of normal dimensions can be tapered, if necessary, to assist in equalizing the width of the space to be filled with strips. Although Fulk went to some pains to minimize the amount of edge set required by planking strips above the garboard, with strips an inch or so wide, moderate edge set offers no problem, provided the sweep of the bend is uniform and fair.

Strips may be wider or narrower depending on the amount of round (from sheer to garboard) in that portion of the hull where they are located — the more round, the narrower the strips. For fastening to the ribs, fine bronze brads no more than ⅝ inch in length should be adequate for strip siding 3/16 inch thick.

Fulk milled the edges of his 3/16-inch strips with a 90° V, one edge standing and the other recessed to match, so that when two lengths of stripping were fitted together, the one fitted the other exactly and they appeared like one smooth, continuous width of stripping.

Another way that works just as well, if not better, is to round one edge slightly and to hollow the other edge to match. The hollow is worked to a slightly quicker radius, so that when two strips are fitted together, the outer edges of the joint press tightly, while there is a bit of space left for glue at the bottom of the hollow, as a precaution against a glue-starved joint.

It should be borne in mind that the edges of these planking strips must be milled with precision, requiring for best results the use of a high-speed electric router or shaper. When a router is used, it is easy to devise a simple jig for cutting the strips accurately.

Short lengths of lumber may be used, for both strips and wider planks. When pieced with properly made scarphs, glued splices are just as strong as a continuous length of uncut lumber, and well-made scarphed joints glued with non-staining epoxy or Aerolite are all but invisible. Scarph joints should be cut in length 12 times the thickness of the lumber to be spliced. They must be accurately fitted and tightly clamped. In clamping, blocks should be used to distribute the clamping pressure evenly over the glued surface while the glue is setting. Of course, splicing is done before the lumber is cut up into strips.

All the patterns required for building a guide-boat can be obtained from the construction drawings reproduced in Appendix C. The order of construction and the building procedures are covered in the preceding chapters describing and explaining the building process. With laminated stems and ribs and glued-strip planking, the construction of a guide-boat of classic form and appearance, capable of creditable performance, and watertight under all conditions, will not be overly difficult for a careful workman of modest woodworking attainments, nor will it be excessively expensive.

Notes

1. Letter, June 2, 1961.
2. Letter, October 18, 1968.
3. Dwight Grant, 1890 pamphlet, in the Adirondack Museum.
4. Letter, January 25, 1965.
5. Letter, March 29, 1965.
6. Letter, March 10, 1965.
7. Letter, March 29, 1965.
8. John Gardner, "An Authentic Guide-Boat," in *National Fisherman*, October 1965, pp. 8-9.
9. Thomas A. Fulk, "Strip Planking Well Adapted for Guide-Boat," in *National Fisherman*, February 1968, pp. 12B-13B.
10. Letter, October 18, 1968.
11. Letter, February 27, 1966.

XXIII/Guide-Boat Handling

He headed his long narrow boat out into the lake, and steadied it between his knees until I was seated in the bow; then, with a slight push, sent the light shell from the beach, vaulting at the same instant, with a motion, airy as a cat's into his own seat astern.

W.H.H. Murray[1]

Dwight Grant demanded of his guide-boats that they be durable, speedy, light, and capacious. In addition he required of them the ability to ride through rough water in safety.

Modifications in the form and construction of boat types take place steadily to answer new demands. No boat is perfect at its inception. Compromises have to be made in which one consideration yields to another, more important one.[2] Like the Indian with his birch canoe and the Eskimo with his kayak, the Adirondack guide sacrificed some stability for essential seaworthiness. The Eskimo perfected the "kayak roll," which enabled him to recover from capsizing by turning over completely. Though the guide-boat at rest on the water does not seem quite steady, it is much harder to upset than a canoe, which, once tipped to a certain point, will turn over instantly. The guide-boat's resistance to tipping increases with the angle of the tip. Even if the gunwale goes six inches under water, the boat will immediately right itself if the weight is shifted slightly to the other side.[3]

The Indian in his canoe learned to cope with whitewater rapids, and the Eskimo in his kayak learned to master an obstreperous sea. The north woods guide, however, had to meet a special hazard unknown to Indian or Eskimo: the perilous and frequently unpredictable behavior of his passenger who, unfamiliar with the guide-boat, found it fragile and cranky. Excited at the landing of a fish, or suddenly afraid of tipping over, he often made unexpected movements, thereby upsetting the boat. In rough water the inexperienced passenger would be asked to sit or lie low in the boat and refrain from grasping the gunwale for support. A skillful oarsman could manage the guide-boat in the roughest water if allowed total control over the boat, occupant, and gear.

A guide-boat should be launched from a shelving sand beach or a slanting dock. "At The Cedars on Forked Lake," remembered Kenneth Durant, "we had shelving beaches, but at the boat house where the shore went down abruptly we built a floating dock." This was a wooden platform, one end of which was hooked by means of chain links or swivel pins to the boathouse or to a log on shore, while the low side dipped with a gentle slant into the water.

Readied for launching, the guide-boat lies with its

Slanting dock at Bisby Lake. (Helen Durant)

bow on the dock or beach and its stern in the water. The oarsman sits or leans astride the bow to hold the boat steady while the passenger steps dry-shod into the middle of the boat and, proceeding carefully over the rib knees, seats himself in the stern. His weight keeps the bow up. Now the oarsman must push the boat out into the water until only the bow remains on the edge of the dock. Standing astride the bow, he grasps the gunwale with both hands. With one leg he pushes the boat out as far as possible without losing his balance and at the same time vaults into the bow seat. This trick may scare the daylights out of the stern passenger, but it settles the oarsman gently into the bow seat in one swoop, while the boat glides on evenly into deep water.

This is the customary method of launching a guide-boat. Without the benefit of counterbalance from a stern passenger, launching requires extra skill: the solitary rower must follow up the vault with a few quick steps to reach the seat amidships before the bow goes down.

If the beach is shoal and the oarsman is alone, the boat must be pushed out into the water as far as possible. With both hands on the gunwale and one foot between bow seat and deck, he gives a quick shove with the other foot to send the boat into deep water while simultaneously swinging aboard. The shove-and-kick pushes the boat into deep water and keeps the weight off the bow as the boat glides out.

Once on the lake the guide-boat must be properly balanced fore and aft. To even bow and stern, especially with a light-weight stern passenger, small bags filled with sand or small rocks are useful as ballast. Sandbags are easier on the boat; a variety of sizes and weights can be kept in the boathouse, but rocks are everywhere available. With three people

aboard, proper balance can also be achieved by adjusting the position of the middle seat.

In shoal water or wherever there is danger from hidden rocks or snags, it is advisable to weigh the bow down slightly. A bow slightly lifted may ride onto a shoal or a log; a low bow will help to keep the boat on course. Proceeding slowly, the boat may slightly bump an obstruction, but it will be easy to back away again. There is nothing more embarrassing than to ride a guide-boat unexpectedly onto a rock in fairly deep water. The boat pivots, neither going over nor backing off, and becomes very tippy. With the rock out of reach under the boat, there is nothing to push against. If the oars can be unshipped, the oarsman can take one in each hand and try to reach bottom with them, thereby raising and freeing the boat. If this does not work, the rower should crawl carefully from bow to stern, grasp the gunwale, and, with an abrupt lurch, throw his body weight toward the stern and then check this movement with a sudden drag. These maneuvers will impart momentum to the boat and it should drift free.

When sunken trunks block a narrow stream, the oarsman can try to hold them down with his paddle, meanwhile pushing his boat across. If this fails, the boat must be taken ashore and carried around the obstruction. The rower can try to slide the boat under a fallen tree resting above the water. Joel T. Headley wrote in *Hours at Home:* "We came upon a fallen tree . . . only a foot or so above the surface. Seizing the trunk in his hands, the hunter pushed the boat down under it, working the boat gradually forward until he got nearly to the stern, when he stepped over into the forward part . . . and soon we were clear of the obstruction. . . ."[4]

In familiar waters the best precaution against running aground is to remember the obstructions and know at what water level they become a menace. "There was a big rock near The Cedars on Forked Lake," remembered Kenneth Durant. "It was named 'Mooley's rock' after a luckless visitor who spent hours pivoting on its top. Even the most experienced rower among us would not hesitate to use it as a convenient excuse when arriving late for dinner."

The guide-boat is excellently suited for trolling but not for fly-fishing. Because bow and stern seats are mounted low, the gunwale obstructs the cast. This difficulty is increased when the fisherman sits facing forward, as he must in small streams. His cast will be blocked by the deck rising in front of him. The paddler at the stern is in danger of being hooked by the back cast. If the fly-fisherman insists on standing to cast, he may tip over the boat. Standing up should always be avoided.

In spite of all precautions, mishaps do occur. When a pointed log pierced his birch canoe, the Indian could repair it in the woods as long as there were spruce trees nearby to supply the necessary gum and fibers. When a guide-boat springs a leak, it's handy to have an awl, a small box of white lead, and a little hammer with a hollow handle in which to keep a few copper tacks. Pieces cut from an old rubber wading boot, or a tin drinking cup, are useful for patches; a felt hat or a frying pan can be used for bailing. If a

guide-boat capsizes and fills with water, a swimmer can empty it by deft rocking. The only way to reenter a guide-boat floating in deep water is over the bow or stern, never over the sides. A more practical solution, however, is to push the boat to the nearest shore, dump out the water, and reenter the boat in the conventional way.

The absence of a floor leaves the ribs exposed to the air and makes any water in the bottom noticeable and inconvenient. On a stormy day or in a leaky boat, one should run ashore now and then and bail out the water or turn the boat upside down to get rid of the bilge water, rather than sit with wet ankles.

The guide-boat is primarily a one-man boat; even with three people aboard, there is only one rower. Two men cannot row a guide-boat conveniently; the boat will build up resistance in a bow wave when forced beyond the speed for which it is designed. Though Dwight Grant in his 1890 pamphlet suggested his boats could accommodate two oarsmen, he did not provide two pairs of oars. Two pairs were seldom seen, and then only in longer boats, such as the family or church boats.

If the oarsman is alone, he rows from amidships. Oars are fastened to the rowlocks with oarpins; the rowlocks turn on a pivot in the gunwale; no tholepins are used. This is a characteristic feature of the guide-boat, observed as unique or peculiar by many writers. Having fixed pins, the oars cannot be feathered on

Charles F. Maurice rowing the Ghost. *Even with three people aboard, there is only one rower. (Helen Durant)*

Kenneth Durant rowing Warren Cole boat. Guide-boats are rowed with the oarsman's arms crossed. (Helen Durant)

the recovery, nor is this essential for small boats on relatively calm water. (Singlehanded management of a boat on a windy day can be a challenging sport.) The oars must be carefully balanced so that, with the least exertion, they can be lifted just far enough to avoid catching snags. Fixed oarpins have an advantage: If the rower needs both hands free to grasp rod or rifle, the oars are held in place, blades trailing in the water, handy when needed again.

For a 16-foot boat, oars are customarily 8 feet long. The distance from the rowlock to the end of the handle is somewhat more than half the boat's beam, so that the oar handles overlap and are rowed with the rower's arms crossed, one wrist in front of and above the other. This brings one loom higher than the other. The rower, accordingly, tips his boat slightly to bring both blades into the water at the same time. The orderly minded passenger who thinks that a boat must always ride on an even keel and shifts his position to compensate for the slight tilt required by the cross-armed oarsman interferes with the rhythm of the strokes. There is nothing for the rower to do but earn the confidence of the passenger to keep him from continuously shifting position.

The only other boat known to us that is rowed cross-handed by one man is the wherry used near Gloucester, mentioned by the Reverend William Bentley in his diary of 1799.[5] Some other boats, such as the racing shell and many lifeboats, have a similar extension of the oar handle to secure the necessary leverage, but these are rowed by more than one man, each rower having two hands on a single oar.

The rower customarily sets his course with a glance over his shoulder, holding it straight by sighting a landmark over the passenger's head, a method observed by Sir Francis Bacon in 1593 when he noted that the Thames wherryman "looketh toward the bridge when he pulleth toward Westminster."[6] If all shores are out of sight during a fog, and one knows the direction, the wake behind the boat is kept in a straight line until it disappears in the fog.

A man afoot has two principal gaits: walking and running. The latter is not merely an acceleration of walking but an entirely different movement. There is a distinct difference, also, between rowing slowly and rowing fast. The Adirondack oarsman uses different strokes according to requirements. For ordinary, unhurried, long distance travel, the slow, short stroke is used, beginning with arms extended and ending on the full sweep. Little body movement is used. With this stroke one can row all day with no more effort than walking. "Of all boats, give me the flat-bottomed, light-built, graceful Adirondack," wrote an admirer. "With a little practice you learn to guide it instinctively, as a bird uses its wings. It obeys the prompting of every impulse, and is so easily propelled in smooth water you need never tire. . . ."[7]

During a long stretch the rower may occasionally use the more relaxed hand-over-hand stroke for a brief, restful change of pace, revolving the oar handles one around the other like slowly twiddling thumbs, dipping the blades alternately. Since no push against the stretchers is required, the rower can comfortably bend one knee into a cross-legged position for further ease. The hand-over-hand method is also used for trolling or as an accompaniment to sustained conversation.

After many hours of rowing it is pleasant, and rather exciting, to change places with the passenger. The smaller of the two occupants crawls to the center of the boat and crouches low while the other one, steadying both hands on the gunwale, steps over him. This is not difficult if done skillfully and without hesitation; nevertheless, it is a precarious operation, one that should be done in shallow water only.

Only in emergencies or, for instance, when chasing a deer, is an extraordinary burst of speed needed. In that case the oarsman will put his back into a quickened stroke, not in the extreme manner of the racer, but with just a slight inclination forward and back, to add body-weight to the muscular pull. The impression this makes on the nonrower is vividly described by Joel T. Headley in *The Adirondack*. Watching his guide, Mitchell Sabattis, in the sudden pursuit of a deer, Headley wrote:

> . . . the Indian sprang to his oars. He stopped, rose to his full length in the boat—stood for a moment like a statue, then, dropping on his seat, seized the oars . . . the energy of ten men seemed concentrated in him. His strokes fell with a rapidity and power I have never before witnessed . . . the strokes of Mitchell seemed each time to lift the cockle-shell from the lake. As he fell back on the oars, so rapid was the passage of the boat, that the water, as it parted before it, rose up on each side as high as his shoulders and foamed like a torrent past me.[8]

Paddling a guide-boat is generally slow. Alone in a boat one man cannot easily control it with a paddle and might tip over. He is better off using oars. With a

passenger seated in the bow facing forward, however, the stern paddler has enough control to bring the boat close to the desired target and back out quickly again, away from snags if need be. The deer, so sensitive to scent or sound, is somewhat defective in sight. It does not easily see an object approaching head-on, though any sideways motion will send it off. A guide-boat propelled straight forward toward a feeding deer by means of a silent paddle can approach very close. Once dipped, the paddle is worked by wrist and elbow, and not withdrawn from the water. It shows no lateral motion as do oars, and does not alarm the deer. The skilled rower can paddle the boat within yards of a fleeting deer in open sight, provided the wind blows from the direction of the animal and the boatman makes not the slightest noise and remains absolutely motionless when the deer raises its head.

When two guides traveled together in one boat, the push of the paddle was a customary aid to the rower. Unless expertly applied in perfect rhythm with oars, however, the paddle throws the rhythm of the oars off balance. A paddle is also useful in streams too narrow for oars, or where the oarsman needs to be able to see where he is going without continually turning his head.

To bring the boat well ashore smoothly, the rower takes a long pull, then releases the oars, and, with both hands on the gunwales, moves quickly to the center of the boat. This shift in weight will generally bring the boat far enough up the dock or beach for the rower to step out dry-shod. A boat beached in this fashion will come to rest at a slant, with the stern lower than the bow. On a wet day rain water will surge down the stern seat before the hapless passenger can rise. Old hands will remember the frantic pleas from female passengers who anticipated the inundation of their feet and legs: "Don't pull it up. Don't pull it up."

To carry a guide-boat around rapids or from one body of water to another, a yoke is used. A permanent accessory aboard every guide-boat, it should never be left behind. The yoke is a hollowed-out neck piece that lies upon the shoulders, like the yoke once used by farmers to carry milk pails. At both ends is a projection that fits into the slots of the yoke cleats mounted on the boat slightly ahead of amidships.

When the boat is carried, paddle, oars, and yoke cleat are fastened with leather thongs. (Helen Durant)

These cleats hold the boat securely on the yoke and provide the bearer with a hand grasp to control balance and direction of the upturned hull. The cleats are mounted inside the hull to save the bearer's knuckles from scraping against trees or other protrusions. The back rest and the paddle and oars, with handles forward and blades aft, are fastened inside the boat with leather thongs before the yoke is put in place.

Guide-boat builders never permitted themselves decorative extensions of the stem like those on Viking boats or Venetian gondolas. Of necessity they could not. The stem is merely made thicker near the top and ends in a projecting stem cap, which has an important function: every time a guide-boat has to be turned over, it pivots on the end of either stem, and when the boat is to be carried, the stern stem cap supports the upended hull.

To prepare for the carry, the bearer leans the boat, bottom side up, against a tree. The bow is propped against a suitable crotch, the tip of the stern rests on the ground. The bearer crouches under the boat, fits the yoke to his shoulders, grasps the yoke cleats with both hands, and lifts. If the boat is properly balanced, the bow is elevated enough to allow him to see ahead while the stern is far enough off the ground to prevent dragging. Skill is more important than muscle. On a strong, erect man, the weight of the boat rests lightly if the yoke fits the shoulders.

To lift the guide-boat, the oarsman, standing at starboard, leans over the boat, grasps the gunwales, and then, with one swing, lifts the boat over his head. (Adirondack Museum)

If no tree with a crotch is handy, the boat is set on the ground, right side up, with all accessories fastened and in place. The bearer, standing at starboard, leans over the boat to grasp the port gunwale with the right hand, the starboard gunwale with the left, and with one swing lifts the boat over his head without touching ground with bow or stern. Once the boat is on his shoulders, the stern is dropped until the point of the stern rests on the ground. This balances the boat and leaves both hands free to adjust the yoke to the shoulders, pull wrinkles out of one's shirt, and otherwise prepare for the carry. If the portage is long and the bearer needs a rest, he can lean the boat's bow against a rock or sapling, withdrawing himself from beneath it.

Through the woods for any distance, one man under the yoke makes better progress than would two men carrying the boat between them; however, when encountering a beaver dam or some such obstruction, two men can take the boat by bow and stern and carry it, with oars and other gear left in the boat, over the short distance.

Putting a boat down is more difficult than picking it up. It takes the last bit of muscle and caution after a tiresome carry. The turnover is again made while pivoting the boat on the point of the stern, protecting decks and gunwale.

The fragile guide-boat also requires protection against sharp pebbles, the hot sun, which can warp the seams, and against sudden and violent mountain squalls. It needs a gentle and protected approach for smooth launchings and landings. Just a roof for shelter will suffice, and a shelving sand beach that can be approached without danger from rocks will do, but when a permanent camp is built, a boathouse should be provided with the typical Adirondack slanting dock.

The guide-boat must be drawn up at every landing, emptied of water, and, if left in the open, turned upside down. The boats of Dwight Grant have a hole in each deck to drain away any water caught under the sheer. If hot sun threatens to open weak seams, a few hours of soaking before departure will usually swell the wood sufficiently to prevent serious leaks. Protected from rot by paint and varnish, the guide-boat in use takes less care than a rider gives his horse.

As children, Kenneth Durant and his brothers were not allowed on the water until they could swim. Kenneth first learned to row in the large, broad-beamed craft built like a guide-boat, which was used at The Cedars every summer to transport the Saratoga trunks containing the gowns of his mother and sister. From this freight boat he graduated to a fairly heavy and steady guide-boat reserved to transport the baggage of camp visitors or for the inexperienced guests. When at the age of 12 he had proved himself experienced and responsible, he was given his own traditional guide-boat.

Notes

1. W.H.H. Murray, *Adventures in the Wilderness* (Boston: Fields, Osgood & Co., 1869), p. 178.
2. T.C. Lethbridge, *Boats and Boatmen* (London and New York: Thames and Hudson, 1952), p. 102.
3. Talbot Bissell, "42 Pounds to Portage," in *The Skipper* XXVII, no. 1 (January 1967).
4. Joel T. Headley, *Hours at Home* IX, August-September 1869, p. 354.
5. *Diary of the Rev. William Bentley of Salem,* in four volumes (Essex Institute, 1907), II, p. 304, entry May 13, 1799.
6. Kenneth Durant, letter to H.K. Hochschild, September 30, 1965.
7. "Ibis," *Forest and Stream,* May 23, 1889.
8. Joel T. Headley, *The Adirondack; or Life in the Woods* (New York: Baker and Scribner, 1849), pp. 137-138.

Afterword

It took a century, more or less, for the guide-boat to reach its apex of development as the most important means of transportation in the Adirondacks, and then to pass into decline. Before anyone ever called it a guide-boat, the crude skiff fashioned by the early settler, after the Indian's canoe disappeared from the north woods, was adequate as long as he remained just a trapper and hunter. When he added guiding to his vocation, the demands upon his boat increased; the requirements became more varied. His boat needed further refinements to make it lighter on the carries and, notwithstanding its lightness, to make it safe and comfortable for the vacationer, With infinite patience, and superb woodcraft, he developed the once strictly utilitarian skiff into a dependable, comfortable, and exquisite craft. It became one of the finest boats ever produced under the inspiration of the wilderness without loss of its essential characteristics as a work boat. There is probably no craft lighter for the work it is meant to perform than the Adirondack guide-boat, yet despite its lightness, in the hands of the skilled oarsman, it is absolutely safe.

The flowering was short-lived. When multitudes of tourists invaded the wilderness, the boat was reduced to an excursion craft. When the guideless amateur and the private camp owner with enough time and leisure became proficient in handling and managing the boat, guiding as a profession came to a close. The guide's boat, appreciated by admirers who recognized the ingeniousness of the craftsmen who had developed it, remained for many years the pleasure craft of those who had the means to maintain a private camp in the wilderness. Many of the finest examples can be found in their boathouses or can be studied in the special small-craft collection of the Adirondack Museum at Blue Mountain Lake, New York.

The art of guide-boat building, suspended by the death of the last of the old guide-boat builders, Lewis L. Grant of Boonville in 1960, and Willard Hanmer of Saranac Lake in 1962, revived when individuals in many different parts of the country began to build guide-boats. Carl Hathaway of Saranac Lake took over the Hanmer shop. The forest ranger Thomas Fulk of Wisconsin built a guide-boat with modern tools and modern materials, as did Laurence Babcock, who built several boats while still a student at Middlebury College. Thomas Bissell of Long Lake experimented with fiberglass guide-boats and Harold Austin, also of Long Lake, built and restored several boats. During the last few years the guide-boat has been a regular part of the Small Craft Workshop conducted annually at Mystic Seaport under the direction of John Gardner.

F.C. Durant's camp, The Cedars, on Little Forked Lake.   (Margaret Bourke-White)

Some of the contemporary builders just mentioned used the classic patterns; some used modern tools, modern materials, and modern methods. Harold Austin built his most recent boat during the summer of 1978. He did not incorporate any innovations of his own, but he did some pattern scrambling. Basically, he used a Warren Cole bottom board pattern, the rib patterns of Charlie Hanmer of Long Lake, and his grandfather's (Merlin Austin) stem pattern. "The reason for this particular conglomerate was because the customer for whom the boat was being made desired good rowing characteristics coupled with a fairly wide boat with the proper deadrise for good stability," wrote Austin. "Looking over the patterns I had on hand I thought that this combination would give us the desired features. Fortunately it worked out very well. When we tried out the boat it was steady as could be."[1]

For years Kenneth Durant had told me about his boyhood vacations at Camp Cedars on Forked Lake and the long journeys he made in a guide-boat. In spite of all the photographs he showed me, and all the details he told me, the guide-boat remained for me a mystery craft. I had always loved crossing the ocean in the great luxury liners before the Second World War. It was a leisurely way to travel. The ocean, the waves, have the same magnetism as a crackling fire; one can watch them for hours, meanwhile letting one's imagination roam. I also liked being out on the seas in comfortably large powerboats. While I was filming the construction of the gigantic dike that was to separate the North Sea from the Zuiderzee in Holland, I spent many months of each year between 1927 and 1932 in the high-powered boats of the construction engineers. But I distrusted small rowboats with the sheer only a few inches above the water.

Then, in the summer of 1958, my husband wanted to make a visit to Camp Cedars, which is accessible only by small boat. When we arrived at the foot of Forked Lake Carry, his guide-boat had already been brought there by the Adirondack Museum. I noticed with what anticipation he looked forward to the two hours of rowing. With great trepidation and a fluttering stomach, I stepped into the fragile craft, almost 17 feet long, and moved toward the stern seat, carefully stepping from rib foot to rib foot as I had been instructed to do. I do not think that any guide could have bettered Kenneth Durant in the way he vaulted the deck while pushing the boat into deep water. Frightening me half to death with his speed and agility, he forthwith lowered himself into the bow seat, took up the oars, and headed toward the distant shore. It was an impression and an experience I shall never forget. Instantly he had become part of the boat and rowed steadily and rhythmically, as if he had never left the woods. It was so fascinating an impression that all my apprehensions disappeared and I began to unwind and enjoy the journey. My reward was his smile showing how happy he was that I shared this experience with him. During our return trip a fog came up and later we were caught in a drenching rain, but this, too, was an exhilarating experience. Wet but happy, we reached shore safely.

Since that first journey I have had a deeper appreciation for the sketches made by Frederick B. Allen in the Adirondacks in 1869 and 1870.[2] Allen was exceptional in catching the charm and manners of the waterways. There are two sketches of the senior Mr. Allen seated in the stern of a square-ended guide-boat, dressed in a dark suit and holding an unfurled parasol over his head. Then there is a sketch of four ladies aboard a guide-boat, elegantly attired in voluminous dresses and charming beribboned hats. In another sketch Allen portrays a guide carrying on his shoulders an early and heavy guide-boat with massive stem posts and thick decks. The weary guide resting on the carry in still another sketch eloquently testifies to the weight of the burden he has just set down. The boatman is usually dressed in somber colors, blending with the natural shades of the woods, the bark of the trees, and the grays of the sand and gravel of the shallows, so that he will not startle the wild life.

Kenneth Durant: "I was one of the few lucky private individuals who had the opportunity to learn the ways of this beautiful and exciting craft." (Helen Durant)

There were so many ways in which a guide-boat could be enjoyed. Nothing gives a deeper feeling of solitude than floating over the wilderness lakes at night. Camping on the shore of Tupper Lake one night in the 1850s, Alfred B. Street took out his guide-boat after supper to explore the sensations of boating by night. It seemed to Street that the boat was gliding of its own volition without a whisper and that the guide's paddle worked as noiselessly "as the fin of a fish." Dark trees mingled with dark rocks, the black woods assumed fanciful shapes, all in the highest degree exciting to fancy. "The black objects above the boulder with a speck of pallid light, some would have said it was a log, with a bit of phosphorescence," wrote Street, "but it seemed to me a panther with his gleaming eye on a slumbering hunter."

Though in his book *Woods and Waters* Street gave only a meager description of the guide-boat, his narrative conveyed unmistakably the subtle motions of the boat, and he described, as no one else had done, the feel and sound of the boat that "wriggles like an eel" through a twisting river. In more open waters the boat proceeded safely, albeit with shifting walls of water on either side and ridges swelling up in front.

Street makes us listen to the ripples from the oars, which "clink along the sides like little muffled bells," and the wake "which makes hollow gurgles." We can hear the rustle of the lilypads "like a shower in the woods." As Street and his guide skimmed over the water, the shadows of some jagged branches were so accurately reflected in the black water that it seemed they would tear the boat apart while it glided over them.[3]

We picnicked along the shore of Long Lake one day, and my husband told me about another phenomenon. "Sometimes," he said, "when rowing along the east shore of a wooded lake just before the sun goes down, when the slanting rays strike the water

at just the right angle, it throws the shadow of the boat, oars and occupants up on the trees, high above the water, completely disengaged from the real form, a refraction never seen on land where a person's shadow always hugs his feet. The passengers in the ghostly craft mimic those in the real boat while both proceed together."

As we rowed back late that afternoon I watched for this faery refraction. My anticipation was too high: the clouds covered the sun. Approaching the Endion landing, my husband said, "I was one of the few lucky private individuals who, from early youth, had the opportunity to learn the ways of this beautiful and exciting craft." After securing our boat on the trailer, we returned it to the Adirondack Museum, where it is now on exhibit in the boathouse, a reminder of a joyful and romantic era.

Notes

1. Harold M. Austin, letter, October 7, 1978.
2. The originals of the F.B. Allen sketches are in the archives of the Adirondack Museum at Blue Mountain Lake, N.Y.; reproductions were published in Kenneth Durant's anthology *Guide-Boat Days and Ways* (Blue Mountain Lake, N.Y.: Adirondack Museum, 1963).
3. Alfred B. Street, *Woods and Waters*, or the Saranacs and Racket, (New York: M. Doolady, 1860), from miscellaneous narratives throughout the book.

Appendix A
The Grant Tally Boards

The tally boards of the Grant boat shop are half-inch pine panels on which Dwight Grant recorded serial numbers, weight, and dimensions, and almost always the names of the purchasers for each boat.

There were no tally boards for the years 1880, 1881, and 1882, but the *Boonville Herald*, March 11, 1880, reported that the Hon. H.D. Grant had begun to build "Saranac boats." It described one, already finished, as about 15 feet long and 4 feet wide, weighing about 80 pounds complete with seats and oars, and capable of carrying three persons and their duffel. "Mr. Henry Stanton is assisting Mr. Grant. . . ," said the *Herald*. "Several boats of this kind for navigating the lakes and streams in the northern wilderness will be built this season. . . ."

In a letter of March 14, 1959, Lewis Grant gave the following account of boats built and sold during the 1880-81 season.

16′ guide-boat	$58	Chris Goodsell, Brown's Tract guide
15′ guide-boat	$55	William Dart, Camp Dart's Lake, Brown's Tract guide
15′ guide-boat	$42	Sylvester Davis, "C.P."
14′6″ guide-boat	$52.75	Paul Jones, Brown's Tract guide
16′ guide-boat	$56	B.P. Graves, Boonville Men's Clothing Store

12′ guide-boat	$40	Fred Hess, guide. Owned boarding house, Cedar Island, Fourth Lake
12′6″ guide-boat	$43.10	Richard Crego, Boonville, farmer and Brown's Tract guide
12′ guide-boat	$40	James Dutton, city man. Camp on Big Moose
12′ guide-boat	$40	John van Valkenburg. Camp on Second Lake. Fulton Chain guide

In the same letter Lewis wrote that there was no doubt that these boats were built in the Rice Brothers' mill. Lewis had found an old account book of his father's, which noted that these boats had been paid for in 1881, before his father's shop was built. According to Lewis, the front part of the shop was built in October, November, and December of 1881, and Dwight Grant started building guide-boats there on January 21, 1882. The following is a list of boats sold during that season.

1881–1882 Season

16′ sail boat	$50	L.H. Taylor, city man, Log camp, L. Moose

13′ guide-boat	$48	L.H. Taylor, city man, camp, Little Moose
13′ guide-boat	$60	Lewis H. Lawrence, summer home, 4th L.
15′ guide-boat	$65	Harvey L. Lewis, Boonville, coal and feed dealer
16′ guide-boat	$58	Geo. Goodsell, Boonville-Old Forge Stage
14′6″ guide-boat	$52.75	A. Tom Griffin, guide, Old Forge
15′6″ guide-boat	$56	Frank Johnson, guide, Old Forge
15′ guide-boat	$54	Mr. Burnham, city man, log camp, L. Moose
16′ guide-boat	$67	Byron P. Graves, Boonville, men's clothing
13′ two boats	$120	A.B. Lamberton, Rochester, NY, camp on 2nd Lake Fulton Chain
18′ guide-boat	$70	John Brinckerhoff, Boonville, guide, game warden
15′ guide-boat	$54	Alonzo Wood, guide, camp 4th Lake
12′ two boats	$84	Edward Arnold, guide, Old Forge
14′6″ guide-boat	$53	Oscar Wood (son of Alonzo), guide, Old Forge
15′ guide-boat	$55	Chris Goodsell, guide, Old Forge
15′ guide-boat	$62	Sidney T. Grant, eldest son of H.D. Grant, died 1884
14′ guide-boat	$65	James Winters, guide, Old Forge
14′ guide-boat	$63	Bart Halliday, guide, "think he had a camp on Fulton Chain"
16′ guide-boat	$48.75	Gus Syphert, Boonville guide, snow-shoe maker
18′ guide-boat	$20	Theodore Seeber

Although there is no tally board for the 1882–83 season, the *Boonville Herald* of May 3, 1883, reported that four of Dwight Grant's Adirondack boats were taken to Moose River to be sent from there to the Fulton Chain. Grant kept one of these for his own use. The other three were sold to Jonathan Meeker, Garry Riggs, and Will Sperry.

These may have been boats built during the spring of 1882. Lewis reasoned that no guide-boats were built in the season of 1882–83 because during the fall of 1882 his father put an addition on the boat shop, and in the winter of 1882–83 he built the steamboat *Hunter* for Jonathan Meeker.

The first tally is headed "Winter 1883–1884." After that the boards carry the year of the spring in which boats were completed. Construction generally began in late autumn or early winter. A note on boat number 18, 1895, says, "This boat set up in June," which was exceptionally late. The boat could have been a special order. By that time Grant and other guides would be in the woods.

The first column in every tally shows the serial numbers for that year. Date and serial number were stamped into the stem under the deck, and on the outside of the yoke cleat, facing the sheer plank. *Shell weight*: taken on a steel yard when the boat came off the stocks, without decks, wales, or any fitting. It was omitted from the record of some of the larger "family boats," which were cumbersome to handle and for which weight was unimportant, since they were not to be carried. *Length bottom*: length of bottom board was the only specified length. For boats after 1894, this was 18 inches less than LOA. *Width bottom*: measured amidships across the top of the bottom board. *Space knees*: distance on centers between adjacent rib feet. *Pairs 0 ribs*: the number of identical center ribs, the 0 ribs. After the center ribs, the frames were numbered 1 to 12 in both directions. The footless scribe ribs, numbers 11 and 12 (which were not fastened to the bottom board but put in after the boat was partly or wholly planked), might be omitted on very short boats, in which case number 10 became a scribe rib. *Depth center*: distance from top of bottom board to horizontal line across top of sheer planks. *Height stems*: height in inches marked in cross lines on stem patterns. *Weight complete*: with three seats, one stern back rest, one neck yoke, one pair oars, one paddle, all metal fittings, painted or varnished. The rack, a removable false bottom or grating, put in after the boat was finished to protect siding against heavy freight or careless heels, was a late development, an accessory never included in the guide's work boat. *Purchaser*: brief notes on the original boards are supplemented by information received from Lewis Grant in a letter of March 14, 1959, and, in some cases, from other sources. Some data found penciled on the wall of the boat shop have been added to the tallies.

Abbreviations and terms

ALC	Adirondack League Club (member or camp)
B	Bisby Lake
BM	Big Moose Lake
FC	Fulton Chain of Lakes
GBDW	*Guide-Boat Days and Ways*
LLG	Lewis L. Grant
LM	Little Moose Lake
OF	Old Forge
4th	Fourth Lake of the Fulton Chain

(All named places are in New York State unless otherwise indicated.)

1884	Shell Weight	Length Bottom	Width Bottom	Space Knees	Pairs 0 Ribs	Depth Center	Height Stems	Weight Complete	Purchaser
No. 1	45	14	8½						
No. 2	46	14	8¼					68	Chris Wagner, New Bremen, guide Beaver River, farmer [LLG]
No. 3	40¼	14	8¼					68	Chris Wagner [see above]
No. 4	40	14	7½					73	
No. 5	42	14½	8					74	G. Riggs, Turin, guide FC
No. 6	42	16	8						Augustus (Gus) Syphert, guide, snowshoe maker [note]
No. 7	42½	16	8					78	Fred Hess, guide FC, built, managed boarding house Cedar Island, 4th
No. 8	39¾	15	7¾					75	
No. 9	36	13	7½					74	William Sperry, OF, guide, carpenter, camp builder
No. 10	38¾	14	7½					73	
No. 11	40	14½	8					74	Taylor [wall]
No. 12	36	13	7						
No. 13	40	14	7½						

1885	Shell Weight	Length Bottom	Width Bottom	Space Knees	Pairs 0 Ribs	Depth Center [wall]	Height Stems	Weight Complete	Purchaser
									Names of purchasers are not listed on tally board this year. *Boonville Herald*, March 26, 1885, reported that Grant made boats for the following:
No. 1	50	15	7¾			12			
No. 2	50	15	7½			12¼			
No. 3	43	14½	7½			12½			A.W. Hooper, New Haven, Conn. (Winchester rifles) [see 90–8]
No. 4	41	14	7½			12¼			Dr. E.S. Gaylord, New Haven, Conn., camp Dollar Island, 4th
No. 5	42	14	7½			12¼			
No. 6	40	14	7½			12¼			Hon. L.H. Lawrence, Utica, camp 4th [note]
No. 7	38	13	7½			12¼			
*No. 8	35	13	7½			12¼			Mr. and Mrs. Fred Hess, boarding house Cedar Island, 4th [see 84-7, 92–1, 93–7]
*No. 9	37	13	7½			12¼			
No. 10	45	15	8			12¼			Chris Goodsell, OF, guide FC [see 87–4, 94–5–7, 01–1–9]
No. 11	42	14	7½			12¼			J.H. Higby, BM, boarding house
No. 12	38	13	7½			12¼			Ed Arnold, OF, guide
No. 13	39	13	7½			12¼			Fred Rivett, guide

*On wall, opposite Nos. 8, 9 is pencil notation "cedar." DG built one boat of Spanish cedar for a customer who provided the lumber. "There is a piece of this cedar still in the shop. When rubbed with sand-paper it gives off a pleasant odor, like a cigar box." [LLG]

1886	Shell Weight	Length Bottom	Width Bottom	Space Knees	Pairs 0 Ribs	Depth Center	Height Stems	Weight Complete	Purchaser
No. 1	43	14	7¾						Lon (Alonzo) Wood, guide, 4th
No. 2	44	16	8					76	George Goodsell, guide, stage driver, ALC camp builder
No. 3	37	14	7⅜					65	Sie Wood, guide FC, ran Cohasset Hotel, 4th, son of Alonzo
No. 4	36	15	7⅜					65½	Dick Crego, Boonville, guide, farmer
No. 5	34	13	7¼						Artemus M. Church, Boonville & OF, guide FC, taxidermist
No. 6	31	12	7½						Jack Sheppard, OF, guide FC, ran steamboat FC
No. 7	30	12	7¼					56	Ned Ball, OF, guide, game warden FC & ALC
No. 8	36	14	7⅜					66	Josiah (Sie) Helmer, Boonville, guide FC, farmer
No. 9	37	14	7⅜					64	Andrew Alexander, Boonville, guide, mgr. Jane Sperry boarding home, BM
No. 10	43	15	7¾						
No. 11	38	14½	7⅜					67	Jack Sheppard [see 86-6]
No. 12	41	15	7¾						

1886 cont.									
No. 13	40	15	7⅝					70	
No. 14		14½	7¼						Henry Covey, BM, guide, builder, mgr. Covey boarding h. [Camp Crag, Wallace '95]
No. 15	37	14½	7¼					66	Chris Wagner

1887	*Shell Weight*	*Length Bottom*	*Width Bottom*	*Space Knees*	*Pairs 0 Ribs*	*Depth Center*	*Height Stems*	*Weight Complete*	*Purchaser*
No. 1	38½	14	7⅜					70	
No. 2	43½	15	7⅜						Jap Johnson, OF, guide FC
No. 3	44	15	7⅜					76	Mr. McCarthy
No. 4	50	17	7⅜						Chris Goodsell, OF, guide FC
No. 5	49	16	7¾					78	Lewis H. Lawrence, Utica, camp 4th [note also Grady]
No. 6	41½	14½	7¼						Chris Wagner [see 84-2]
No. 7	41½	14½	7¼					71	James Dunbar, from Beaver River section
No. 8		18	10						Fred Hess [see 84-7]

1887 cont.	Shell Weight	Length Bottom	Width Bottom	Space Knees	Pairs 0 Ribs	Depth Center	Height Stems	Weight Complete	Purchaser
No. 9	$38\frac{1}{2}$	14	$7\frac{1}{2}$					68	Riley Parsons, Boonville, carpenter, guide-boat builder, OF
No. 10	32	11	$7\frac{1}{2}$					57	
No. 11	39	14	$7\frac{1}{2}$						

1888	Shell Weight	Length Bottom	Width Bottom	Space Knees	Pairs 0 Ribs	Depth Center	Height Stems	Weight Complete	Purchaser
No. 1	41	14	$7\frac{1}{2}$	$5\frac{3}{4}$	5		$22\frac{1}{2}$-$23\frac{1}{2}$	71	NO NAMES
No. 2	$42\frac{1}{4}$	$14\frac{1}{2}$	$7\frac{3}{8}$	$5\frac{1}{8}$	9		$22\frac{1}{2}$-$23\frac{1}{2}$	70	
No. 3	$39\frac{3}{4}$	$14\frac{1}{2}$	$7\frac{3}{8}$	$5\frac{1}{2}$	7		$22\frac{1}{2}$-$23\frac{1}{2}$	69	
No. 4	$41\frac{1}{2}$	$14\frac{1}{2}$	$7\frac{3}{8}$	$5\frac{1}{2}$	7		$22\frac{1}{2}$-$23\frac{1}{2}$	69	
No. 5	44	15	$7\frac{1}{2}$	$5\frac{5}{16}$	9		23-24	74	
No. 6	$40\frac{1}{4}$	$14\frac{1}{2}$	$7\frac{3}{8}$	$5\frac{1}{2}$	7		$22\frac{1}{2}$-$23\frac{1}{2}$	69	
No. 7	35	12	$7\frac{3}{8}$	$5\frac{1}{8}$	3		$22\frac{1}{2}$-23	60	
No. 8	$34\frac{1}{4}$	12	$7\frac{3}{8}$	$5\frac{1}{8}$	3		$22\frac{1}{2}$-23	59	

1888 cont.									
No. 9	40	14	7⅜	5 5/16	7		22½-23½	69	
No. 10	41¼	14	7⅜	5 5/16	7		22½-23½	69	
No. 11	45	15	7⅛	5 5/16	9		23-24	72	
No. 12	45	15	7⅛	5 5/16	9		23-24	74	
No. 13	36	13	7¼	5 7/32	5		22½-23	64	Bill Dart [LLG letter, Aug. 30, 1959]
No. 14	40	14½	7⅛	5½	7		23-24	70	
No. 15	40	14	7¼	5¼	7		23-23½	64	

1889	*Shell Weight*	*Length Bottom*	*Width Bottom*	*Space Knees*	*Pairs 0 Ribs*	*Depth Center*	*Height Stems*	*Weight Complete*	*Purchaser*
No. 1	46	14½	7¼	5⅛	9		23-24		NO NAMES
No. 2	45	14½	7¼	5⅛	9		23-24		
No. 3	43	14½	7¼	5⅛	9		22½-23½		
No. 4	41	14	7¼	5¼	7		22½-23½		
No. 5	39	14	7¼	5¼	7		22½-23½		
No. 6	40	14	7¼	5¼	7		22½-23½		

1889 cont.	Shell Weight	Length Bottom	Width Bottom	Space Knees	Pairs 0 Ribs	Depth Center	Height Stems	Weight Complete	Purchaser
No. 7	42	14½	7¼	5⅛	9		22½-23½	71	NO NAMES
No. 8	32	12	7¼	5½	3		22-22½		
No. 9	33	12	7⅝	5½	3		22-22½		
No. 10	37	13	7¼	5⁷/₃₂	5		22½-23		
No. 11	40	14½	7¼	5⅛	9		23-24		
No. 12	42	14¾	7¼	3³/₁₆	13		22½-23½		
No. 13	36	13	7¼	5⁷/₃₂	5		22½-23		
No. 14	41	14¾	7¼	3³/₁₆	13		22½-23½		

1890	Shell Weight	Length Bottom	Width Bottom	Space Knees	Pairs 0 Ribs	Depth Center	Height Stems	Weight Complete	Purchaser
No. 1	47	15	7¼	5	11	12½	23-24	73	
No. 2	37	13	7¼	5⁷/₃₂	5	12¼	22½-23	66	Geo. Barber, White Lake Corners, carpenter, guide ALC, B, LM
No. 3	41	14	7¼	5¼	7	12¼	22½-23½	73	
No. 4	41	15	7¼	5	11	12½	23-24	72	Mr. Anderson, city man, camp Eagle Bay 4th

No.									
No. 5	37	13	7¼	5⁷⁄₃₂	5	12	22-22½	67	Mr. Cook, Boonville businessman
No. 6	42	14	7¼	5½	7	12	22½-23½	72	Merrill White, Boonville, guide FC & LM, farmer
No. 7	46	15	7⅜	5	11	12	23-24	76	Gus Syphert, Boonville [see 84-5]
No. 8	29	11	7½	5³⁄₁₆	3	11¾	23-24	58	Mr. Hoper, city man, summer tourist FC
No. 9	42	15	7½	5	11	12	23-24	73	
No. 10	38	14	7¼	5	9	12	22½-23½	70	R.W. Roberts, Talcottville, farmer, guide ALC, LM
No. 11	32	12	7⅜	5⅛	3	11¾	22-22½	62	W.C. Augur, mgr. Cedar Island Camp 4th [Wallace 1895]
No. 12	39	14½	7⅜	5⅛	7-0 4-1	12	23-23½	71	
No. 13	40	14½	7⅜	5⅛	7-0 4-1	12	23-23½	72	Dennis Fraula, OF, guide, caretaker Wm. S. De Camp
No. 14	32	12	7⅜	5	3	11¾	22½-23½	62	

1891	*Shell Weight*	*Length Bottom*	*Width Bottom*	*Space Knees*	*Pairs 0 Ribs*	*Depth Center*	*Height Stems*	*Weight Complete*	*Purchaser*
No. 1	37	13	7⅜	5 7/32	5	12	22-22½	60	Harry L. Spinning, Woodhull Lake, guide ALC, carpenter, B
No. 2	38	13′7″	7⅜	5 1/16	7	12	23-23½	69	V. Gilbert, Boonville, later Inlet, guide FC
No. 3	37	13′8″	7⅝	5⅛	7	12	22½-23	70	Samuel J. Bryant, New Haven, Conn., ALC, camp B
No. 4	57	15	7⅜	5	11	12¼	23-24	104	J. Porter, bought Cedar Island of F. Hess
No. 5	58	15	7¾	5	11	12¼	23-24	104	J. Porter
No. 6	84	18	10	5¾	13	13	24½-25	138	Alonzo Wood, 4th [see 86-1]
No. 7	29	11	7⅝	5 1/16	3	11¾	21-21	55	W.H. Boardman, ALC president 1889-1899, camp B
No. 8	29	11	7⅝	5 1/16	3	11¾	21½-21½	53	
No. 9	41	14′7″	7¾	5⅛	9	12	23-24	73	
No. 10	38	13′10″	7⅞	3⅜	11	12	22½-23	71	Chris Wagner, New Bremen [see 84-2]
No. 11	39	14′7″	7⅞	5⅛	9	12	23-23½	71	Peter Rivett, OF, carpenter, guide ALC, LM
No. 12	41	14′7″	7⅞	5⅛	9	12	23-23½	72	Lewis L. Lawrence [see 87-5]
No. 13		13′1″	7⅞	5¼	5	12	23-23½	64	Mr. Bowers
No. 14	39	14′7″	7⅞	5⅛	9	12	23-23½	70	Val Grosjean, Boonville, father ran a woodworking mill

No.									
No. 15	37	14	7⅞	5¼	7	12	23-23½	69	Josiah (Sie) Wood, guide FC, son of Lon Wood [see 86-3]
No. 16	37	14	7¹⁵⁄₁₆	5¼	7	12	23-23½	70	Ed. Arnold, son of Otis Arnold, Thendara
No. 17	29	12	7¾	5⅛	3	11¾	22-22½	59	J. Porter, owner Cedar Island [see 91-4-5]
No. 18	29½	12	7¾	5⅛	3	11¾	22-22½	60	J. Porter
No. 19	34	13′1″	7¾	5¼	5	11¾	22½-23	64	Abner Blakeman, Inlet, guide FC, brother-in-law of Fred Hess
No. 20	30	12′1″	7¾	4¾	5	11½	22½-23		
No. 21	45	15′1″	7⅞	5	11	12	23-23½	60	F.J. Brown
No. 22	40	14′7″	7⅞	5⅛	9	12	23-23½		G. Riggs, Turin, guide L.H. Lawrence camp 4th
No. 23	35	14′3″	7¾	5	9	11¼	23-23½	63	A.M. Church, Boonville, OF, guide, taxidermist
No. 24	35	14′7″	7⅞	5⅛	9	11¼	23-23½		Dick Crego, Boonville guide, farmer [see 86-4]
No. 25	25	11	7¾	5⅛	3	11	21-21		Dr. E.S. Gaylord [see 85]

1892	Shell Weight	Length Bottom	Width Bottom	Space Knees	Pairs 0 Ribs	Depth Center	Height Stems	Weight Complete	Purchaser
No. 1	43	14′7″	8½	5⅛	9	11½	23-23½	72	Fred Hess, Inlet builder, mgr. Arrowhead & Hess Inn [see 84-7]
No. 2	41	14′7″	8½	5⅛	9	11½	23-23½	73	Lewis L. Lawrence [see 87-5]
No. 3	39	14	8	5¼	7	11½	23-23½	71	
No. 4	42	14′7″	8½	5⅛	9	11¾	23-23½	73	
No. 5	42	14′7″	8½	5⅛	9	11¾	23-23½	73	L.W. Fiske, Boonville, lawyer, camp 4th
No. 6	41	14′7″	8½	5⅛	9	11¾	23-23½	73	
No. 7	39	14′1″	8¼	5¼	7	11¾	23-23½	74	Vernon Gilbert, Inlet, guide FC, brother of V. Gilbert [see 91-2]
No. 8	39	13′7″	8½	5⅛	7	11¾	23-23½	70	A.M. Collier, summer tourist from NYC
No. 9	37	13′7″	8½	5 1/16	7	11¾	22½/3	69	Cornelius B. Erwin, Boonville, farmer
No. 10	42	14′1″	8¼	5¼	9	11¾	23-23½	73	
No. 11	42	14′7″	8½	5⅛	9	11¾	23-23½	75	
No. 12	40	14′1″	8¼	5½	7	11¾	23-23½	71	
No. 13	41	14′1″	8¼	5¼	7	11¾	23-23½	71	Lewis L. Grant: "school days! Mother and I did a lot of fishing, vacations, 4th!"
No. 14	42	14′7″	8½	5⅛	9	11¾	23-23½		H.D. Grant, Boonville, farmer, millwright, Assemblyman, camp builder, guide FC, guide-boat builder

1892 cont.

	Shell Weight	Length Bottom	Width Bottom	Space Knees	Pairs 0 Ribs	Depth Center	Height Stems	Weight Complete	Purchaser
No. 15	34	12'1"	8½	5¼	3	11¾	22-22½		Emmet Marks, OF, many years in charge State Fish Hatchery
No. 16	34	12'1"	8½	5⅛	3	11¾	22-22½		
No. 17	37	14'1"	8¼	5¼	7	11¾	23-23½		Henry Covey, guide [see 86-14]

1893*	Shell Weight	Length Bottom	Width Bottom	Space Knees	Pairs 0 Ribs	Depth Center	Height Stems	Weight Complete	Purchaser
No. 1	46	14'7"	8⅛	5⅛	9	11½	23-23½	73	Milo Bull, stage driver Boonville to OF, camp 4th
No. 2	45	14'7"	8	5⅛	9	11	23-23½		
No. 3	43	14'7"	8½	5⅛	9	11¼	23-23½	71	
No. 4	43	14'7"	8	5⅛	9	11¼	23-23½	73	Mr. Harper, city man, summer tourist FC
No. 5	48	15'7"	7¾	5	11	11¼	23-24	81	James C. Dunbar [see 87-7]
No. 6	90	18	10	6¼	9	12¼	24½-25		Henry H. Covey, 18' freight boat [see 86-14]
No. 7	46	16	8	5⅜	11	11	24-24½	77	Fred Hess, builder, mgr. Arrowhead, Woods and Cedar Island hotels [see 84-7]
No. 8	43	14½	8	5⅛	9	11¼	23-23½		Al D. Barber, Boonville, feed & coal dealer

*The changeover: No. 1 marked "model 92"; No. 3, "old model"; Nos. 4 to 8, "model 92."

1894	Shell Weight	Length Bottom	Width Bottom	Space Knees	Pairs 0 Ribs	Depth Center	Height Stems	Weight Complete	Purchaser
No. 1	41	14	8½	5⅛	7	11	23-23½	74	Peter Rivett, OF, guide, carpenter, house builder, ALC, FC, LM
No. 2	33	11	7½	5 1/16	3	11	22-22 (new model)	60	Chris Wagner [see 84-2]
No. 3	50	16	8	5 1/16	13	11¼	23½-24	82	James C. Dunbar [see 87-7]
No. 4	52	16	8	5 1/16	13	4¼	23½-24	84	Chris Wagner [see 84-2]
No. 5	48	14½	8	5⅛	9	11½	23-23½	76	James Higby, guide, hotel BM
No. 6	24	9	8½	5⅛	1	10¾	20-20	43	L.W. Fiske [see 92-5]
No. 7		15	8½	5¼	11	11½	23-23½	78	James Higby [see 94-5]
No. 8	41	14	8½	5¼	7	11½	23-23½	73	James Pullman, Thendara mill owner, camp builder FC
No. 9	43	14½	8½	5⅛	9	11½	23-23½	74	Walter Briggs, OF, fire watcher Rondaxe Mountain
No. 10	42	14	8½	5¼	7	11½	23-23½	73	Frank Sperry, OF, guide LM & FC
No. 11	26	9½	8½	5⅛	3	10⅞	21-21	52	Ned Ball [see 86-7]
No. 12	39	13½	8½	5 1/16	7	11½	23-23½	71	Harry L. Spinning [see 91-1]

1895	*Shell Weight*	*Length Bottom*	*Width Bottom*	*Space Knees*	*Pairs 0 Ribs*	*Depth Center*	*Height Stems*	*Weight Complete*	*Purchaser*
No. 1	38	12	8	5 1/8	3	11 1/4	22-23 1/2		
No. 2	46	14 1/2	8 1/2	5 1/8	9	11 1/4	23-23 1/2		
No. 3	45	14 1/2	8 1/2	5 1/8	9	11 1/4	23-23 1/2		
No. 4	43	14 1/2	8 1/2	5 1/8	9	11 1/4	23-23 1/2		
*No. 5	44	15	7	5	11	12	23-23 1/2		Frank Williams, guide B & LM
**No. 6	43	14 1/2	8 1/2	5 1/8	9	11 1/4	23-23 1/2		
No. 7	42	14	8	5 5/16	7	11 3/4	23-23 1/2		
No. 8	32	11	8	5 1/16	3	11 1/4	22-23		Homer Traffern, Boonville young man; father had camp 7th
No. 9	32	11	8	5 1/16	3	11	22-23		G. Riggs [see 84-5, 91-22]
No. 10	43	14 1/2	8 1/2	5 1/8	9	11 1/4	23-23 1/2		George Smith, worked at camps on 4th
No. 11	45	15	8 1/2	5 1/4	9	11 3/4	23-23 1/2		Chris Wagner [see 84-2]
No. 12		18	11 1/2	6 1/4	9	13	24-24 1/2		
No. 13	32	11	8	5	7	11 1/4	22-22		Dick Crego [see 86-4]
No. 14		18	12	6 1/4	9	13	24-24		W.H. Boardman [see 91-7]
No. 15	46	15	8 3/8	5 5/16	9	11 1/4	22-22		
No. 16	39	14	8	5 1/4	7	11 3/4	23 1/2		
No. 17	41	14 1/2	8 1/2	5 1/8	9		23 1/2		

1895 cont.	Shell Weight	Length Bottom	Width Bottom	Space Knees	Pairs 0 Ribs	Depth Center	Height Stems	Weight Complete	Purchaser
No. 18	44	14½	8½	5⅛	9	11¼	23½	74	Harry Costello, New York City, young man in Boonville for his health

* Letters KD July 31, 1958; June 2, 1959, with notes LLG
** Diary August 5, 1959

1896	Shell Weight	Length Bottom	Width Bottom	Space Knees	Pairs 0 Ribs	Depth Center	Height Stems	Weight Complete	Purchaser
*No. 1	32	11	8	4¹³⁄₁₆	3	11	22½	61	W.D. Baldwin, NYC (Otis Elevator), ALC, camp Bisby
*No. 2	31	11	8	5	3	11	22½	61	W.D. Baldwin
No. 3	44	14½	8½	5⅛	9	11¼	23½	74	W.D. Baldwin
*No. 4		18	12	6¼	7-0 4-1	13	25		W.D. Baldwin [see 96-1]
No. 5	44	14	8⅜	3⁵⁄₁₆	7	11½	23½	75	
No. 6	41	14	8½	5⁵⁄₁₆	7	11½	23½	72	
No. 7	41	14	8½	5⁵⁄₁₆	7	11½	23½	72	
No. 8	40	14	8½	5⁵⁄₁₆	7	11½	23½	72	
No. 9	43	14½	8½	5⅛	9	11½	23½	73	
*No. 10	41	14½	8½	5⅛	9	11¼	23½	73	William Commerford,* Boonville, guide

* LLG March 14, 1959, p. 7

1896 cont.

	Shell Weight	Length Bottom	Width Bottom	Space Knees	Pairs 0 Ribs	Depth Center	Height Stems	Weight Complete	Purchaser
No. 11	42	14	8½	5 1/16	9	11¼	23½	72	Fred Hess, Inlet [see 84-6]
No. 12	44	14½	8½	5⅛	9	11¼	23½	75	George Parkhurst, Buffalo, ALC camp LM
No. 13	44	14½	8½	5⅛	9	11¼	23½	75	

1897

	Shell Weight	Length Bottom	Width Bottom	Space Knees	Pairs 0 Ribs	Depth Center	Height Stems	Weight Complete	Purchaser
No. 1	39	13½	9	5 1/16	7		23	68	J.H. Wright, ALC, Camp Bisby
No. 2	36	13½	9	5 1/16	7		23	67	J.H. Wright
No. 3	36	13½	8½	5 1/16	7		23	67	J.H. Wright
No. 4	35	13½	8½	5 1/16	7		23	66	Chris Wagner [see 84-2]
No. 5	38	14½	8⅛	5⅛	9		23½	72	Chris Wagner
No. 6	42	16	8½	5 5/16	11		24	74	Fred Hess [see 84-6]
No. 7	40	15	8½	5¼	9		23½	70	George Goodsell [see 86-2]
No. 8	36	13½	8½	5 1/16	7		23	64	William Commerford [see 96-10]
No. 9	37	13½	8½	5 1/16	7		23	69	Alexander White, OF, ALC guide and camp builder, LM
No. 10	34	12½	8½	5	5		23½	65	D.H. Weston
No. 11	39	14½	8½	5⅛	9		23½	70	G. Riggs [see 84-5]

1897 cont.	Shell Weight	Length Bottom	Width Bottom	Space Knees	Pairs 0 Ribs	Depth Center	Height Stems	Weight Complete	Purchaser
No. 12	36	13½	8½	5 1/16	7		23	67	Walter ("Coon") Briggs, guide, fire watcher
No. 13	74	18	11	6¼	7-0 4-1		25	116	Frank Williams [see 95-5]
No. 14	39	14	8½	5⅛	7		23½	71	
No. 15	43	14½	8½	5⅛	9	11¼	23½	74	John Starin (?)

1898	Shell Weight	Length Bottom	Width Bottom	Space Knees	Pairs 0 Ribs	Depth Center	Height Stems	Weight Complete	Purchaser
No. 1	41	15	8½	5¼	9	11⅜	23½		Hank Hart, Inlet, guide FC, boarding house 4th
No. 2	43	15	8½	5¼	9	11⅜	23½		Arch Delmarsh, Inlet, guide FC, Rocky Point Inn
No. 3	39	13½	8½	5 1/16	7	11½	23		Miss H. Wyncoop, NYC, at F.A. Booth camp LM
No. 4	31	11	8	4¾	3		22½	56	George W. Parkhurst, Buffalo, ALC, camp LM
No. 5	30	11	8	5	7 no. 10 scribe		22½	59	Charles L. Pine, Troy, ALC, summers at Club House LM
No. 6	31	11	8	5	7	11	22	59	Dan Ainsworth, BM, guide
No. 7	31	11	8	5	7	11	22	60	Charles Bratten, city man who spent summers BM (?)

1898 cont.

	Purchaser	Weight Complete	Height Stems	Depth Center	Pairs 0 Ribs	Space Knees	Width Bottom	Length Bottom	Shell Weight
No. 8	Dick Crego, caretaker Theodore Page, camp BM [see 86-4]	59	22	11	7	5	8	11	31
No. 9	J.A. Delanoy, NYC, ALC, camp B		23	11¼	7	5 1/16	8½	13½	38

1899

	Purchaser	Weight Complete	Height Stems	Depth Center	Pairs 0 Ribs	Space Knees	Width Bottom	Length Bottom	Shell Weight
No. 1	James Douglas, NYC, ALC, camp LM	68	23	11¼	7	5 1/16	8½	13½	39
No. 2	Fred Kristzer, Morehouseville, guide	68	23	11¼	7	5 1/16	8½	13½	38
No. 3	Wm. G. DeWitt, NYC, broker, ALC, camp LM	78	24	11¾	9-0 4-1	5 5/16	8½	16	47
No. 4	Peter Rivett [see 94-1]	65	22½	11¼	5	5¼	8½	13	37
No. 5	Wm. G. DeWitt [see 99-3]	59	22	11¼	3/11	5 1/16	8½	11	32
No. 6	Melvin Oley, White Lake, guide LM, forest ranger	70	23½	11¼	7	5¼	8½	14	38
No. 7	ALC, LM boathouse, for rent to members	150	25	12	7-0 4-1	6¼	12	18	
No. 8	James Douglas [99-1]	150	25	12	7-0 4-1	6¼	12	18	
No. 9	Frederick A. Booth, NYC, ALC, camp LM	150	25	12	7-0 4-1	6¼	12½	18	

1899 cont.	Shell Weight	Length Bottom	Width Bottom	Space Knees	Pairs 0 Ribs	Depth Center	Height Stems	Weight Complete	Purchaser
No. 10	41	14½	8½	5⅛	9	11¼	23½	72	Charles Brown, Boonville, guide, carpenter, B, LM
No. 11	39	13½	8½	5 1/16	7	11¼	23	70	W.H. Boardman [see 91-7]
No. 12	42	14½	8½	5⅛	9	11¼	23½	72	W.E. Lowe, NYC, broker, ALC, camp LM
No. 13	38	13½	8½	5 1/16	7	11¼	23	68	Dr. Alfred Meyer, NYC, camp LM

1900	Shell Weight	Length Bottom	Width Bottom	Space Knees	Pairs 0 Ribs	Depth Center	Height Stems	Weight Complete	Purchaser
*No. 1	35	12½	8½	5	5	11¼	22½	65	H.L. Spinning [see 91-1]
*No. 2	28	10½	8	4⅞	3 no. 10 scribe	11	22	55	H.L. Spinning
*No. 3	52	16' 1⅝"	8½		7-0 4-1	11½	24	90	H.L. Spinning
No. 4	37	13½	8½	5 1/16	7	11¼	23	68	F.M. Johnston, Poughkeepsie, ALC, LM
No. 5	32	11	8½	5 1/16	3 no. 10 scribe	11	22½	60	B.D. Folwell
No. 6	39	13	8½	5¼	7 no. 10 scribe	12¾	24	68	Frank Williams, guide BM [see 95-5]
No. 7	31	11	8½	5 1/16	3 no. 10 scribe	11	22½	59	Dr. Charles W. Stimson, NYC, ALC, camp LM

1900 cont.									
No. 8	30	11	8	5 1/16	3 no. 10 scribe	11½	22	58	George Ravick, Inlet, guide
No. 9	41	14½	8½	5⅛	9	11¼	23½	71	Charles Brown [see 99-10]
No. 10	40	13½	8½	5 1/16	7	11¼	23	72	Dr. Ritter
No. 11	48	16	9½	5 5/16	9-0 4-1	12	24½	87	Dr. Charles W. Stimson [see 00-7]
No. 12	40	14	8½	5¼	7	11¼	23½	71	Arthur Irwin, "I think this was a young man in the woods for his health." [LLG]
No. 13		18	12½	6¼	7-0 4-1	12	25	137	L.W. Brown, Utica, "Warnick & Brown Tobacco," camp BM
No. 14		18	12½	6¼	7-0 4-1	12	25	137	Dr. Ritter
No. 15	39	14	8½	5¼	7	11¼	23½	69	William Commerford [see 96-10]
No. 16	40	14	8½	5¼	8½	11¼	23½	74	H.D. Grant, "a new boat for Dad" [LLG]
No. 17	36	13½	8½	5 1/16	13½	11¼	23	68	J.W. Norton, Otter Lake, gift shop
No. 18	43	14½	8½	5⅛	14½	11¼	23½	74	D.R. Sperry, OF, built telephone line to Old Forge
No. 19	41	13½	8½	5 1/16	13½	11¼	22½	72	Thomas Husted, ALC Honnedaga(?)
No. 20	55	16	10¾	5 5/16	10¾ 4-1	12⅛	24		Thomas R. Proctor, Utica, NY, President ALC 1905–1906

* LLG: "I think he got these boats for ALC members."

1901	*Shell Weight*	*Length Bottom*	*Width Bottom*	*Space Knees*	*Pairs 0 Ribs*	*Depth Center*	*Height Stems*	*Weight Complete*	*Purchaser*
No. 1	44	15	8½	5	11	12	23½	76	James Higby [see 94-5]
No. 2	38	13½	8½	5 1/16	7	11¼	23	67	James M. Taylor, Poughkeepsie, Pres. Vassar College, ALC, camp LM
No. 3	36	13′4½″	8½	5	7	11¼	23	65	Miss Martha Williams, Buffalo, ALC, camp LM
No. 4	36	13′4½″	8½	5	7	11¼	23	65	W.P. Smith
No. 5	29	11	8½	5 1/16	3 no. 10 scribe	11	22½	60	Martha Williams [see 01-3]
No. 6	29	11	9½	5 1/16	3 no. 10 scribe	11	22½	59	Leslie Brown [see 00-13]
No. 7	36	13′4½″	8½	5	7	11¼	23	65	William Commerford, fish hatchery owner [see 96-10]
No. 8	68	16½		5¾	7-0 4-1	13	25	128	John U. Fraley, NYC, ALC, camp LM
No. 9	44	15	8½	5	9-0 4-1	12	24	76	Mrs. James Higby [see 94-5]
No. 10	38	13′4½″	8½	5	7	11	23	67	Charles Martin, BM, guide, boarding house BM
No. 11	75	18	13	6¼	7-0 4-1	12¼	25	138	Martha Williams [see 01-3]
No. 12	30	11	8½	5 1/16	3 no. 10 scribe	11	22½	58	John B. Chambers, NYC, ALC, camp LM
No. 13	75	18	12¾	6⅜	7-0 4-1	12	25	149	William G. DeWitt [see 99-3]

1901 cont.

	Shell Weight	Length Bottom	Width Bottom	Space Knees	Pairs 0 Ribs	Depth Center	Height Stems	Weight Complete	Purchaser
No. 14	73	18	12¾	6⅜	11	12	25	147	John B. Chambers [see 01-12]
No. 15	37	13′4½″	8½	5	7	11¼	23	68	Henry F. Taylor, NYC, broker, ALC, Mountain Lodge LM

1902

	Shell Weight	Length Bottom	Width Bottom	Space Knees	Pairs 0 Ribs	Depth Center	Height Stems	Weight Complete	Purchaser
No. 1	40	13½	8½	5 1/16	7	11¼	23	73	James Douglas, NYC, ALC, camp LM
No. 2	37	13′4½″	8½	5	7	11¼	23	68	Wm. E. Lowe [see 99-12]
No. 3	38	13½	8½	5 1/16	7	11¼	23	69	George Commerford, Boonville, farmer, guide for W.P. Hall, Bisby
No. 4	75	18	12	6⅜	7-0 4-1	12⅛	25	151	F.S. Woodbury
No. 5	76	18	12	6⅜	7-0 4-1	12½	25	153	W.H. Albright
No. 6	39	14	8½	5¼	7	12	23½	70	Dan Ainsworth [see 98-6]
No. 7	29	11′2¾″	8	5 3/16	3	11⅛	23	54	William P. Smith, ALC president, 1907-1910, camp LM
No. 8	27	10	8½	5	1	11	22	52	Melvin J. Oley [see 99-6]
No. 9	26	10	8½	5	1	11	22	42	Nelson Chandler, White Lake, guide ALC

1902 cont.

	Shell Weight	Length Bottom	Width Bottom	Space Knees	Pairs 0 Ribs	Depth Center	Height Stems	Weight Complete	Purchaser
No. 10	31	11½	8½	5⁵/₁₆	3	11¼	22½	61	Chris Wagner [see 84-2]
No. 11	38	13½	8½	5¹/₁₆	7	11¼	23	69	Edward Turk, White Lake, farmer, guide Bisby, LM
No. 12	37	13½	8½	5¹/₁₆	7	11⅝	23	68	Charles Bratten [see 98-7]
No. 13	37	13½	8½	5¹/₁₆	7	11½	23	68	Miss S.W. Masters, Dobbs Ferry, ALC, camp LM

1903

	Shell Weight	Length Bottom	Width Bottom	Space Knees	Pairs 0 Ribs	Depth Center	Height Stems	Weight Complete	Purchaser
No. 1	39	13½	8½	5¹/₁₆	7	11¼	23	69	S.D. Stockton, Poughkeepsie, ALC, camp Bisby
No. 2	44	14½	8½	5⅛	9	11¼	23½	83	William P. Hall, NYC, ALC president 1911-22, camp Bisby
No. 3	35	12	8½	5⅛	3	11¼	23	61	William P. Hall
No. 4	75	18	12	6⅜	7-0 4-1	12	25	150	William P. Hall
No. 5	75	18	12	6⅜	7-0 4-1	12	25	150	Richard Crego [see 86-4, 98-8]
No. 6	38	13½	8½	5¹/₁₆	7	11¼	23	68	Arthur Talmage, Netherwood, N.J., son of ALC member, LM
No. 7	38	13½	8½	5¹/₁₆	7	11¼	23	69	William Commerford [see 96-10]
No. 8	38	13½	8½	5¹/₁₆	7	11¼	23	69	Alvin Wood, OF, caretaker camp LM

No. 9	38	13½	8½	5 1/16	7	11¼	23	69	Roy Crego, OF, guide and caretaker, ALC, LM (son of Dick)
No. 10	38	13½	8½	5 1/16	7	11¼	23	69	James Dalton, Boonville, guide and caretaker, ALC, LM
No. 11	38	13½	8½	5 1/16	7	11¼	23	69	Mrs. F.G. Mead, Plainfield, NY(?), ALC, LM
No. 12	38	13½	8½	5 1/16	7	11¼	23	67	Alex White [see 97-9]
No. 13	65	16	10¾	5 5/16	9-0 / 4-1	12⅛	24	105	T.R. Proctor [see 00-20]
No. 14	38	13½	8½	5 1/16	7	11¼	23	69	Frank Perkins, OF, guide ALC, LM
No. 15	45	15	8½	5	11	12	24	88 w/rack	Leslie W. Brown [see 00-13]
No. 16	30	10½	8½	4⅞	1	11	22	53	L.B. Smith, son of ALC member Wm. P. Smith, camp LM
No. 17	31	11	8½	5 1/16	3 no. 10 scribe	11	20½	59	Richard Crego [see 86-4, 98-8]

1904	Shell Weight	Length Bottom	Width Bottom	Space Knees	Pairs 0 Ribs	Depth Center	Height Stems	Weight Complete	Purchaser
No. 1	39	13½	8½	5 1/16	7	11¼	23	69	J.S. Frelinghuysen, NJ Senator, insurance broker, ALC, camp LM
No. 2	39	13½	8½	5 1/16	7	11¼	23	69	L.F. Stanton, Beaver River man
No. 3	39	13½	8½	5 1/16	7	11¼	23	67	William Commerford [see 97-8]
No. 4	39	13½	8½	5 1/16	7	11¼	23	68	Will Sperry [see 84-9]
No. 5	40	14	8½	5¼	7	11¼	23½	70	Charles Wood, carpenter and guide BM(?)
No. 6	31	11'9"	7½	5 1/16	3	11¼	22½	58	Charlot F. Lowe, daughter of W.E. Lowe, ALC, camp LM
No. 7	41	14'2"	8½	5 5/16	9	11¼	23½	71	Charles E. Miller, NYC, lawyer, camp LM
No. 8	46	16	9	5 5/16	9-0 4-1	11¾	24	78	Theodore A. Page, large land-owner BM, camp BM
No. 9	42	14½	7½	5⅛	9	11¼	23½	71	Melvin J. Oley [see 99-6]
No. 10	43	14½	8	5⅛	9	11¼	23½	72	Thomas Barrett, BM, guide, bought Cohasset Hotel of Sie Wood
*No. 11	38	12½	8½	5	5	11¼	23	65 rack 8	T.P. Kingsford, Kingsford Corn Starch, camp BM
No. 12	71	18	12	6⅜	7-0 4-1	12	24½	114	J.S. Frelinghuysen [see 04-1]
*No. 13	71	18	12	6⅜	7-0 4-1	12	23½	112 rack 15	T.P. Kingsford [see 04-11]
No. 14	43	14½	8½	5⅛	9	11¼	23½	73	Chris Wagner [see 84-2]

1904 cont.

	Shell Weight	Length Bottom	Width Bottom	Space Knees	Pairs 0 Ribs	Depth Center	Height Stems	Weight Complete	Purchaser
No. 15	32	10½	8½	5¼	1 no. 10 scribe	11	22	59	Ed Griffith, Boonville, guide, caretaker H.J. Wright, Bisby
No. 16	39	13½	8½	5¼	7	11¼	23	68	Lewis L. Grant

* Nos. 11 and 13 at Camp Tokenka, Mr. O.W. Hubbell, Big Moose. The camp and boats purchased by Mr. Hubbell from T.P. Kingsford. The boats, having been scarcely used, were in perfect condition when seen on July 26, 1961.

1905

	Shell Weight	Length Bottom	Width Bottom	Space Knees	Pairs 0 Ribs	Depth Center	Height Stems	Weight Complete	Purchaser
No. 1	43	14½	8¾	5⅛	9	11½	23½	75	Mrs. A.H. Harris, NYC, ALC, camp LM
No. 2	42	14½	8¾	5⅛	9	11½	23½	72	Noah C. Rogers, NYC, ALC, camp LM
*No. 3	42	14½	8¾	5⅛	9	11½	23½	72	Robert M. Jeffress, Richmond, Virginia, camp BM
No. 4	37	13½	8½	5 1/16	7	11¼	23	67	W.W. Porter, Syracuse, camp Gull Rock Bay, 4th
No. 5	38	13½	8½	5 1/16	7	11¼	23	66	Sanford Sherman, Alder Creek, farmer, camp caretaker Bisby
No. 6	37	13½	8½	5 1/16	7	11¼	23	69	L.F. Stanton [see 04-2]
**No. 7	38	13½	8½	5 1/16	7	11¼	23	67	W.D. Baldwin [see 96-1]
No. 8	37	14	8½	5¼	7	11¼	23½	67	Theodore A. Page [see 04-8]

1905 cont.	*Shell Weight*	*Length Bottom*	*Width Bottom*	*Space Knees*	*Pairs 0 Ribs*	*Depth Center*	*Height Stems*	*Weight Complete*	*Purchaser*
**No. 9	36	13½	8½	5¹⁄₁₆	7	11¼	23	66	W.D. Baldwin [see 96-1]
No. 10	37	13½	8½	5¹⁄₁₆	7	11¼	23	67	James Puttney(?), Boonville, guide and camp caretaker BM
**No. 11	71	18	12	6⅜	7-0 4-1	12	24½	114 rack 15	W.D. Baldwin [see 96-1]
No. 12	37	13½	8½	5¹⁄₁₆	7	11¼	23½	69	Ervin Crego, Boonville, guide with father Richard, BM
No. 13	32	11	8½	5¹⁄₁₆	1	11¼	22½	59	F.L. Smith, son of ALC pres. 1907-10, William P. Smith, camp LM

* *Virginia*, LLG, Sept. 21, 1959.,
** LLG, Mar. 14, 1959, p. 7.

1906	*Shell Weight*	*Length Bottom*	*Width Bottom*	*Space Knees*	*Pairs 0 Ribs*	*Depth Center*	*Height Stems*	*Weight Complete*	*Purchaser*
No. 1	40	13½	8½	5¹⁄₁₆	7	11¼	23	70	William P. Hall [see 03-2]
No. 2	39	13½	8½	5¹⁄₁₆	7	11¼	23	70	William P. Hall
No. 3	44	14½	8¾	5⅛	9	11¼	23½	75	James Dalton [see 03-10]
No. 4	47	15	9⅝	5⁵⁄₁₆	9	11¾	24½	73 without rack	Thomas R. Proctor [see 00-20]
No. 5	75	18	12	6⅜	7-0 4-1	12¾	25	142 with rack	Charles F. Roe, NYC, ALC, camp LM

1906 cont.

	Shell Weight	Length Bottom	Width Bottom	Space Knees	Pairs 0 Ribs	Depth Center	Height Stems	Weight Complete	Purchaser
No. 6	40	14½	7½	5⅛	9	11¼	23½	72	Melvin Oley [see 99-6]
No. 7	44	14½	8¾	5	9	11¼	23½	86 with rack	Ira A. Place, NYC, camp LM
No. 8	29	10	8½	5	1	11	22	58	Roy Crego [see 03-9]

NOTE: Shop closed 1906–1916

1917	Shell Weight	Length Bottom	Width Bottom	Space Knees	Pairs 0 Ribs	Depth Center	Height Stems	Weight Complete	Purchaser
No. 1	45	14½	8¼	5¼	9	11½	23½	81	John J. Riker, NYC, ALC, camp LM
No. 2	43	14½	8¼	5⅛	9	11½	23½	78	John J. Riker
No. 3	45	14½	8¼	5⅛	9	11½	23½	81	John J. Riker
No. 4	33	10½	8¼	4⅞	1	11	22	60	John J. Riker
No. 5	30	10	8¼	5	1	10¾	22	45	F.M. Woolworth, Niagara Falls, ALC, club houses
No. 6	45	14½	8¼	5⅛	9	11¼	23½	81	W.G. Gallowhur, Scarsdale, ALC, camp LM

1918

	Shell Weight	Length Bottom	Width Bottom	Space Knees	Pairs 0 Ribs	Depth Center	Height Stems	Weight Complete	Purchaser
No. 1	44	14½	8½	5⅛	9	11¼	24	80	R.A. Cowles, NYC, ALC, camp LM
No. 2	33	10	8½	5	1	11	22	59	J.S. Frelinghuysen [see 04-1]

1919

	Shell Weight	Length Bottom	Width Bottom	Space Knees	Pairs 0 Ribs	Depth Center	Height Stems	Weight Complete	Purchaser
No. 1	47	14½	8½	6⅛	9	11¼	23½	78	J.B. Terbell, NYC, ALC, camp LM
No. 2	44	14½	8½	5⅛	9	11¼	23½	87 with rack	ALC for boathouse LM to rent to members
No. 3	45	14½	8½	5⅛	8-0 4-1	11¼	23½	88 with rack	ALC for boathouse LM to rent to members
No. 4	47	14½	8½	5⅛	9	11¼	23½	90 with rack	ALC for boathouse LM to rent to members

1920

	Shell Weight	Length Bottom	Width Bottom	Space Knees	Pairs 0 Ribs	Depth Center	Height Stems	Weight Complete	Purchaser
No. 1	52	16	8¾	5⁵⁄₁₆	9-0 4-1	11¼	24	100 with rack	W.G. Gallowhur [see 17-6]

	Shell Weight	Length Bottom	Width Bottom	Space Knees	Pairs 0 Ribs	Depth Center	Height Stems	Weight Complete	Purchaser
1921									
No. 1	33	10½	8½	4⅞	1	11¼	22	59	Alfred G. Smith, Greenwich, Conn., ALC, camp Bisby
No. 2	43	14½	8½	5⅛	9	11¼	23½	77 rack 11	Alfred G. Smith
No. 3	45	14½	8½	5⅛	9	11¼	23½	80 rack 11	Alfred G. Smith
1922									
No. 1	48	16	8½	5⁵⁄₁₆	9-0 4-1	11¼	24	79	L.T. Warner, M.D., NYC, ALC, camp LM
No. 2	32	10½	8½	4⅞	1	11¼	22	59 rack 7½	J.H. Wagoner, Boonville, mgr. Boonville Sand & Gravel Co., "my next door neighbor" [LLG]
1923									
No. 1	44	14½	8¾	5⅛	9	11½	23½	77	Mrs. A.H. Harris [see 05-1]
NOTE: 10-year interruption									
1934									
No. 1	35	12	8½	5⅛	3	11¼	23½	61	Ray Schweinsberg, Boonville coal and feed dealer

Appendix B
Lewis Grant's Boat Shop Diary

In the chapter entitled "Warren Cole," Talbot Bissell gave us an intimate glimpse of the atmosphere in the Cole boat shop at Long Lake. The meticulous Lewis Grant kept a diary, now in the Adirondack Museum. It is a record of various tasks, of comings and goings, of the death of a friend, and of the many odd jobs and free carpentry and repair work done for his neighbors. The diary served as a time book by which the self-employed carpenter would reckon his hours on any job. Being a countryman, Lewis began each day with a description of the weather, followed by temperature readings taken at 7:30 a.m. (8 a.m. on Sundays) and at bedtime, generally 10 p.m. The following extracts are taken from the period when Lewis was building his last guide-boat. We have concentrated on his activities in the boat shop, omitting most repetitious details.

1934

Wed. Feb. 28	Fine day & little warmer. 18 below Z at 7:30 AM & 4 above at 10 PM. Spent most of the day cleaning up shop and getting ready to build a guide-boat. 1 hr on stems for guide-boat. Looked after Hough's hens for Walt McClusky.
Thur. Mar. 1	Zero at 7:30 AM. 27 above at 10 PM. 5 hrs making stems for guide-boat. Let Clayton Brazie take pipe wrench.
Fri. Mar. 2	Started to rain at 8 PM. 5 hrs on ribs for guide-boat. Glued up chair for neighbor, Mrs. Goodsen. Got in lumber from back room to dry out.
Sat. Mar. 3	Fine day & thawing. Got down and cleaned up boat patterns and cleaned up shop in forenoon. Made a coffee-pot handle for McClusky.
Sun. Mar. 4	Fine day, foggy at night. Wrote up books.
Mon. Mar. 5	5 hrs on ribs and bottom board for guide-boat. Mary Jane [his cousin and housekeeper] and I went to a show in the evening, "Wallace Beery in the Bowery."
Tue. Mar. 6	All kinds of weather. 5 hrs on boat, working on ribs, bottom board and putting on ribs. Went shopping and to bank in afternoon.
Wed. Mar. 7	7 hrs on guide-boat. Putting ribs on bottom board and setting boat on stock.

200

Thur. Mar. 8	6 hrs on boat, truing up ribs and getting out siding.
Fri. Mar. 9	Fine forenoon, cloudy afternoon. 7 hrs getting out and putting on siding.
Sat. Mar. 10	7 hrs getting out and putting on siding. Mary Jane went to Lowville.
Sun. Mar. 11	Fine day. Wrote up books and answered Nellie's letter.
Mon. Mar. 12	7 hrs getting out and putting on siding.
Tue. Mar. 13	Went shopping in the forenoon. Martins from Big Moose in for a visit and to ask about material for a launch. 2 hrs getting out and putting on siding.
Wed. Mar. 14	Fine day. Snowed in night. 7 hrs getting out and putting on siding.
Thur. Mar. 15	Fine day & warmer. 7 hrs on boat getting out and putting on siding. First good sap day in this section.
Fri. Mar. 16	6 hrs on boat, getting out and putting on siding. Bought a second-hand car of Bronson garage for Camp Grant.
Sat. Mar. 17	7 hrs on boat, getting out and putting on siding. Mary Jane and I went shopping in the evening.
Sun. Mar. 18	Sent order to Sears, Roebuck for typewriter ribbons, dictionary and a file.
Mon. Mar. 19	Fine day . . . and it was thawing at noon. Another good sap day. 7 hrs on boat getting out and putting on siding.
Tue. Mar. 20	Went shopping for oil burner for kitchen range in forenoon. 6 hrs on boat, getting out and putting on siding.
Wed. Mar. 21	Cloudy and snowed about two inches the first day of spring. 7 hrs on boat, getting out and putting on siding.
Thur. Mar. 22	Fine day but cold. Zero at 7:30 AM & 2 below 10 PM. 5 hrs on boat, putting on siding and getting out wales.
Fri. Mar. 23	Had an oil burner put in kitchen range. 4 hrs on boat, getting out and putting on wales.
Sat. Mar. 24	5 hrs on boat, putting in extra screws and working on decks. Half sick with a headache all day.
Sun. Mar. 25	Wrote up books to date. Russell & Mildred Moran here for visit in afternoon.
Mon. Mar. 26	Cloudy and light snow in forenoon. 6 hrs on boat working on decks.
Tue. Mar. 27	Rained most all day. 7 hrs on boat, on decks, seat and yoke cleats and cutting off ends of ribs.
Wed. Mar. 28	Went to mill to get oak for decks. 5 hrs on boat, working on decks.
Thur. Mar. 29	7 hrs on boat, finishing decks and working on false bottom.
Fri. Mar. 30	7 hrs on boat, on bottom rack and sandpapering boat.
Sat. Mar. 31	Partly cloudy but nice until 5 PM and then light rains. 7 hrs on boat, finished sandpapering and varnished boat outside first coat.
Sun. Apr. 1	Easter. Cloudy but nice day. Wrote up books to date. R. Peterson in for a visit in afternoon and Ada and Eunice in for a visit in the evening.
Mon. Apr. 2	6 hrs on boat, finishing rack, filling decks, varnishing boat inside 1st coat & oiling rack.
Tue. Apr. 3	Spent forenoon writing orders for material, paying bills and shopping. Went shopping for varnish and worked one hour for Emmet [Brazie, his next-door neighbor and fishing companion] and worked one hour varnishing boat second coat outside in afternoon.
Wed. Apr. 4	7 hrs for Emmet Brazie, casing up his office doors, windows, putting on mop-boards, etc.
Thur. Apr. 5	7 hrs on boat. Varnished boat inside 2nd coat and worked on seat frames.
Fri. Apr. 6	Cloudy & misty all day. Went shopping and to bank for Floyd in forenoon. 4 hrs making seat frames for boat.
Sat. Apr. 7	7 hrs, finished seat and back frames and varnished boat outside, third coat.

Sun. Apr. 8   Fine day. Wrote to Clara and to Ben Parsons.

Mon. Apr. 9   Went to the bank to see Geo. Traffern about sending to New York some papers for Nellie. 4 hrs varnishing boat, 3rd coat inside.

Tue. Apr. 10   Spent about 6 hrs today putting in a new toilet and tank in bath room. Got car running afternoon & Mary Jane and I went shopping with it.

Thur. Apr. 12   Snowed about 6 inches in forenoon. Shoveled walks in afternoon. 5 hrs making and varnishing yoke for boat.

Fri. Apr. 13   Cloudy & light snows at times. 5 hrs today caning stern seat for boat. Cleaned up shop. Ruth & Miss Jones arrived from Schenectady at eleven o'clock tonight.

Sat. Apr. 14   Took a ride with Ruth, Miss Jones, Mary Jane and Floyd to Locust Grove to get maple syrup for Ruth to take home. Went to Miller's for a limberg [limber?].

Sun. Apr. 15   Snow all gone tonight. Nothing doing today.

Mon. Apr. 16   2 hrs finishing caning stern seat. Spent balance of the day answering letters and shopping.

Tue. Apr. 17   7 hrs caning a back rest and started a bow seat.

Wed. Apr. 18   Brought camp truck home from Walt's and put it in my barn this forenoon and put my car in the shop. 2 hrs caning bow seat.

Thur. Apr. 19   7 hrs caning seats, finished bow seat and middle seat.

Fri. Apr. 20   6 hrs putting foot brass in boat & varnishing seats.

Sat. Apr. 21   4 hrs sanding & varnishing boat outside 4th coat & varnished rack and seat cleats. Varnished Lydia's [Brazie] chair a third coat. Raked leaves off yard in afternoon.

Sun. Apr. 22   Fine day but cold. Donald Ryder took pictures in the shop at 2 PM.

Mon. Apr. 23   7 hrs on boat, putting on stem bands, three shoes and putting on seat cleats. Looked after Hough's hens and got 22 eggs.

Tue. Apr. 24   Mowed the lawn. 3 hrs on boat, putting in seats and putting on row locks.

1935

Mon. June 17   Sold my guide-boat this forenoon to Ray Schweinsberg and spent most of the day fitting false bottom rack into the boat.

Mon. June 24   Tied fixtures into guide-boat and got it ready to ship.

Thur. June 27   Schweinsberg's truck came after the boat before I had my breakfast, and I loaded the boat on the truck and they left with it for Bald Mountain House, Third Lake, at 9 AM.

Lewis Grant estimated that it took his father approximately 210 working hours to make a 16-foot guide-boat. For Lewis's 13½-foot guide-boat the diary recorded 241 hours. Dwight Grant had the advantage of yearly production in a well-organized shop with experienced assistants. Lewis, who had not made a guide-boat for 11 years, started this boat from scratch and worked alone. He received $175 for the boat. For the time recorded in the diary, this represented about 75 cents per hour, without any provision for time spent making oars and paddle (which were made in advance), or digging the spruce roots, or for the cost of lumber, varnish, tacks, screws, and metal fittings.

Lewis Grant's price list of 1921 included a 13½-foot boat with the same finish at $195.50, including 10 percent federal tax. His cost accounting remains a mystery. It is not surprising that his account book for 1934, with the guide-boat he had built still unsold and carried on the inventory at $125, showed a net return "for boatbuilding and other work" of $21.28 for the year.

Appendix C
The Guide-Boat Drawings, with Accompanying Remarks, by John Gardner

The drawings that follow record in print for the first time the complete details for replicating an authentic and representative Adirondack guide-boat. The boat that Kenneth Durant selected for our model in 1959 came from the Boonville shop of H. Dwight Grant and was built by his two sons, Lewis and Floyd, in 1905, for Robert M. Jeffress, who had a camp at Big Moose, New York. Although produced somewhat late in the time span of guide-boat evolution, the *Virginia* is a fine example of a guide's full-size work boat at the peak of its development, before decadence set in, as evidenced in part by the fact that the *Virginia*, as a true working boat, was painted, not varnished.

It might seem strange that no lines for a craft as distinctive as the Adirondack guide-boat were ever published until *Outdoor Maine* printed the first draft of lines of the *Virginia* in August 1960. The principal reason is that guide-boats were built from patterns, not from lines. The guides, in building their boats, had no use for lines, and no building plans were ever drawn.

When the guides ceased to be in demand in the north woods, early in this century, the production of guide-boats all but came to an end, and outside the Adirondacks the guide-boat was quickly and completely forgotten. Not until the Adirondack Museum sparked a revival of interest in the guide-boat in the 1950s was the attention of a few marine historians and naval architects directed to this remarkable wilderness craft.

It has seemed incredible to some that a craft as sweetly and as delicately lined as the guide-boat could have been devised by untutored woodsmen without benefit of training in naval architecture, although the fact is that all our classic native small craft were developed by working boatbuilders without assistance from professional architects. Indeed, naval architecture in this country did not begin to pay attention to small craft until well along toward the end of the last century, when the guide-boat had already attained its final and perfected form. However, a story has gained currency that a "naval architect" from Syracuse by the name of Salisbury came up to Long Lake, where he assisted local builders in smoothing out and fairing up the lines of their boats. An H.L. Salisbury & Bro. apparently did build boats for a time at Long Lake, New York. A guide-boat with certain deviant characteristics bearing the Salisbury name plate is in the Mystic Seaport Museum's collection. The same Salisbury either designed or built the *Cub* (perhaps both), an over-size guide-boat that Franklin Brandreth commissioned for his three daughters.

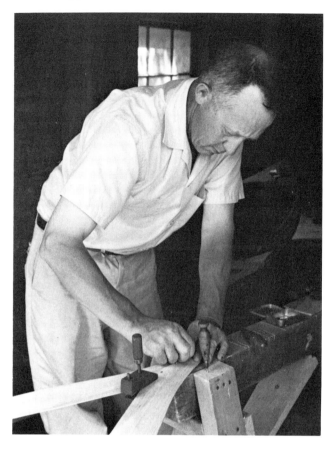

John Gardner measuring the Virginia

Salisbury also is credited with having instructed Willard Hanmer's father as a young man in guide-boat building at Saranac Lake. All of this seems to have taken place in the middle 1880s. A Herbert L. Salisbury, pattern maker, apparently the same man, is listed in the Syracuse city directory for 1883–84 and again at the same address in 1886–87. The key here is the occupation of pattern maker. Apparently, to Franklin Brandreth, pattern maker and naval architect were one and the same, inasmuch as the Adirondack boats he was familiar with were built from patterns. The trade of pattern making, as hardly needs explaining, involves the making of patterns from wood or other materials for metal castings, and has nothing to do with boat design.

When J. Henry Rushton of Canton, New York, included what he called an "Adirondack or Saranac Lake Boat" in his 1888 catalogue, he illustrated the descriptive text with a schematic drawing of what might seem to be the lines of a guide-boat, but these were too small and incomplete to be considered guide-boat lines in any true or useful sense of the term.

While the first preliminary draft of lines for the *Virginia* published in *Outdoor Maine* in August 1960 was not accompanied by a table of offsets, nevertheless, these lines were accurate enough and large enough to allow building lines to be scaled from them, and the following September issue included a fully detailed construction drawing of the *Virginia's* midsection, which in revised form appears here as Plate V. This drawing diagrammed for the first time Grant's unique improved lap with matching shoulders recessed .028 inch.

To follow up the work begun in 1959 and reported in *Outdoor Maine* in 1960, Durant arranged for me to spend a week at the Adirondack Museum in August 1963, rechecking the lines of the *Virginia* and making a complete record of construction details for inclusion in his work on the guide-boat then in progress. This was done, and from the data obtained, the drawings reproduced here were prepared over the course of the following year. During that time, the work as it proceeded was carefully checked by Durant and revised where needed to make it as correct and as complete as possible. Everything a builder might need is included and fully detailed. Few small craft types, if any, have been more fully, or more precisely, drawn.

Not so with the only other plan of guide-boat construction so far produced. In 1965 E.I. Schock paid a hurried visit to the Adirondack Museum, where he measured a 13-foot 1-inch guide-boat built by John Blanchard, a Raquette Lake guide. His plan has no offsets. The planking lap shown is Grant's improved lap, never used by Blanchard, who, like most guide-boat builders, planed his laps to a feather edge. Furthermore, the distinctive Adirondack method of fastening delicate guide-boat laps with two rows of copper tacks is not shown. Plank or siding thickness is given as ¼ inch throughout, when only the garboard is ¼ inch: all planks above the garboard are thinned to ³⁄₁₆ inch, or slightly less in some 13-foot boats. No siding dimension for the ribs appears. We could continue in the same vein. Admittedly, Schock's lines are neatly and expertly laid down, and what is drawn is quite handsome and looks like a Blanchard boat as far as the casual eye can see, but not enough correct information is given to build a

Blanchard boat, and that is where the difference lies.

The drawings of the *Virginia* that follow speak for themselves and are intended to be self-sufficient, without requiring explanation. Yet a few introductory comments will not be amiss. Plates I and II give lines and offsets according to the practice and conventions of naval architecture. These are provided mainly for study, the lines for visual comparison with other hull shapes by trained professionals and others accustomed to making such comparisons. Of course an accurate reproduction of the *Virginia*'s hull can be built from these lines and offsets, but instead of going through the lengthy procedure of making and fairing a full-size laydown of the lines, and lifting building molds, and so forth, it will be

simpler, easier, and more accurate to do as the guide-boat builders did; that is, to work directly from rib patterns. These can be accurately obtained from the diagram and dimensions given in Plates III and IV. Accurate dimensions for all the patterns required for forming the guide-boat hull are provided, namely, the patterns for the stock plank, the bottom board, the ribs, and the stems. These basic shapes, strictly adhered to and correctly assembled, virtually assure a correctly formed hull, and to this extent, guide-boat construction is not particularly difficult. Where difficulty lies is in the exact and expert workmanship required in shaping and thinning the delicate planking or "siding," and in fitting the precise laps. The skill and careful workmanship required here are of the very highest order.

Plate I

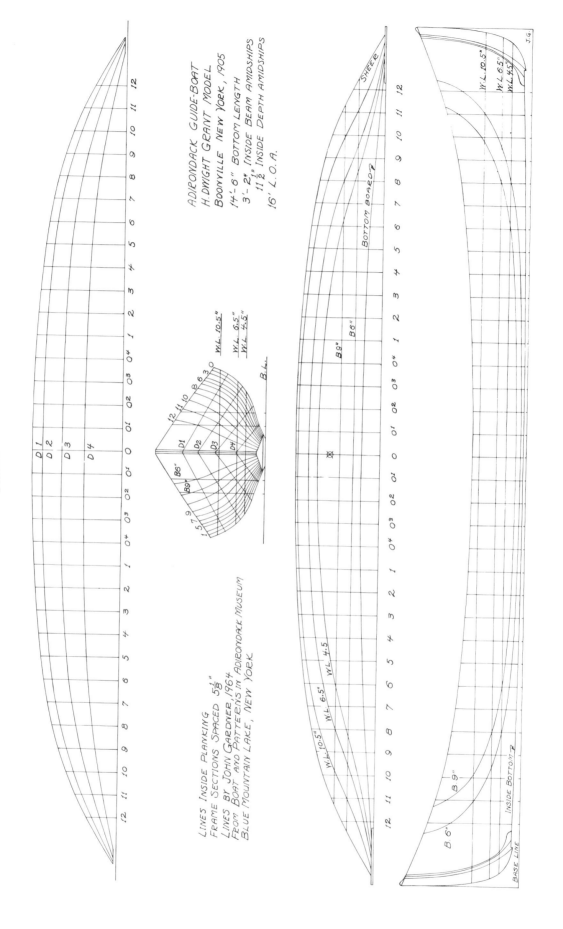

ADIRONDACK GUIDE-BOAT
H. DWIGHT GRANT MODEL
BOONVILLE NEW YORK, 1905
14'-6" BOTTOM LENGTH
3'-2" INSIDE BEAM AMIDSHIPS
11½" INSIDE DEPTH AMIDSHIPS
16' L.O.A.

LINES INSIDE PLANKING
FRAME SECTIONS SPACED 5⅛"
LINES BY JOHN GARDNER, 1964
FROM BOAT AND PATTERNS IN ADIRONDACK MUSEUM
BLUE MOUNTAIN LAKE, NEW YORK

Plate II

Offsets — 16' Grant Guide-Boat. Inches and Thirty-Seconds.

	STATIONS	0	O¹	O²	O³	O⁴	1	2	3	4	5	6	7	8	9	10	11	12	STEM
HEIGHTS ABOVE BASE LINE	SHEER	12-0	12-1	12-3	12-6	12-10	12-14	12-22	13-0	13-10	13-23	14-6	14-25	15-16	16-12	17-17	19-0	20-20	25-12
	BOTTOM	0-16	0-16	0-16	0-17	0-18	0-19	0-20	0-21	0-23	0-25	0-28	0-30	1-2	1-6	1-11	1-16	1-22	—
	6" BUTTOCK	1-8	1-9	1-10	1-11	1-13	1-16	1-21	1-26	2-1	2-11	2-23	3-11	4-9	5-21	7-20	10-11	15-12	21-16
	9" BUTTOCK	2-8	2-9	2-11	2-12	2-16	2-21	2-26	3-1	3-10	3-24	4-10	5-7	6-15	8-10	11-2	16-17	—	19-15
HALF-BREADTHS	SHEER	19-0	19-0	18-30	18-27	18-20	18-14	18-2	17-22	17-4	16-23	16-3	15-10	14-13	13-7	11-24	9-24	7-9	0-13
	BOTTOM	4-10	4-9	4-8	4-6	4-4	4-1	3-28	3-24	3-19	3-11	3-4	2-26	2-16	2-4	1-22	1-8	0-26	—
	10.5" WATER L.	18-15	18-15	18-11	18-7	18-0	17-23	17-9	16-26	16-9	15-21	14-28	13-27	12-18	10-26	8-19	6-4	3-28	0-13
	6.5" WATER L.	16-2	16-2	15-30	15-26	15-19	15-10	14-27	14-10	14-25	12-31	12-1	11-24	9-2	7-0	5-0	3-14	2-5	0-13
	4.5" WATER L.	13-26	13-26	13-22	13-17	13-9	12-31	12-15	11-29	11-10	10-12	9-11	7-28	6-10	4-26	3-15	2-14	1-17	0-13
DIAGONALS	DIAGONAL 1	20-12	20-12	20-9	20-6	19-31	19-23	19-10	18-30	18-13	17-27	17-4	16-6	15-1	13-19	11-24	9-16	6-31	0-15
	DIAGONAL 2	18-2	18-2	17-31	17-28	17-22	17-16	17-6	16-26	16-13	15-26	15-5	14-8	13-4	11-21	9-28	7-30	5-27	0-15
	DIAGONAL 3	13-23	13-23	13-21	13-19	13-15	13-10	13-2	12-25	12-17	12-1	11-16	10-22	9-24	8-15	7-2	5-18	4-1	0-16
	DIAGONAL 4	8-14	8-14	8-13	8-12	8-9	8-5	8-0	7-27	7-20	7-10	7-0	6-16	5-27	5-3	4-6	3-8	2-9	0-17

DIAGONAL 1	19-0 ABOVE B.L.	FROM C.L. ON W.L. 10.5	14-20	ON W.L. 6.5	21-19
DIAGONAL 2	15-18 ABOVE B.L.	FROM C.L. ON W.L. 10.5	7-13	ON W.L. 6.5	13-7
DIAGONAL 3	11-16 ABOVE B.L.	FROM C.L ON W.L. 4.5	8-22	ON B.L.	14-8
DIAGONAL 4	6-26 ABOVE B.L.	FROM C.L ON W.L. 4.5	2-27	ON B.L.	8-12

Offsets Measured Inside Plank — Inside Bottom and from the Bearding Line on the Stem.

J.G.

Plate III

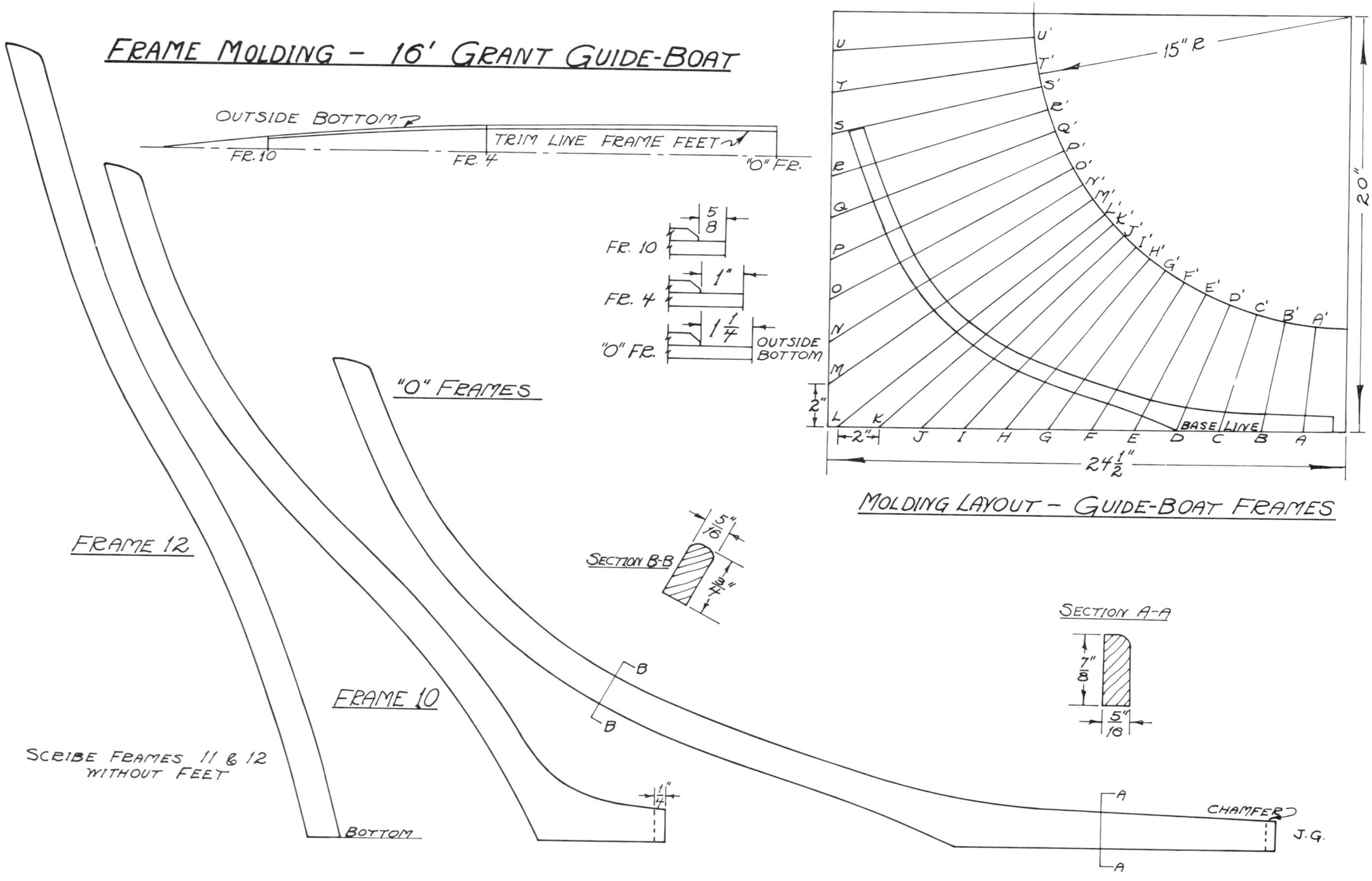

FRAME MOLDING - 16' GRANT GUIDE-BOAT
OUTSIDE BOTTOM
TRIM LINE FRAME FEET
FR. 10
FR. 4
"O" FR.
5/8
1"
1 1/4
OUTSIDE BOTTOM
"O" FRAMES
FRAME 12
FRAME 10
SECTION B-B
5/16"
3/4"
SECTION A-A
7/8"
5/16"
SCRIBE FRAMES 11 & 12 WITHOUT FEET
BOTTOM
1/4"
CHAMFER
J.G.
15" R
20"
2"
24 1/2"
BASE LINE
MOLDING LAYOUT - GUIDE-BOAT FRAMES

Plate IV

MEASUREMENTS — MOLDING LAYOUT — GUIDE-BOAT FRAMES FROM GRANT PATTERNS — INCHES AND THIRTY-SECONDS

J.G.

DISTANCE ON LINE	AA'	BB'	CC'	DD'	EE'	FF'	GG'	HH'	II'	JJ'	KK'	LL'	MM'	NN'	OO'	PP'	QQ'	RR'	SS'	TT'	UU'
FR. 0 OUTSIDE	B.L.	B.L.	B.L.	B.L.	6-18	6-27	7-8	7-22	8-5	8-16	8-24	8-31	9-6	9-11	9-13	9-12	9-10	9-10	9-14	—	—
FR. 0 INSIDE	4-10	4-18	4-30	5-12	5-24	6-3	UNIFORM 3/4″ MOLDING														
FR. 1 OUTSIDE	B.L.	B.L.	B.L.	B.L.	6-17	6-25	7-5	7-20	8-2	8-13	8-22	8-29	9-4	9-8	9-9	9-8	9-7	9-7	9-11	—	—
FR. 1 INSIDE	4-10	4-17	4-30	5-12	5-23	6-1	UNIFORM 3/4″ MOLDING														
FR. 2 OUTSIDE	B.L.	B.L.	B.L.	B.L.	6-15	6-22	7-2	7-16	7-28	8-7	8-15	8-21	8-28	8-31	8-30	8-28	8-28		9-0	—	—
FR. 2 INSIDE	4-10	4-17	4-30	5-11	5-20	5-30	UNIFORM 3/4″ MOLDING														
FR. 3 OUTSIDE	B.L.	B.L.	B.L.	B.L.	6-13	6-19	6-30	7-9	7-21	7-31	8-6	8-12	8-18	8-21	8-21	8-19	8-16		8-18	—	—
FR. 3 INSIDE	4-10	4-17	4-30	5-10	5-18	5-26	UNIFORM 3/4″ MOLDING														
FR. 4 OUTSIDE	B.L.	B.L.	B.L.	B.L.	6-12	6-17	6-26	7-5	7-16	7-25	7-31	8-4	8-9	8-11	8-10	8-8	8-5		8-3	—	—
FR. 4 INSIDE	4-11	4-17	4-30	5-10	5-18	5-24	UNIFORM 3/4″ MOLDING														
FR. 5 OUTSIDE	B.L.	B.L.	B.L.	B.L.	6-9	6-12	6-20	6-30	7-7	7-15	7-21	7-26	7-31	8-1	8-1	7-31	7-28	7-25	7-24	—	—
FR. 5 INSIDE	4-11	4-17	4-29	5-8	5-15	5-20	UNIFORM 3/4″ MOLDING														
FR. 6 OUTSIDE	B.L.	B.L.	B.L.	B.L.	6-7	6-7	6-13	6-21	6-29	7-4	7-9	7-14	7-19	7-21	7-21	7-19	7-16	7-13	7-11	—	—
FR. 6 INSIDE	4-11	4-18	4-30	5-8	5-10	5-13	UNIFORM 3/4″ MOLDING														
FR. 7 OUTSIDE	B.L.	B.L.	B.L.	B.L.	6-3	5-31	6-0	6-6	6-14	6-21	6-26	6-30	7-2	7-4	7-5	7-3	7-1	6-31	6-31	—	—
FR. 7 INSIDE	4-11	4-18	4-30	5-8	5-8	5-6	UNIFORM 3/4″ MOLDING														
FR. 8 OUTSIDE	B.L.	B.L.	B.L.	B.L.	5-28	5-18	5-16	5-18	5-22	5-27	5-31	6-2	6-7	6-9	6-9	6-7	6-6		6-7	—	—
FR. 8 INSIDE	4-10	4-17	4-29	5-5	4-31	4-23	UNIFORM 3/4″ MOLDING														
FR. 9 OUTSIDE	B.L.	B.L.	B.L.	B.L.	5-19	5-2	4-26	4-24	4-25	4-27	4-31	5-2	5-6	5-8	5-10	5-10	5-11		5-14	—	—
FR. 9 INSIDE	—	4-20	5-0	5-7	4-22	4-7	UNIFORM 3/4″ MOLDING														
FR. 10 OUTSIDE	B.L.	B.L.	B.L.	5-6	4-13	3-30	3-22	3-19	3-17	3-18	3-19	3-21	3-23	3-24	3-25	3-26	3-30	4-6			
FR. 10 INSIDE	—	4-19	4-31	5-0	4-8	3-17	UNIFORM 3/4″ MOLDING														
FR. 11 OUTSIDE	—	No Foot		B.L.	4-25	3-22	2-16	2-8	2-3	2-0	1-30	1-29	1-27	1-26	1-25	1-24	1-23	1-25	1-29	2-6	
FR. 12 OUTSIDE	—	No Foot		B.L.	4-15	3-6	2-10	1-23	1-11	1-3	0-29	0-25	0-20	0-16	0-12	0-8	0-5	0-4	0-6	0-12	

DISTANCES FROM FRAME LINES TO ARC ON 15″ RADIUS. SCRIBE FRAMES 11 & 12 MOLDED A UNIFORM 3/4″ THROUGHOUT.

Plate V

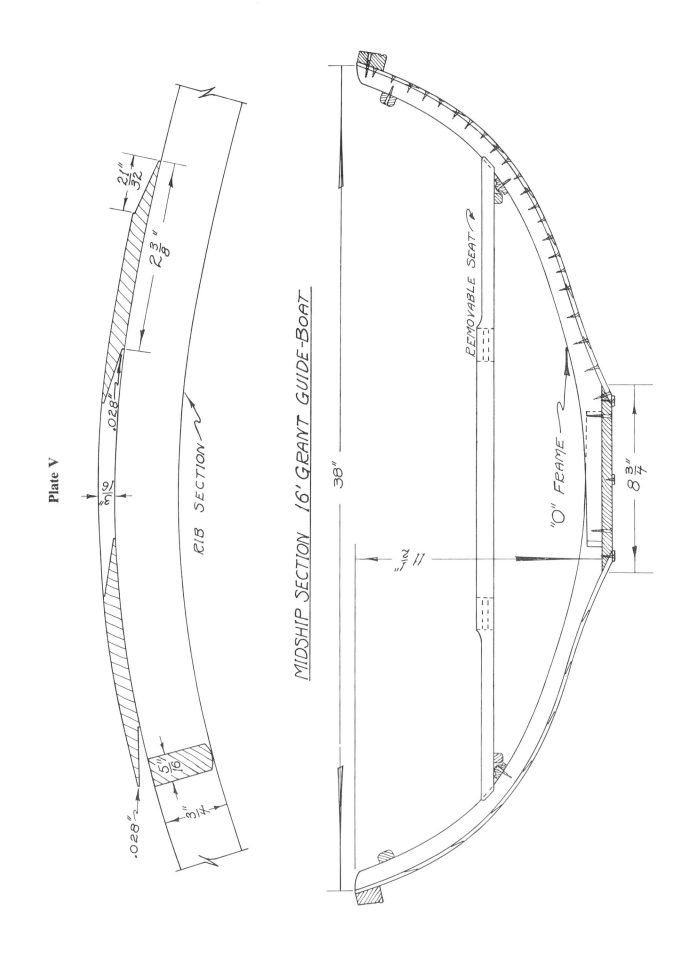

$\frac{21"}{32}$

$2\frac{3"}{8}$

.028"

$\frac{3"}{16}$

RIB SECTION

$\frac{5"}{16}$

$\frac{3"}{4}$

.028"

38"

REMOVABLE SEAT

"O" FRAME

$8\frac{3"}{4}$

$11\frac{1"}{2}$

MIDSHIP SECTION 16' GRANT GUIDE-BOAT

Plate VI

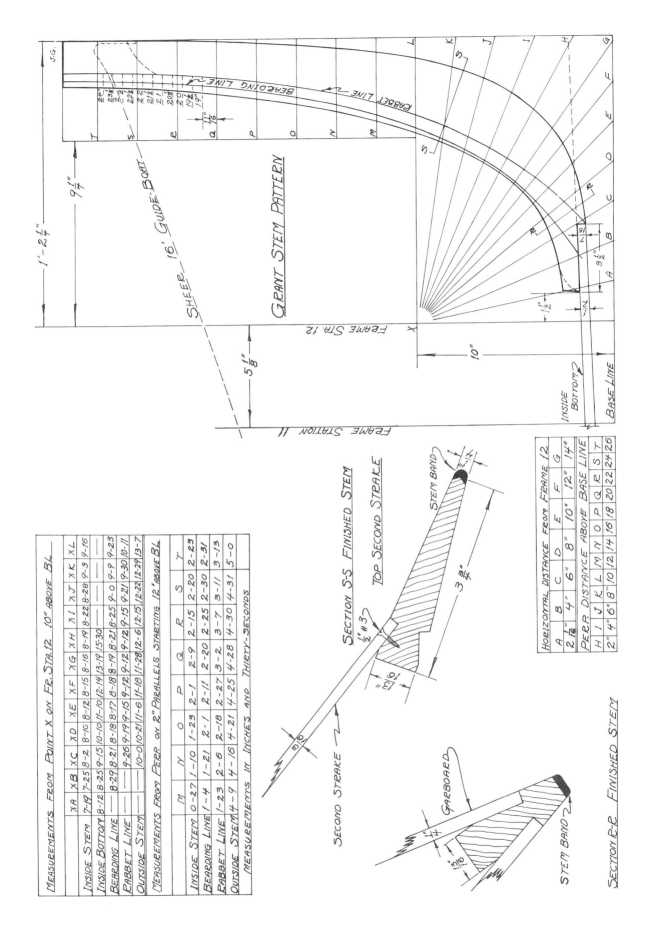

GRANT STEM PATTERN

SHEER 16' GUIDE-BOAT

FRAME STA. 12

FRAME STATION 11

BASE LINE

INSIDE BOTTOM

BEARDING LINE

RABBET LINE

10"

$9\frac{1}{4}"$

$1'-2\frac{1}{4}"$

$5\frac{1}{8}"$

J.T.G.

SECTION S-S FINISHED STEM

TOP SECOND STRAKE

STEM BAND

SECOND STRAKE

$3\frac{3}{4}"$

SECTION R-R FINISHED STEM

GARBOARD

STEM BAND

MEASUREMENTS FROM POINT X ON FR. STA. 12, 10" ABOVE BL.

	XA	XB	XC	XD	XE	XF	XG	XH	XI	XJ	XK	XL
INSIDE STEM	7-19	7-25	8-2	8-10	8-12	8-15	8-16	8-19	8-22	8-28	9-3	9-16
INSIDE BOTTOM	8-12	8-25	9-15	10-10	11-10	12-14	13-19	15-30				
BEARDING LINE		8-29	8-21	8-18	8-17	8-18	8-19	8-21	8-25	9-0	9-9	9-23
RABBET LINE			9-26	9-19	9-15	9-12	9-12	9-12	9-15	9-21	9-30	10-11
OUTSIDE STEM				10-0	10-2	11-6	11-8	11-28	12-6	12-15	12-22	12-29	13-7

MEASUREMENTS FROM PERP. ON 2" PARALLELS STARTING 12" ABOVE BL.

	M	N	O	P	Q	R	S	T
INSIDE STEM	0-27	1-10	1-23	2-1	2-9	2-15	2-20	2-23
BEARDING LINE	1-4	1-21	2-1	2-11	2-20	2-25	2-30	2-31
RABBET LINE	1-23	2-6	2-18	2-27	3-2	3-7	3-11	3-13
OUTSIDE STEM	4-9	4-16	4-21	4-25	4-28	4-30	4-31	5-0

MEASUREMENTS IN INCHES AND THIRTY-SECONDS

HORIZONTAL DISTANCE FROM FRAME 12							
A	B	C	D	E	F	G	
$2\frac{1}{16}"$	4"	6"	8"	10"	12"	14"	
PERP. DISTANCE ABOVE BASE LINE							
H	I	J	K	L	M	N	O	P	Q	R	S	T
2"	4"	6"	8"	10"	12"	14"	16"	18"	20"	22"	24"	26"

Plate VII

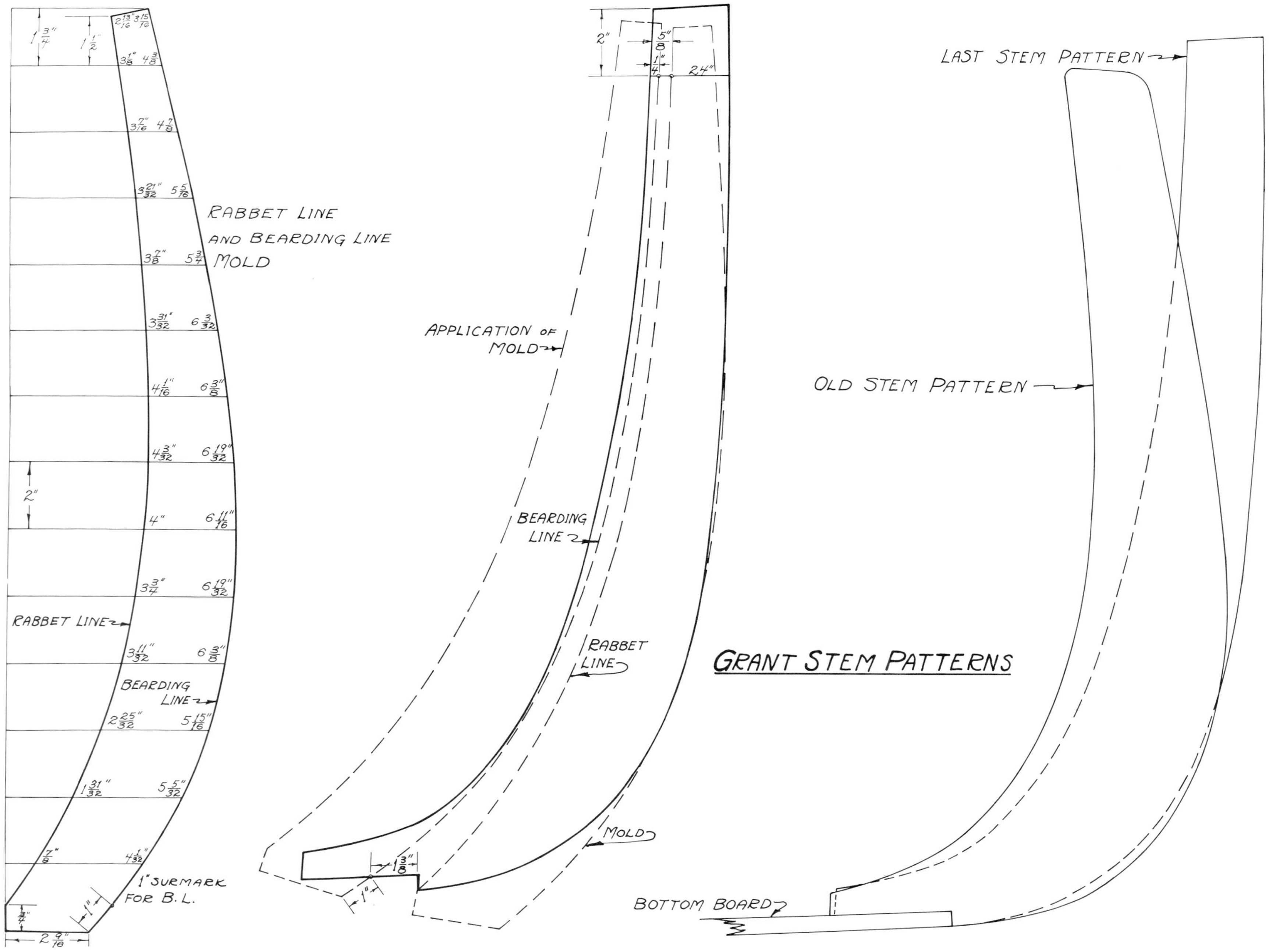

GRANT STEM PATTERNS

LAST STEM PATTERN

OLD STEM PATTERN

BOTTOM BOARD

APPLICATION OF MOLD

BEARDING LINE

RABBET LINE

MOLD

RABBET LINE AND BEARDING LINE MOLD

RABBET LINE

BEARDING LINE

1" SUEMARK FOR B.L.

Plate VIII

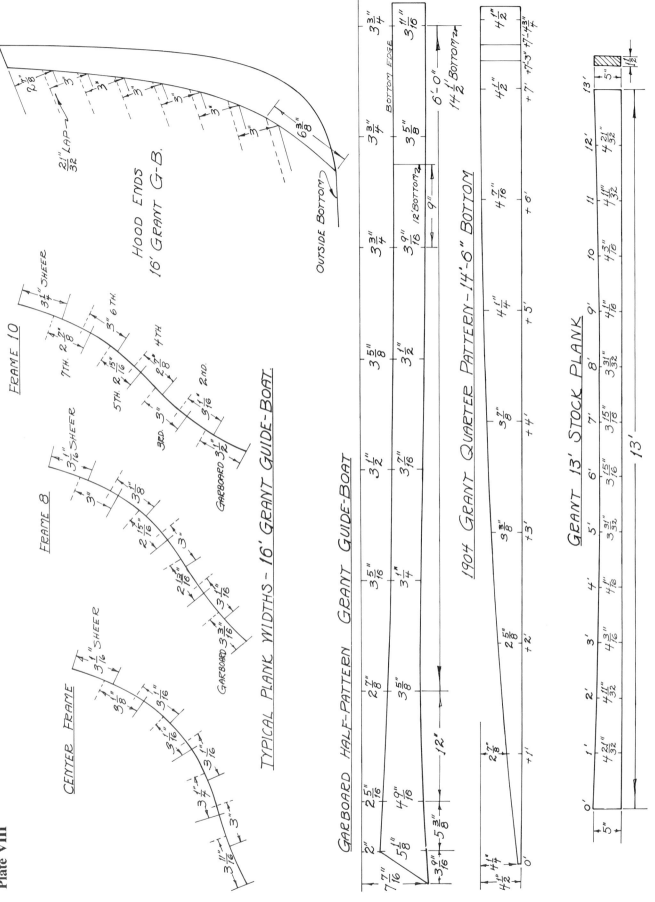

HOOD ENDS
16' GRANT G-B.

$2\frac{7}{8}$"

21" LAP

3"

3"

3"

3"

3"

3"

$6\frac{3}{8}$"

OUTSIDE BOTTOM

FRAME 10

$3\frac{1}{4}$" SHEER

$2\frac{7}{8}$" 7TH.

3" 6TH.

$2\frac{15}{16}$" 5TH.

$2\frac{7}{8}$" 4TH.

3" 3RD.

$3\frac{1}{16}$" 2ND.

GARBOARD $3\frac{1}{2}$"

FRAME 8

$3\frac{1}{16}$" SHEER

3"

$3\frac{1}{8}$"

$2\frac{15}{16}$"

$2\frac{13}{16}$"

3"

$3\frac{1}{16}$"

GARBOARD $3\frac{3}{16}$"

CENTER FRAME

$3\frac{1}{16}$" SHEER

$3\frac{3}{8}$"

$3\frac{1}{16}$"

$3\frac{3}{16}$"

$3\frac{1}{16}$"

$3\frac{1}{4}$"

3"

$3\frac{1}{16}$"

TYPICAL PLANK WIDTHS – 16' GRANT GUIDE-BOAT

GARBOARD HALF-PATTERN GRANT GUIDE-BOAT

$3\frac{3}{4}$" $3\frac{3}{4}$" $3\frac{3}{4}$" $3\frac{5}{8}$" $3\frac{1}{2}$" $3\frac{5}{16}$" $2\frac{7}{8}$" $2\frac{5}{16}$" 2"

$3\frac{11}{16}$ $3\frac{5}{8}$ $3\frac{9}{16}$ 12 BOTTOM 2 $3\frac{7}{16}$ $3\frac{1}{4}$ $3\frac{5}{8}$ $4\frac{9}{16}$ $5\frac{1}{8}$

BOTTOM EDGE

9"

12"

$5\frac{3}{8}$" $3\frac{9}{16}$" $7\frac{7}{16}$"

$6'-0$"

$14\frac{1}{2}$" BOTTOM 2

1904 GRANT QUARTER PATTERN – 14'-6" BOTTOM

$4\frac{1}{2}$" $4\frac{1}{2}$" $4\frac{7}{16}$" $4\frac{1}{4}$" $3\frac{7}{8}$" $3\frac{3}{8}$" $2\frac{5}{8}$" $2\frac{7}{8}$" $4\frac{1}{4}$" $4\frac{1}{2}$"

$+7'-4\frac{3}{4}$" $+7'-3$" $+7'$ $+6'$ $+5'$ $+4'$ $+3'$ $+2'$ $+1'$ $0'$

GRANT 13' STOCK PLANK

$1\frac{1}{2}$"

5"

$13'$ $4\frac{21}{32}$ $4\frac{11}{32}$ $4\frac{3}{16}$ $4\frac{1}{16}$ $3\frac{31}{32}$ $3\frac{15}{16}$ $3\frac{31}{32}$ $4\frac{1}{16}$ $4\frac{3}{16}$ $4\frac{11}{32}$ $4\frac{21}{32}$

$0'$ $1'$ $2'$ $3'$ $4'$ $5'$ $6'$ $7'$ $9'$ $10'$ $11'$ $12'$ $13'$

5"

$-13'-$

Plate IX

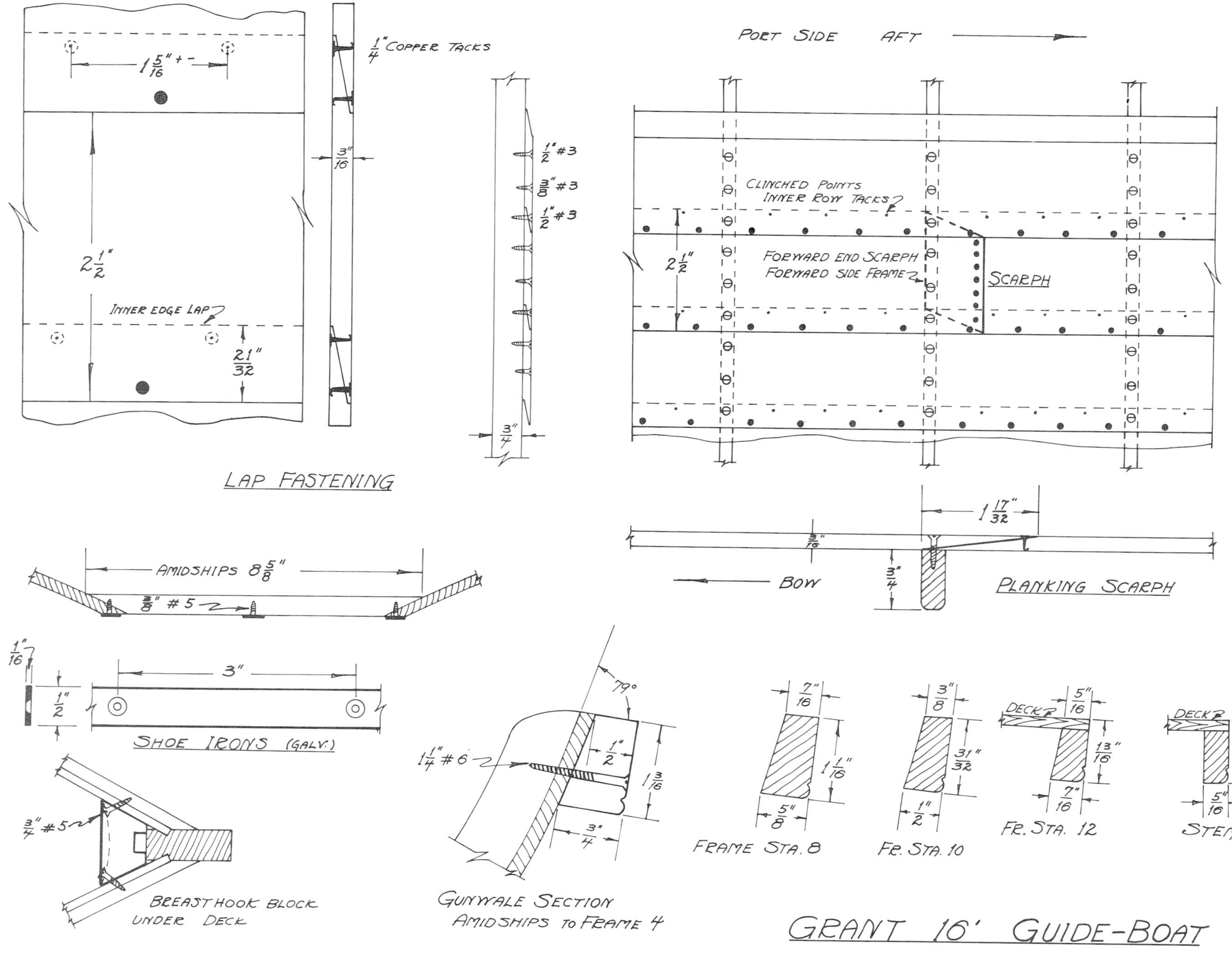

POET SIDE   AFT

SCARPH

CLINCHED POINTS
INNER ROW TACKS

FORWARD END SCARPH
FORWARD SIDE FRAME

$2\frac{1}{2}$"

$\frac{1}{2}$" # 3 $\frac{3}{8}$" # 3 $\frac{1}{2}$" # 3

$\frac{3}{4}$"

$\frac{1}{4}$" COPPER TACKS

$\frac{3}{16}$"

$1\frac{5}{16}$" +

$2\frac{1}{2}$"

$\frac{21}{32}$"

INNER EDGE LAP

LAP FASTENING

$1\frac{17}{32}$"

$\frac{3}{4}$"

$\frac{3}{16}$"

BOW

PLANKING SCARPH

AMIDSHIPS $8\frac{5}{8}$"

$\frac{3}{8}$" # 5

3"

$\frac{1}{2}$"

$\frac{1}{16}$"

SHOE IRONS (GALV.)

BREAST HOOK BLOCK
UNDER DECK

$\frac{3}{4}$" # 5

$79°$

$\frac{1}{2}$"

$1\frac{3}{16}$"

$\frac{3}{4}$"

$1\frac{1}{4}$" # 6

GUNWALE SECTION
AMIDSHIPS TO FRAME 4

$\frac{13}{16}$"

$\frac{5}{16}$"

DECK

STEM

$\frac{5}{16}$" $\frac{13}{16}$"

DECK $\frac{7}{16}$"

FR. STA. 12

$\frac{3}{8}$" $\frac{31}{32}$"

$\frac{1}{2}$"

FR. STA. 10

$\frac{7}{16}$" $1\frac{1}{16}$"

$\frac{5}{8}$"

FRAME STA. 8

GRANT 16' GUIDE-BOAT

Plate X

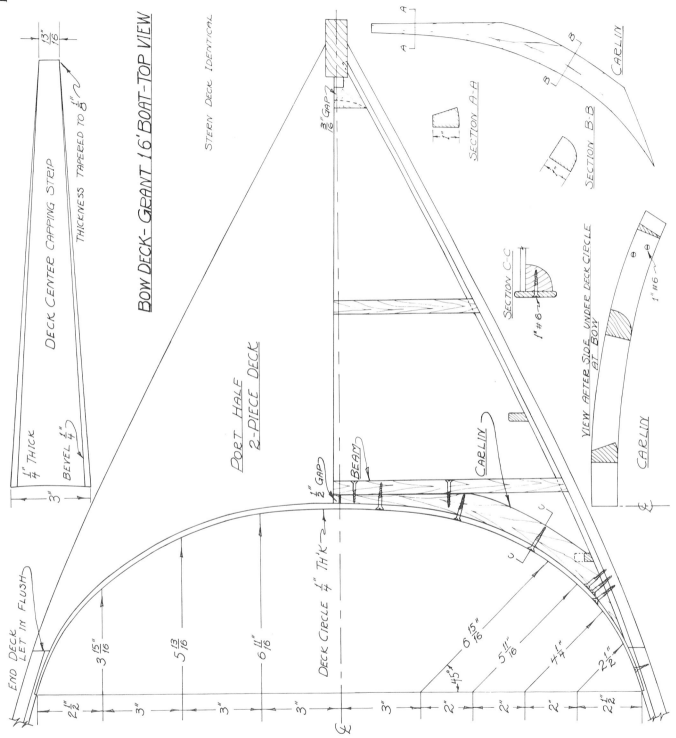

BOW DECK - GRANT 16' BOAT - TOP VIEW

STERN DECK IDENTICAL

DECK CENTER CAPPING STRIP

THICKNESS TAPERED TO ⅛"

¼" THICK

BEVEL ¼"

3"

13/16

SECTION A-A

1"

SECTION B-B

CARLIN

CARLIN

SECTION C-C

1" #6

VIEW AFTER SIDE, UNDER DECK CIRCLE AT BOW

CARLIN

1" #6

PORT HALF
2-PIECE DECK

BEAM

CARLIN

½" GAP

DECK CIRCLE ¼" TH'K

3/16 GAP

END DECK LET IN FLUSH

2½"
3"
3"
3"
3"
2"
2"
2"
2½"

3 15/16"
5 13/16"
6 11/16"
6 15/16"
5 11/16"
4 ¼"
2 ½"

45°

Plate XI

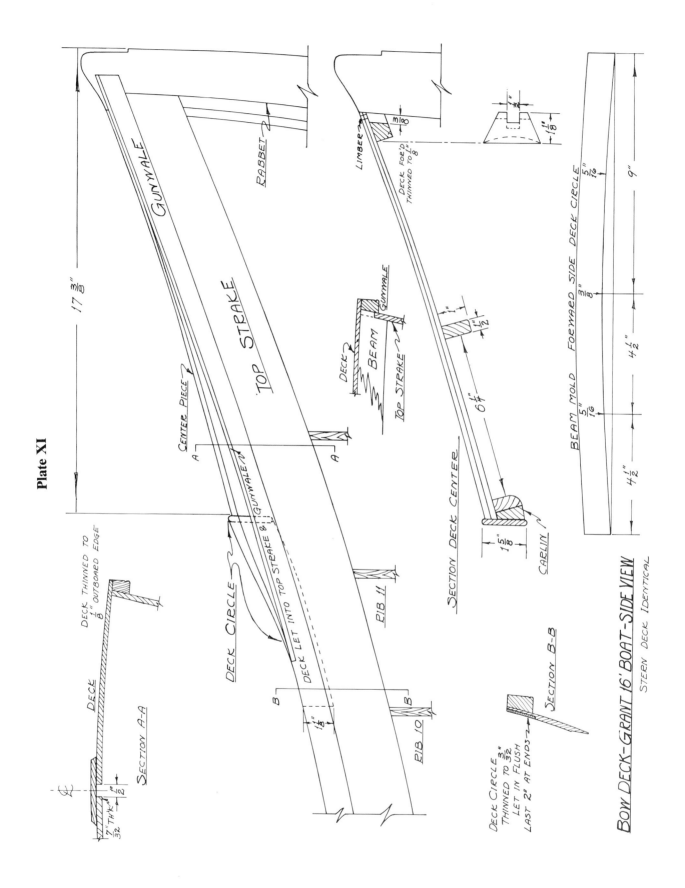

DECK THINNED TO ⅛" OUTBOARD EDGE

DECK

⅞" THK   ½"

₣

SECTION A-A

CENTER PIECE

GUNWALE

TOP STREAKE

RABBET

DECK CIRCLE

DECK LET INTO TOP STREAKE & GUNWALE

17 ³⁄₈"

A   A

DECK LET INTO TOP STREAKE

RIB 11

B

1⅛"

B

RIB 10

DECK CIRCLE THINNED TO ³⁄₃₂"
LET IN FLUSH
LAST 2" AT ENDS

SECTION B-B

LIMBER

DECK FOR'D THINNED TO ⅛"

³⁄₈"

½"   1⅛"

DECK

BEAM

GUNWALE

TOP STREAKE

1"   ½"

6⅔"

1⅝"

CARLIN

SECTION DECK CENTER

BEAM MOLD   FORWARD SIDE DECK CIRCLE

⁵⁄₁₆"   ³⁄₈"   ⁵⁄₁₆"

4½"   4½"   9"

BOW DECK-GRANT 16' BOAT-SIDE VIEW

STERN DECK IDENTICAL

Plate XII

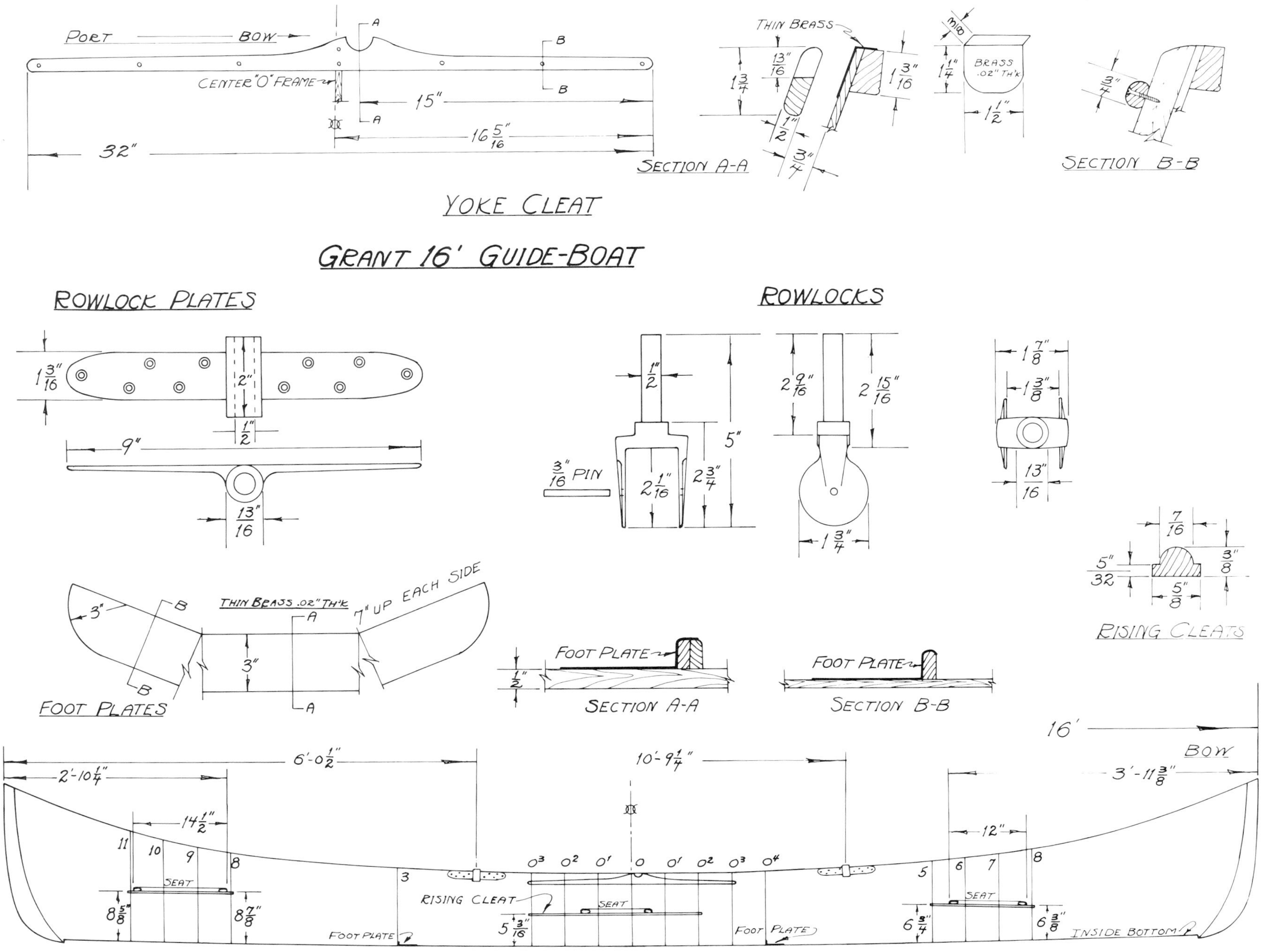

YOKE CLEAT

SECTION B-B

SECTION A-A

BRASS .oz THK.

THIN BRASS

$\frac{3}{4}$"

$\frac{13}{16}$"

$1\frac{1}{4}$"

$1\frac{1}{2}$"

$\frac{3}{16}$"

$\frac{13}{16}$"

$1\frac{3}{4}$"

$1\frac{1}{2}$"

$\frac{3}{4}$"

PORT

BOW

CENTER "O" FRAME

A

A

B

B

15"

$16\frac{5}{16}$"

32"

GRANT 16' GUIDE-BOAT

ROWLOCKS

$2\frac{9}{16}$"

$2\frac{15}{16}$"

$1\frac{3}{4}$"

$\frac{1}{2}$"

5"

$2\frac{3}{4}$"

$2\frac{1}{16}$"

$\frac{3}{16}$" PIN

$1\frac{7}{8}$"

$\frac{3}{8}$"

$\frac{13}{16}$"

ROWLOCK PLATES

2"

$1\frac{1}{2}$"

9"

$1\frac{3}{16}$"

$\frac{13}{16}$"

FOOT PLATES

THIN BRASS .oz THK.

1" UP EACH SIDE

3"

3"

A

A

B

B

RISING CLEAT

$\frac{7}{16}$"

$\frac{3}{8}$"

$\frac{5}{8}$"

$\frac{5}{8}$"

$\frac{5}{32}$"

FOOT PLATE

SECTION B-B

FOOT PLATE

SECTION A-A

$\frac{1}{2}$"

BOW

$3'-11\frac{3}{8}$"

16'

INSIDE BOTTOM

$10'-9\frac{1}{4}$"

$6'-0\frac{1}{2}$"

$2'-10\frac{1}{4}$"

O³ O² O¹ O O⁴

O O¹ O² O³ O⁴

O³ O² O¹ O

SEAT

SEAT

SEAT

RISING CLEAT

FOOT PLATE

FOOT PLATE

8

12"

5 6 7

$6\frac{3}{8}$"

$5\frac{1}{4}$" $6\frac{1}{4}$"

$5\frac{3}{16}$"

8

$14\frac{1}{2}$"

11 10 9

$8\frac{7}{8}$"

$8\frac{5}{8}$"

Plate XIII

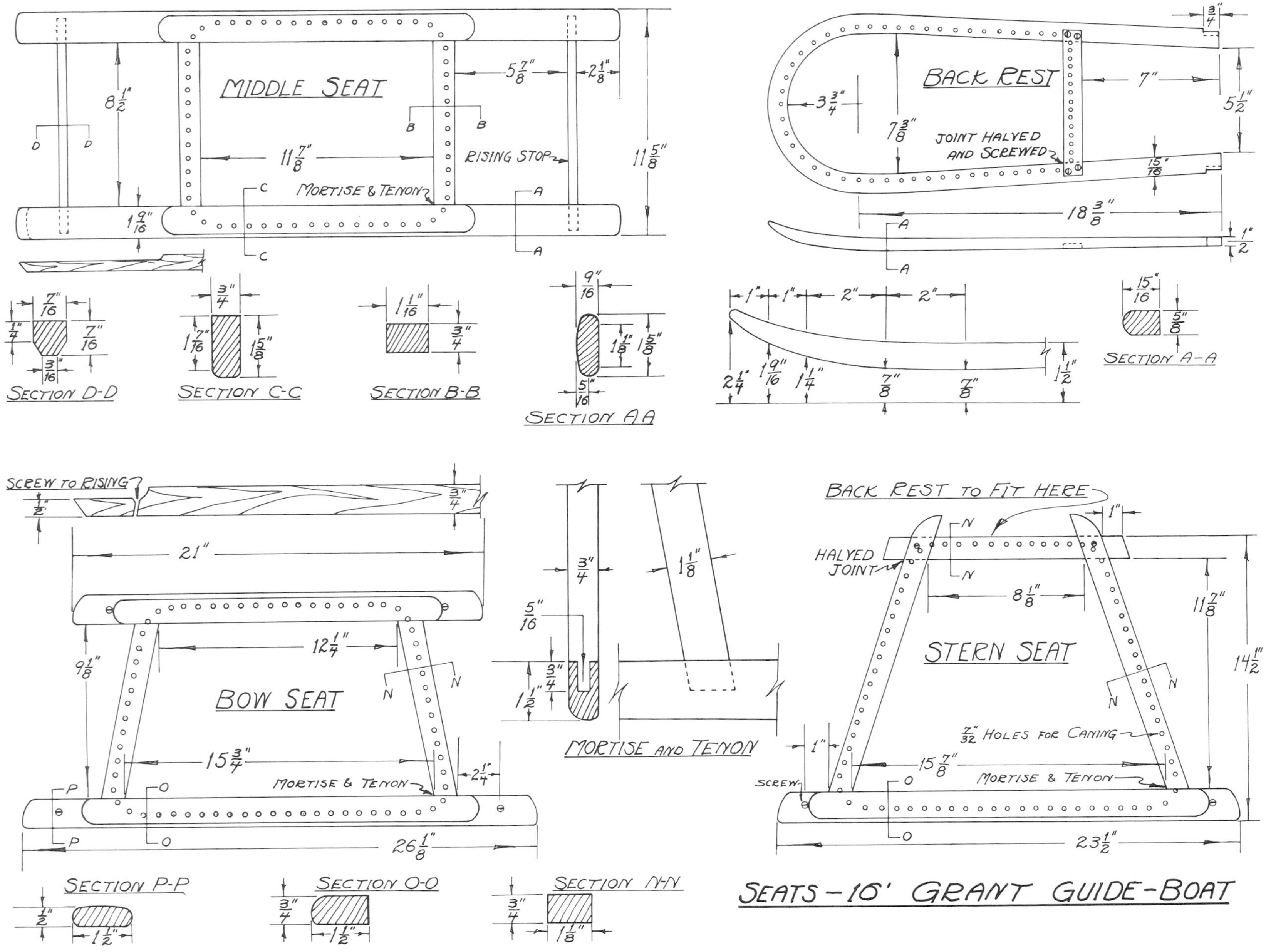

BACK REST

JOINT HALVED AND SCREWED

SECTION A-A

MIDDLE SEAT

RISING STOP

MORTISE & TENON

SECTION A-A

SECTION B-B

SECTION C-C

SECTION D-D

STERN SEAT

BACK REST TO FIT HERE

HALVED JOINT

MORTISE & TENON

SCREW

$\frac{7}{32}$" HOLES FOR CANING

MORTISE AND TENON

SECTION N-N

BOW SEAT

MORTISE & TENON

SCREW TO RISING

SECTION O-O

SECTION P-P

SEATS — 16' GRANT GUIDE-BOAT

Plate XIV

STEM BAND

$\frac{1}{4}"$ $\frac{1}{4}"$

RING - BOW ONLY

$\frac{7}{8}"$ $\frac{5}{8}"$ $\frac{1}{4}"$ $\frac{1}{2}"$

JOINT - BOTTOM AND STEM

$\frac{1}{16}"$ THK $\frac{1}{8}"$ THK C.S. $\frac{3}{4}"$ $\frac{1}{2}"$ $2"$ $4"$

BOTTOM - STEM BAND

$\frac{7}{16}"$ $\frac{1}{4}"$

GRANT STEM BAND

$2\frac{1}{8}"$ $1\frac{5}{8}"$

STEM SECTIONS

$\frac{1}{8}"$ CAP $\frac{3}{4}"$ $\frac{1}{4}"$

GRANT STEM CAP $\frac{1}{8}"$ N.P. BRASS

$\frac{7}{32}"$ LIMBER HOLE $\frac{3}{4}"$ $\frac{13}{16}"$

TOP - STEM TAPER $\frac{1}{4}"$

RABBET LINE

8' OAR - GRANT PATTERN

$+91"$ $\frac{7}{16}"$ $2"$

$+72"$ $1\frac{3}{8}"$ $1\frac{13}{16}"$

$+27$ TO $+42"$ $1\frac{1}{16}"$

$+24"$ $1"$ $1\frac{1}{4}"$

$\frac{15}{16}"$ $1\frac{1}{4}"$

$1\frac{1}{4}"$ $\frac{7}{8}"$ $4\frac{1}{4}"$

$+66"$ $\frac{1}{4}"$ $1\frac{1}{4}"$ $1\frac{1}{4}"$

$+47"$ $\frac{1}{4}"$ $1\frac{3}{16}"$ $1\frac{3}{16}"$

HORIZONTAL SECTION

PIN

$+20"$ $\frac{1}{8}"$ $\frac{13}{16}"$ $3\frac{1}{4}"$ $\frac{1}{8}"$

$+12"$ $\frac{1}{8}"$ $2\frac{1}{4}"$ $\frac{1}{2}"$

$+6"$ $\frac{1}{8}"$ $2\frac{9}{16}"$ $\frac{9}{32}"$

$+0"$ $\frac{1}{8}"$ $2\frac{11}{16}"$ $\frac{1}{4}"$

VERTICAL SECTION

J.G.

$+0"$ $+6"$ $+12"$ $+20"$ $+24"$ $+27"$ $+42"$ $+47"$ $+66"$ $+71"$ $+72"$ $+91"$ $+91\frac{3}{4}"$ $+96"$

Plate XV

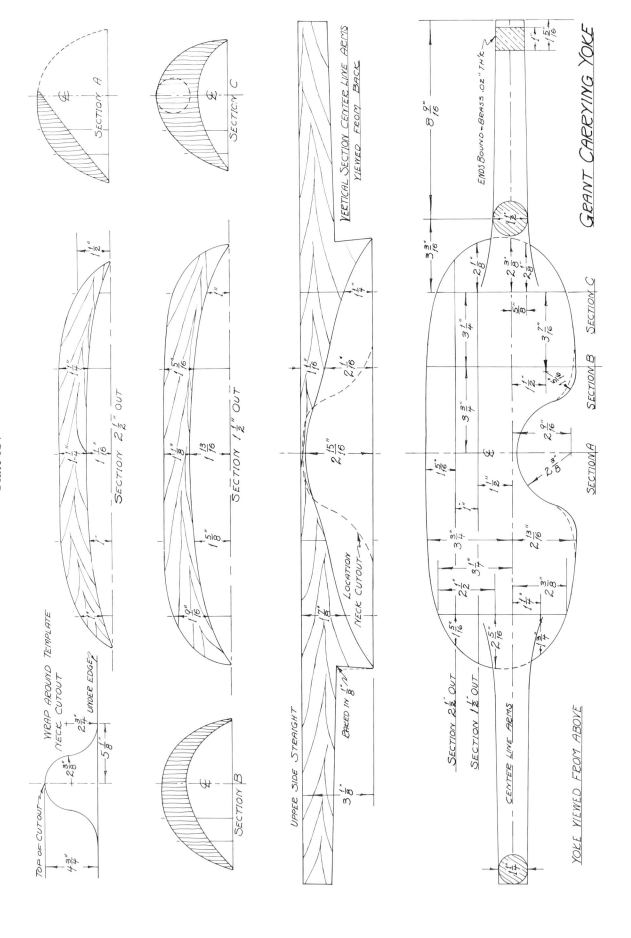

GRANT CARRYING YOKE

Plate XVI

GRANT PADDLE

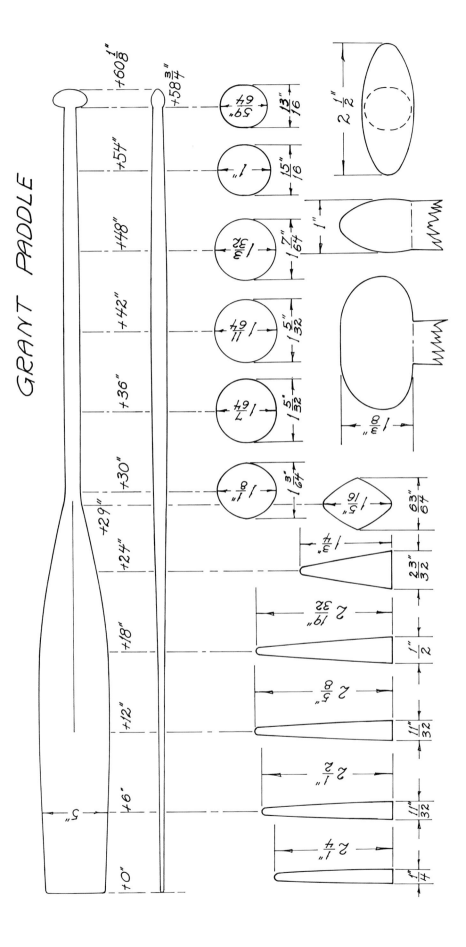

Appendix D
Count of Tacks and Screws

These counts of tacks and screws and their sizes for the guide-boat and accessories are averaged from several Grant boats of 16 feet LOA, each with 8 strakes on 33 pairs of ribs: 9 pairs of center (0) ribs, 20 pairs of footed ribs numbered 1 to 10, and 4 pairs of footless scribe-ribs numbered 11 and 12. Numeration follows Grant's system; the strakes are numbered from the bottom up: the garboard is strake number 1 and the sheer plank is strake number 8.

TACKS

Fastening garboard to bottom board from center rib to rib 7, fore and aft (beyond no. 7 the angle of the bevel requires screw fastenings); in each space between ribs, three ⅝″ tacks are driven from the outside, two ½″ from the inside; five tacks in each of 22 spaces on a side; 44 for whole boat: 220

From top of garboard to bottom of sheer, seven seams have regular arrangement of tacks in all spaces between ribs from center to no. 12, fore and aft. In each space four tacks from the outside close to lower edge of bevel, three from inside close to upper edge (Gardner Plate IX). Between ribs 12 and 12 are 32 spaces, with seven tacks in each of seven seams; 32 x 7 x 7 x 2, for both sides: 3136

Between ribs 12 and stem where setting hammer cannot be used, both rows are driven from the outside. In one quarter, 118 tacks; for whole boat: 472

A single tack is driven from inside through sheer plank, midway between ribs, into wale with 2 or 3 additional under deck: 72

Tacks continued

Scarphs are fastened with seven tacks at the after end (Plate IX). One scarph in each strake 1–6; two in 7–8; ten scarphs to the side, both sides: 140

Accessories

Brass foot-plates are held to the bottom board with 34 tacks in each set and 36 escutcheon pins into the top of rib feet, making 70; 2 sets of plates: 140

Small brass plates to protect sheer plank against chafing by end of yoke are held with five tacks each, the pair: 10

The grooved stem band is fastened to the stem with five finish nails: 10

Total tacks and nails: 4200

TACK SIZES

(Tack weights in ounces per thousand)

Through garboard into bottom board: $\frac{5}{8}''$
Through bottom board into garboard: $\frac{1}{2}''$
Fastening lap of garboard and second strake: $\frac{5}{16}''$, $2\frac{1}{2}$ oz.
Fastening all seams on strakes 3 to 8, $\frac{3}{16}''$ planking: $\frac{1}{4}''$, 2 oz.
For planking thinner than $\frac{3}{16}''$: $\frac{7}{32}''$, $1\frac{1}{2}$ oz.

SCREWS

1. Through three shoe irons into bottom board, screws on 3″ centers: 169

2. Through bottom into rib feet, each pair, 4 screws: 29 pairs: 116

3. Through siding (not wale)
	one quarter
into stem:	35
into ribs 12, 11, 10, 9:	74
into ribs 8 to 1, 0-4, 0-3, 0-2, 0-1:	252

   361 x 4   1444
   into center ribs 0 :   42

4. Through wale into stem: 2 (one quarter)
   into cross pieces under deck (Gardner plate X): 2
   into 16 ribs 0-1 to 12: 16

   20 x 4   80
   into center ribs: 2

5. Through garboard into bottom board between stem and rib no. 7
   24 + 25: 49 x 2:   98

6. Through bottom into stems: 4

7. Decks
through circles into carlins:	20
through decks into wales:	40
through decks into cross pieces:	12
through decks into carlins:	12
through center strip:	16

   100   100

8. Under decks
through inside blocks into siding and wale (Gardner Plate IX):	4
through cross pieces into carlins:	8
through carlins into wales:	8

   16   16

Screws continued

9. Accessories
   stem band into bottom
      of stem: 1
   stem band into
      bottom board: 3
   stem band into top
      of stem (Gardner
      Plate XIV):   2
   stem cap into deck: 1
                              _____
                              7 x 2   14

   seat cleats into ribs,
      bow 8, middle 12,
      stern 8 (Gardner
      Plate XII):   28
   yoke cleats into ribs
      (Gardner Plate XII):   16
   rowlock straps into wales: 40
   cross pieces of back rest
      (Gardner Plate XIII):   4
   seats into cleats: bow
      4, stern 4 (Gardner
      Plate XIII):   8
                                      _____
                                       110   110

                   Total screws: 2185

SCREW SIZES

1. Shoe irons into bottom board: $\frac{3}{8}''$ #5 (when screw hole is under rib: $\frac{5}{8}''$ #5)

2. Bottom into rib feet: at heel, $1\frac{1}{4}''$ #6; at toe, $1''$ #6

3. Siding into stem: $\frac{1}{2}''$ #3
   Garboard through bevel into rib foot: $\frac{7}{8}''$ #3; upper edge into rib: $\frac{3}{4}''$ #3
   Second strake, lower edge into rib: $\frac{3}{4}''$ #3; upper edge: $\frac{5}{8}''$ #3.
   Third to eighth strakes ($\frac{3}{16}''$) upper and lower screws: $\frac{1}{2}''$ #3; middle screw: $\frac{3}{8}''$ #3

4. Wale into stem: $1''$ #5
   Wale into cross pieces: $1\frac{1}{4}''$ #6
   Wale into ribs: $1\frac{1}{4}''$ #6

5. Through garboard into bottom board: first three screws at ends: $\frac{1}{2}''$ #3;
   Fourth and fifth screws: $\frac{5}{8}''$ #3; remainder: $\frac{3}{4}''$ #3

6. Bottom to stem, toe: $1''$ #6; heel: $1\frac{1}{4}''$ #6

7. Deck circles into carlins: $\frac{3}{4}''$ #4
   Deck into cross pieces: $\frac{1}{2}''$ #4
   Decks into carlins: $\frac{1}{2}''$ #3
   Center strip into deck: $\frac{3}{4}''$ #4

8. Cross pieces into carlins: $1''$ #6
   Through carlins into wales: $1''$ #6

9. Stem band into bottom of stem: $\frac{7}{8}''$ #6
   Stem band into bottom board: $\frac{7}{8}''$ #5
   Stem band into top of stem: $1''$ #5
   Stem cap into deck: $1''$ #5
   Seat cleats into ribs: $\frac{7}{8}''$ #5 brass flat head
   Yoke cleats into ribs: $\frac{7}{8}''$ #5
   Rowlock straps into wales: $\frac{3}{4}''$ #7
   Seats into cleats: $1\frac{1}{4}''$ #6, round head brass; except back of stern seat: $1\frac{1}{2}''$ round head brass

Appendix E
Contents of the Grant Boat Shop

I. Items donated by Kenneth and Helen Durant, September 1970.

The following are all from the Boonville, N.Y., shop of H. Dwight Grant:

PLANE, for cutting boat plank lap, designed by H. Dwight Grant.
MODEL, for casting steel sole of above plane.
OARLOCK PINS, pair, brass.
GUNWALE SECTION, wood, beaded.
STEM BAND, piece (bow iron).
FOOT-PLATES, brass—2 samples.
CLEAT, section, molded wood.
SHOE IRONS—2 samples.
GAUGE, for turning oar handles.
GAUGE, showing oar handle sizes for the round.
STRAKES, sections, 6, showing Grant lap.
STEM PATTERN, scribed with rabbet and bearding line.
STEM PATTERN, with rabbet and bearding lines.
PATTERN, for rabbet and bearding lines.
BOAT RIB (no. 7).
BOAT RIB (no. 10).

The following are various items prepared by Lewis L. Grant, Boonville, N.Y., to show details of guide-boat construction:

GARBOARD AND BOTTOM BOARD, section, joined, with metal shoe, tacks and screws.

STRAKES, 2, showing lap fastening.
STRAKES, 2, showing dry lap fastening.
STRAKES, 2, showing spar varnish fastening.
STRAKE, section, 2nd round of siding.
STRAKE, sections, 2, showing rounding and flat finish.
STRAKE, sections, 2, showing scarphing.
STRAKE, section, showing hollow and round and flat of stem.
STRAKE, wide section, showing lap and scarph.
TACKS, boat, copper.
SCREWS, brass, flat head, ½—4.
SCREWS, brass, flat head, ⅝—4.
SCREWS, brass, flat head, ⅜—3.

The following are miscellaneous items pertaining to guide-boat construction:

STRAKE, piece, from Parsons boat left for repair at Hathaway shop, Saranac Lake.
STRAKE, piece, origin unknown, showing thinness of wood.
PATTERNS, guide-boat, 12, scribed from Grant patterns in AM collection, pressboard.
BOAT RIB, Grant no. 6, blocked out on laminated stock.
BOAT RIB, preparatory lamination.
BOAT RIB, preparatory lamination.
BOAT RIB, cut from laminated stock.
BOAT RIB, finished from laminated stock.
BOAT RIB, unfinished, cut from laminated stock.
PLANKING, strip, 5 sections.
NAILS, bronze, annular, ¾—14.

PHOTOS, by Thomas A. Fulk, Loana, Wisconsin, showing his boat under construction and in use.
   Seventy 3 x 3 black-and-white prints and fifteen 5 x 5 black-and-white enlargements, with notes by Fulk.
DRAWINGS, by Lewis L. Grant.
LETTERS, between J.C.A. Gerster and Kenneth Durant.
LETTERS, between Lewis L. Grant and Kenneth Durant.
DRAWINGS, boat details, by Lewis L. Grant.
LETTERS, from Lewis L. Grant, re steamboat he built.
NOTES, by Lewis L. Grant, on draft by Kenneth Durant.
LETTERS, from Kenneth Durant to Lewis L. Grant.
DIARIES, Lewis L. Grant.
CHECK STUB BOOK, Lewis L. Grant.
SCRAPBOOK, miscellaneous clippings, Lewis L. Grant.
ACCOUNT BOOKS, 4, Lewis L. Grant.

II. Items donated by Mr. and Mrs. William D. Gillespie, Schenectady, N.Y., July 1966. (Mrs. Gillespie was the daughter of Floyd Grant and the niece of Lewis L. Grant. She was also Lewis L. Grant's heir.)

FLAT-BOTTOMED BOAT FORMS:
   A. Bow form for narrow boat.
   B. Two patterns on one form: center form for narrow boat and bow form for wide outboard boat.
   C. Center form for wide boat.

RIB PATTERNS, probably for a Lewis L. Grant flat-bottomed boat.
SIDING PATTERNS FOR GUIDE-BOAT (these patterns are now missing).
SIDING PATTERNS FOR FLAT-BOTTOMED BOAT:
   A. 63½″ x 3½″.
   B. 56″ x ⅝″.
   C. 102½″ x 3½″.
   D. 113″ x 4¾″.
QUARTER PATTERNS FOR GUIDE-BOAT BOTTOM BOARDS (these are now missing).
OAR PATTERNS:
   A. Oar loom pattern, 23⅞″.
   B. Oar loom pattern, 28⅛″.
   C. Oar pattern, 64⅝″ LOA.
   D. 6-foot oar pattern.
   E. Oar pattern, 98½″ LOA.
   F. 8-foot oar pattern.
   G. Oar pattern, 86″ LOA.
   H. 7-foot oar pattern.
   I. 7½-foot oar pattern.
   J. Oar pattern, 104″ LOA.
TAPERED OAR PATTERN, for use in planer.
7-FOOT OAR, unfinished and imperfect grain.
7-FOOT 7-INCH OAR, unfinished, black, without pin.
PADDLE PATTERNS:
   A. 54⅛″ LOA.
   B. 54″ LOA.
   C. 29½″ LOA.
   D. 66″ LOA.
   E. 71⅞″ LOA.
RABBET MOLD AND LAST PATTERN.
RIB PATTERNS, "first Grant pattern" for a 16-foot boat.
RIB PATTERNS, 13 patterns on 12 pieces, last Grant patterns similar to *Virginia* ribs, stamped
   1906-1916.
RIB PATTERNS, of the *Virginia* type, labeled "last Grant patterns."
UNIDENTIFIED RIB PATTERNS, numbered 0-6.
RIB PATTERNS, unidentified:
   A. Has 10½ and Chris Wagner written on the back.
   B. Has 9½ written on the back.
   C. Has 6½ X marked on the back.
   D. Has 4½ marked on the back.
   E. Has 9½ X marked on the back.
FIRST GRANT STEM PATTERN.
GUIDE-BOAT YOKE BLOCKS, two, of unfinished wood.
TALLY BOARDS:
   A. For the years 1884–1887, 1888, and 1889.
   B. For the years 1890–1894.
   C. For the years 1896–1900.
   D. For the years 1901–1906, 1917, and 1918.
   E. For the years 1919–1923 and to 1934.

TEMPLATES FOR SEAT HEIGHTS:
   A. Stern seat.
   B. Bow seat.
   C. Middle seat.
   D. Bow seat.
   E. Stern seat.
GUIDE-BOAT BOTTOM BOARD, with rib feet attached. Made by Lewis L. Grant to demonstrate rib attachment.
GUIDE-BOAT MIDDLE SEATS, unfinished, wooden with caning holes and long side thwarts to attach to seat cleats.
BOW AND STERN SEATS, unfinished:
   A. Bow seat.
   B. Stern seat.
   C. Bow seat.
   D. Stern seat.
MIDDLE, BOW, AND STERN SEATS, varnished, without cane:
   A. Middle seat.
   B. Stern seat.
   C. Bow seat.
PATTERNS FOR MIDDLE, BOW, AND STERN SEATS:
   A. Stern seat pattern.
   B. Bow seat pattern.
   C. Middle seat pattern.
SUPPORTS FOR MIDDLE BACK RESTS, unfinished, for guide-boats.
BLOCKS FOR GLUING SEAT FRAMES.

GUIDE-BOAT RIB PATTERNS:
   A. through D. Bow or stern ribs, without feet.
   E. through M. End (extreme bow or stern) ribs, without feet.
   N. through Q. Midsection ribs, with feet.
   R. and S. Footed ribs, approximately no. 7.
   T. Footed rib, approximately no. 9.
   U. Footed rib, approximately no. 10.
CLEAT STOCKS, beaded, for guide-boats.
CRADLE BIN, for storing guide-boat ribs.
BOAT STERN, cut off to make square stern for outboard.
POST WITH THREE IRON BRACES, part of boat stock.
STEAM BOX AND COVER:
   A. Steam box.
   B. Cover.
YOKE PATTERNS:
   A. Boat yoke pattern made of tin and wood.
   B. Yoke arm pattern.
   C. Plywood yoke pattern.
   D. Cardboard yoke pattern.
DECK PIECES.
DEVICE FOR SCRIBING DECK CIRCLES, wooden, in the form of a T-square.
JIG TO HOLD OAR BLADE WHILE SHAVING OFF SUPERFLUOUS THICKNESS.

GRANT PAPER PATTERNS:
  A. Bow stem for 18-foot boat.
  B. Pattern labeled "back."
  C. Stern form.
  D. Bow quarter.
  E. Pattern labeled "center."
PLANK STOCK.
CANING, bundle of strips for guide-boat seats.
STERN BACK SUPPORTS AND JIG:
  A. Stern back support.
  B. Stern back support.
  C. Jig for forming ribs for flat-bottomed boats, ca. 1933.
UNIDENTIFIED CLAMP.
OUTBOARD MOTOR BRACKET.
SNOWSHOES, bearpaw.
SEAT PATTERNS:
  A. 17″ x ¾″.
  B. 16½″ x ¾″.
  C. 16½″ x ¾″.
FRAME WITH DRAWKNIVES:
  A. Wooden frame for 5 drawknives.
  B. Drawknife 14½″ x 6″ x 1⅝″.
  C. Drawknife 15½″ x 6½″ x 1⅜″.
  D. Drawknife 15½″ x 7¼″ x 1¾″.
  E. Drawknife 21″ x 6¼″ x 2⅝″.
  F. Drawknife 19½″ x 6″ x 2¼″.
PUNCH, made of black metal for making holes in bottom irons.
FRAME SAW, wooden, self-jointed by mortise and tenon.
ROUGHED-OUT RIB PIECE.
CAST IRON GLUE POT.
BOAT SHOP SIGN, "Lewis L. Grant" in black on a yellow-green background.
SEGMENTS OF RIB PATTERNS AND SMALL-SCALE GUIDE-BOAT (CARDBOARD) IN A BOX:
  A. and B. Top section of rib.
  C. Rib foot.
  D. Small board with outlined rib end.
  E. Cardboard guide-boat.
  F. Cigar box containing A. through E.

FRAMING AUGER, used by Dwight Grant in dam construction and log structures.
STEM PATTERNS.
STEAM BOX AND COVER:
  A. Steam box.
  B. Cover.
SPRUCE-ROOT FLITCHES:
  A. and B. Cut by chain saw probably supplied by Gallagher.
  C. Original Grant flitch.
SHEER BATTENS, for guide-boats.

BOAT IRONS AND FOOT-PLATE PATTERNS:
  A. and B. Brass stem irons.
  C. Bottom iron.
  D. Brass strip for foot-plates.
  E. and F. Galvanized metal foot-plate patterns.
MISCELLANEOUS WOOD PIECES, including one wedge, one short octagonal piece, and a block with a hole.
CANE SEATS, middle seats for guide-boats.
WOODEN TRUNK, now empty.
TEMPLATES FOR SEATS AND BACK RESTS:
  A. Bow and stern seats.
  B. Middle seat.
  C. Stern back.
  D. For caning middle back.
  E. Rectangular shape with 2 notches at ends.
  F. Back of stern seat.
  G. Bow and stern seat.
  H. Bow seat.
SMALL WOODEN GAUGES FOR SIDING.
JIGS AND BLOCK, for use with Lewis L. Grant machines:
  A. Jig.
  B. Block.
  C. Board.
WEDGES FOR HOLDING BACK REST FRAMES AFTER STEAMING, 47, of unfinished wood.
WEDGING BENDING FRAMES:
  A. 17 wooden blocks for wedging and bending frames of guide-boat seat back rests.
  B. Wooden trunk.
  C. 10 metal wedges for bending frames of guide-boats.
JIGS:
  A. and B. Bending clamp.
  C. Brace.
  D. Board.
GAUGE FOR END OF OAR BLADE.
PAPER PROTRACTOR.
GARBOARD PATTERNS FOR GUIDE-BOATS.
PLANK PATTERNS FOR GUIDE-BOATS.
QUARTER PATTERNS FOR GUIDE-BOAT BOTTOM BOARDS.
BOAT YOKE PATTERNS (originally there were 5 patterns):
  A. Made of thin wood, rectangular.
  B. Elliptical-shaped, with 2 arms.
BOAT YOKE PATTERNS:
  A. Oblong, of light wood.
  B. Elliptical-shaped.
  C. Made of tin and wood.
  D. Elliptical-shaped, with handles.
  E. Oblong, made of plywood.
NECK YOKE CLEATS, half finished, 2 together, made by Lewis L. Grant for the Museum to show construction.

STERN SEAT FOR PARSONS BOAT, plywood, with penciled pattern; also marked "L.L. Grant."

SLICK, which belonged to Dwight Grant, made of iron and used in framing heavy timbers in building water-powered sawmills and log buildings.

MEASURING STICKS, 33 in all.

EXHIBITION NECK YOKE, half finished, one half rough block; other half, finished yoke. Made by Lewis L. Grant for the Museum.

CLAMP FOR BENDING MIDDLE BACK REST SUPPORT.

CLAMP WITH MIDDLE BACK REST SUPPORT IN PLACE.

SHIPWRIGHT'S ADZE, with reverse wooden helve (haft) and peg-shaped poll. "A.D. Barton/Rochester" is stamped on the underside of bit. Adze belonged to Dwight Grant.

HAIRPIN CLAMP, wrapped with leather and held tight by chain links. Used by Dwight Grant for putting ribs on one side of a guide-boat from 1880; made by a blacksmith.

PART OF AN OAR ADAPTED FOR WEIGHING GUIDE-BOATS.

STEELYARD, 200 lbs., stamped near hook, "Chatillon, New York." Used by Grant to weigh his guide-boats from 1880:

    A. Curved bar with hooks.

    B. Weight with #8 stamped on the handle.

    C. Weight with #2 stamped on the side of hook.

CROSS ARM OR LIFTING TOGGLE, adjusted to fit under wale in hanging boats on steelyard.

GUIDE-BOAT RIB FOOT PATTERNS:

    A. through K. Last Grant patterns, numbered 0 through 10.

    L. and M. Paper patterns copied from guide-boat brought in for repair; not necessarily Grant patterns.

SMALL STEELYARD WITH ONE WEIGHT.

WOODEN GAUGE FOR OARS, to gauge width of loom at pin; to set pinhole; and to sight through slot to keep blade in line.

PATTERNS AND PIECES FOR TIMBERS TO SUPPORT "RACK" OR GRATING, as in Grant family boat from Covewood Lodge:

    A. through F. Patterns.

    G. through J. Pieces.

GUIDE-BOAT DECK PATTERNS, of the *Virginia* type.

PADDLE BLADE TEMPLATE.

CLAMP FOR BENDING BACK REST SUPPORT.

WOODEN CLAMP.

PUNCH FOR HOLES IN BOTTOM IRON.

IRON CLAMPS, of cast steel of the C-clamp screw type.

CLENCHING IRONS.

BOAT CLAMPS.

WOODEN CLAMPS.

PLANES:

    A. Moulding plane adapted by H.D. Grant to serve as a lap plane with a concave sole and blade.

    B. Moulding plane adapted by H.D. Grant to serve as a lap plane with a broad curved sole.

    C. Moulding plane adapted by Grant to serve as a lap plane forming a narrow, raised, rounded channel.

    D. Moulding plane adapted by Grant to serve as a lap plane. Sole is cut to form 2 rectangular strips, one of which has been channeled.

    E. Moulding plane adapted by Grant to serve as a lap plane with a concave sole similar to A above.

    F. Rabbet plane, without fence.

    G. Rabbet plane, without fence.

CHISEL OR SLICK, stamped "Keaton & Dencela Cast Steel," used for cutting scarphs.

STEEL NAME PUNCH, used by H.D. Grant on his tools; changed by his son Lewis to L.L. Grant.

SPOKESHAVES.

OARPINS, bronze.

OARPIN SOCKET PLATES, bronze.

OARPIN SOCKET PLATES, cast steel.

YOKE-TYPE OARLOCK, cast steel

OARPIN SOCKET PLATE, cast steel; fits yoke-type oarlock above.

BOW IRON.

METAL PLANES:
  A. $2\frac{1}{2}''$ x $1''$.
  B. $3\frac{7}{8}''$ x $1\frac{1}{2}''$ x $1\frac{1}{4}''$.
  C. With convexed bottom and blade $3\frac{3}{8}''$ x $1\frac{1}{4}''$ x $1\frac{1}{8}''$.
  D. $3\frac{1}{2}''$ x $1\frac{1}{4}''$ x $1\frac{1}{4}''$.
  E. Convexed $3\frac{3}{8}''$ x $1\frac{1}{4}''$ x $1\frac{1}{4}''$.

SANDER, sanding block with 2 metal handles.

LAP PLANES:
  A. Without a blade and with metal fence.
  B. With an iron sole patented by Grant.

CONCAVE STEEL SMOOTHER PLANE.

CONVEX STEEL JACK PLANE.

CONCAVE AND CONVEX WOODEN PLANES.

NUMBER STAMPS.

BOAT PATTERNS AND STOCK:
  A. Stock roughed out from a piece of wood.
  B. Boat pattern.
  C. Boat pattern.

CHISEL, with a wooden handle stamped "Marlestock Cast Steel," for making scarph plank-end joints. This "was the most precious tool in the Grant shop, kept in a secret drawer to prevent 'borrowing'; maintained razor-edged and pushed only by hand; never struck with a mallet." — K. Durant.

SCRAPER.

AWLS IN A CIGAR BOX:
  A. Pear-shaped handle with 2 flat sides.
  B. Oblong handle and bent point.
  C. Diamond-shaped point used only in guide-boat building.
  D. Without a point.
  E. Handle flat on 2 sides and painted black.
  F. Chisel-shaped point.
  G. Diamond-shaped point used only in guide-boat building with rounded handle.
  H. Cigar box.

WOODEN MALLET.

SETTING HAMMER.

DRAWKNIVES:
  A. $14''$ x $4\frac{1}{2}''$ x $\frac{1}{4}''$.
  B. $12''$ x $5''$ x $\frac{1}{2}''$.

JOINTER PLANE, with a convexed blade, $24''$.

JOINTER PLANE, with a blade missing, $21''$.

BLOCK FOR CHISEL, chisel missing.

GUIDE-BOAT STERN SEAT PATTERNS.

TRACING GAUGE FOR STEM CAP AND FOOT-PLATES.
GAUGE FOR OAR LOOMS.
GAUGE FOR SCRIBING CIRCUMFERENCES OF OAR HANDLES.
UNIDENTIFIED PIECES, for bow and stern seats.
GAUGE FOR HEIGHT OF THE MIDDLE AND STERN SEAT CLEATS.
GAUGES, to measure cross-section of the gunwales.
GAUGES:
   A. Caning bow seat back and front.
   B. Caning bow seat ends.
   C. Caning bow.
   D. Caning bow seat.
   E. Caning back rest.
   F. Caning back rest of bow.
   G. Caning stern seat.
   H. Caning bow seat.
BACK REST FOR BOAT SEAT.
JIGS FOR STERN SEATS OF FLAT-BOTTOMED BOAT.
PATTERN FOR GUIDE-BOAT DECK CONSTRUCTION.
BRACES USED IN OAR CONSTRUCTION, according to Durant used to brace loom when cutting
   oar blade with a circular saw.
   A. $15\frac{7}{8}$″ x $3\frac{1}{4}$″ x $\frac{3}{4}$″.
   B. $9\frac{1}{4}$″ x $3\frac{7}{8}$″ x $1\frac{1}{4}$″.
   C. 9″ x 2″ x 2″.
   D. 9″ x $3\frac{1}{2}$″ x $2\frac{3}{4}$″.
   E. $6\frac{7}{8}$″ x $3\frac{1}{2}$″ x $2\frac{3}{4}$″.
   F. $3\frac{1}{8}$″ x $6\frac{5}{8}$″ x $3\frac{3}{8}$″.
WEDGES, possibly for flat-bottomed boat construction.
GAUGE FOR OAR BLADE THICKNESS.
UNIDENTIFIED GAUGES.
UNIDENTIFIED ROUND PEGS.
UNIDENTIFIED JIGS.
TOP HALF OF RIB REMOVED FROM A GUIDE-BOAT, not necessarily Grant's.
CLAMP, possibly used in oar construction.
JIG, possibly used in oar or paddle construction.
OAR OR PADDLE BLADE.
PATTERNS FOR FLAT-BOTTOMED BOAT:
   A. (1-2) $32\frac{3}{8}$″ x $9\frac{7}{8}$″ x $\frac{3}{4}$″.
   B. (1-4) 22″ x $4\frac{5}{8}$″ x $\frac{1}{4}$″.
   C. (1-2) 23″ x $5\frac{5}{8}$″ x $\frac{1}{2}$″.
   D. $22\frac{3}{8}$″ x $5\frac{1}{2}$″ x $\frac{1}{2}$″.
   E.   21″ x $4\frac{3}{4}$″ x $\frac{3}{4}$″.
   F. $21\frac{1}{2}$″ x 4″ x $1\frac{5}{8}$″.
BATTENS.
STEAMED RIB, probably for flat-bottomed boat.
SIDING GAUGES.
TRACING GAUGE FOR STEM BEVELS.
GAUGES FOR ROUNDS.
UNIDENTIFIED OAR BLOCKS.
UNIDENTIFIED PIECES.
TWO MIDDLE SEATS, finished.
TRACING OF RIB AND STEM PATTERNS.

Appendix F
Adirondack Boatbuilders

List compiled January 1979 by T. Warrington. Additional information from the files of the Kenneth and Helen Durant Collection in the archives of the Adirondack Museum.

This list represents an attempt to combine information from the various sources within the Adirondack Museum, including the Boats and Boat Builders file in the registrar's office, selected accession folders, Library Vertical Files, discontinued periodicals, guidebooks, etc.

The division of builders into three groups (guide-boat builders, probable guide-boat builders, and other builders of miscellaneous craft) is only a heuristic device. This list is intended as a guide to further study, and as such will undoubtedly undergo drastic changes, additions, deletions, as more facts are uncovered.

Unless other sources are given, the names may all be found on individual folders in the Museum registrar's office.

Abbreviations used:
AM – Adirondack Museum
KD/HD Coll. – Kenneth and Helen Durant Collection at the Adirondack Museum

I. Guide-Boat Builders

Anderson, Leonard	1873–1941, Tupper Lake Built several boats. His patterns are in the AM.
Austin, Hank	1835–1925, Long Lake
Austin, Lewis	1866–1901, Long Lake
Austin, Merlin	ca. 1875–ca. 1951, Long Lake

Austin, Harold

Long Lake
For details on the activities of the members of the Austin family as boat-builders, see the following folders of the Kenneth and Helen Durant Collection at the Adirondack Museum: 5-15, page 41; 16-24, #28 and #29; 50-19; and 50-46A, #90A, #94A, #99A, and #100A.

Billings, Albert Henry

1853-1903, Lake Placid
Billings boat in possession of James H. Higgins at the Brunson S. McCutchen Camp, Lake Placid: KD/HD Coll. folder 5-27, #42 and #43. Place of his first boat shop, destruction of patterns and records in fire; description of Billings boat found in the Hanmer shop, etc., see folder 50-24.

Blanchard, Arthur

Raquette Lake

Blanchard, John

Blue Mountain Lake

Blanchard, Paul

Raquette Lake

For details see KD/HD Coll. folders 3-29, #19; 16-13, #1-3; 50-39, #14-16; 50-47, #58-62; 50-64, #4; 70-11, #5; 70-18, #88-89; 70-20, #78-79

Burns, Fred

1892-?, Long Lake
Built very few boats.

Buyce, John F.

1870-1947, Speculator
Was also blacksmith and wagon maker. Represented in AM boat collection. Background information and biographical data: KD/HD Coll. folder 3-22.

Carey, Reuben

ca. 1845-1933, Long Lake/Brandreth Lake/Raquette Lake
Represented in AM collection.
See also: *Forest and Stream*, March 9, 1876, p. 74, letter to D.W. Mandell; KD/HD Coll. folder 50-51, #4 and #7; Extract 10th U.S. Census 1880, Long Lake: folder 8-13, #11; Reuben Carey square stern, transom and stern post carved from a single block: folders 5-6; 50-19; 50-24; 50-27; 70-7, #17; 70-9, #29; 70-18.

Chapman, Earl B.

?-ca. 1958, Busch's Landing
Patterns in AM.

Chase, Caleb

1830-1911, Newcomb
One of the famous builders. Represented in AM boat collection. *Forest and Stream*, March 9, 1876, p. 74, letter to D.W. Mandell; *Field and Stream*, September 1901. *Conservationist*, June/July 1948: change from square stern to double-ender. Biographical data: KD/HD Coll. folders 16-11, #1-11; 50-42, #131- 23; 50-47, #27-31; 50-51, #29; 50-54, #70; 65-5, #24-29; 70-10, #31; 70-11; 70-20, #17. Builder: 50-3; 50-55, #9. Guide: 65-25, #4. Patterns: 50-47, #47-48; 70-20, #15-17.

Chase, Edmund J.

?-1927, Newcomb

Cole, Charles

Long Lake

Cole, Warren

1854–1922, Long Lake
Renowned builder. Represented in AM boat collection. *Forest and Stream*, February 4, 1899. Biographical data: KD/HD Coll. folders 3-24; 3-29, #8–15 and #24-31; 50-33, #38-46; 50-43. Working methods: 3-29, #18–19 and #51-57; 5-10; 50-19. Miscellany: 3-29, #1–6; 50-54; 70-19, #13.

Emerson, Wallace F.

ca. 1874–1953, Long Lake
Made some extra-wide boats for fishing. Represented in the AM collection. Biographical data: KD/HD Coll. folders 5-6; 16-12, #3–5; 65-5.

Fish, Elijah

1842–?, Sabael

Fish, Ernest

1877–1910, Sabael and Indian Lake

Fish, Raleigh

1904–1977, Sabael

Grant, Floyd

1866–1941, Boonville

Grant, H. Dwight

1833–1911, Boonville
Father of Floyd and Lewis L. Grant. Represented in AM boat collection. Contents of Grant boat shop in AM.

Grant, Lewis L.

1878–1960, Boonville

Hanmer, Theodore S.

1860–1957, Saranac Lake
Adirondack Daily, April 20, 1957; *Adirondack Daily Enterprise*, February 26, 1957; *North Country Life*, Spring 1957; *The Conservationist*, June-July 1948. Biographical data: KD/HD Coll. folder 16-6, #4–12. Notes on construction, prices, etc.: folders 3-32; 16-6, #13-15; 50-10; 50-29A, #3–7, 50-33, #36–37.

Hanmer, Willard

1902–1962, Saranac Lake
Son of Theodore. Represented in AM boat collection. Construction model, 16 mm. film, and taped interview in AM. *Guide-Boat Days and Ways*, by Kenneth Durant; *Adirondack Daily Enterprise*, March 5, 1958; *Times-Union*, October 5, 1958; *Watertown Daily Times*, April 20, 1957; *Warrensburg News*, May 31, 1962; *Conservationist*, Dec./Jan. 1962; *Adirondack Life*, August 20, 1964. General information: KD/HD Coll. folders 3-6; 16-6; 30-2, #16–22; 50-19; 70-19. Construction: folders 3-23; 16-6; 70-20. Transcript of tape: folder 16-4.

Hathaway, Carl

Now living in Saranac Lake
Took over the Hanmer shop.

Hurst, Isaac

Canton

Kerst, William   1874–1950, Sabael

Martin, H. Kilburn   Saranac Lake

Martin, William A.   1849–1907, Saranac Lake
Well-known builder. Represented in AM boat collection. Biographical data: KD/HD Coll. folders 16-8, #4–5. Construction: folder 70-9, #39. AM display of guide carrying boat: folders 50-24; 50-47; 70-9; 70-11, #10.

Moody, Alric B.   Saranac Lake
Some information in KD/HD Coll. folders 14-4 and 14-6.

Nickerson, Myron A.   See KD/HD Coll. folders 14-4; 14-11; 50-46, #2; 70-6; 70-12.

Palmer, Cyrus H.   1845–1897, Long Lake
Patterns attributed to him are in the AM collection. General information: KD/HD Coll. folders 3-24; 8-13; 50-19; 50-32; 50-55, #25–26 and #37.

Parsons, Ben   Old Forge

Parsons, Ira   Old Forge

Parsons, Riley   Old Forge
Father of Ben and
Ira Parsons

Represented in AM boat collection. KD/HD Coll. folders 5-10; 10-8; 16-10, #4–10; 50-10; 50-32, #53; 50-43, #72–87; 50-45, #56–65; 50-62, #2–7; 70-3; 70-7, #15–18; 70-15, #19–23; 70-20. Patterns: folder 70-15, #20.

Rice, Fred   1852–1934, Bloomingdale and Saranac Lake
Biographical notes: KD/HD Coll. folders 16-25, #8–13. Undated catalogue: folder 16-25, #1–7.

Ricketson, G.   Bloomingdale
Represented in AM boat collection.

Smith, George W.   1866–1926, Long Lake
Represented in AM boat collection. Biographical data: KD/HD Coll. folder 50-34, #27. Patterns: folder 16-22, #4–5. General information: folders 16-22; 50-32.

Stanton, George B.   1847–1935, Long Lake
See KD/HD Coll. folder 3-24.

Stanton, Henry   ca. 1844–1881, Long Lake
Represented in AM boat collection. Brother of George B. Stanton. Biographical notes: KD/HD Coll. folders 3-24; 8-13, #11; 16-15, #4–7; 16-16, #7–8; 50-19; 50-32.

Vassar, William (& Son)   Bloomingdale

II. Probable Guide-Boat Builders

Alden, William   1848–1885, Newcomb
                                Son-in-law of Caleb Chase. Biographical data: KD/HD Coll. folders
                                3-23; 50-42; 70-20.

Bissell, Harvey   Newcomb
                                Mentioned in Rev. H.S. Huntington diary, 1853. Extract 9th U.S. Census 1870, Newcomb, in KD/HD Coll. folder 8-13, #6.

Bliss, C.H.   Lake Placid
(George & Bliss)

Craig   Blue Mountain Lake

George, Th. H.   Lake Placid
(George & Bliss)

Graves, Nathaniel S.   Blue Mountain Lake
                                Forest and Stream, October 17, 1903. Apparently taught John Blanchard.

Hamner, Charles   1882–1956, Long Lake
                                Sometimes also spelled Hanmer. See also KD/HD Coll. folder 50-19.

Hinkson, Daniel   1861–1946, Tupper Lake

Marsha, C.H.   Long Lake
                                Successor to H.L. Salisbury & Bro.

McCaffrey, William   Saranac Lake and Bloomingdale
                                Extreme ram bow a characteristic of his boats.

McLenathan, Wm.(?)   Upper Saranac Lake
                                Various spellings of name. Taught W.A. Martin, N.S. Graves. Mentioned in Donaldson, Vol. I, p. 305.

Owen, Dyton   1908– ?, Tupper Lake   Luther worked for Rushton, set
                                Grandson of Luther.   up own shop in West Potsdam,
                                                              then Tupper Lake. Owen's
Owen, Earl   1881–1943, Tupper Lake   Boat & Motor Co. Biographical
                                Son of Luther.   notes on Owen family: KD/HD
                                                              Coll. folder 50-43, #54.
Owen, Luther   Tupper Lake

Palmer, Ransom   Long Lake

Peck, Robert J.	Long Lake Builder of boat accessories. S.R. Stoddard, *The Adirondacks*, 1887, p. 116. Copy of 1887 catalogue in KD/HD Coll. folder 3-23.
Plumbley, John	Long Lake Boatbuilder when not acting as a guide. Wallace's *Guide to the Adirondacks*, 1875.
Rushton, J. Henry	1843-1906, Canton Mainly a canoe builder. Biographical data: KD/HD Coll. folders 14-4; 16-21, #39; 60-63. Construction: folders 16-21, #29-59; 14-4. Catalogues: folder 16-21, #131.
Sabattis, Isaac	Long Lake
Sabattis, Mitchell	1824-1906, Long Lake *Spirit of the Times*, Vol. 19, November 3, 1849.
Salisbury, H.L., & Bro.	Long Lake Mystic Seaport has 14′4″ boat with name plate; keel instead of bottom board.
Seiber, Theodore	Moose River and Old Forge Name also spelled Seeber or Seber. Originally with Dwight Grant, later partner with Riley Parsons, 1890-1896.
Shaw, Robert	Long Lake Mentioned in AM accession folder 60-37. See also KD/HD Coll. folder 50-43A, #16-25.
Spaulding St. Lawrence Boat Co.	Ogdensburg 1895 catalogue lists "Adirondack Skiff *Ampersand*."
Thompson, Albert	Cranberry Lake
Thompson, George L.	Cranberry Lake
Thompson, John	Cranberry Lake
Villeneuve, Joe	Tupper Lake
Wood, Jerome	

III. Other North Country Boat Builders

Bain, A., & Co.	Clayton, N.Y. After moving to Ogdensburg in 1896, they became Spaulding St. Lawrence Boat Co. Copies of catalogues in KD/HD Coll. folders 16-24, #4-11; 70-5.

Baker, Freeman J.	Saranac Motorboats and paddle boats.	
Barlow, William	Horicon Flat-bottomed fishing boats.	
Barnum, "Unk"	Malone	
Bates, George	Lake George	
Boardway, Charles	Malone	
Bolton, William	Horicon Flat-bottomed boats.	
Bowdish, Edward	Skaneateles	According to 1889 catalogue, operated under name of Bowdish Manufacturing Co., Engines, Boilers, Launches, Boats, Canoes & Fittings. See also KD/HD Coll. folder 3-23.
Bowdish, Nelson S.	Skaneateles	
Brasher Boat Co.	Brasher Falls	
Brown, Delbert	Lake George	
Brown, Everett "Cyce"	Canton Rushton workman; may have had own shop.	
Brown, Nelson	Canton Rushton's foreman 1878–1916. See also KD/HD Coll. folder 14-4.	
Cantwell, Joseph J.	Saranac Lake Boat livery.	
Clute Bros. & Co.	Schenectady Builders of steamboat *Osprey*, 1881.	
Crandell, Will	Lake George	
Demerse, Russell	Saranac Lake	
Denner, E.T.	Chippewa Bay St. Lawrence skiffs.	
Duell, Charles	Horicon Brant Lake fishing boat; partner E. Streeter.	

Durand Mfg. Co.	Rochester Canoes.
Durrin, Henry	Lake George
Durrin, Sherm	Lake George
Duso, Harry	Saranac Lake
Emmett, Dan	Bark canoes.
Flagy, Arlo C.	Saranac Lake
Flanders, A.B.	Tupper Lake
Fulton Pleasure Boat Co.	Fulton Canoes, etc. Advertised in 1892 A.C.A. yearbook.
Grant, William	Edwards
Green, Harry	Hermon Canoes.
Hayes, Dennis	Westport
Hitchcock, John	Crystal Lake
Huntington, Henry E.	Tupper Lake
Jackson, Alfred	Brushton Few boats to order.
Jacob, C.A., Jr.	Chestertown Duckboat.
Joyner	Glens Falls/Schenectady Canoes, launches, skiffs. Sold 82 rowboats in 1882 to the Prospect House in Blue Mountain Lake. General: KD/HD Coll. folders 14-12; 16-7; 16-21; 20-1; 50-12; 50-12A, #45–49. Joyner lap: folders 4-21; 14-4; 14-8; 50-5A, 50-9.
Kingsley, Willis	Chestertown Associated with Duell, Streeter.
Leonard, John T.	Morley
Leyare, Joseph	Ogdensburg

Mead, George   Lake George

Morrow, Ralph   Saranac Lake
                                    Worked with Hathaway. Now on his own.

Morse, Jim   Essex

Patnode, David   Saranac

Perkins, C.E.   Malone

Rivett, Jack   Old Forge
                                    Launches.

Roberts, John   Old Forge
                                    Associated with Parsons for several years.

Rogers, J.H.   Ogdensburg/Brasher Falls

Sexton, Jesse   Hague
                                    Launches.

Smith, Everett   Parishville

Smith, Fred R., & Sons   Bolton Landing

Smith, Olie   Lake George

Sprague, Herbert M.   Parishville
                                    See KD/HD Coll. folders 14-4; 16-16; 40-13.

Streeter, Asa   Horicon

Streeter, Elmer   Horicon

Thomas, Willard   West Bangor

Waters, E., & Son   Troy
                                    Paper boat builders. See also KD/HD Coll. folder 16-20, #1-14.

Watertown Boat & Canoe Co.   Watertown

Westcott, Jim

Wheelock & Wilbur   Canton

Index

ERRATA

Added words or changed phrases appear in italic (Edited 1986)

Page 2
Left column, second paragraph, last sentence.
Now reads: Thousands of these craft were built during the late 1800s and 1900s. . .
Should read: . . .were built during the late 1800s and *early* 1900s. . .

Page 6
Left column, middle of second full paragraph.
Now reads: Ten miles above Albany, where three rivers unite. . .
Should read: Ten miles above Albany, where *the Hudson and Mohawk Rivers* unite. . .

Page 11
Right column, middle of first full paragraph.
Now reads: Foster was caulking his boat when threatened by the Indian. . .
Should read: . . .when *allegedly* threatened by the Indian. . .

Page 38
Right column, end of second paragraph.
Now reads: . . . such as the Raquette Lake House on Tioga Point, Mother Johnson's at Raquette Falls, and Palmer's on Long Lake.
Should read: . . .such as *Palmer's on Long Lake,* Mother Johnson's at Raquette Falls, and *the Raquette Lake House on Tioga Point.*

Page 63
Right column, line 13.
Now reads: . . .built for Messmuk.
Should read: . . .built for *Nessmuk.*

Page 67
Caption for photograph.
Now reads: Paul Smiths on the Lower St. Regis
Should read: *Paul Smith's* on the. . .

Right column, first line of last paragraph.
Now reads: At Paul Smiths on the Lower St. Regis. . .
Should read: At *Paul Smith's.* . .

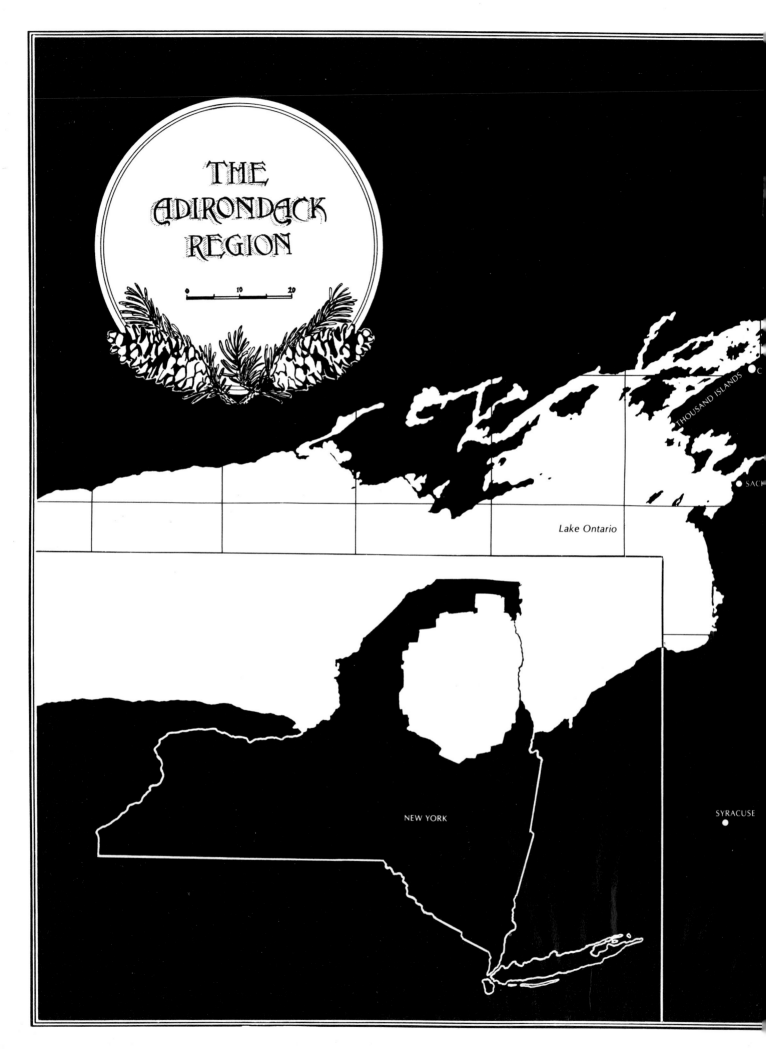

THE ADIRONDACK REGION

0   10   20

THOUSAND ISLANDS   C

SACK

Lake Ontario

NEW YORK

SYRACUSE